Democracy and Social Policy

Social Policy in a Development Context

General Editors: **Thandika Mkandawire and Huck-Ju Kwon**, both at UNRISD

Social Policy in a Development Context is a new series which places social policy at the centre of research while maintaining the United Nations Research Institute for Social Development (UNRISD)'s unified approach to social development. The series provides a new and exciting contribution to the literature in economic development and social policy. In economic development, social policy has been recognized as an integral part of development, but the literature often falls short of elaborating social policy for a unified approach to economic and social development. In social policy, analysis has concentrated mainly on European and North American countries, and studies on developing countries often lack comparative rigour. The bridge between economic development and social policy will not only contribute to the academic research but also inform the policy debate at the international and national levels.

Titles include:

'Jìmí O. Adésínà (*editor*)
SOCIAL POLICY IN SUB-SAHARAN AFRICAN CONTEXT
In Search of Inclusive Development

Yusuf Bangura (*editor*)
DEMOCRACY AND SOCIAL POLICY

Giovanni Andrea Cornia (*editor*)
PRO-POOR MACROECONOMICS
Potential and Limitations

Olli Kangas and Joakim Palme (*editors*)
SOCIAL POLICY AND ECONOMIC DEVELOPMENT IN THE NORDIC COUNTRIES

Massoud Karshenas and Valentine M. Moghadam (*editors*)
SOCIAL POLICY IN THE MIDDLE EAST
Political, Economics and Gender Dynamics

Huck-Ju Kwon (*editors*)
THE DEVELOPMENTAL WELFARE STATE AND POLICY REFORMS IN EAST ASIA

Maureen Mackintosh and Meri Koivusalo (*editors*)
COMMERCIALIZATION OF HEALTH CARE
Global and Local Dynamics and Policy Responses

Thandika Mkandawire (*editor*)
SOCIAL POLICY IN A DEVELOPMENT CONTEXT

Shahra Razavi and Shireen Hassim (*editors*)
GENDER AND SOCIAL POLICY IN A GLOBAL CONTEXT
Uncovering the Gendered Structure of 'the Social'

Manuel Riesco (*editor*)
LATIN AMERICA
A New Developmental Welfare State Model in the Making?

Social Policy in a Development Context
Series Standing Order ISBN 1–4039–4295–1 (hardback) 1–4039–4296–X (paperback)
(*outside North America only*)

You can receive future titles in this series as they are published by placing a standing order. Please contact your bookseller or, in case of difficulty, write to us at the address below with your name and address, the title of the series and the ISBN quoted above.

Customer Services Department, Macmillan Distribution Ltd, Houndmills, Basingstoke, Hampshire RG21 6XS, England

Democracy and Social Policy

Edited by

Yusuf Bangura

palgrave macmillan

UNRISD
United Nations Research Institute for Social Development

First published 2007 by
PALGRAVE MACMILLAN
Houndmills, Basingstoke, Hampshire RG21 6XS and
175 Fifth Avenue, New York, N.Y. 10010
Companies and representatives throughout the world

PALGRAVE MACMILLAN is the global academic imprint of the Palgrave Macmillan division of St. Martin's Press, LLC and of Palgrave Macmillan Ltd. Macmillan® is a registered trademark in the United States, United Kingdom and other countries. Palgrave is a registered trademark in the European Union and other countries.

ISBN-13: 978-0-230-54695-0 hardback
ISBN-10: 0-230-54695-1 hardback

This book is printed on paper suitable for recycling and made from fully managed and sustained forest sources.

A catalogue record for this book is available from the British Library.

A catalogue record for this book is available from of the Library of Congress.

10 9 8 7 6 5 4 3 2 1
16 15 14 13 12 11 10 09 08 07

Printed and bound in Great Britain by
Antony Rowe Ltd, Chippenham and Eastbourne

Contents

List of Tables

List of Figures

Foreword

Democracy and concerns about improvements in citizens' well-being have gained importance in the international development agenda. The prevailing normative discourse assumes that development processes should no longer be anchored in authoritarian rule, but should respect human rights and citizen participation in policy making. There is concern, however, that even when democracies appear consolidated, improvements in voters' well-being have not materialized. Governments seem unwilling or unable to respond to the interests of poor voters even when urged to develop poverty reduction strategies as a condition for receiving financial support.

This book is part of the UNRISD series, *Social Policy in a Development Context*, which examines the multiple roles of social policy in supporting economic development, welfare protection and equity under democratic conditions. It seeks to understand how democracy and social policy can be mutually reinforcing, the conditions under which democracies can deliver good social outcomes, why some democracies have a better record than others in welfare development, and the role social policy has played in strengthening democracies. It focuses on countries or regions whose democracies have been consolidated or are relatively stable. This includes both developed and developing countries, and covers three different periods or phases of global democratic expansion.

The book makes three broad arguments. First, economic development is a necessary but insufficient condition for social policy development. Even though there is a wide gap in welfare provision between countries classified according to income levels, considerable variations exist among countries within each income group to suggest the importance of non-income factors in explaining welfare outcomes. Second, sustained welfare development in democracies requires interest group organization and mobilization, strategic interactions between groups and political parties, and pro-welfare parties in government. In highly industrialized democracies, welfare variation is explained by differences in the national reach and organizational structures of unions, the presence of left-oriented parties in government, and social pacts that reconcile the conflicting interests of government, business and employees. Social security provision tends to be limited in countries with low levels of industrialization, even though a few countries, such as Costa Rica and Mauritius with a social democratic orientation, seem to have done well. The India case suggests that low-income countries with long traditions of political rights, improvements in electoral competitiveness, and a welfare-sensitive or proactive judiciary may enable social movements to pressure governments to introduce progressive social reforms even when the broad thrust of social policy itself is restrictive or lopsided.

The book also shows that social policy has played an important role in legitimizing complex transitions to democracy. These transitions often involve negotiated pacts. Social policy can be useful in democratic transitions that are highly polarized, such as early twentieth-century democratization in advanced industrial societies, and Southern Europe in the 1970s, in transitions that involve both political and market liberalization as in Central and Eastern Europe; and in multi-ethnic societies, such as in Mauritius. In such cases, social policies improved the security of most citizens, contributed to the development of a culture of social solidarity, and encouraged excluded or disadvantaged groups to have faith in the democratic regime by delegitimizing violent alternatives.

UNRISD is grateful to the Swedish International Development Cooperation Agency (Sida) and the United Kingdom Department for International Development (DFID) for their financial support for the research on which this volume is based. As is the case with all UNRISD projects, work on the Social Policy in a Development Context project would not have been possible without core funding provided by the governments of Denmark, Finland, Mexico, Norway, Sweden, Switzerland and the United Kingdom. Let me once again take this opportunity to express our gratitude.

THANDIKA MKANDAWIRE
DIRECTOR, UNRISD

Notes on the Contributors

Yusuf Bangura is a Research Co-ordinator at the United Nations Research Institute for Social Development for a programme on Democracy, Governance and Well-being. His research interests are in the fields of public sector reform, democratization, welfare policies and ethnic conflict. He received his undergraduate and doctoral degrees from the London School of Economics and Political Science in 1974 and 1978. He has taught in universities in Nigeria and Canada and worked as a visiting researcher in Sweden. He has published widely on the politics of economic relations, the African crisis, structural adjustment and livelihood strategies, democratization, and ethnic conflict. His recent publications include *Public Sector Reform in Developing Countries* (co-edited, Palgrave Macmillan, 2006), *Ethnic Inequalities and Public Sector Governance* (edited, Palgrave Macmillan, 2006), and *Racism and Public Policy* (co-edited, Palgrave Macmillan 2005).

Sheila Bunwaree is Associate Professor in the Department of Sociology at the University of Mauritius. She has also headed the Gender Bureau of the Ministry of Women's Rights and is a member of various Gender networks in Africa and overseas. From 2000 to 2003, she was the Director of the Research and Documentation Center at the Council for the Development of Social Science Research in Africa-CODESRIA, based in Dakar (Senegal). She co-directed the CODESRIA Gender Institute of 2002 on the theme of 'Globalisation, Gender and Trade'. Bunwaree has been a consultant for FAWE, IFAD, SADC, UNICEF and UNDP. She has published widely on gender, human capital formation and social policy.

Neera Chandhoke is Professor of Political Science, University of Delhi, where she also serves as Director of the Developing Countries Research Centre. She received her MA (1968) and PhD (1984) degrees from the University of Delhi. Her main teaching and research interests are political theory, comparative politics, and the politics of developing societies, with special focus on India. She is the author of *The Conceits of Civil Society* (2003); *Beyond Secularism: The Rights of Religious Minorities* (1999), and *State and Civil Society: Explorations in Political Theory* (1995). She is currently directing two projects: 'Conflict and Institutional Change in India' in partnership with the London School of Economics and Political Science, and 'Globalization and the State in India', with a focus on the capacity of the state to provide basic goods and services to the poor.

Terry Cox is Reader in Central and East European Studies at the University of Glasgow and has been appointed editor of *Europe-Asia Studies* (from summer 2005). His research interests include the social impact of economic transformation and state–society relations in Eastern Europe. He also maintains a long-standing interest in Russian peasant society. He currently holds a Leverhulme Research Fellowship for a project on 'Governance and State–Society Relations in Hungary'. Recent publications include: 'Changing Societies: Class and Inequality in Central and Eastern Europe', in S. White, J. Batt and P. Lewis (eds), *Developments in Central and East European Politics 3* (Macmillan: 2003); 'Civil Society and Interest Representation' (with Laszlo Vass), in G. Lengyel and Z. Rostovanyi (eds), *The Small Transformation: Society, Economy and Politics in Hungary in the New European Architecture* (2001); and *Social and Economic Transformation in East Central Europe: Institutions, Property elations and Social Interests* (with Bob Mason) (UNRISD, 1999).

Maurizio Ferrera is Professor of Comparative Public Policy at the State University of Milan. He also directs the Research Unit on European Governance – URGE – (Moncalieri, Turin). He formerly taught at the University of Pavia and has been visiting professor at several universities, including UC-Berkeley, the LSE, McGill, the Juan March Institute and the European University Institute. He is a member of several academic and editorial boards, including the Research Council of the European University Institute (IUE) and the Executive Committee of the ECPR. He has worked as a consultant for the European Commission, the ILO and the OECD. Ferrera's field of research is comparative social policy. His recent publications include *The Boundaries of Welfare* (2005); *Rescued by Europe? Social and Labour Market Reforms from Maastricht to Berlusconi* (with E. Gualmini) (2004); *Recasting the European Welfare State* (co-edited with Martin Rhodes), and *The Future of Social Europe,* a report commissioned by the Portuguese Presidency of the EU in 2000.

Fernando Filgueira has a Master's degree and a PhD in Sociology from the University of Northwestern, USA. He has been the co-ordinator of the evaluation programme in Education Management at the Research Unit of the National Administration of Public Education in Uruguay and academic coordinator at the Research Institute of Integration, Poverty and Social Exclusion at the Catholic University. He has participated as visiting researcher in various projects at the Columbia University (ILAIS), Western Ontario, Notre Dame (Kellog Institute), the University of North Carolina and as docent in various research centres and universities in the USA and Latin America. He has also worked as a consultant for the World Bank, BID, UNDP, ILO, ECLAC, IDRC and UNICEF. Filgueira has published several books and articles in journals specialized in the fields of social policy, poverty and development models.

Carl-Johan Hedberg is a Research Assistant at the United Nations Research Institute for Social Development (UNRISD). Before joining UNRISD in 2004 he received a scholarship from the Swedish International Development Cooperation Agency (Sida) and undertook two months of field research on democracy and policy making in Ghana. He holds an MSc degree in Economics from

Stockholm University where he also studied Political Science, focusing on democratization in the developing world. He has also studied in the United Kingdom and France. His research interests include comparative research on democratization and on the political economy of social policy.

Jennifer Jones has a Master's degree in sociology from the University of the West Indies (UWI) and a Bachelor's degree in English from the University of Cambridge. Presently, she is Social Monitoring Specialist in the Jamaica Social Policy Evaluation (JASPEV) project. She has been involved in social research and community development work, in the latter area working mainly in NGOs but also, more recently, with the Jamaica Social Investment Fund (JSIF). She has participated in, and co-written, a number of internationally funded social research studies, including a CIDA/Government of Jamaica (GOJ) socioeconomic study, and a study on social conditions and social relations in small enterprises funded by the GOJ and the Government of the Netherlands. She is the author of the chapter on Jamaica in *Structural Adjustment and the Public Sector in Central America and the Caribbean*, published in 1995 by CRIES and funded by Public Services International (PSI).

Keitseope Nthomang has a Master's degree and a PhD in Social Work from McGill University, Canada and the University of Queensland, Australia respectively. He lectures on Social Policy and Community Practice at the University of Botswana. He has been the coordinator of the Collaborative (University of Botswana and University of Tromso, Norway) Programme on Basarwa/San/Bushmen Research and Capacity building at the University of Botswana. He has participated in various research projects, including: a social policy project sponsored by the International Development Research Centre (IDRC), Canada, focusing on Southern and Eastern Africa; an HIV/AIDS project sponsored by the Human Sciences Research Centre, Capetown, South Africa; and a project on Capacity Development for Delivery of Remote Area Dweller Programme, sponsored by the Botswana Institute for Development Policy Analysis (BIDPA). He has been a consultant for the UNDP, BIDPA, Government of Botswana, African Comprehensive HIV/AIDS Programme (ACHAP) and NGOs/CSOs in Botswana. He has published several journal articles, book chapters and professional reports in the field of community practice, social policy and HIV/AIDS in Botswana.

Toshimitsu Shinkawa is Professor of Political Science at the Faculty of Law, Kyoto University. His major research interests lie in the fields of comparative welfare states and labour politics. His major publications include *Nihon-gata Fukushi no Seiji-Keizaigaku* (The Political Economy of Japanese-Style Welfare) and *Sengo Nihon Seiji to Shakai Minshushugi* (Social Democracy in Postwar Japan). The excerpt of the latter work appears in English as 'Failed Reform and Policy Changes of the SDPJ', in H. Otake (ed.), *Power Shuffles and Policy Processes* (2000), distributed outside Japan by the Brookings Institution Press.

John D. Stephens is the Gerhard E. Lenski Jr. Distinguished Professor of Political Science and Sociology, University of North Carolina. He received his BA (1970) from Harvard University and his PhD (1976) from Yale University. His main interests are comparative politics and political economy, with area focus on Europe and the Caribbean. Stephens teaches European politics and the political economy of advanced industrial societies. He is the author or co-author of four books, including *Capitalist Development and Democracy* (with Evelyne Huber and Dietrich Rueschemeyer, 1992) and *Development and Crisis of the Welfare State* (with Evelyne Huber, 2001). He has also contributed articles to, among others, *The American Political Science Review, American Journal of Sociology, American Sociological Review, The British Journal of Sociology, Comparative Politics, Comparative Political Studies, Comparative Social Research* and *World Politics*. Stephens is currently working on a study of the impact of neoliberal economic reform of social policy in Latin America, Iberia, and the Antipodes.

List of Abbreviations and Acronyms

ACP	African, Caribbean and the Pacific
AIDS	Autoimmune Deficiency Syndrome
ALDP	Arable Land Development Programme
BDP	Botswana Democratic Party
BFTU	Botswana Federation of Trade Unions
BHC	Botswana Housing Corporation
BPL	Below Poverty Line
CAFFE	Citizens' Action for Free and Fair Elections
CHI	Clerks' Health Insurance
CSA	Commonwealth Sugar Agreement
CSO	Central Statistics Office
DB	Defined Benefits
DC	Defined Contributions
DC	Democrazia Cristiana (Christian Democrats)
DNVP	German National People's Party
DPEP	District Primary Education Programmes
EAC	Electoral Advisory Committee
EAP	economically active population
EC	European Community
ECCE	Early Child Care and Education
EMU	Economic and Monetary Union
EPF	Employees' Pension Fund
EPI	Employees' Pension Insurance
EPP	Employees' Pension Plan
EPZ	Export Processing Zone
EU	European Union
GCT	General Consumption Tax
GDP	Gross Domestic Product
GER	Gross Enrolment Rate
GNP	Gross National Product
GoB	Government of Botswana
HDI	Human Development Index
HEART	Human Employment and Resource Training
HI	Health Insurance
HIV	Human Immunodeficiency Virus
IADB	Inter-American Development Bank
ILO	International Labour Organization
IMF	International Monetary Fund
INP	Institute for Social Provision

ISI	Import Substitution Industrialization
JEA	Japan Employers' Association
JFJ	Jamaicans for Justice
JFU	Japan Farmers' Union
JLP	Jamaica Labour Party
JSP	Japan Socialist Party
JSY	Janani Suraksha Yojana
KPH	Kingston Public Hospital
LDP	Liberal Democratic Party
LRIDA	Labour Relations and Industrial Disputes Act
MDGs	Millennium Development Goals
MFA	Multi-Fibre Agreement
MHW	Ministry of Health and Welfare
MLAs	Multilateral Lending Agencies
MLP	Mauritius Labour Party
MMM	Mouvement Militant Mauricien
MSI	Movimento Sociale Italiano
MSM	Mouvement Socialiste Mauricien
NBA	Narmado Bachao Andolan
NER	Net Enrolment Rate
NFBS	National Family Benefit Scheme
NGOs	Non-governmental organizations
NHI	National Health Insurance
NHF	National Health Fund
NPA	National Planning Agency (Jamaica)
OAS	Organization of American States
OECD	Organization for Economic Cooperation and Development
PASOK	Greek Socialist Party
PAYG	Pay as You Go
PCI	Partito Comunista d'Italia
PDS	Public Distribution System
PMSD	Parti Mauricien Social Democrate
PNP	People's National Party (Jamaica)
PPL	Police Peace Law
PRI	Institutional Revolutionary Party (Mexico)
PSB	Brazilian Socialist Party
PSOE	Partido Socialista Obrero Espanol
PSI	Partito Socialista Italiano
PUCL	People's Union for Civil Liberties
QCA	Qualitative Comparative Analysis
RADP	Remote Area Development Programme
RMI	*reddito minimo d'inserimento* (minimum insertion income)
SAPs	Structural Adjustment Policies
SCAP	Supreme Commander Allied Powers

SEWA	Self-Employed Women's Association
SHHA	Self-Help Housing Agency
SIIC	Social Insurance Investigation Commission
UGT	Union General de Trabajadores
UNDP	United Nations Development Program
UNESCO	United Nations Educational, Social and Cultural Organization
UNRISD	United Nations Research Institute for Social Development
UWI	University of the West Indies
VRS	Voluntary Retirement Scheme
WPJ	Workers' Party of Jamaica

1
Democracy and Social Policy Development: Introduction and Overview[1]

Yusuf Bangura and Carl-Johan Hedberg

Introduction

Since the 1980s, there has been a dramatic increase in the number of countries classified as democracies. The need to build democratic institutions and values as organizing principles of government underpins current development initiatives such as the anti-poverty agenda and the Millennium Development Goals (MDGs). Democracy is seen as a good instrument of accountability and for improving public policy outcomes. But globalization, market-driven policy prescriptions and the fragmentation of labour markets and collective bargaining raise questions about whether new democracies can pursue social polices that improve the welfare of the majority of their citizens.

Evidence suggests that the performance of many countries in promoting basic rights, public services and welfare development is inadequate. Many new democracies retain elements of authoritarian practices and seem unresponsive to voters' interests. Increasingly, researchers and development practitioners are adopting the view that it is not enough for countries to be democratic; the substance or quality of their democracies matters a great deal (O'Donnell 2001; Whitehead 2002; UNDP 2002; O'Donnell *et al.* 2004; Mkandawire 2004; Ringen 2005). What has been the record of democracies in social policy development? What are the intrinsic properties of democracy that can facilitate or constrain effective social policies? How do different democracies promote the well-being of citizens? And under what conditions can democratic regimes deliver adequate social protection?

This volume examines the complex relations between democracy and social policy development. It focuses on countries or regions whose democracies have been consolidated or are relatively stable: advanced western industrial societies, Japan, Southern Europe, Central and Eastern Europe, India, Latin America, Jamaica, Mauritius and Botswana. Welfare development is related to economic development. Developing countries with a GDP per capita of less than US$2,000 (in purchasing power parity terms) have not attained universal levels of education or adequate levels of life expectancy, let alone the range and coverage of the welfare programmes of high-income countries. However, some countries have been able to obtain fairly high scores in their health and education indexes with low levels of per capita income, while others have failed to convert high levels of income into commensurate levels of human development. This suggests that economic development is a necessary but not a sufficient condition for effective social provision.

The book underscores the importance of interest group (especially union) organization, strategic interactions of interest groups and political parties, and the partisan composition of government in explaining variations in welfare development in democracies. Countries with encompassing unions and left-oriented governments and that score highly on indexes of corporatism produce higher welfare outcomes than other countries. In countries where industrial unions are relatively weak, it is important that the political system is competitive and that pro-welfare parties are in government for long periods of time. In medium- and low-income democracies, where a substantial proportion of the labour force is in agriculture and the informal sector, social policy is still very much focused on providing basic services, such as education, health and water. Despite numerous programmes aimed at helping vulnerable groups, the monetary value of social security provision is still very low in these democracies. Medium-income democracies with relatively higher levels of urbanization, industrial employment, unionization, and competitive party systems, have combined substantial basic service provision with reasonable levels of social security. However, even in these countries, some core welfare policies (such as unemployment benefits) are still non-existent or poorly developed; and segmented industrialization has produced dualist and stratified welfare regimes in which organized groups in the labour market enjoy superior benefits.

The franchise had a relatively strong redistributive element during the early periods of democratization when organized groups used it strategically to influence public policy reforms. The link between the organized working class (and social groups more generally), the franchise and pursuit of substantive welfare policies became much weaker as more agrarian economies became democratic and national economies experienced deregulation. The vote has increasingly come to be seen, especially by rational choice perspectives that focus on the individual voter, as a weak instrument for promoting redistribution or holding governments to account. However, insights from the literature on the political budget cycle suggest that uncertainties associated with competitive elections provide incentives for some kind of governmental responsiveness to voters that have implications for welfare. But the conversion of interests into welfare outcomes often requires additional institutions, such as social pacts and those that improve the knowledge base of voters and the competitiveness of the political system.

The next section of this introduction provides an overview of development, labour markets, social expenditures and welfare in high-, medium- and low-income countries. Then we explore conceptual issues surrounding the potential and limits of democracy in promoting responsiveness and redistribution in four areas: the redistributive quality of the franchise in historical perspective; the rational voter and problems of accountability; the political budget cycle; and institutions, competitiveness and welfare. This is followed by a discussion of the main insights from the nine studies within a framework that divides countries according to different phases of democratization, and then a discussion of the effects of social policy development on democracy. Finally, the sixth section concludes the introduction.

Development and welfare

Economic development correlates with social development when countries are grouped according to their GDP per capita. Table 1.1 provides data on urbanization, formal labour force, sectoral distribution of employment, and union density for low-, middle- and high-income countries. It shows that high-income countries have the highest levels of urbanization, formal employment and union density, as well as the lowest numbers of people employed in agriculture. Middle-income countries occupy an intermediate position, and low-income countries are at the other end of these indicators.

Table 1.2 shows that levels human development, educational attainment, life expectancy, social security expenditure, income security and poverty correlate with the broad income group categories. Low-income countries have, on average, the lowest indexes on human development, education, life expectancy and income security, spend the least on social security, and have the highest number of people living on less than $2 a day. The positive correlation between countries' GDP per capita and their HDI scores has long been recognised by scholars in development studies (see, for example, McGillivray 1991). Least developed countries have not attained universal levels of education or adequate

Table 1.1 Labour force characteristics of low-, medium- and high-income countries

Country[1]	*% of urban formal labour force*	*% in agriculture*[2]	*% in industry*	*% in services*	*% urban population (2002)*	*Union density*[3]
Low income	—	51.85	13.27	31.81	33.36	10.94
Middle income	49.95	19.54	24.96	53.99	59.13	24.37
High income	82.94	4.68	25.96	65.92	76.09	32.72

Sources: World Bank 2004; ILO 2004; ILO 1997.
Notes:
[1] All countries are grouped by income using World Bank classifications: high income (GNI/c of US$ 9,076 or more in 2002), middle income (US$736–$9,075) and low (US$735 or less).
[2] Sectoral data for low-income countries are from World Bank 2004.
[3] Union membership as a percentage of non-agricultural labour force, 1995.

Table 1.2 Social outcomes in low-, medium- and high-income countries

Country groups	*GDP per capita, ppp US$*[a]*, 2002*	*Human Development Index*[b]*, 2002*	*Education index*[b]	*Life expectancy index*[b]	*Social security expenditure as % of GDP*[c]	*ILO's income security index*[d]	*Population living on less than US$ 2 per day*[a]
Low-income countries	1,330	0.50	0.59	0.47	4.51	0.37	31.78
Middle-income countries	6,075	0.75	0.83	0.73	10.47	0.53	8.28
High income countries	22,906	0.91	0.93	0.87	20.61	0.80	<1

Sources: World Bank 2004; UNDP 2004b; ILO 2000; ILO 2005.

levels of life expectancy, let alone the range and coverage of welfare programmes in high-income countries. The combined average index for life expectancy and education of the top 21 high-income countries with income per capita of more than US$23,000 is 0.93 (UNDP 2002); that for low-income countries is 0.59; and for the least developed countries is 0.48. The combined index for middle-income countries, at 0.79, compares favourably with that for high-income countries, but the welfare programmes of the former are well below those of high-income countries. These outcomes underscore the importance of economic development in understanding social policy development.

Despite the close links between GDP per capita and social outcomes, there are significant variations in social policy efforts in countries at similar levels of development as the welfare state literature has shown even for high-income countries (Esping-Anderson 1990; Huber and Stephens 2001; Hicks 1999). Hicks (1999) finds that although a threshold level of income per capita (US$2,000) explains early welfare programme consolidation in Europe, above a certain level income per capita does not explain variations in welfare development. Studies have also shown that countries have been able to obtain fairly high scores in their health and education indexes with low levels of national income, while others have failed to convert high levels of income into commensurate levels of human development (Ghai 2000; Mehrotra and Jolly 2000; Moore *et al.* 1999). For instance, some countries with per capita incomes of less than US$2,000 have very high scores in their combined indexes for life expectancy and education – Tajikistan (0.84), Vietnam (0.78), Mongolia (0.74), Sao Tome and Principe (0.71) and Solomon Islands (0.70). Indeed, 73 countries would lose points, 87 would gain points, and there would be no change in only eight countries if HDI rank is subtracted from

GDP rank (UNDP 2002). Similarly, although there is a high overall correlation between countries' GDP per capita and their income security index as measured by the ILO (2004), some countries with low or medium incomes have been able to attain fairly high levels of income security, while others have not been able to achieve levels of income security commensurate with their levels of income. These variations suggest that economic development alone is not enough to explain variations in social welfare efforts across countries.

Democracy and redistribution

Social policy development has occurred in both authoritarian and democratic regimes. The experiences of communist and East Asian developmental states suggest that policy makers can respond to the welfare needs of citizens even when civil rights are curtailed, leaders do not have to renew their mandates or gain office through competitive elections, interest groups are denied autonomy, and power is monopolized by a political elite. This book is concerned, however, with the links between democracy and social policy. In examining non-income factors that explain variations in welfare development, we will ignore factors that enable authoritarian regimes to pursue effective social policies and concentrate only on those that are specific to democratic regimes.

Any study on democracy and welfare requires conceptual clarification of the intrinsic properties of democracy that are conducive to social policy development. It also has to define the universe of democratic countries. There is much disagreement about the number of countries that can be classified as democratic, although all datasets point to a sharp increase in the last 25 years. The Polity IV dataset suggests an increase in democratic countries from about 40 in 1980 to more than 80 in 2003, and a corresponding decrease in authoritarian regimes in the same period from more than 80 to about 30. Freedom House reports similar developments and describes liberal and electoral democracies as the dominant regime form in the world today: 62.5 per cent of countries are reported to be democratic at least in the electoral sense by 2000. Yet in both these widely used datasets, there are a large number of countries that are classified as not fully democratic: 'restricted/partial democracies' in Freedom House language, or 'anocracies' according to Polity IV. Different scholars also question the democratic status of some of the countries classified as full democracies in both datasets. With the exception of Botswana, which is classified as a 'bureaucracy' by Przeworski *et al.* (2000) because of its lack of alternation of parties in government, our case studies are generally regarded as democratic in virtually all major academic studies. Apart from Central and Eastern Europe, most have also experienced uninterrupted democratic rule of at least 25 years. This time period is long enough to associate welfare changes to dynamics in the democratic regime.

Two defining features of democracy are the periodic renewal of the mandates of leaders through free, fair and competitive elections; and a set of basic rights of expression and organization that facilitate the exercise of political choice and for holding leaders to account. In the next four sections we explore in more detail the intrinsic properties of democracy and their potential to deliver or constrain good welfare outcomes.

The franchise and redistribution in historical perspective

Theories on the political economy of public expenditures and the growth of government expect societies where the median voter is poor or at the lower end of the income distribution to have big governments and strong pressures for income redistribution, including extensive social provisioning (Meltzer and Richard 1981). Since the *raison d'être* of political parties is to win or retain office, it is believed policies will gravitate towards the median voter. Although this hypothesis has been challenged by some recent data on OECD democracies, in the nineteenth and early twentieth centuries, democratization, or extension of the franchise to non-propertied classes, was strongly associated with redistribution. Representatives of the landed gentry and rising industrial classes believed extension of the vote to the rising working-class majority would be harmful to private property owners as popularly elected parliaments would greatly increase taxes on the rich. Democracy was perceived as 'a battle, not of parties, but of classes' and 'a struggle between property… and mere numbers'.[2] Even liberal thinkers, such as John Stuart Mill (1946), worried about the redistributive potential of democracy and advocated plural votes for industrialists, bankers, merchants and professionals (Therborn 1977).

Much of the literature on the early history of democracy highlights a close link between democratization, redistribution and welfare development (Rueschemeyer *et al.* 1992; Huber and Stephens 2001; Hicks 1999; Acemoglu and Robinson 2000; Boix 2003). Rapid industrialization, trade union power and mass politics defined democracy's redistributive quality. Industrialization was associated with the mass production of goods and services, reduction of the contribution of agriculture to the gross domestic product and employment, high levels of population growth and urbanization, and emergence of a new class of producers – workers – whose survival depended on their ability to sell their labour power for wages. These developments introduced new social risks, such as workplace accidents; unemployment; long working hours and child labour; low pay; and old age insecurities. Trade unions – acting either independently or in coalitions with other groups in mass parties – emerged as pressure groups to force employers and the state to act on those risks. Universalization of the franchise was seen as a strategic tool in achieving social objectives. One of the leading Marxists of the time, Frederick Engels (1960), drew positive lessons from the use of the franchise by German workers to press for change, and wrote that if electoral reforms were sustained 'by the end of the century we … shall grow into the decisive power in the land before which all other powers will bow, whether they like it or not' (Therborn 1977; Hicks 1999). Indeed, historians of the welfare state link its early development in Germany under Bismarck to strategies aimed at avoiding revolutionary outcomes and reconciling working-class interests to those of the state.

Redistribution implies that achievement of universal suffrage, now mostly taken for granted in new democracies, was staggered rather than a once-and-for-all phenomenon, or something offered without contestation. Lenz and Ladd (2003) identify 26 cases of suffrage reform that increased the size of the electorate between 1807 and 1972 in 13 western democracies. The major reforms occurred between 1897 and 1922 when the franchise was extended to more than 50 per cent of the adult population in most countries. Most of these democracies were still largely male democracies before the First World War. Popular pressures of various forms influenced the politics of franchise extension. Sometimes, reforms were introduced from above to win working-class votes (Collier 1999) or stave off revolts. The revolutionary posture of sections of the working class movement may not have been successful in overturning existing political arrangements, but they surely added to the pressure for change and the need to incorporate the demands of workers in the political economy. Democratization was closely tied to industrialization and various forms of political unrest that have been identified for that period.

As Chapter 2 by John Stephens in this book suggests, democratization and welfare development in advanced industrial societies were driven by interrelated, though distinct, processes in which the working-class movement, acting through trade unions and social democratic and clerical parties, played a substantial role. Hicks (1999) finds that Socialist/labour voting in 1920 correlated highly at 0.606 with 1920 welfare programme consolidation;[3] and mobilization, which includes union density and labour voting, correlated 0.764 with programme consolidation. Acemoglu and Robinson contend that 'extending the franchise acted as a commitment to future redistribution and prevented social unrest' (p. 1). They posit that without a commitment to redistribution, democratization, which still allowed the ruling classes to hold on to power, would not have been credible in the eyes of the newly enfranchised and disadvantaged majority. Their study, drawing on data from Lindert (1994), Williamson (1985), Flora (1983), Morrison (2000) and Kraus (1981) shows that social spending, social programmes and taxation in Britain, France, Germany and Sweden increased and Gini coefficients declined after countries embarked on democratization. Their data suggest that the peak of the Kuznets curve, or rising inequality, coincided with democratization, which subsequently led to redistribution or a reduction of inequalities. Boix (2003) also relies on these data to arrive at a similar conclusion about a drop in inequality in the European cases of democratization.

The rational voter and accountability

A striking feature of the current wave of democratization is the seeming erosion of the redistributive quality of the franchise. Universal suffrage is almost taken for granted in new democracies even when the integrity of the vote is still a contested issue. Many new democracies have been described as 'choiceless democracies', 'disempowered democracies' (Mkandawire 2004), or simply 'electoral democracies', implying a distinct loss of capacity to respond to the needs of the populace. Even though industrialization became a worldwide phenomenon in the twentieth century, not many countries experienced a transformation of their economies and social structures leading to a large and independently organized working class with a capacity to influence decisions at the workplace and in public policy. Even long-established democracies witnessed a flexibilization of their labour markets, fragmentation of the working class movement, and capital mobility. These developments have enhanced the security of property owners and made large-scale redistributions difficult (Boix 2003). In addition, most of the older democracies were relatively homogenous nation-states. The rise of complex cleavages of a non-class nature may have served to weaken collective action in some contexts (Vershney 1999). Indeed, in polarized ethnic settings, voters may support leaders on ethnic grounds rather on the basis of their governmental record or ability to deliver good social or economic policies. It seems, then, that in this new dispensation, citizens, who have become a highly heterogeneous group, do not always vote for redistribution or welfare development; and policy makers and the dominant interests they may represent do not need to be afraid of democratization.

The literature on the rational voter and policy makers' responsiveness questions the redistributive quality of the franchise. One branch of this literature links low voter turnout in, for instance, advanced democracies with the relative insignificance of the marginal voter's choices in electoral outcomes. It is also believed that policy convergence among major political parties makes low voter participation rational. The focus on the individual voter deviates from the view of voting as collective action mediated by organized groups with clear preferences on the economy and on welfare policies and a strategic interest in voting irrespective of perceived outcomes. It challenges the assumed power of organized groups to mobilize their putative constituencies in electoral contests.

Indeed, recent work on accountability from a rational choice perspective views elections as a blunt or insufficient instrument for extracting accountability from leaders or forcing them to maximize citizens' welfare. According to Przeworski, Stokes and Manin (1999), elections are not enforceable contracts. In reviewing the Latin American experience, Stokes (2001) observes that politicians repeatedly violate their mandates on non-market approaches to economic reform when they get elected. It is not surprising that Fearon (1999) sees mandates, at best, as instruments to choose good leaders rather than to sanction or hold office holders accountable. Voters do not have adequate information to make correct judgements on government performance, and may have inconsistent policy preferences in the electoral cycle (preferring a policy at one end of the cycle and rejecting it at the other end).

These constraints suggest that governments may not be responsive to voters' interests, and may pursue policies they believe are best for citizens even if they turn out to be not welfare enhancing. They also leave scope for self-serving policies (and corruption) that bear no relation to the needs of the population or the economic interests of investors. In addition, citizens judge governments on a broad range of issues with only one instrument: the vote. In such situations, they may downgrade the performance of a government on the economy or on welfare development in their scale of preferences in making decisions about how to use their single vote. This body of literature suggests that additional 'accountability agencies' may be needed to get policy makers to be responsive to the needs of the populace.

The political budget cycle

Problems associated with converting voter preferences into welfare outcomes do not mean, however, that politicians are immune to pressures for redistribution. Free and competitive elections always have elements of uncertainty, which may induce responses, however minimal, from incumbents. The literature on political budget cycles highlights fluctuations in governments' public expenditures and tax policies that are linked to electoral cycles. The models on which this literature is based indeed perceive the vote as an instrument for social choice. Early research, pioneered by William Nordhaus (1975), focused on the effects of elections on the macroeconomy. It assumed that incumbents would reflate the economy during election years on the expectation that voters would support incumbents when economic conditions improve and support the opposition when they deteriorate. But the empirical evidence of political business cycles, as observed in OECD democracies, was ambiguous, because of the time it takes for monetary and fiscal policies to impact the real economy, or, as most analysts now believe, the seeming impossibility of leveraging economic policies to deliver results when they are required (Shi and Svensson 2003; Drazen 2000). Attention subsequently shifted away from macroeconomic outcomes to the policy instruments themselves and their budgetary implications. In election years, as Rogoff (1990: 21), who led the new line of research affirmed, 'governments often engage in a consumption binge': they cut taxes and/or increase expenditures and social transfers. Both models assume information asymmetries between voters and incumbent policy makers. In the Rogoff model, incumbents shift public expenditure towards consumption spending to signal competence to voters.[4]

The existence of political budget cycles is supported by numerous empirical studies.[5] One widely cited study (Alesina *et al.* 1997) on 13 OECD countries found an increase of 0.6 per cent of GDP in the budget deficit between 1961 and 1993 during election years. Schuknecht (1996) reports this same level of deficit for 35 developing countries. Barry Ames's (1987) study on politicians and public policy in Latin America records a 6.3 per cent increase in government expenditure during pre-election years. In the case of Africa, Block

(2002) finds that the fiscal deficits of 44 countries where multi-party competitive elections have been held increased by 1.2 per cent of GDP during election years. Significantly, he finds no cycles in countries with non-competitive elections. Hallerberg and de Souza (2000) also report that the budget balance worsened in 10 Central and East European countries by 1.5 per cent of GDP in elections between 1990 and 1999, and that the type of exchange rate regime determined whether governments used fiscal or monetary policies to manipulate the economy.[6] Block (2003) also finds, on the basis of data from a sample of 69 countries, that the composition of public expenditure changes during election years in favour of current consumption expenditures and away from public investment. Based on a study of 123 developing and developed countries covering a period of 21 years, Shi and Svensson (2002) report that cycles are caused by both a reduction in taxes and an increase in government expenditure.

One interesting insight in the political budget cycles literature is that cycles are much greater in developing than in developed countries. Shi and Svensson (2003) find that cycles in developing countries double those found in developed countries: the deficit increased by 1.3 per cent of GDP in the average developing country and 0.6 per cent of GDP in the average developed country. And Brenda and Drazen (2004) report that new democracies account for the large cycles found in samples that include both developed and developing countries.

There has been much discussion about the causes of variations in budget cycles. Explanations include issues related to differences in transparency and voter education on the competence of incumbents as more elections are held (Akhmedov *et al.* 2002; Gonzalez 2002 and Shi and Svensson 2003), the extent of rent-seeking opportunities enjoyed by office holders (Shi and Svensson 2002) and the existence of institutional restraints, such as governmental checks and balances and independent central banks (Brenda and Drazen 2004; Akhmedov *et al.* 2002; Hallerberg and de Souza 2000).

Most studies treat political budget cycles as pathological. Voters are assumed to be myopic and incumbents manipulative or opportunistic. Since economists have dominated this field of enquiry, the focus has tended to be on the negative effects of political budget cycles on the fiscal balance rather than on their potential to act as a mechanism for getting governments in competitive environments to respond to the welfare of voters.[7] The impact of political budget cycles on economic reform programmes has also been a subject of concern by the multilateral financial institutions. Yet, in Nordhaus's initial formulation, political budget cycles, which seem inevitable in competitive environments where social investment is a scarce good, can only be successfully regulated through a 'planning framework' that 'broadens the base of participation in policy-making'. His planning framework echoes corporatist negotiations between 'the government, opposition parties, labour, management and other interest groups' (p. 189). Rogoff (1990), in fact, saw political budget cycles as 'a socially efficient mechanism for diffusing up-to-date information about the incumbent's administrative competence'; and that 'efforts to curtail the cycle can easily reduce welfare, either by impeding the transmission of information or by inducing politicians to select more socially costly ways of signalling' (p. 22).

The higher incidence of political budget cycles in developing countries may not be fully explained by the myopia of voters, opportunistic behaviour of incumbents and weak regulatory institutions. In situations where the track record or credibility of governments on the provision of public goods is inadequate, voters may very well act rationally by demanding immediate 'returns' or 'payoffs' in election years: 'it's either now or never' in popular parlance. These returns or payoffs may vary from supply of consumer goods and cash transfers (the political bribery literature) to wage increases, public works and provision of clinics, schools and production inputs. And they may be targeted to different voters depending on the calculations of incumbents and pressures by voters. Khemani (2000) finds that spending on public works, such as road construction, is not only higher in Indian state governments in election years, but that the management of these programmes also improves. As he puts it 'it is only in the election year that incentives to woo the majority of voters is the greatest'. This is consistent with Tufte's (1978) argument that political business cycles may be beneficial; and that most major improvements in social benefits in the US occur during presidential or congressional election periods.

Politicians may surely behave in fiscally irresponsible ways, as Maurizio Ferrera argues in Chapter 3 of this volume in the case of Italy where votes were traded with individual welfare before the major reforms in that country's welfare system. It is also the case that politicians in many new democracies may personalize expenditures in election years by bribing voters with money and goods rather than providing common services or social welfare. In the absence of party manifestoes that are credible, individual politicians may have good reason to prefer targeted welfare since that is the only service they can credibly provide, monitor and control. Recent work by Susan Stokes (2005) has raised the issue of *perverse accountability* as a feature of many new democracies – i.e. situations where voters do not hold leaders to account; instead, parties provide targeted welfare and monitor and control the behaviour of voters to ensure that what they provide translates into votes.

It is difficult to measure the proportion of individually targeted and corrupt forms of social expenditures to the overall expenditures in the budget cycle. However, the existence of large political budget cycles in developing countries suggests that democracy does matter to voters and governments: they signal a need for redistribution. Policy makers will have to find effective ways of meeting the needs of the electorate if economies are to be freed from these cycles.

Institutions, competitiveness and welfare

The three perspectives on democracy and redistribution reviewed here often require institutions to convert preferences into welfare. The literature on the rational voter and accountability highlights two broad types of institutions for improving responsiveness. The first deals with institutions that correct informational asymmetries. As Manin, Przeworski and Stokes (1999: 23) put it, 'the main difficulty both in instructing governments what to do and in judging what they have done is that we, citizens, just do not know enough'. Voters will be unable to act strategically or defend their interests if they lack adequate information about the economy and how decisions are made. This problem is structural and not just a reflection of voter preferences to elect autonomous leaders with superior knowledge. Despite being public agents, rulers enjoy enormous powers, including the power to withhold information from the public. The situation is complicated in poor democracies with low literacy rates. Recommended institutions include independent boards for transparency of campaign financing to ensure that the rich do not enjoy an overwhelming advantage in public policy; independent auditing agencies; independent sources for information on the economy; and participation of opposition parties in the regulation of the public media (p. 50).[8]

The second set of institutions addresses ways of improving the effectiveness of the vote. It is premised on the view that although governments may make thousands of decisions that affect the welfare of individuals, citizens have only one instrument – the vote – to influence those decisions. Manin, Przeworski and Stokes (1999) suggest that some key policies, such as monetary policy, may be separated from other public policies by asking individuals to vote on these policies separately – in effect granting voters multiple instruments to deal with multiple targets or problems that affect individual welfare.[9] These reforms may need to be complemented by policies that improve the competitiveness of the political system, especially in ethnically polarized societies. Multiple votes and improved voter information may be meaningless if voting simply reflects ethnic affiliations. Where voting is ethnic, some kind of accountability can still be extracted from leaders when voters in the same ethnic group are presented with multiple parties with real choices.[10] Accountability may be severely compromised when only one party controls the votes of a group. Responsiveness is improved in both plural and homogenous societies when there are high probabilities that incumbents would lose elections.

The literature on organized interests and the redistributive quality of democracy, on the other hand, highlights the significance of corporatist institutions or social pacts in improving social welfare efforts. This literature suggests that democracy delivers high welfare outcomes when left parties with strong union links are in government for extended periods, and are backed up by corporatist arrangements in industrial relations and in macroeconomic policy making. Under corporatism, independent, centrally organized unions authoritatively bargain on behalf of members and, together with pro-welfare parties, play central roles in defining the social agenda and resolving the conflicting interests of employers and workers in the macro-economy. In regimes of corporatism, all parties, including governments, are expected to abide by decisions on wages, employment and social security more generally; and although a central objective of corporatism is to reduce the incidence of industrial unrest, labour retains the strike option to ensure compliance from government and business.[11] Empirical studies suggest that although the impact of corporatism on employment, inflation and growth is ambiguous (Vergunst 2004), social democratic regimes, which score highly on indexes of corporatism, have produced higher welfare efforts than other regimes (Hicks 1999; Huber and Stephens 2001; Esping-Andersen 1990).[12]

Phases of democratization and social policy

The countries discussed in the nine chapters of this book fall under three phases of democratization. The first phase deals with the experiences of western industrial societies in the nineteenth and early twentieth centuries. Although 33 countries, including four from Latin America, experienced democratic transitions during this period, they survived in only 11 by the outbreak of the Second World War (Huntington 1991). This period is associated with the early stages of social policy development. A new phase of democratization emerged after the Second World War, and covers the experiences of Japan, Costa Rica, India, Jamaica, Mauritius and Botswana. This phase is associated with high rates of economic growth, promotion of full employment, pursuit of national development strategies, corporatism in industrial relations, and expansion of welfare programmes in advanced industrial democracies. The diffusion of welfare policies to the new developing democracies was limited, although there were differences among countries. The third phase of democratization started in Southern Europe in the mid-1970s and engulfed Latin America, Central and Eastern Europe, Africa and Asia in the 1980s and 1990s. It coincided with the crisis of established welfare states, deregulation of labour markets, long-running economic crises in developing countries, the collapse of communism, and the ascendancy of neoliberal ideas in economic and social policy making.

First phase of democratization: western industrial societies

In Chapter 2, John Stephens provides an overview of the forces that propelled the transitions to democracy and social policy development in western industrial societies between 1870 and 1950. His survey includes nine West European countries, Australia, Canada, New Zealand, and the United States. Drawing on his previous works and those of other scholars, he posits a unified theory that explains the links between democratization and social policy. Central to this linkage is the role of the organized working class. Urbanization, factory production, and new forms of communication and transportation improved the capacity of the working and middle classes for self-organization. He adds that democratic consolidation needed a strong, relatively autonomous state and a well-organized civil society that counter-balanced the power of the state. His explanation also involves understanding changes in international power relations, which, for the period covered, were the effects of the First World War and British colonial rule.

By 1920, most of the countries under review were full democracies, with Switzerland, France and Norway the first to democratize in the mid-to-late nineteenth century. Switzerland and Norway were smallholding agrarian democracies without powerful land-owning classes. Except in France, where artisanal workers were active, organized labour was not a significant actor in the democratization of these countries. However, by the turn of the century, the working class had become ascendant in much of Europe through the social democratic labour movement. The First World War strengthened the position of labour in the power equation: workers were needed in the production effort and at the war front. The size of organized labour more than doubled from 11 per cent to 27 per cent. However, labour needed allies as it was unable to effect democratic change on its own. Though workers constituted a majority in all countries, working-class parties could not receive electoral majorities even after the universalization of the franchise. Socialist parties' share of the vote averaged 30 per cent. In the Scandinavian countries workers collaborated with small farmers and segments of the middle classes. In the Netherlands and Belgium, unions and working-class organizations worked through clerical parties. In Britain, the reforms were spearheaded by upper-class-led parties, which in part were responses to working-class pressure and competition for working-class votes in the absence of a strong Labour party. Stephens reports that the European labour movement, acting through the Second International, ultimately adopted universal suffrage as a key demand in their programme for social change. He argues that democracy subsequently broke down in Germany and other countries because of their highly concentrated agrarian relations. He suggests that Britain's changing role as a colonial power and in the international system influenced patterns of democratization in the United States, Canada, Australia and New Zealand where high levels of suffrage were achieved before self-government.

Welfare development was shaped by variations in working-class power, as demonstrated by union organization or density as well as the strength of Left parties and participation in government. In some cases working-class demands for welfare reform were articulated through clerical parties – Christian democracy – whose Catholic ideology supported social policies to moderate the negative effects of markets. He argues that social policy development contributed to the consolidation of democracy in the inter-war period and to the 'class compromise' in the post-Second World War period. He highlights Hicks's (1999) three routes to early welfare consolidation to underscore the role of labour in welfare reform: a 'lib-lab' route of labour and liberal party government (Britain, Sweden and Denmark); a labour-Catholic route (Belgium and the Netherlands) and a Bismarckian authoritarian route with subordinated but organized working-class associations (Germany). The data suggest that working-class organization was necessary but not sufficient in bringing about early welfare programme consolidation. Significantly, the early agrarian democracies or those with no strong labour participation (Switzerland, Norway, France, New Zealand, Canada and north and west of the USA) were laggards in welfare development. The depression in the interwar period slowed down social policy development as countries adopted austerity measures. However, wide-ranging social unrest across countries subsequently produced the building blocks of corporatism, especially in the Scandinavian countries where social democrats were in government for extended periods.

Postwar democratization: Japan, Costa Rica, India, Jamaica, Mauritius and Botswana

Many countries around the world experienced democratization or redemocratization after the Second World War. Huntington (1991) describes this phase, which, in his estimation, spans the period 1943–62, as the second wave of democratization. Przeworski *et al.* (2000) have questioned the notion of a 'democratic wave' for this period since, in their own estimates, the 'reverse wave' was stronger than the democratic wave. Both Huntington and Przeworski *et al.* exclude a large number of countries, especially in Africa, that they incorrectly claimed entered statehood as authoritarian regimes.[13] The Allied occupation promoted democracy in West Germany, Italy, Austria, Japan and Korea. In Latin America, Uruguay experienced redemocratization; Brazil and Costa Rica established democratic governments; and some forms of democratic rule were briefly experienced in Argentina, Colombia, Peru and Venezuela. Decolonization in Asia, Africa and the Caribbean produced a host of democratic regimes, even though they survived only in the Caribbean and a few countries in Africa and Asia. In our case studies, democratic government was established in India in 1947; in Costa Rica in 1950; in Jamaica in 1962; in Botswana in 1966; and in Mauritius in 1968. Cross-class nationalist movements led by middle classes, who privileged national sovereignty over everything else, were responsible for most of these transitions.[14]

This second period of democratization occurred in a context of sustained growth in the world economy between 1950 and 1973. The average annual growth rate for 15 European countries and the United States and Japan was 4.96 per cent, with 'catch-up countries', such as Japan, Germany, Spain, Greece and Portugal recording growth rates of more than 6 per cent. Developing countries also experienced high rates of growth and rising per capita incomes. High growth led to a transformation of European economies as workers left agriculture for industry on a massive scale. Additional features of this period were the expansion of the state's role in the economy, the emergence of Keynesian methods of demand management in stabilizing economies, the consolidation and expansion of corporatist methods of collective bargaining, and innovative and expansive programmes in social policy. The international environment was thus favourable for social policy development in the new postwar democracies. The constraints on, or differences in, welfare effort can be explained by differences in the structure and development of national economies and labour markets, the formation and organization of salaried classes, the competitive nature of the democratic regime, and the extent to which parties in government were committed to comprehensive welfare policies.

Japan, as Toshimitsu Shinkawa points out in Chapter 3, experienced limited democratization when a two-party system emerged between 1924 and 1932. However, sovereignty still rested with the emperor during this period and the military was not subordinated to civil control. The shift from light to heavy industry increased the number of male workers, who challenged the state's paternalistic style of labour relations that were prevalent when the labour force was largely female, through increased levels of unionization and collective action on wages, working conditions and social insurance. Union militancy encouraged liberal-minded bureaucrats to advocate progressive social legislation. However, the labour movement was suppressed by the military in the 1930s and plant-level industrial patriotic units replaced unions. Social policies during this period took the form of mutual aid schemes; retirement allowances of varying quality; poor relief to foundlings, orphans and the aged; compensation for work injuries; health insurance for manual workers; and a rudimentary pension plan. Employers and conservative elites in the bureaucracy and the party system consistently opposed unemployment insurance. Employers perceived social policy as a gift for workers' loyalties.

The occupying power, the United States, was the main driver for democratization and social policy development after the Second World War. Political and social citizenship rights were protected in the new constitution and a major land reform empowered small holders. Although 70 per cent of farmers did not own the land they tilled at the end of the war, by 1950 more than 60 per cent did. Japan experienced sustained economic growth of more than 8 per cent between 1950 and 1973 and a profound transformation of its economy. The salaried component of its labour force expanded in leaps and bounds. Unionization reached an all-time high of 55 per cent in 1949. The combination of free peasants and expansion of organized labour helped the socialist party to win a plurality of the votes and to form a centre-left coalition government in 1947. However, this government lasted only a year. Divisions within the ruling party, the dominance of anti-capitalist forces in the largest union, hard-hitting policies against radical unionists by the occupying power and employers, and withdrawal of support by farmer groups from the coalition ensured that social policy developed within a framework of occupationally structured and fragmented programmes. The unionization rate declined to about a third in the early 1950s and to less than 20 per cent in recent times. Japan has the lowest ratio of social security expenditures to GDP (14.1 per cent in 1996) in OECD countries.[15] Shinkawa concludes that in the corporate welfare regime that prevailed, the level of social protection for a worker is, in general, a function of company size and length of service.

The economic and labour force characteristics of India, Costa Rica, Mauritius, Jamaica and Botswana were different from Japan's. The former were largely agrarian economies when they attained statehood or established democratic forms of rule. The process of industrialization in these countries was not as profound as in Japan; and high levels of informalization accompanied their urbanization. The proportion of their salaried labour force and levels of unionization were relatively low compared to those of the advanced democracies. Mass parties with strong union links did not develop in these countries to the level experienced in OECD democracies. The contribution of social expenditure as a proportion of GDP was also lower in the developing democracies than in the OECD ones. The emphasis in social policy development in these developing democracies tended to focus on basic social services. However, there are differences among them in terms of their economic and labour force characteristics, political dynamics, and welfare efforts.

According to World Bank classification, Costa Rica, Mauritius and Botswana are upper-middle-income countries; Jamaica is a lower-middle-income country; and India is a low-income country. As Table 1.3 shows, despite strong efforts at industrialization through import-substitution strategies and a more open economy in recent years, more than two-thirds of India's labour force is still in the agricultural sector. Industry accounts for about 13 per cent of its labour force and services 20 per cent. Even though India's economy grew at a rate of more than 5 per cent after market reforms were introduced in the early 1990s, the corresponding growth in formal employment has been disappointing. Indeed, as Neera Chandhoke shows in Chapter 7, growth in employment in the manufacturing sector has remained stagnant; and the bulk of employees in the urban areas are found in the informal sector. Union density

Table 1.3 Labour force characteristics of Costa Rica, Mauritius, Jamaica, India and Botswana (2000 if not otherwise indicated)

Country	*% informal labour force*	*% in agriculture*[1]	*% in industry*	*% in service*	*urban pop % of total*	*Union density*[2]
Costa Rica	18.9[3]	20.4	22.3	56.5	59	13.1
Mauritius	38.8[3]	14.5	39.8	45.7	41	25.9
Jamaica	23.5[3]	21.4	18.5	60	56	25
India	55.7[4]	66.7	12.9	20.3	28	5.4
Botswana	19.3[4]	19.7	20.9	58.1	49	11.5

Sources: ILO 2002; World Bank 2004; ILO 1997; and Cowell and Singh 2001.
Notes:
[1] Sectoral employment observations for India and Mauritius are from 1995, Jamaica from 1998. Observation for wage and salaried workers in Mauritius is from 1995, Jamaica from 1999.
[2] Union membership as a percentage of non-agricultural labour force, 1995.
[3] Small or micro-enterprises (national definition), Costa Rica 2000, Mauritius 1997, Jamaica 1996.
[4] National definition, India 2000, Botswana 1996.

is only 5.4. It has been estimated that collective bargaining agreements cover less than 2 per cent of formal and informal sector workers; and that patronage relations have tended to define union–government relations, especially during the long rule of the Congress party (Bhattacherjee 2002).

Botswana, Costa Rica, Mauritius and Jamaica have comparatively less labour in agriculture than India. As Table 1.3 shows, the majority of the labour force of these countries is found in the service sector. However, Mauritius has a very high proportion of its employees (39.8 per cent) in industry, followed by Costa Rica (22.3 per cent), Botswana (20.9 per cent) and Jamaica (18.5 per cent). Both Mauritius and Costa Rica have pursued export-led industrialization strategies; whereas Botswana is a mineral-based economy; and Jamaica derives more than two-thirds of its foreign exchange from bauxite and tourism. Keitseope Nthomang shows in Chapter 8 that although Botswana's diamond industry has provided enormous revenues to the state, its effects on employment have been dismal. The state is still the largest single employer. Employment in the services sectors of Botswana and Jamaica is high, but much of this is informal or small-scale activity, or in the case of Jamaica tourism-related. In Chapter 10, Jennifer Jones highlights the failure of the dominant sectors of the Jamaican economy – bauxite, tourism, large sugar estates, hotels and other services – to absorb the country's unskilled labour. A populist regime in the 1970s that tried to promote redistributive policies faced strong resistance from the international financial institutions and private capital.

The level of union density also varies across the four countries. Union density is higher in Mauritius (25.9 per cent) and Jamaica (25 per cent), followed by Costa Rica (13.1 per cent) and Botswana (11.5 per cent). Jones discusses the strong divisions within Jamaica's trade union movement, with the main labour federations linked to ideologically opposed political parties, as a factor in labour's weak impact on policy making. In Mauritius, however, as Sheila Bunwaree points out in Chapter 9, unions have been influential in industrial relations and public policy. A tripartite system of collective bargaining governs industrial relations; and unions are involved in shaping the agendas of the main parties, which are commited to welfare. However, unions do not enjoy the right to strike. Nthomang reports in Chapter 8 that Botswana's unions are very weak and are not affiliated to any of the political parties. In addition, the government has prevented public sector employees from joining or forming unions. Unions in Costa Rica are also weak, although solidarity associations complement labour participation in industrial relations.[16] The political system has tended to be very competitive in Costa Rica, Mauritius, Jamaica and, recently, in India. It is less competitive in Botswana where only one party has governed since independence. Voter participation rates are highest in Mauritius and Costa Rica, followed by India and Jamaica. They are low in Botswana.[17]

These differences may explain variations in social policy development, especially in social security effort. Two of the three upper-middle-income

Table 1.4 Social outcomes in Costa Rica, Mauritius, Jamaica, India and Botswana

Country	*GDP per capita, ppp $, 2002*	*Human Development Index, 2002*	*Education index*	*Life expectancy index*	*GINI Index*	*Social security expenditure as % of GDP (1996)*[1]	*Population living on less than 2 S/day*
Costa Rica	8,840	0.834	0.87	0.88	46.5	13	9.5
Mauritius	10,810	0.785	0.79	0.78	38.7	6	na
Jamaica	3,980	0.764	0.83	0.84	37.9	4.5	13.3
India	2,670	0.595	0.59	0.64	32.5	2.6	79.9
Botswana	8,170	0.589	0.76	0.27	63	2.7	50.1

Source: UNDP 2004b; ILO 2000; ILO 2005 and World Bank 2004.
Notes:
[1] Costa Rica 2000, Jamaica 2000, India 1999–2000, Botswana 1993.

countries, Costa Rica and Mauritius, are the high performers in provision of basic social services. As Table 1.4 shows, Costa Rica's performance in HDI, and education and life expectancy indexes is comparable to those of OECD democracies; and Mauritius is a medium human development country. However, for its level of per capita income, Mauritius should have registered a higher HDI score. Jamaica's scores place it at the medium human development level, at a lower level than Mauritius. India and Botswana are further down in the medium human development level. For its level of per capita income, Botswana's HDI should have been closer to that of Mauritius. Botswana's education index is high, but its life expectancy index has fallen dramatically due to the AIDS crisis. Without the AIDS crisis it might still be registering a higher HDI, as in 1993 when it ranked 71 out of 178 countries. If all countries have done relatively well in basic services, the picture is different in social security. Table 1.4 shows that Costa Rica is the best performer in this area: it spent 13 per cent of its GDP on social security in 1996. This is followed by Mauritius with 6 per cent; and Jamaica 4.5 per cent. Botswana and India are the laggards, spending a mere 2.7 per cent and 2.6 per cent of their GDPs respectively on social security.

Costa Rica's welfare generosity has been linked to the early emergence of a dominant, though non-hegemonic, social democratic party (Mesa-Lago, 2000; Huber, 1996); consensus by the two main parties on social policy; existence of a high proportion of salaried employees (67.5 per cent of the labour force in 1995); and development of a highly competitive party system where the two main parties alternate in government and voter participation has consistently been above 75 per cent between 1970 and 1998. Costa Rica enacted many liberal reforms in the 1940s, including recognition of workers' rights and minimum wages. Following a brief civil war over disputed elections in 1948, a new constitution was adopted that extended the franchise to women and the small black population, and the national army was abolished. The newly elected government, which was in office for about 10 years, pursued a radical socialist-oriented programme by nationalizing the banks and introducing a social security system. It seems that these issues make up for the relatively weak levels of unionization in explaining the very positive social policy outcomes. Mauritius's welfare development can be explained by factors related to the high proportion of its labour force in manufacturing; it's relatively high union density and tripartite bargaining regime; the commitment, as Sheila Bunwaree explains in Chapter 8, of its main parties to some form of social democracy; and the competitive nature of its party system. However, in contrast to Costa Rica, more than 50 per cent of its population is still rural and about 40 per cent of its labour force is in the informal sector. Such differences may explain the relatively less generous outcomes in Mauritius when compared to Costa Rica despite the former's higher per capita income.

India's low performance in social security seems connected to its low-income status, large proportion of its labour force in agriculture and informal sector as well as its low levels of unionization and absence of pro-welfare parties.[18] And Botswana has been less generous in social security because of the structure of its labour market, low levels of unionization and relatively low level of political competition as measured by the lack of alternation in government of the main parties and low voter participation in elections. As Nthomang reports in the case of Botswana, the government feels less pressured by social forces; although opposition parties have increased their share of the popular votes in urban areas, the government continues to enjoy a large majority of seats in parliament thanks to its strong rural support and the first-past-the-post electoral rules; and pursuit of development programmes and governmental relations with social groups has tended to be paternalistic. Botswana's Gini index (63) is also the highest among the five countries.

Despite low social security expenditures as a proportion of GDP in India, Botswana and Jamaica, all five countries have supported a wide range of programmes in social security. The five countries have a pension system, although those of Costa Rica and Mauritius are the most generous. Coverage of the self-employed is voluntary, and Jamaica's excludes casual workers and unpaid family labour. In India, only workers in firms with more than 20 employees are covered. There is almost complete coverage of the population in health care in Costa Rica, Mauritius and Botswana, although the level of provision varies; and in Botswana and Mauritius coverage is supplemented by mutual aid schemes funded by both workers and employees. Varying forms of support for work injury also exist in the five countries, as well as maternity leave and limited family allowances. A major gap in all countries is unemployment insurance. Some countries have severance pay schemes or retirement benefits, and limited income support for a number of work-days per year as in India. Neera Chandhoke reports in Chapter 6 that even though India has been a laggard in welfare development, democracy and a very progressive judiciary have recently empowered a wide range of advocacy groups to compel governments to firm up the rights on food, employment, health and education embedded in its constitution.[19]

The third phase: Southern Europe, Latin America, and Central and Eastern Europe

Scholars generally agree that the third phase of democratization started in Southern Europe when the authoritarian regimes of Spain, Portugal and Greece were dismantled in the mid-1970s. By 2000, most regions of the world had experienced some form of democratization, even if there are questions about the quality and sustainability of some of the democracies. The long period of growth enjoyed by the world economy ended with the first oil crisis of 1974; and economies experienced high levels of fiscal deficits, inflation and unemployment. Calls for welfare state retrenchment as well as residualism and targeting in social provision became prominent; Keynesianism was discredited; and neoliberal ideas that privilege inflation control, liberalization and privatization over full employment and state intervention emerged as a framework for managing economies in both developed and developing countries. The third wave of democratization thus occurred in a global environment that is less favourable to the pursuit of effective social policies. Mkandawire (2004) has observed that the new democracies have been much more orthodox in their macroeconomic policies than established or older democracies.

Southern Europe experienced rapid industrial transformation in the period 1950–73 when its average growth rate of 8 per cent surpassed the average of the European OECD countries (4.6 per cent). However, the three Southern European countries' average growth rate of 1.7 per cent[20] was much lower than the OECD average of 2.3 per cent between 1973 and 1979 – the period of democratization in the region. These countries also had a significant proportion of their workforce in agriculture at the time of their transitions: 22 per cent in Spain and 35 per cent in Portugal and Greece against an EU average of 10 per cent. As Maurizio Ferrera reports in Chapter 4, these countries had a highly segmented labour market: a core/regular sector with strict rules on employment conditions and job security; a peripheral/irregular sector of small enterprises with flexible rules of employment and job instability; and an underground sector. Female labour force participation was also low in Spain and Greece. Labour market segmentation produced an insider-outsider cleavage in welfare policy development.

Unlike developing country democracies consolidated in the second phase of democratization, Southern Europe had a long history of ideological polarization related to the compressed nature of its transition to capitalism in the late nineteenth and early twentieth centuries. Compressed industrialization exacerbated social conflict, radicalized the working class, and facilitated the growth of communist and fascist movements. Authoritarian rule in the three countries was unable to wipe out the radical, anti-systemic traditions in politics; they survived until much later after democratic rule was established.

The average density of unionization for the three countries (39.4 per cent)[21] in 1975 compared favourably with the average for the United Kingdom, Belgium, Austria, Ireland, Germany, Switzerland, France, Italy and Netherlands estimated at 43.2 per cent. Only the Nordic group of countries had a much higher average (65.5 per cent) (Ebbinghaus and Visser 1998). Despite the unfavourable global economic environment, Southern European countries were compelled by the polarized nature of their transitions to use social policy as an instrument to consolidate their democratic regimes. European Union cohesion funds helped ease the transition burden.[22]

Social security transfers as a percentage of GDP averaged 7.3 per cent in 1974 (compared to an EU average of 13.3 per cent); by 1990 this has jumped to 14 per cent against an EU average of 17 per cent. A pension system with varying degrees of coverage was introduced or expanded in places where it already existed; and a national health service was established in all three countries. Especially in Portugal and Spain, unions participated in the management of welfare programmes through social pacts that helped ease the transition to democracy and European Union membership. However, social protection followed the logic of the segmented labour market; transfers enjoyed a priority over services; and the welfare system in general was fragmented into various schemes linked to occupational status. Ferrera reports that before the market-oriented reforms of the 1990s that rationalized the welfare system, democracy provided a basis for parties and voters to personalize the welfare delivery system and trade welfare with votes when faced with high unemployment. Invalidity pensions and unemployment subsidies, especially in backward sectors and regions, such as agriculture in the impoverished South, were the most affected.

The third wave of democratization reached Latin America in the late 1970s, and by the 1990s most countries in the region were at least formally democratic. A recent study suggests substantial progress in democracy in the region as measured by the electoral democracy index[23] (UNDP 2004a). This rose from 0.28 in 1977 to 0.93 in 2002. A notable feature is the seemingly routine alternation of power among parties, which contrasts sharply with the practice between 1920 and 1980 when some countries experienced periods of democratic rule. In examining the historical links between democracy and social policy, Fernando Filgueira suggests in Chapter 6 that countries that experienced long periods of democratic rule before the current transitions to democracy demonstrate levels of social spending that are higher than should be expected given their GDP; and countries whose histories were largely marked by authoritarian rule, with few or no democratic interludes, demonstrate levels of social expenditure that are lower than should be expected given their levels of GDP.

Filgueira highlights three distinct types of social states in Latin America before the democratic transitions. These are based on the nature of their import substitution industrialization strategies, and the way different social strata were included or excluded in social programmes. Argentina, Uruguay and Chile[24] are categorized as cases of universal or near-universal social states: social security covered most of the economically active population; primary education was universal; and basic health services were available to almost all of the population. However, with the exception of education, their welfare system was highly stratified. Brazil, Mexico and, to some extent, Venezuela, Panama, and Colombia are classified as cases of dualism: a large proportion of the population had access to social services and income maintenance schemes, although in a highly stratified manner; and another very large part of the population did not enjoy social protection. The third type refers to the exclusionary social states of El Salvador, Honduras, Bolivia, Ecuador and Guatemala: only a small privileged elite enjoyed social protection. Filgueira reports that long periods of democracy in Chile, Uruguay and Argentina empowered pro-welfare social forces, such as trade unions, that helped advance the social states. He also suggests that dualism and exclusion were a product of authoritarian rule or lack of electoral competitiveness in those countries: only segments of the population incorporated in the modern sector enjoyed social protection, albeit in a stratified way.

The new wave of democratization coincided with fiscal deficits of about 8 per cent of GDP in the 1980s (some countries, such as Brazil and Mexico had deficits of between 10 per cent and 20 per cent of GDP). Most of these countries had also accumulated large private debts. Stabilization and debt rescheduling brought them under the supervision of the Bretton Woods Institutions. A liberal route to economic and social reform gained dominance, and social spending decreased in the 1980s. However, the deepening of the social crisis and the threat it posed to the new democracies led to an increase in social spending in the 1990s. Filguiera suggests that the liberal reforms on social security partly maintained previous privileges based on the type of social state in existence. However, only Chile among the stratified universal countries opted for a full-blown privatization of social security. Uruguay, Argentina and Costa Rica pursued mild forms of privatization of their social security systems. Among the dualist countries, only Mexico opted for radical private provision. And the exclusionary states, such as Bolivia and El Salvador, experimented with large-scale privatization of social security. He concludes that opportunities for new social policy initiatives have been offered by the recent backlash against neoliberal reforms and the electoral victory of left-leaning parties in many countries in the region.

Democratization reached Central and Eastern Europe towards the end of the 1980s and early 1990s with *perestroika* and *glasnost* and the subsequent collapse of the Soviet Union. This region had a relatively developed industrial economy and an extensive welfare regime during communist rule. However, the transition to a market economy, large-scale privatization, and use of market principles in social policy resulted in the loss of some social rights and a decline in well-being in many countries. Terry Cox reports in

Chapter 5 that the main social policy innovations were the introduction of unemployment benefits, services for job search, poverty relief, and separation of social funds – for pensions and health care, for instance – from the state budget. Tripartite pacts of varying effectiveness, involving employers, employees and government emerged in all countries to mediate the transition to democracy and the market as well as to govern the social funds.

Effects of social policy on democracy

The nine studies in this book suggest that democracy and social policy can be mutually reinforcing. Democracy promotes rights and facilitates participation in the policy process; and governments periodically have to renew their mandates to citizens, who may reward or punish contestants depending on how well they perform on welfare. However, as we have seen, for democracy to deliver effective social protection to citizens, it needs some level of economic development; a competitive political environment; organized movements, especially labour unions, with encompassing interests; pro-welfare political parties; and social pacts.

Social policy can, in turn, affect the development of democracy. It can contribute to its *consolidation* as well as improve its *quality*.[25] Consolidation and quality are not the same, although regimes have to be consolidated before their quality can be deepened. A democracy can be consolidated at a very low level of welfare or income security as the example of India and, indeed, the experiences of many new democracies in the third wave suggest. Democratic consolidation involves behavioural and attitudinal changes in which the overwhelming majority of citizens uphold the intrinsic values and procedures of democracy in settling differences. The democratization literature highlights several factors that help consolidation. These include the quality of civil society, degree of consensus among elites on the rules of contestation and alternations of power, and development of an effective bureaucracy and rule of law. It is not always easy to determine when a democracy has been consolidated. Analysts often fall back on the cliché that a democracy is consolidated when 'it is the only game in town' (Linz and Stepan 1996) – i.e. when citizens and politicians accept mutually acceptable rules of political competition. The number of free competitive elections held after the founding election often measures this.

What role does social policy play in the consolidation of democracy? It is not easy to separate out the effects of social welfare provision on democratic consolidation from issues such as incomes, employment and economic growth. Some correlation has been established between levels of income and democratic consolidation. The data by Adam Przeworski *et al.* (2000), which covers the period 1950–1990, suggest that although high income is not a strong predictor of democratization, it plays an important role in consolidating democracies. Democratization can occur at any level of income, but it is almost certain to survive only in countries with per capita incomes that are higher than US$4,000. The second part of this finding confirms a key prediction of modernization theory formulated in the late 1950s by Lipset (1959). In addition, Boix's study (2003) on democracy and redistribution suggests that high levels of equality and capital mobility are also conducive to democratic survival.

It may be overly ambitious and, perhaps, questionable to attempt to derive political outcomes from precise income measurements. However, it is crucial to understand the sociological and political meaning of the links between high income, redistribution and democratic consolidation. High income produces more enlightened citizens; helps the development of social classes, interest groups and civil society more generally; improves the capacity of citizens to discipline policy makers, politicians and administrators; and supports the development of an effective state. In addition, initial redistributions to incorporate the working-class in the political economy and capital mobility may reduce the tax burden on the rich or the scale of subsequent redistributions (as the tax base expands), and may encourage dominant groups to embrace democracy (Boix 2003).

The problem arises when we narrow the focus of analysis to social policy or welfare provision. It has long been assumed that extensive welfare provision has a positive effect on the consolidation of liberal democracy. This point has been highlighted by the literature on the so-called 'historic class compromise'. As Przeworski (1985) puts it, 'social democrats trade off the abolition of private property in the means of production for cooperation of capitalists in increasing productivity and distributing its gains'. However, empirical studies on these linkages, especially as they relate to non-western democracies, are in short supply. The UNDP's Human Development Report of 2002 has shown that even though all western democracies enjoy high HDIs, there is no automatic link between human development and democracy. There are many fairly stable democracies with medium or low human development indexes. One can hypothesize, however, that a social policy that improves the security of the overwhelming majority of citizens improves social solidarity (a cornerstone of citizenship), locks in disadvantaged groups to the democratic regime by undermining revolutionary or violent alternatives, weakens clientelist social relations, and enhances the capacity of citizens to participate in public life as autonomous actors. In other words, social policy impacts the political system and democracy through social cohesion.

The chapters in this book suggest that social policy has been used to advance the cause of democracy in transitions that are highly polarized, such as in advanced industrial societies at the beginning of the twentieth century, and Southern Europe in the 1970s; in democratizations that coincide with a transition to a market economy with high social costs, as in Central and Eastern Europe; in societies whose initial attempts at democracy were threatened by civil unrest or war as in Costa Rica in the late 1940s; or in multi-ethnic societies with small open economies, as in Mauritius.

Conclusion

In conclusion, we restate the point that economic development is a necessary but not a sufficient condition for social policy development. Differences in the quality of industrialization; structure of labour markets; strength of civil society, especially organized interests, such as labour unions; existence of pro-welfare parties in government; and competitive nature of political systems explain variations in social policy efforts across democracies. The vote had a redistributive quality during early periods of democratization: it was used to stave off expropriations and to incorporate working-class interests in the political economy. The uneven quality of industrialization that underpinned subsequent democratizations, especially in developing countries, served to weaken the link between the franchise and redistribution. Concerns for fiscal prudence, deregulation of labour markets, privatization and globalization of production systems have made it increasingly difficult to link the growing networks of civil society groups to the basic capital–labour cleavage that informed the process of democratization and redistribution in earlier periods. It is not surprising that rational choice perspectives, which focus on the individual voter rather than on organized groups, have come to see the vote as a weak instrument for promoting redistribution or holding governments accountable. However, the existence of large political budget cycles in developing countries suggests that competitive elections do matter to voters and politicians and that there is need for some redistribution if economies are to be freed from such cycles.

Although there is no strong correlation between democracy and social policy development, it is important to note that the 22 countries with the highest human development index are all democracies; and no developing country democracy that was consolidated during the second phase of democratization is in the category of countries classified as low human development. In our case studies, developing countries that have demonstrated superior efforts in welfare development have highly competitive political systems and/or reasonable levels of unionization, pro-welfare political parties that have enjoyed governmental office, and elite consensus (sometimes backed by social pacts) on welfare development. Unfortunately, the current international anti-poverty agenda and strategies for attaining the Millennium Development Goals more generally eschew issues related to political contestation and promote a sanitized version of participation in which actors lack real power to effect change or hold policy makers accountable.[26] Economic growth, especially in least developed countries, is certainly a *sine qua non* for meeting these international development targets. However, it has been shown that when growth is combined with redistribution, the chances are much higher for many countries to meet these targets (Cling *et al.* 2005; World Bank 2004). Redistribution, as this book demonstrates, is strongly political.

Notes

1. We would like to thank Lasse Lindström of Stockholm University for comments on this chapter.
2. Views of a leading Conservative MP, Viscount Cranborne. (quote in Acemoglu and Robinson 1999; from Smith 1967).
3. Programme consolidation is defined as when countries have adopted at least three of the four main social insurance programmes: work accident, health, pension and unemployment.
4. The assumption of different types of competent incumbents has been relaxed to include all incumbents in Shi and Sevensson (2002), and Persson and Tabellini (2000) without deviating from the core hypothesis that governments will engage in expansionary fiscal policies before elections.
5. For a general review see Svensson and Shi (2003).
6. A fixed exchange rate regime encourages regimes to manipulate the economy through large budget deficits; countries with non-independent central banks and flexible exchange rates adopt looser monetary policies in election years.
7. Block recognizes the accountability value of political budget cycles but seems largely concerned about how to integrate political and economic reforms in developing countries.
8. Keefer and Khemani (2003) highlight the significance of information and credible political competition in explaining the marked differences between Kerala and Uttar Pradesh in the provision of education and health services despite comparable per capita incomes.
9. In the case of monetary policy, they suggest that voting could be at staggered intervals for the directors of central banks, for instance.
10. In ethnically bipolar Belgium, there are no national political parties, but each of the two ethnic groups, the Flemish and the Walloons, have multiple political parties. In such a situation, parties may not take the ethnic vote for granted.
11. The relative autonomy and political rights enjoyed by organized labour distinguishes this type of corporatism from the corporatism that flourished under Fascist, Nazis and authoritarian governments.
12. Noel Vergunst's doctoral dissertation (2004) on consensus democracy, corporatism and socioeconomic policy making in 20 developed democracies found that it is only in social expenditures that corporatism makes a big difference: in other words, countries with corporatist arrangements have larger welfare states.
13. Huntington (1991) includes only Botswana, Nigeria and Ghana in Africa in the list of formal democracies. Przeworski *et al.* (2000) list only Congo, Mauritius, Nigeria, Sierra Leone and Somalia. The fact is most African countries, especially those ruled by Britain, gained independence with multi-party political regimes. In any case, one fails to see why, for instance, Przeworski *et al.* list (on page 42, footnote 24) Botswana, Gambia, Kenya, Uganda, Zambia, Senegal and Lesotho as dictatorships, and Somalia and Congo as democratic during this period.
14. Kwame Nkrumah's (first president of Ghana) most famous statement 'seek ye first the political kingdom and everything else will be added unto it' is instructive in this regard.
15. Excludes the Republic of Korea.
16. These are less antagonistic towards employers.
17. Mauritius: average of 82.37 per cent (for 7 elections between 1976 and 2000); Costa Rica: average of 77.37 per cent (for 8 elections between 1970 and 1999); India: average

of 62.25 per cent (for 9 elections between 1971 and 1999); Jamaica: average of 54.8 per cent (for 6 elections between 1972 and 1997); and Botswana: average of 42.68 per cent (for 7 elections between 1969 and 1999). Source: Institute for Democracy and Electoral Assistance (IDEA), 2005.

18. Contrast with Kerala where communist party rule has produced high social indicators.
19. Having a progressive judiciary and political parties that are not strongly committed to social provision may not yield substantive welfare development.
20. Spain's rate of growth was 1.4 per cent, Greece's was 2.9 per cent and Portugal's was 0.8 per cent.
21. Portugal's union density was 52.4 per cent, Spain's was 30.4 per cent and Greece's was 35.8 per cent.
22. Between 1989 and 1993, these funds contributed 2.6 per cent of GDP in Greece, 3 per cent of GDP in Portugal and 0.7 per cent of GDP in Spain. Between 1994 and 1999, they went up to 3 per cent of GDP in Greece, 1.5 per cent of GDP in Spain and 3.3 per cent of GDP in Portugal (Dunford 2005).
23. The Electoral Democracy Index is based on measures of four factors: the right to vote, fair elections, free elections, and elections as a means of gaining access to public office.
24. And Costa Rica in the 1980s. Otherwise, Costa Rica is treated as a special case that combines democracy with a less stratified universalism.
25. The issues that inform discussion on the quality of democracy are many and there is little consensus on how to measure quality. Some authors focus strictly on political factors, such as electoral equality, effectiveness of citizen control of government, and freedom of political competition; others combine political factors with issues of rights and group equality; and others emphasize welfare protection and poverty reduction. At the same time there are authors who believe that the protection of property rights and economic performance should be at the heart of efforts to evaluate the quality of democracies. It may be more fruitful to study what different democracies deliver by way of welfare and other public goods than trying to rank countries according to some elusive measure of quality. Studies on the political economy of welfare states and on comparative analysis of the performance of Western democracies already do this very well. In high-income countries with high literacy levels and health provision and drastically reduced poverty, ranking democracies on the basis of their 'quality' will be a very subjective exercise. For instance, we may agree that social democracy provides better welfare outcomes, but it is contestable whether its democracy is of a higher quality than, say, that of liberal welfare states (for a discussion on measurement and conceptual problems on quality of democracy see Schmitter 2004; O'Donnell *et al.* 2004; Whitehead 2002; Ringen 2005; Diamond and Morlino 2005; Baker 1999; and Pasquino 2005).
26. The IMF/World Bank-inspired poverty reduction strategies are top-down despite their support for civic participation in defining the programmes. Governments are not bound to accept the demands of civic groups, and the IMF and World Bank are not bound to accept the views of governments or those that arise out of the 'participatory' process.

References

Acemoglu, D. and J. A. Robinson. 2000. 'Why did the West Extend the Franchise? Democracy, Inequality and Growth in Historical Perspective', *Quarterly Journal of Economics*. 115 (4): 1167–99.

Akhmedov, A, A. Ravichev and E. Zhuravskaya. 2002. 'Opportunistic Political Cycles: Test in a Young Democratic Setting'. Mimeo. 20 December.

Alesina, A., N. Roubini, and G. Cohen. 1997. *Political Cycles and the Macroeconomy.* Cambridge, MA: MIT Press.

Ames, B. 1987. *Political Survival: Politicians and Public Policy in Latin America.* Berkeley: University of California Press.

Baker, B. 1999. 'The Quality of Democracy in the Developing World: Why and How it Should be Measured.' Paper delivered at the 27th ECPR Joint Sessions of Workshops, Mannheim, 26–31 March.

Bhattacherjee, D. 2002. 'Organized Labour and Economic Liberalization in India: Past, Present and Future', in A. V. Jose, *Organized Labour in the 21st Century.* Geneva: International Institute for Labour Studies, the International Labour Organization.

Block, S. 2002. 'Political Business Cycles, Democratization, and Economic Reform: The Case of Africa', *Journal of Development Economics*, 67, 205–28.

Block, S. 2003. 'Elections and the Composition of Public Spending in Developing Countries'. Mimeo. January.

Boix, C. 2003. *Democracy and Redistribution.* Cambridge: Cambridge University Press.

Brenda, A. and A. Drazen, 2004. 'Political Budget Cycles in New versus Established Democracies'. Draft mimeo. August.

Cling, J.-P., P. De Vreyer, M. Razafindrakoto and F. Roubaud. 2006. 'The Impact of Economic Growth and Inequalities on Poverty', translated version of 'L'mpact de la croissance et des inégalités sur la pauvreté', in F. Mourji, B. Decaluwé, A. Diaw et P. Plane (eds), *Le développment face à la pauvreté.* Paris: Economica.

Collier, R. B. 1999. *Paths Toward Democracy: The Working Class and Elites in Western Europe and South America.* Cambridge: Cambridge University Press.

Cowell, N. and G. Singh. 2001. 'Strategic Choices and De-collectivization of the Employment Relationship in the Commonwealth Caribbean'. CIBER Working Paper No. 18, San Diego State University.

Diamond, L. and L. Morlino (eds). 2005. *The Quality of Democracy.* Baltimore: Johns Hopkins University Press.

Drazen, A. 2000. 'The Political Business Cycle after 25 Years.' Paper for the NBER Macroeconomics Annual Conference, 7–8 April.

Dunford, M. 2005. 'Old Europe, New Europe and the USA: Comparative Economic Performance, Inequality and Market-led Models of Development', *European Urban and Regional Studies*, 12(2), 149–76.

Ebbinghaus, B. and J. Visser. 1998. 'When Institutions Matter: Union Growth and Decline in Western Europe, 1950–95', Mannheimer Zentrum für Europäische Sozialforschung. Arbeitsbereich I/Nr. 30.

Engels, F. (1890) 1960. 'Introduction', In K. Marx, *The Civil War in France, 1848–1850.* Moscow: Progress Publishers.

Esping-Andersen G. 1990. *Three Worlds of Welfare Capitalism.* Princeton, NJ: Princeton University Press.

Fearon, J. D. 1999. 'Electoral Accountability and the Control of Politicians: Selecting Good Types Versus Sanctioning Poor Performance', in Przeworski *et al.*, *Democracy, Accountability, and Representation.* Cambridge: Cambridge University Press.

Flora, P. 1983. *State, Economy and Society, 1815–1975.* Frankfurt: Campus Verlag.

Ghai, D. (ed.) 2000. *Social Development and Public Policy: A Study of Some Successful Experiences.* London: Macmillan Press in collaboration with UNRISD

Gonzalez, M. 2002. *On Democracy, Transparency and Economic Policy: Theory and Evidence.* Dissertation. Princeton University.

Hallerberg, M. and L. V. de Souza. 2000. 'The Political Business Cycles of EU Accession Countries'. *Tinbergen Institute Discussion Paper*. TI 2000-085/2

Hicks, A. 1999. *Social Democracy and Welfare Capitalism: A Century of Income Security Policies*. Ithaca: Cornell University Press.

Huber, E. 1996. 'Options for Social Policy in Latin Amercia: Neoliberal versus Social Democratic Models', in G. Esping-Andersen, *Welfare States in Transition: National Adaptations in Global Economies*. London: UNRISD and Sage.

Huber, E. and J. D. Stephens. 2001. *Development and Crisis of the Welfare State: Parties and Policies in Global Markets*. Chicago, IL: The University of Chicago Press.

Huntington, S. P. 1991. *The Third Wave: Democratization in the Late Twentieth Century*. Norman: University of Oklahoma Press.

Institute for Democracy and Electoral Assistance (IDEA). 2005. *Voter Turnout Database*. Stockholm. Accessed on 13 June 2005.

International Labour Organization (ILO). 2005. *Socio-Economic Security Database*. Geneva. Accessed on 5 June 2005.

International Labour Organization (ILO). 2004. *Key Indicators of the Labour Market 3rd edition*. Geneva.

International Labour Organization (ILO). 2002. *ILO Compendium of Official Statistics on Employment in the Informal Sector*. STAT Working Paper No. 1. Geneva.

International Labour Organization (ILO). 2000. *World Labour Report 2000: Income Security and Social Protection in a Changing World*. Geneva.

International Labour Organization (ILO). 1996–1997. *World Labour Report 1997–1998: Industrial Relations, Democracy and Social Stability*. Geneva.

Keefer, P. and S. Khemani. 2003. 'Democracy, Public Expenditures, and the Poor'. World Bank, Policy Research Working Paper 3164. November.

Khemani, S. 2000. 'Political Cycles in a Developing Economy: Effect of Elections in Indian States'. World Bank. Policy Research Working Paper 2454.

Kraus, F. 1981. 'The Historical Development of Income Inequality in Western Europe and the United States', in P. H. Flora and A. Heidenheimer (eds), *The Development of the Welfare State in Europe and America*. New Brunswick, NJ: Transaction Books.

Lenz, G. and J. Ladd. 2003. 'A Quantitative Investigation of the Extension of the Franchise in the West'. Paper presented at the annual meting of the American Political Science Association, 28–31 August. Philadelphia.

Lindert, P. H. 1994. 'The Rise in Social Spending, 1880–1930', *Explorations in Economic History*, 31, 1–37.

Linz, J. L. and A. Stepan. 1996. *Problems of Democratic Transition and Consolidation: Southern Europe, South America, and Post-Communist Europe*. Baltimore, MD: Johns Hopkins University Press.

Lipset, S. M. 1959. 'Some Social Requisites of Democracy: Economic Development and Political Legitimacy.' *American Political Science Review*, 53(1), 69–105.

Manin, B., A. Przeworki and Susan C. Stokes. 1999. 'Elections and Representation.' In Przeworski, A., S. C, Stokes and B. Manin (eds), *Democracy, Accountability and Representation*. Cambridge: Cambridge University Press.

McGillivray, M. 1991. 'The Human Development Index: Yet Another Redundant Composite Indicator?' *World Development*, 19(10), 1461–8.

Mehrotra, S. and R. Jolly. 2000. *Development with a Human Face: Experiences in Social Achievement and Economic Growth*. Oxford: Oxford University Press.

Meltzer, E. and S. Richard. 1981. 'A Rational Theory of the Size of Government.' *Journal of Political Economy*, 89(5), 914–27.

Mesa-Lago, C. 2000. 'Achieving and Sustaining Social Development With Limited Resources: The Experience of Costa Rica', in D. Ghai (ed.), *Social Development and Public Policy: A Study of Some Successful Experiences*. London: UNRISD and Macmillan.

Mill, J. S. 1946. 'Considerations on Representative Government.' in *On Liberty and Considerations of Representative Government*. Oxford.

Mkandawire, T. 2004. 'Disempowering New Democracies and the Persistence of Poverty', in M. Spoor (ed.), *Globalization, Poverty and Conflict*. Dordrecht: Kluwer Academic Publishers, pp. 117–53.

Moore, M., J. Leavy, P. Houtzager and H. White. 1999. 'Polity Qualities: How Governance Affects Poverty'. Paper for the Governance Department of the United Kingdom Department for International Development, September.

Morrison, C. 2000. 'Historical Perspectives on Income Distribution: The Case of Europe', in A. B. Atkinson and F. Bourguignon (eds), *Handbook of Income Distribution*. Vol. 1. Elsevier.

Nordhaus, W. 1975. 'The Political Business Cycle.' *Review of Economic Studies*, Vol. 42, Pp. 169–90.

O'Donnell, G. 2001. 'Human Development, Human Rights, Democracy.' Paper prepared for discussion in a workshop on the 'Quality of Democracy', sponsored by the UNDP. Regional Division for Latin America and the Caribbean, and the Progama de la Nacion, Costa Rica.

O'Donnell G., J. V. Cullell, O. M. Iazzetta (eds). 2004. *The Quality of Democracy: Theory and Applications*. Lafayette, in: University of Notre Dame Press.

Pasquino, G. 2005. 'The Quality of Democracy'. The 2005 Isaiah Berlin Visiting Scholar Lectures. Lecture One. Centre for the Study of Democratic Government, Department of Politics and International Relations, University of Oxford. Working Paper Series. No. 002-1. February.

Persson, T. and G. Tabellini, 2000. *Political Economics: Explaining Economic Policy*. Cambridge MA: MIT Press.

Przeworski, A. 1985. *Capitalism and Social Democracy*. New York: Cambridge University Press.

Przeworski, A., S. Stokes and B. Manin. 1999. *Democracy, Accountability and Representation*. Cambridge: Cambridge University Press.

Przeworski, A., M. Alvarez, J. A. Cheibub and F. Limongi. 2000. *Democracy and Development: Political Institutions and Well-Being in the World, 1950–1990*. Cambridge: Cambridge University Press.

Ringen, S. 2005. 'What is Democratic Quality?' Mimeo. University of Oxford.

Rogoff, K. 1990. 'Equilibrium Political Budget Cycles', *American Economic Review*, 80, 21–36.

Rueschemeyer, D., E. H. Stephens and J. D. Stephens. 1992. *Capitalist Development and Democracy*. Chicago: University of Chicago Press.

Schmitter, P. C. 2004. 'The Quality of Democracy: The Ambiguous Virtues of Accountability'. Mimeo. Istituto Universitario Europeo. September.

Schuknecht, L. 1996. 'Political Business Cycles and Fiscal Policies in Developing Countries', *Kyklos*, 49, 155–70.

Shi, M. and J. Svensson. 2002. 'Conditional Political Budget Cycles'. CEPR Discussion Paper, No. 3352.

Shi, M. and J. Svensson. 2003. 'Political Budget Cycles: A Review of Recent Developments', *Nordic Journal of Political Economy*, 29(1), 67–76.

Stokes, S. 2001. *Mandates and Democracy: Neoliberalism by Surprise in Latin America*. Cambridge: Cambridge University Press.

Stokes, S. 2005. 'Perverse Accountability: A Formal Model of Machine Politics with Evidence from Argentina', *American Political Science Review*, 99(3), 315–26.

Shi, M. and J. Svensson. 2003. 'Political Budget Cycles: A Review of Recent Developments', *Nordic Journal of Political Economy*, 29(1), 67–76.

Therborn, G. 1977. 'The Rule of Capital and the Rise of Democracy', *New Left Review*. 103, 3–41.

Tufte, E. R. 1978. *Political Control of the Economy*. Princeton, NJ: Princeton University Press.

United Nations Development Programme (UNDP). 2002. *Human Development Report: Deepening Democracy in a Fragmented World*. Oxford: Oxford University Press.

United Nations Development Programme (UNDP). 2004a. *Ideas and Contributions: Democracy in Latin America*. New York: United Nations Development Programme.

United Nations Development Programme (UNDP). 2004b. *Human Development Report: Cultural Liberty in Today's Diverse World*. Oxford: Oxford University Press.

Vergunst, N. 2004. 'The Institutional Dynamics of Consensus and Conflict: Consensus democracy, corporatism and socio-economic policy-making and performance in twenty developed democracies (1965–1998)'. PhD dissertation. Department of Political Science, University of Amsterdam. The Netherlands.

Varshney, A. 1999. 'Democracy and Poverty'. Paper for the conference on the World Development Report 2000, England, 15–16 August.

Whitehead, L. 2002. 'Notes on Human Development, Human Rights, and Auditing the Quality of Democracy'. Revised comments for UNDP workshop on the Quality of Democracy. San José, Costa Rica. February.

Williamson, J. G. 1985. *Did British Capitalism Breed Inequality?* Boston: Allen and Unwin.

World Bank. 2004. *World Development Indicators*. Washington, DC: World Bank.

2

Democratization and Social Policy Development in Advanced Capitalist Societies*

John D. Stephens

In a number of works stretching back twenty-five years, my co-authors and I have argued that similar social, political, and historical factors are behind the development of political democracy and generous and redistributive social policy (Stephens 1979, 1989, 1995; Rueschemeyer, Stephens, and Stephens 1992; Huber, Rueschemeyer, and Stephens 1993, 1997; Huber, Ragin, and Stephens 1993; Huber and Stephens 1999, 2001; Stephens and Kümmel 2002; Bradley *et al.* 2003). While the factors leading to democracy and generous social policy are not identical, they are sufficiently similar to suggest that a relatively unified theory can explain both sets of social change. In this essay, I reconsider the development of democracy and social policy in western advanced capitalist democracies, primarily focusing on the period 1870 to 1950.[1]

Following the analytic strategy of Rueschemeyer, Stephens, and Stephens, I examine the universe of cases that fits the selection criteria, which are partly analytic and partly practical, the latter related to the fact that the other possible cases are covered by other chapters in this book. My analytic criteria for choosing these countries are that (i) they were national states in 1900; (ii) they were western developed capitalist democracies as of 1950; and (iii) they were stable democratic regimes as of 1950 (which we know only in retrospect). The countries included in the analysis are nine countries in Western Europe: Belgium, Denmark, France, Germany, Netherlands, Norway, Sweden, Switzerland, and the United Kingdom; and the four British settler colonies: Australia, Canada, New Zealand, and the United States.[2]

The period is chosen for analytic reasons. At the initial date, none of these countries had initiated any of the social policies which are generally thought to constitute the modern welfare state. In Europe, only Switzerland was democratic by the conventional definitions of democracy. For France, Switzerland, Britain, and the British settler colonies, I do extend the analysis of

* I would like to thank James Cronin and Evelyne Huber for helpful comments on this chapter.

democratization further back into the nineteenth century since developments in that period are an essential part of the explanation of the political outcome. In the initial two sections of the essay, I present our theories of democratic development and social policy development. The third and fourth sections cover the development of democracy in Europe and the British settler colonies respectively. The fifth, sixth, and seventh sections cover the development of social policy in both regions up to 1920, in the interwar period, and the immediate post-Second World War period respectively.

The theory of democratic development

In *Capitalist Development and Democracy*, we adopt a conventional definition of democracy; regular free and fair elections of representatives on the basis of universal suffrage, responsibility of the state apparatus to the elected representatives of the people; and guarantees for freedom of expression and association. We argue that the development of democracy is the product of three clusters of power: (i) the balance of class power; (ii) the nature of the state and state–society relations; and (iii) transnational structures of power, or the international economy and system of states.

The central thesis of our book is that capitalist development is related to democracy because it shifts the balance of class power by weakening the power of the landlord class and strengthening subordinate classes. The working and the middle classes – unlike other subordinate classes in history – gain an unprecedented capacity for self-organization due to such developments as urbanization, factory production, and new forms of communication and transportation. The working class was the most consistently pro-democratic force, whereas the middle classes took an ambiguous position. As to the role of the bourgeoisie,[3] we dispute the claims of both liberal and Marxist political theory that democracy is the creation of the bourgeoisie. The bourgeoisie made important contributions to the move towards democracy by insisting on its share in political power in the form of parliamentary control of the state, but the bourgeoisie was also hostile to further democratization when its interests seemed threatened.[4]

The structure of the state and state–society relations are clearly relevant for the chances of democracy. The state needs to be strong and autonomous enough to ensure the rule of law and avoid being the captive of the interests of dominant groups; the state's authority to make binding decisions in a territory and the state's monopoly of coercion must be settled. However, the power of the state needs to be counterbalanced by the organizational strength of civil society to make democracy possible; the state must not be so strong and autonomous from all social forces as to overpower civil society and rule without accountability.

Recent work on democratization has revived the notion developed by de Tocqueville in his discussion of the role of autonomously organized social groups in the sustaining of American democracy, namely, that a strong or dense civil society is favourable for the development and sustenance of democracy. This clearly fits well with our argument that development of organization of the middle classes and working class is the most important determinant of democratic development. However, as Gramsci reminds us, in more advanced capitalist societies, a dense civil society can be a conduit for inculcation of upper class ideologies in lower classes. Indeed, Hagtvet (1980), arguing against the mass society thesis, contends that German middle classes were thoroughly organized but the values propagated by these organizations were authoritarian and militaristic.

The third power cluster involves international power relations. For the European countries analysed here by far the most decisive impact of international relations has been war, which created a need for mass support both at home for production and on the front for fighting, and which discredited ruling groups in case of defeat. In the case of British settler colonies, it is not surprising that the posture of the colonial power was a critical influence on the course of events.

The theory of social policy development

The class power element of our theory of democratic development has its exact counterpart in the power resources theory of welfare state development (Stephens 1979; Korpi 1983; Esping-Andersen and Korpi 1984). According to this theory, variations in working-class power, as indicated by the strength of union organization, the strength of parties of the left, and the governmental role of parties of the left is the primary explanation for variations in the size and redistributive impact of welfare states across advanced industrial countries. There is copious empirical evidence to support this theory for the post-Second World War period (e.g. see Hicks 1999; Huber and Stephens 2001; Swank 2002; Bradley *et al.* 2003) and Hicks (1999) has extended the argument to the period covered in this chapter.

Wilensky (1981) presents evidence that Christian democracy also encourages the development of a generous welfare state. Not only is Catholic ideology sympathetic to market-correcting policy, Christian democracy aspires to be a multi-class party mediating the differing class interests and thus attempts to appeal to, and organize, the working class in competition with the left (van Kersbergen 1995). Esping-Andersen (1990) and van Kersbergen (1995) argue that the Christian democratic welfare state has characteristics which distinguish it from the social democratic: It is less redistributive and it reinforces the traditional gender inegalitarian male breadwinner family.

The hypotheses about the impact of social democracy and Christian democracy on welfare state development have strong affinities with the arguments for the importance of civil society for democratic development because it is assumed that the impact of these two forces is mediated by the associational life created by these two movements: unions, parties, women's organizations, youth associations, sports leagues, choral societies, etc. That is, it is not enough to have a large working-class proportion or a large Catholic proportion of the population; it must be organized to have an effect on social policy. In some variants of the argument, it is of pivotal importance that the social democratic and Christian democratic parties be in government (Huber and Stephens 2001). However, in addition, opposition parties often influence the social policy agenda and electoral competition may stimulate governing parties to coopt some of the issues of the opposition. This is particularly true of the competition between Christian democracy and social democracy as both parties attempt to appeal to and mobilize working class voters (Huber and Stephens 2001; Wilensky 2002).

The literature on early welfare state development points to another role that working-class movements have had on welfare state development: These movements were often the objects of early reformist legislation, legislation which was often opposed by working-class leaders because of its co-optative design or intent or because it was too meagre. Bismarck's attempt simultaneously to repress social democracy and to co-opt workers with social policy initiatives is the most famous example of this. This dynamic is not limited to conservative governments in authoritarian regimes, but also occurs in Catholic and liberal governments in democratic regimes.

A number of studies have shown that aspects of state structure, such as state centralization, federalism, or the number of constitutionally mandated veto points affect social spending (Immergut 1992; Hicks and Misra 1993; Maioni 1998). State centralization, unitary government, unicameralism or weak upper chambers, and absence of an executive veto have been found to be favorable to social policy innovation.

In the literature on social policy development, there are frequent references to transnational influences, but the nature of these influences is quite variable dependent on the region and time period. In the case of the countries and time period under consideration, the two world wars are without a doubt the most important influence for much the same reason that war influenced the development of democracy in these countries: These mass mobilization wars created a need for mass support at home and on the front and they discredited ruling groups in case of defeat.

Democratization in Western Europe[5]

By the definition of democracy offered above, in 1870, only one country in Europe was democratic. By 1920, the overwhelming majority were, including all nine under study here. Two decades later, democratic rule had crumbled again in a number of these countries. What had brought democracy about? What separated the democratic survivors from the cases of breakdown?

Moore's (1966) analysis of the role of 'labour repressive' landlords in accounting for breakdown cases focuses heavily on the type of agricultural arrangements and labour-force control adopted by the landed aristocracy. Had Moore included the smaller European countries, his analysis would certainly have begun with the existence (or absence) of a politically powerful landed class. This, in turn, is largely a product of the pattern of concentration of landholdings itself: In all of the small countries, there were too few large estates to support the development of a politically significant class of large landowners. This factor already prevents the development of the class coalition that Moore argues is fatal for democracy. The fact that democracy broke down in not only Germany (which is analyzed here) but also in all countries in Western, Central, and Eastern Europe which contain a large body of landholders dependent on a large supply of cheap labour, save one, and survived in the other eight countries under study here indicates that this factor provides a powerful explanation for the survival or demise of democracy.[6] Britain stands out as one deviant case in terms of landholding. While Moore (1966) argues that the type of commercialized agriculture is the factor that explains British exceptionalism, we point to a number of other features which contributed to the outcome. It is also accurate to classify Germany as a case in which 'labor-repressive' agriculture dominated.

The early democratizers

By the eve of the First World War, a handful of European countries had become democratic: Switzerland (1848) was the trailblazer, followed by France (1877) and Norway (1898). In 1915, Denmark joined this group. These are all nations of smallholders, urban petty bourgeoisie, and with a significant though not nearly dominant industrial sector (and therefore significant working and capitalist classes) at the time of democratization.

The roots of Swiss democracy reach relatively far back and are grounded in Swiss social structure. Swiss history is punctuated with successful intervention of family farmers in political developments. Such autonomous and successful intervention on the part of small farmers only occurs in countries without a powerful landed upper class and it is certainly this characteristic of the social structure of the Swiss countryside that was responsible for early political influence of farmers. Norway was similar in this respect and in both countries small farmers, artisanal workers and the urban middle classes were the main agents of democracy. The industrial working class, in both countries, was quite small at the time of the democratic transition and played little or no role in the transition. These were agrarian democracies.

In France, the various Republican factions of the late 1860s and 1870s, which provided the final push to democracy, were supported by the working class, the petit bourgeoisie, segments of the peasantry (depending on local economic organization, the influence of the Catholic clergy and revolutionary traditions), and segments of the bourgeoisie, especially in the provinces. The events of the late Second Empire clearly built on earlier democratic advances (particularly 1848) which, though thwarted, continued to influence the course of events. In these developments, the bourgeois influence was weaker, and rebellions of the largely artisanal working class played a much larger role.

The ascendance of the social democratic labour movement as the primary force pressing democratization

In Denmark, an alliance of the working class, small and medium farmers, and urban middle-class segments as represented by the Social Democratic–Venstre coalition pressed through the 1901 introduction of parliamentary government. The driving force behind the 1915 introduction of universal suffrage were the Social Democrats and the Radikale Venstre, representing the working class, small farmers, and segments of the middle class. It is important to note here that, though the Scandinavian peasantry was divided on the issue of universal suffrage and the medium and larger farmers not supportive of the final push to universal suffrage, they generally contributed to the process of democratization by supporting earlier suffrage extensions.

In the rest of Western Europe, but particularly among the antagonists in the First World War, the social dislocations caused by the war contributed to the breakthrough of democracy. The war and its outcome changed the balance of power in society, strengthening the working class and weakening the upper classes. The ruling class was discredited, particularly in the defeated countries. Labour support was necessary, at home for the production effort, on the front for the first mass mobilization, mass conscription war of this scale and duration. And, finally, the war economy and mass conscription strengthened the hand of labour in the economy, enabling it to extract concessions for the coming period of peace. One indicator of the change in class power was the swell in labour organization from an average prewar level of 11 per cent of the labour force to a postwar peak of 27 per cent in the antagonists, which experienced the transition to democracy in this period (see Table 2.1). Organization more than doubled in the two non-participants (Sweden and the Netherlands) which experienced the same transition at this time. In all these countries (with the partial exception of Britain, see below), working-class forces played a key, usually the key, role in the transition to democracy. In all cases, social democracy and affiliated unions were an important contributor and, in the Netherlands and Belgium, unions and working-class leagues in the clerical parties also contributed to the pro-democratic posture of those parties. But, as Therborn (1977) notes, the working class was not strong enough on its own. It needed allies or unusual conjunctures of events to effect the introduction of democracy. As an indicator of this it could be pointed out that in no case did the working-class parties receive electoral majorities even after the introduction of universal suffrage.

In Sweden, Belgium, and the Netherlands, it can be argued that the war only accelerated the introduction of democracy. In each country, the pro-democratic coalition – the parties and the underlying alignment of social forces – had formed before or was in the process of formation. In most cases,

Table 2.1 Democratization and union membership in advanced capitalist societies, 1848–1950

	Full democracy	*Previous reform*	*1905*	*1913–14*	*Post-war Peak*	*1930*	*1939–40*	*1950*
Early democratizers								
Switzerland	1848		7	5	12	17	19	29
France	1877	1848	4	5	8	7	17	22
Norway	1898	1884	2	7	13	12	26	34
Social Democratic dominance								
Denmark	1915	1901	7	13	27	21	28	33
Netherlands	1917	1896	4	11	25	20	22	31
Belgium	1918	1893	2	7	27	18	24	36
Sweden	1918	1909	5	6	11	20	36	51
British exceptionalism								
UK	1918	1884	11	22	43	23	31	40
Breakdown cases								
Germany	1918		6	11	30	18		29
Italy	1919	1912	1	2	12			37
British settler colonies								
New Zealand	1891	1852	8	15	19	17	39	38
Australia	1901	1860	10	25	30	38	35	50
Canada	1920	1867	6	6	12	8	8	19
United States	1965	1832	6	7	11	7	16	22
Mean			5.6	10.1	20.0	17.4	25.1	33.6

Source: Stephens 1979: 115.

this coalition had been responsible for previous suffrage extensions, such as the 1907 reform in Sweden or the 1893 reform in Belgium. In these countries, the agrarian elites were too weak to be a significant political force. In Belgium, the Workers' Party, after decades of struggle, including six general strikes, found support in the Social Christian wing of the Catholic party, which was based on working-class Catholics. In the Netherlands, similar divisions among the religious parties and the liberals produced possibilities of alliances for the Social Democrats. It is worth emphasizing that the accounts of the transition in both low countries make it clear that the growing importance of the working class created the pressures that moved the clerical parties towards a more democratic posture. In part, this pressure was transmitted by workers and artisans, already mobilized by self-help societies and trade unions, who joined these parties, and, in part, the pressure was a result of the efforts of these parties to compete with the Social Democrats for the loyalties of unmobilized workers.

The prevailing view of suffrage extension in the British case is that segments of the British upper classes had settled into a pattern of peaceful political competition by the mid-nineteenth century, and this extended to competition for working-class votes, which resulted in the suffrage extensions of 1867 and 1884. On deeper examination, this view of the development of democracy in Britain misses significant contributions of early working-class agitation. The reforms were in part a response to working-class pressure beginning at least as early as the Chartist movement, the main demand of which was universal suffrage, and which was extended throughout the nineteenth century. Nonetheless it is a British peculiarity that the final political initiation of the reforms came from upper-class-led parties without a strong working-class base. A large part of the explanation for this peculiarity lies in the late development of the Labour party itself. The Liberals and the Tories were willing to extend the right to vote to workers only because they hoped to benefit from the votes of the newly enfranchised groups. Had a substantial Labour Party already commanded the loyalty of workers, the established parties would have certainly been reluctant to make such a move.

Full democracy was established by the reform of 1918, which established male suffrage and eliminated all but minor provisions for multiple voting. As Collier (1999: 97–101) argues, the 1918 bill was not the result of the extension of prewar lib–lab cooperation, contrary to our assertion in earlier work (Rueschemeyer, Stephens, and Stephens 1992: 97). The war produced consensus among the parties in the three-party national unity government that disenfranchised workers deserved the vote for their support in the war effort at home and abroad. Thus, the 1918 suffrage reform was uncontroversial.

What can be said so far concerning the development of democracy in Western Europe as has been outlined here? Therborn's (1977) argument seems to be confirmed. He stresses the important role played by the working class – that is, by its organizational representatives, the trade unions and the socialist parties. One can add the role of artisan agitation and early craft unions in the French and British cases and the role of workers in the confessional parties in the Netherlands and Belgium in pressing those parties towards a more democratic posture. The rapid development of industrial capitalism in the second half of the last century stimulated working-class organization that first gradually, and then with the war and its outcome, decisively changed the balance of class power in the entire core of the world capitalist system. In no country in 1870 were the socialists a significant mass-based party and the trade unions organized a miniscule proportion of the labour force; by the eve of the First World War, the parties affiliated with the Second International garnered an average of 24 per cent of the vote (despite suffrage restrictions in a number of countries) and the trade unions organized an average of 10 per cent of the labour force (see Tables 2.1 and 2.2). In the immediate postwar elections, the socialists' electoral share increased to an average of 30 per cent, while trade union organization grew spectacularly, increasing two fold. The organized working class was also the most consistently pro-democratic force during the period under consideration: at the onset of the First World War, European labour movements, all members of the Second International, had converged on an ideology which placed the achievement of universal suffrage and parliamentary government at the centre of their immediate programme. One must add to this the pro-democratic working-class wings of the clerical parties in the low countries.

However, Therborn's (1977) focus on the last reforms in the process of democratization leads to an exaggeration of the role of the working class. First, in the two agrarian democracy cases (Switzerland and Norway), the role of the working class was secondary even in the final push to democracy. Second, in other cases, not only did the working class need allies in the final push, in earlier democratic reforms, multi-class alliances were responsible for the success of the reform (France, Britain, Denmark, Sweden, and Belgium).

However, as the experience of Germany shows most clearly, none of these other social classes were as consistently pro-democratic, both across countries and through time, as the working class.[7] Both the urban middle class and/or segments of the peasantry provided the mass base for authoritarianism in the breakdown cases. The bourgeoisie whose role in the introduction of democracy has been emphasized in so many accounts, from Marxist to liberal, played a positive role in only three cases: Switzerland, Britain and France. Moreover, in Britain and France, it was only segments of the class that cooperated in the push for democracy, and then only after earlier histories of popular agitation for democracy and bourgeois resistance to it. In all of the others, the bourgeoisie was one of the centres of resistance to working-class political incorporation. It did make an indirect contribution to the outcome, however. In the cases discussed so far, the bourgeoisie sought entry into the corridors of power and in all cases, except for Denmark and Sweden, it supported the drive for parliamentary government. Bourgeois political forces established parliamentary government with property, tax, or income qualifications for voting – that is, democracy for the propertied.

The breakdown of democracy in Germany

Thus, the working class needed allies, its power alone was insufficient. In the cases with powerful landed upper classes dependent on cheap labour, no alliance strong enough to overcome their opposition could be constructed in the prewar period. It was only the change in the balance of class power caused by the war that allowed for the democratic breakthrough. This surge in the strength of labour and the political left was quickly, though not completely, rolled back. A quick glance at union membership and voting statistics indicates that this was a general European pattern (Tables 2.1 and 2.2). Where this surge of working-class strength was the essential ingredient in the transition to democracy, the working class and its allies (where it had any) were unable to maintain democracy when a new conjuncture of forces

Table 2.2 Democratization and left percentage of the total vote

			1890s	*1900s*	*Last Pre war Election*	*First postwar election*	*1920s*	*1930s*	*1945–50*
Early democratizers									
Switzerland	1848		8.2	15.0	20.0	23.0	27.4	29.3	31.3
France	1877	1848	9.9	10.2	16.8	21.2	19.1	20.2	20.9
Norway	1898	1884	0.3	12.6	32.1	30.5	34.9	39.3	52.2
Social Democratic dominance									
Denmark	1915	1901	10.3	22.9	29.5	29.7	34.9	45.6	45.4
Netherlands	1917	1896	1.4	11.5	18.5	21.6	24.2	25.7	36.1
Belgium	1918	1893	15.4	25.1	30.3	36.6	37.9	37.9	41.4
Sweden	1918	1909	0.0	9.2	30.1	36.1	42.4	51.8	52.4
British exceptionalism									
UK	1918	1884	0.5	3.1	6.4	22.5	32.9	34.9	47.5
Breakdown cases									
Germany	1918		21.5	30.4	34.8	45.5	37.8	35.4	35.0
Italy	1919	1912	7.9	17.8	22.8	34.3	29.9		38.8
British settler colonies									
New Zealand	1891	1852	0.0	2.5	8.5	23.8	25.7	45.5	49.5
Australia	1901	1860		29.0	48.5	42.5	45.2	41.4	50.2
Canada	1920	1867	0.0	0.2	0.1	2.3	1.9	1.0	1.4
United States	1965	1832	0.0	1.8	6.4	3.2	0.7	1.9	0.0
Mean			5.8	13.7	21.8	26.6	28.2	31.5	35.9

Source: Mackie and Rose 1974.

presented new problems (the depression, worker and peasant militance, and so on) and new alliance possibilities for the upper classes moved the bourgeoisie and the landlords from passive to active opposition to the democratic regime.[8]

As was pointed out, in Germany, on the eve of the First World War, the Social Democrats were the only supporters of parliamentary government and full suffrage reform at all levels of government. Consequently, it seems eminently plausible to argue that the transition to democracy was a direct result of the war. The defeat in the First World War, the discrediting of the ruling class, and the temporary power vacuum on the right that this created changed the balance of class power in Germany. Without the defeat, it seems quite likely that Germany would not have become a democracy for decades, until something created a decisive shift in the balance of class forces.

The Junker landlords and most of heavy industry, primarily coal and steel, supported the authoritarian German National People's Party (DNVP) throughout the Weimar Republic. Other segments of business, export-oriented industry, finance and so on, tended to support the centre right secular parties. These segments of business gradually moved to the right, moving to favour the exclusion of the Social Democrats from any influence and the rolling back of *Sozialpolitik* and other pro-labour measures. This drive to exclude the Social Democrats, combined with the rise of the Nazi vote, left business with two options: supporting a parliamentary government with Nazi support or an extra-parliamentary cabinet of the right, either of which would move the government in an authoritarian direction. Business as a whole supported the chancellorship of DNVP leader Papen, whose government not only began to roll back the Weimar labour legislation and *Sozialpolitik* but also suspended the Prussian Landtag and drew up plans to revise the constitution in a decidedly more authoritarian direction. In all these developments, business used its money, political contacts, and media to influence events in the desired direction. There can be little question that, objectively, the Papen government was a groundbreaker for the Nazis. Papen himself was a key actor in the formation of the first Nazi-led government (a coalition with the DNVP) and a minister in that government. Thus, it is clear that objectively business intervention in the political process contributed to the breakdown of democracy.

To explain the breakdown of democracy in interwar Germany, one must explain not only the action of elites but also why so many people were open to voting for the Nazis (37 per cent in 1932) or, adding the DNVP (6 per cent in July 1932) for authoritarian parties in general. The Nazi vote increased from only 3 per cent in 1928. This increase came almost entirely at the expense of the conservative monarchist (DNVP) and National Liberal (DVP and DDP) blocs, whose mass base was the protestant middle classes and peasantry. The socialist/working-class blocks and the Catholic blocks by and large maintained their support. I contend that the authoritarian and militaristic ideology of the ruling groups of Imperial Germany contributed to the susceptibility of every other sector of the population to the reactionary appeals of Nazism.[9] Under the impact of the increasingly desperate economic conditions of the depression, these social groups turned from the traditional conservative authoritarianism of their old parties to the radical racist authoritarianism of the Nazis.

The British Settler Colonies

This group of countries – the United States, Canada, Australia, and New Zealand – differs from the European countries in that they were characterized by broad suffrage before they achieved self-government, either in independence or within the British Empire. Thus, the relationship with the colonial power and Britain's changing role in the international political and economic system are an essential part of the story of democratization.

By conventional definitions of democracy (including ours), the United States did not become a full democracy until the late 1960s when the Voting Rights Act of 1965 allowed the federal government to insure that blacks in the

South could exercise the right to vote. Given state and local control of suffrage requirements and coercive power until 1965, it is more appropriate to classify the North and West of the country as a full democracy from the Jacksonian period and the South as a constitutional oligarchy or restricted democracy, depending on the time period and state in question, until the late 1960s.

The American colonies' suffrage qualifications followed the prevailing British pattern of property qualifications for voting. The main qualification in Britain was the '40 shilling freehold' – that is, anyone owning land bringing in an annual income of 40 shillings could vote. Despite the similarity of suffrage requirements in Britain and the American colonies, the colonial electorate was vastly larger in proportionate terms than the British: In the colonies, the proportion of adult white males entitled to vote varied from 50 to 80 per cent, while only 15 per cent of adult males could vote in Britain due primarily to the much greater concentration of agricultural property ownership in Britain. In the South, the existence of a large class of black slaves and greater concentration of rural property holding resulted in a political system characterized by not only a much higher degree of political exclusion but also a higher degree of de facto concentration of power among the politically included. The movement from this already broad suffrage to universal white male suffrage in the North and West occurred in three phases: the revolutionary era, the Jeffersonian period, and the Jacksonian period. Each phase pitted roughly the same social groups against one another. Those opposed to suffrage extension were generally men of property, wealth, and prestige. Small and medium farmers, artisans, and manual laborers favoured suffrage extension.

The Civil War and the end of slavery brought only a temporary period of democracy to the Southern United States. The end of occupation of the South in 1877 paved the way for the installation of a new system of labour control based on the crop liens and debt peonage and progressive disenfranchisement of blacks. The completion of American democracy required the enfranchisement of blacks and this was delayed until the post-Second World War period. Though in the last instance black enfranchisement was the achievement of the civil rights movement, structural changes in the economy and polity allowed this movement to develop and facilitated its success. First, the need for tenant labour began to decline due to declining profitability of cotton production and then to the mechanization of Southern agriculture, which allowed blacks to exit plantation labour and move to cities in the North and South. Second, the New Deal realignments and power shifts meant that political forces in the rest of the country became allies of Southern blacks. In part due to the previous changes mentioned which increased blacks' capacity for self-organization, blacks began to organize and to demand political and social rights, first in the North, then in the South. The end result was the passage of the Civil Rights Act of 1964 and the Voting Rights Act of 1965, which gave the federal government the responsibility of enforcing black voting rights in the South and eventually resulted in the inclusion of Southern Blacks in the electorate.

As they did in the case of the 13 American colonies, the British granted representative assemblies to the Canadian colonies with suffrage requirement based on the prevailing British criteria, but, as in the United States, these qualifications resulted in a vastly larger proportion of adult males with suffrage rights than they did in Britain due to the wider diffusion of agricultural property. Around 70 per cent of adult males were qualified to vote under the property qualification. Beginning in the 1820s, one sees the beginning of consistent pressure for representative government and suffrage extension by the liberals and their forerunners. The social bases of the democratic movements are similar to the United States. Abortive rebellions in 1837 led to the appointment of a royal commission which recommended the establishment of representative government, which was indicative of the change in British posture towards the demand for self-government since the time of the American Revolution. With this change in attitude, self-government was easily achieved in 1867, with the property or tax franchise requirement extending suffrage to 70 per cent to 90 per cent of adult males depending on the province. The step to full democracy came as a result of the First World War, with suffrage extensions in 1917 and 1920.

Australia is of great interest because it is one of the few cases in which the countryside was dominated by large estates and in which democracy developed at a comparatively early stage of industrialization. The large sheep estates established after the first white settlement in 1788, with origins in land grants to officers and in purchases by immigrant capitalists, were manned by 'assigned' convict labour. Thus, the agricultural system was labour repressive and so it is not surprising that the landed oligarchy, though favouring self-government, demanded a restricted franchise along with the continuation of convict transportation and assignment. Arrayed against the oligarchs was a variety of groups created by the convict system and the wool economy. Small holders, often ex-convicts, producing wheat and other products for the domestic market, favoured broader democratic rights and opposed squatter attempts to monopolize crown lands. The urban centres created by the need to transport wool and service the domestic economy contained growing classes of artisans, labourers, and various middle strata which opposed the landed oligarchs' demands and organized to end the transportation and assignment of convicts.

The key factor that prevented the development of authoritarianism was that the landed upper classes did not control the state; the colonial state was still controlled by London. Following the liberal climate of opinion in British politics in the 1840s, the Colonial Office moved to grant the self-government demanded by factions in the colony in a way in which the landed oligarchy would not be allowed exclusive political influence. In 1839, the Colonial government ended assignment of convict labour and then in 1840 terminated the transportation of convicts, marking the end of the labour repressive system in Australia. These developments helped ensure the initial victory of the moderate liberal alliance and the introduction of a wide franchise, though not manhood suffrage, and responsible government.

The political arrangements in the Australian colonies remained essentially the same from this period until the rise of the labour movement in the 1880s and 1890s. The Labour parties made dramatic gains in elections in all colonies in the early 1890s except Tasmania which followed suit a decade later. Labour–Liberal coalitions pushed through electoral reforms which (i) introduced manhood suffrage for the lower house where it had not already been the rule; (ii) abolished property qualifications for office holding; (iii) introduced payment for members of parliament; (iv) eliminated plural voting for property holders; and (v) in many colonies, introduced female suffrage. With the introduction of federation in 1901, universal suffrage was adopted at the federal level.

The colonization of New Zealand did not begin until 1840 and, thus, at its initial stages its whole development – economic, social, and political – was shaped by post-mercantilist Britain, specifically, by the liberal free trade philosophy that had penetrated the Colonial Office at this time. The availability of land made it difficult to deny labourers land. The consequence was the dominance of small family farming along North American lines. True, there were a number of large sheep estates, but these employed very little labour; even the largest were populated by no more than a score of people, including the owner and his family. With the addition of the goldminers in the 1860s, the social structure of New Zealand was favourable to democracy. However, the unquestionably pro-democratic forces created by these economic arrangements did not have to fight very hard for democracy. The initial constitution in 1846 authored by the Colonial Office provided for household suffrage. In response, the colonists demanded self-government with broad suffrage, and the 1852 constitution contained suffrage provisions which excluded few males. The liberals proceeded to complete the process of democratization by eliminating plural voting with two laws in 1891 and 1893.

Social policy development, 1880–1950

It is the consensus among students of welfare state development in the now advanced industrial countries that the first modern welfare state legislation – that is, legislation which departed from the poor law tradition – was Bismarck's 1883 sickness insurance legislation (see Table 2.3). From this point until 1950, there is a deep interplay between the history of social policy development and the history of democratic development in the European countries analysed in this chapter. In the period up to 1920, most of these countries were in the process of establishing democracy and, in a significant number of them, the same social forces which established democracy were also responsible for social policy reforms. In the interwar period, social policy developments were part of the process of democratic stabilization and class

Table 2.3 Adoption of welfare programmes in advanced industrial societies

	Welfare programme					*No. of programmes adopted by*			
	Old Age, disability and survivors	*Sickness and Maternity*	*Workers' compensation*	*Unemployment compensation*	*Family allowance*	*1920*	*1930*	*1940*	*1950*
Early democratizers									
Switzerland									
Binding or extensive	1946	1911	1911	1924	1960	2	3	3	4
Binding and extensive	1946	1911	1911	1976	1960	2	2	2	3
France									
Binding or extensive	1946	1930	1946	1967	1938	0	1	2	4
Binding and extensive	1946	1930	1946	1967	1938	0	1	2	4
Norway									
Binding or extensive	1936	1909	1895	1938	1946	2	2	4	5
Binding and extensive	1936	1909	1895	1938	1946	2	2	4	5
Social Democratic dominance									
Denmark									
Binding or extensive	1922	1892	1890	1907	1952	3	4	4	4
Binding and extensive	1922	1933	1916	1907	1952	2	3	4	4
Netherlands									
Binding or extensive	1913	1930	1913	1916	1939	3	4	5	5
Binding and extensive	1913	1930	1913	1949	1939	2	4	5	5
Belgium									
Binding or extensive	1924	1894	1903	1920	1930	3	5	5	5
Binding and extensive	1924	1945	1971	1945	1930	0	2	2	4
Sweden									
Binding or extensive	1913	1891	1916	1934	1948	3	3	4	5
Binding and extensive	1913	1891	1916	1934	1948	2	3	4	5
British exceptionalism									
UK									
Binding or extensive	1908	1911	1897	1920	1945	4	4	4	5
Binding and extensive	1925	1911	1946	1920	1945	2	3	3	5

(Continued)

Table 2.3 (Continued)

	Welfare programme					*No. of programmes adopted by*			
	Old Age, disability and survivors	*Sickness and Maternity*	*Workers' compensation*	*Unemployment compensation*	*Family allowance*	*1920*	*1930*	*1940*	*1950*
Breakdown cases									
Germany									
Binding or extensive	1889	1883	1884	1927	1954	3	4	4	4
Binding and extensive	1889	1883	1884	1927	1954	3	4	4	4
Italy									
Binding or extensive	1919	1928	1898	1919	1943	3	4	4	5
Binding and extensive	1945	1946	1898	1919	1943	2	2	2	5
British settler colonies									
New Zealand									
Binding or extensive	1898	1938	1908	1930	1941	2	3	4	5
Binding and extensive	1898	1938	1908	1930	1941	2	3	4	5
Australia									
Binding or extensive	1908	1944	1902	1944	1941	2	2	2	5
Binding and extensive	1908	1944	1902	1944	1941	2	2	2	5
Canada									
Binding or extensive	1927	1971	1908	1940	1944	1	2	3	4
Binding and extensive	1927	1971	1908	1940	1944	1	2	3	4
United States									
Binding or extensive	1935	None	1912	1935	None	1	1	3	3
Binding and extensive	1936	None	1912	1935	None	1	1	3	3

Source: Hicks 1999: 51.

compromise in most of the European democratic survivors, and opposition to social legislation was at least a contributing reason to democratic eclipse in Germany. Finally, the initial postwar years witnessed the consolidation of the postwar class compromise in all of these counties. Except for Australia and the American South, the relationship between social policy development and democratic developments is not so intimate in the British settler colonies, but the interwar period, particularly, the depression, is pivotal in the welfare state development in all of them, so this periodization is useful in all four of these countries.

1880–1920

The period of rapid industrialization in Europe in the last half of the nineteenth century created significant industrial working classes in all countries and with it the gradual development of working-class organization and concern among intellectual and political elites for the 'worker question'. The first response of political elites was co-optative: Authoritarian monarchist governments in Germany and then Austria-Hungary passed social legislation aimed at co-opting workers and fending off the growing social democratic workers' movements. The response of the Catholic Church to the growing working class and the rise of the atheistic social democratic parties was to attempt to organize their own workers movement, unions and working-class wings of Catholic parties, and, beginning with the Papal Encyclical Rerum Novarum in 1893, to appeal to workers with their own anti-capitalist ideology, which rejected the market but also rejected the notion of class conflict. While the basic relationship between the social democrats and Catholics was competitive and often hostile, this did not stop them from cooperating on specific issues, as we saw in the case of suffrage reform in the Netherlands and Belgium.

A similar relationship existed between the centrist liberals and the social democrats. Though the liberals infrequently set up their own unions and even more rarely were very successful at it, they did simultaneously compete with the social democrats for political supporters and voters among workers and cooperate with them on some issues, as we saw in the case of democratizing reforms in Britain, Sweden, and Denmark.

For the period under examination here, there are no comparable data on social spending, the most common measure of social policy generosity. However, Hicks (1999) has assembled a comprehensive and comparable data base on the passage of the first significant social legislation in the five areas covered by the US Social Security Administration's (USSSA) publication, *Social Security Programs Throughout the World*. Hicks (1999: 50–3) supplements the USSSA data by requiring that the legislation be 'binding' and/or that it result in extensive coverage. Hicks' (1999: 53) definition of these terms follows:

> *Binding* here refers to programs that are (a) legally compulsory for some set of national actors (citizens, firms, and so on) or (b) virtually binding, as in

> the case of Ghent unemployment programs … *Extensive and funded* programs are programs that cover a notable share of potential target groups … and are adequately funded to begin provision within some period of two or three years (after the passage of the legislation).

For his analysis of 'early program consolidation', Hicks employs Qualitative Comparative Analysis (QCA), an analytic technique based on Boolean algebra developed by Ragin (1987). Hicks' criterion to qualify as an 'early consolidator' is that a country must adopt three programmes that were binding or extensive by 1920. He cross-checks this with an analysis for 1930 in which the country must have three binding *and* extensive programmes. He finds that there are three paths to early consolidation: a 'lib–lab' path, which combines strong working-class organization and frequent liberal party government (Britain, Sweden, and Denmark); a labour-Catholic path, which combines strong working-class organization and Catholic government (Belgium and the Netherlands); and finally a Bismarckian path, which combines authoritarian government with strong working-class organization (Germany). Thus, strong working-class organization is a necessary but not sufficient condition for early programme consolidation.

QCA can only demonstrate association and one must go to the historical sequence to determine whether the configurations correspond to actual historical causal sequences. In at least two of the three pieces of legislation in these countries, the configurations do conform to the causal sequences. In Germany, the reforms of 1883–89 were in fact an attempt by a conservative monarchist government to co-opt the rising working class and consolidate the authoritarian regime. In Belgium and the Netherlands, reforms were passed by Catholic-led governments either faced with rising working-class movements or, in the case of the legislation after the turn of the century, by the same cooperation between Catholic governments and social democratic parties and unions responsible for the reforms that brought full democracy to these two countries. Similarly, in Sweden, Denmark, and Britain, the reforms were passed by liberal governments faced with rising working-class movements or, in the case of the post-1900 reforms, the same lib–lab cooperation responsible for the democratic reforms.

It is striking that none of the early democratizers or the former British colonies were 'early consolidators' by Hicks' criterion. Even more striking is the lag between the adoption of full democracy (using the 1832 date for the United States) and the adoption of three binding and extensive programmes (Hicks' post-1920 criterion). It is important to remember that five of these countries were 'agrarian democracies' (Switzerland, Norway, New Zealand, Canada, and the north and west of the United States), countries dominated by family farms with no significant agrarian upper class and no legacy of feudalism, weak or no legacy of monarchism, not to speak of absolutism. In these countries and in France, there were no or weak modern social democratic labour movements at the time of transition. Working-class contributions to democratization, if any, came from the pre-industrial working class. Hicks (1999) points precisely to the weakness of the working-class movement to account for the welfare state laggard status of these countries. Amenta (1998) would add that the undemocratic American South was a significant obstacle to social policy innovation in the United States.

In Hicks' (1999) analysis, Australia was the one country with a strong labour movement prior to 1920 which was not an early consolidator by either his 1920 or 1930 criteria. In part, this represents a reality in that national legislation existed only in the two areas indicated in Table 2.3. The reason for this is simple: The Australian federal constitution of 1901 reserved power in all other areas of social policy to the states. However, even before independence, the Labour Party had become the largest or second largest party and, with liberal cooperation, passed social legislation in every colony except Tasmania. More important, as Castles (1985) has argued, was the development of 'social protection by other means', namely via the system of compulsory arbitration, in both Australia and New Zealand. In Australia, the Harvester judgment of 1908, which guaranteed the unskilled worker a sufficient wage to support himself, his wife, and three children, was the critical turning point and, in 1920, this was complemented by a decision guaranteeing workers 100 per cent wage replacement in sick pay for short sick absences. If one counts this along with the legislative reforms, then Australia qualifies as an early consolidator and also a lib–lab case since the social legislation and the arbitration court were products of cooperation between the Labour Party and the protectionist faction of the liberals.

By 1930, New Zealand rises into both Hicks' strong labour movement and early consolidator categories. Hicks' placement of New Zealand in the lib–lab path is supported by the historical events of the period. Moreover, as in Australia, the arbitration system guaranteed workers a living wage for their family.

There can be little doubt that relatively high levels of social reform legislation in the nascent European democracies following the lib–lab and Catholic–labor paths (Denmark, Sweden, Britain, Belgium, and Netherlands) helped to stabilize the democratic systems in these countries. It continued a virtuous cycle of working-class integration and moderation begun by the earlier democratizing reforms. The working-class victories in the struggle for political and then social rights reinforced the dominant reformist wings of these movements. This, in turn, led to acceptance of democracy and social reform by conservative upper class groups.

Interwar period

Among our nine European countries, only Germany suffered a democratic breakdown in the interwar period. However, among the ten Eastern and Southern European countries not examined here, democracy survived only in Czechoslovakia and Finland, and in the latter only in restricted form due to exclusion of the numerically significant Communists. With the advent of the Depression and the resultant additional political pressures, the political climate for the remaining democratic regimes was not particularly favourable. Moreover, as one can see from Table 2.4, this was a period of great industrial unrest in many of these countries. Nevertheless, not only did they weather the period as democracies, in five of these eight countries, the Scandinavian and the low countries, profound class and political compromises which prefigured the post-Second World War development of neocorporatism emerged. In all of these countries, social policy innovations figured as one element of these compromises.

After the postwar surge of union organization and industrial unrest subsided, an impasse in the area of social policy emerged in most of these countries. At the heart of this impasse was the pre-Keynesian economic orthodoxy, which prescribed budget austerity and real wage decreases as a response to prevailing high levels of unemployment. The first break with orthodoxy came with the 1929 Social Democratic election victory in Denmark and the striking of a political deal with the Radical Liberals, the junior partner in the ensuing coalition government, who represented small farmers, and the opposition Liberals, representing large farmers, which traded agricultural subsides for farmers for support for the Social Democrats' active crisis policy and social legislation. Sweden and Norway followed suit with the advent of Social Democratic government with similar policies in 1932 and 1935, respectively. In all three countries, the events of the 1930s ushered in extended periods of social democratic governmental dominance.

In the Netherlands, the Social Democrats did not join the government until the outbreak of the Second World War, but the country experienced many of the steps towards class compromise due to the dominant position of the Catholics, who had a very strong trade union wing, in most governments. A turning point came in 1937, when, under pressure from Social Democrats and left Catholics, the Catholic-led government initiated an extensive programme of public works and purchased both agricultural and industrial goods in order to support prices and boost consumption; a move reminiscent of the red-green compromises in Scandinavia. In Belgium, it was the 'national unity' government of the three major parties – Social Democrats, Catholics, and Liberals – that took power in March 1935 that marked the new turn toward deepening class compromise.

Katzenstein (1985: 136) points out that the cross-collaboration of the 1930s in these five countries 'played the midwife at the cradle of democratic corporatism', the highly institutionalized postwar system of political exchange, which featured highly centralized employer organizations and union federations and bargaining over a wide range of social and economic objectives. The events in the social policy arena and cross-party compromises outlined above were complemented in industrial relations by agreements between employers and unions that paved the way for the development of centralized bargaining and a dramatic decline in strikes, which had been very high in most of these countries in the interwar period, in the post-war period (see Table 2.4).

Though the Swiss Social Democrats entered the Federal Council, the seven-member collegial executive, in 1935 and a peace agreement between employers and unions was struck two years later, Switzerland stuck with economic orthodoxy and did not experience a new breakthrough in social policy, a pattern which continued after the Second World War (see Table 2.3). As Immergut (1992) argues, the Swiss constitutional structure, which provides for multiple veto points necessitating the construction of very large coalitions to pass any legislation, is the reason for the laggard status of the Swiss welfare state, especially when compared to Belgium and the Netherlands, the two other consociational democracies with similar social cleavage structures.

Social policy development in France was strikingly backward at the outbreak of the Second World War (Table 2.3), due to the exclusion of the left from power, with the exception of the short-lived Popular Front period in 1936–37. After establishing itself as an early consolidator, Britain also made little progress in the field of social policy in the interwar period due to Conservative Party domination of the political scene.

By contrast, the two North American welfare state laggards did experience major departures in this period. As Hicks (1999) argues, the two cases are similar in that the social democratic parties are small and politically uninfluential at the national level and it was centrist parties, which enjoyed very large political majorities, that carried through the reforms. Amenta (1998) adds that, in the United States, the New Deal reform burst required not only a Democratic and reform-minded president but also a Congressional majority of non-Southern democrats. Despite this, the Southern representatives retained sufficient power to ensure that the reforms did not threaten the agrarian labour control system in the South: Agricultural workers were excluded entirely and the states controlled the level of compensation in the unemployment insurance system.

In New Zealand, the Labour Party won the 1935 election and stayed in office until 1949. The Labour government passed a comprehensive social security bill in 1938 and it was complemented by other measures, such as increases in the means-tested pension, a flat rate universal superannuation benefit, a universal family allowance with a flat rate benefit for each child, and essentially free medical care during Labour's period in office. In Australia, Labour was shut out of office in the interwar period and no progress was made in the social policy arena.

Postwar Compromise

The Second World War and its outcome stimulated class compromises, the cornerstones of which were Keynesian economic policy, social policy innovation, and the routinization of industrial relations, across the advanced industrial world, but most intensively in the European countries. During the war in the democratic European countries, the war and the struggle against fascism stimulated national cross-class solidarity, which expressed itself in wartime grand coalitions, even in neutral Sweden and Switzerland. The defeat in war discredited the fascists and the ruling classes who had collaborated with fascists. This eliminated the most powerful opponents of democracy. The class compromise further strengthened democracy as it (further) integrated the working-class movements into the system and thus moderated their demands, which served to reassure any potential upper-class opponents of democracy.

In Scandinavia and the Low Countries, the immediate postwar period consolidated the work of the 1930s as the same coalitions ruled these countries and pushed through the postwar legislation. From Table 2.3, we can see that these countries completed the laying of the foundations for the basic welfare state transfer programmes. In addition, they also passed national health insurance in this period. Finally, as I mentioned in the previous section, these five countries developed centralized bargaining systems and broader patterns of neo-corporatist bargaining among labour market and political actors in the early postwar period and, as a consequence, experienced dramatic declines in industrial conflict. Here the class compromise was most complete and, in the long run, the outcomes most egalitarian (Bradley *et al.* 2003). In the areas of social policy and macroeconomic management, the Labour government of 1945–51 moved Britain in a similar direction.

In Germany, the class compromise was less favourable to labour, which might be expected given the exclusion of the Social Democrats from government. Nonetheless, the Christian Democratic government, in part because of its pro-welfare ideology, in part because of pressure from its labour wing, and in part because of competition with the Social Democrats, did implement significant social reforms, which propelled it to the position of highest social spender among the countries analysed here, though the programme structures were less egalitarian than those in Britain, Scandinavia, and the Low Countries. On the industrial relations front, postwar development led to more inclusionary arrangements for labour. The collaboration of coal, iron, and steel entrepreneurs with the Nazis led to the introduction of co-determination in which labour received full parity in the management boards in these industries. In 1952, this was extended to other large businesses, but labour received only one-third of the seats on the boards of these businesses. The result in terms of its effect on industrial conflict was similar to neo-corporatist countries: dramatic declines in strikes (Table 2.4).

The compromises struck in Switzerland and France were less inclusionary for labour in different ways and for different reasons. In Switzerland, an industrial peace accord between employers' associations and unions was struck prior to the war, but the multiple veto points in the legislative process continued to impede the progress of social legislation and the resulting social policy regime was the least generous and least redistributive in Europe. In France,

Table 2.4 Strikes: man hours lost per 1,000 workers

	1900–13	*1919–38*	*1946–76*
Early democratizers			
Switzerland		55	11
France	309	404	566
Norway	491	1,853	90
Social Democratic dominance			
Denmark	272	681	173
Netherlands	251	379	34
Belgium	722	665	255
Sweden	1,286	1,440	43
British exceptionalism			
UK	460	1,066	213
Breakdown cases			
Germany	489	875	31
Italy	293	126	631
British settler colonies			
New Zealand		146	191
Australia	399	684	381
Canada	471	296	509
United States		356	585
Mean	495	645	265

Source: Korpi 1983: 165.

the Communists became the largest left party due to their successes during the Resistance. After the war, broad popular front coalitions, including the Communists, passed important pieces of social legislation. With the beginning of the Cold War and the exit of the Communists from the government, the largest working-class party became politically isolated. One manifestation of this was the level of industrial unrest, which was higher than in the interwar period, in sharp contrast to all of the other European countries.

In Australia, the Labour Party came to power in 1941 but was in a tenuous parliamentary situation until it emerged victorious in the 1943 election. The Labour governments of 1943–49 passed legislation providing for child allowances, unemployment benefits, sick pay, and health care benefits for the first time at the federal level and they passed legislation improving pensions and maternity allowances.

In Canada and the United States, there were no postwar compromises, at least in regard to social policy. The progress in social legislation of the 1930s and early 1940s came to a halt. After the unions failed to extend the welfare state, they turned to collective bargaining to achieve the benefits in health care, supplementary pensions, and sick pay, which most European workers received (or would receive) from the welfare state. Of course, these benefits only went to organized workers and, even among them, they were unequally distributed due to differences in bargaining power and labour productivity. The reliance on the strike weapon can clearly be seen in Table 2.4.

As I pointed out in the discussion of democracy, the United States did not become a full democracy until the mid-1960s, a period which also witnessed new social policy initiatives. As we have found at many other points in this analysis, the politics of democratization and the politics of social policy are again linked as the coalition of social political forces behind national support for the Southern civil rights movement were much the same as those that pushed through President Johnson's Great Society legislation. Still, the US initiative fell short of developments elsewhere among the advanced capitalist democracies.

Conclusion

This historical overview has shown that the development of democracy and the development of the welfare state were deeply interwoven, but distinct processes. As of 1870, there was only one full democracy among our 13 countries and in none of them had a single piece of modern social legislation been passed. By 1950, all of them were democracies and nascent welfare states. The feature that ties the two together is the development of the modern working-class movement, which was critical in many of the democratic transitions and central, either as an agent or object, in the development of modern social policy.

However, the processes were hardly identical. In the countries which moved to democracy before substantial industrialization, the agrarian democracies (Switzerland, Norway, New Zealand, Canada, and the north and west of the United States) as well as France, any participation of the working class in the transition to democracy came in the form of artisanal, pre-industrial workers, and they were at best partners in a much larger coalition. In these countries, there was a very long delay between the transition to democracy and the development of the first modern social policies.

By contrast, in the remaining countries, the final transition to democracy came after substantial industrialization, the coalitions for democracy and welfare state reform were closely related, and substantial social reform came simultaneous with democratization or followed it closely. In all of these the modern working class, in the form of unions, social democratic parties, or working-class wings of Catholic parties, was a central actor in the historical drama. In Sweden, Denmark, Australia, Belgium, and the Netherlands, the two processes were practically identical; labour–liberal or labour–Catholic party coalitions championed social reform and democratic reform. In Britain, labour was not as central to democratic reform, but lib–lab coalitions were responsible for the early social legislation. In Germany, early social reforms were sponsored by an authoritarian government in an effort to co-opt growing working-class movements. Democracy came as a result of the dislocations caused by the First World War and it did not survive the interwar period.

The paths to the postwar compromise can be read off these early twentieth-century democratic transition/welfare reform cases. In the Low Countries, the social democratic–Catholic alliances continued or were reformulated after a hiatus. In Sweden, Denmark, Britain, and Australia, there is a shift to social democratic dominance of the reform process. Among the early democratizers, Norway and New Zealand join this latter group. In these eight societies, the postwar compromise is most favourable to labour.[10] In these countries, on average, over half of the labour force was covered by sick pay legislation and more than 60 per cent by unemployment compensation and pension legislation. The average income replacement rate for the average production worker was 37 per cent in the case of unemployment compensation and sick pay, and 24 per cent in the case of pensions. Public health care was available at no or modest cost to all or nearly all citizens, except in Australia (see above).

In France, the post-Second World War liberation coalition of Catholics, social democrats, and communists installed the social legislation pillar of the postwar compromise. In Germany, the compromise between the unions and the Social Democrats and future dominant Christian Democrats was worked out under the shadow of the occupation and a power vacuum on the right and followed Christian democratic lines in social policy and social democratic lines in industrial relations. In Switzerland, an inclusionary industrial relations accord was struck, but the multiple veto points in Swiss political structures blocked the development of more generous social policy. Finally, in Canada and the United States, the period of innovation occurred before the end of the Second World War, and social policy and industrial relations were least favourable to labour, certainly a product of the fact that neither country had a social democratic party capable of competing for national power.

In the recent literature on democratic transitions, it has become routine to attribute successful democratic transition and consolidation to strong civil societies. In my accounting of the events, the term 'civil society' appears infrequently. Secondary associations do figure prominently in the analysis, but they are differentiated by their position in the cleavage structure instead of lumped together under the umbrella term 'civil society'. The strong social democratic movements are strong not simply because they get many votes, but also because the party, the unions, their women's associations, their cooperatives, their youth organizations, their sports clubs, and so on, enlisted many members. Likewise, underlying the strength of the agrarian parties of Scandinavia was a network of farmers' organizations. For the Liberals, it was the dissenting churches and the temperance movement. Similarly, and in part in reaction to the rising labour movements, the Catholic Church built a parallel network of organizations. The advantage of analysing the impact of strong civil societies through the lens of the cleavage structure is that it allows one to recognize that a network of secondary organizations can be a conduit for authoritarian values as was the case in the German middle class, and thus not contribute to democratic transition – on the contrary.

I contend that not only did social policy and democracy develop hand in hand, social policy was necessary for democratic stability. If democracy is not a sham, then the less privileged must be able to use the democratic process to influence the outcome of the policy making. If they are unable to do this, they will either become alienated from the political system or move to oppose it. This is etched in the history recounted here; the labour movements in Western Europe were initially quite radical; their ultimate goal was the complete transformation of the capitalist system. Once they were successful in their demand for political democracy, they became, in practice, reformists – they accepted the decisions that emerged from the democratic process. As they were able to achieve some of the distributive goals within capitalist democracy, those long-term socialist goals began to recede in importance, eventually to be put on the shelf forever. The integration of the working-class movements also reconciled the nineteenth- and early-twentieth-century upper-class opponents of democracy as they began to see that democracy would not result in expropriation.

Is the experience of the advanced capitalist democracies relevant to less developed countries now? Sceptics might contend that the level of affluence of these countries makes their experience irrelevant to the less developed countries of today. However, at the end of the historical processes outlined here, these countries were not much more affluent than the more advanced parts of the less developed world today, such as Latin America and the Caribbean. The average per capita income in constant dollars corrected for purchasing power parities of the 14 countries examined here was $7,583 in 1950 compared to $6,538 in Latin America and the Caribbean in 1998. The overlap in the distribution is impressive: Eight of the 29 Latin American and Caribbean countries for which Penn World Tables data are available in 1998 are above the 1950 industrial country mean and another eight are within one standard deviation of the 1950 industrial country mean. Moreover, the social spending levels were very similar: In 1950, these 14 advanced industrial countries spent 7.6 per cent of GDP on social security, welfare, and health benefits; in 1994, 20 Latin American and Caribbean countries for which data are available spent 6.6 per cent of GDP in these areas.

Let us be clear, social spending and entitlement in the 14 advanced capitalist democracies would not qualify them as being the advanced welfare states they became 25 years later. By 1975, social security benefit expenditure had risen to 18 per cent of GDP in these countries; income replacement rates in sickness and unemployment insurance and pensions had doubled and coverage had increased by at least half. Moreover, the similarity in spending levels between Latin America and the Caribbean in 1998 and the advanced industrial democracies in 1950 hides as much as it reveals, because it ignores differences in employment structure and the distribution of benefits. In Latin

America and the Caribbean, anywhere from 20 to 60 per cent of the labour force is in the informal sector where they are not covered by most social security programmes. Moreover, public pensions are often highly inegalitarian in their structure, with privileged groups, such as military officers, judges, and higher civil servants receiving much better pensions than manual workers. Thus, it is not surprising that social security and welfare spending, which is very highly egalitarian in its impact in advanced industrial democracies, is highly inegalitarian in Latin America and the Caribbean. By contrast, health and education spending, which does benefit informal sector workers, is modestly egalitarian in Latin America and the Caribbean (Huber *et al.* 2004). My point here is that, as indicated by their per capita GDPs, these countries have adequate national resources to provide basic welfare state provisions. What is lacking is social and political movements with sufficient power to push through the required social policy legislation.

Notes

1. For most of the analysis, I draw on, extend, and revise our previous work but for the analysis of social policy development, I also rely heavily on Hicks' (1999) award-winning book, the only work which covers all of the countries covered here.
2. Italy is included in Ferrera's essay, so I do not include it here. Democratization and breakdown in Austria, Finland, Italy, and Spain are covered in Stephens (1989); Austria, Italy, and Spain in Rueschemeyer, Stephens and Stephens (1992); and Austria, Czechoslovakia, Estonia, Finland, Greece, Hungary, Italy, Poland, Portugal, and Spain in Stephens and Kümmel (2002). Social policy development in Austria and Finland is covered in Huber and Stephens (2001).
3. In our terminology, the bourgeoisie refers to only large capitalists, not to small capital owners and urban middle classes. Looser usages of the term often include one or both of these groups.
4. In the extended version of this paper available on the UNRISD website (http://www.unrisd.org/), I address the criticism of Rueschemeyer, Stephens, and Stephens (1992) in Ertman (1998) and Collier (1999). These criticisms have resulted in some clarification of our argument and substantial revisions of the treatment of one case, Britain.
5. The citations to the historical sources for the analysis in this essay are available in the extended version of this chapter which can be accessed at http://www.unrisd.org/ and http://www.unc.edu/~jdsteph/. For a complete listing of sources for the analysis of democracy, see Rueschemeyer, Stephens, and Stephens (1992) and Stephens (1989, 1995).
6. In Stephens and Kümmel (2002), I extend this analysis to all of interwar Europe and show that 16 of 18 cases of democracy breakdown or survival can be predicted (of rather post-dicted) on the basis of agrarian class relations.
7. In the interwar period this generalization about the working class is harder to sustain, since the splits in the working class induced by the war and the Russian Revolution created anti-democratic minorities, above all the Communist Parties, whose political posture clearly contributed to the breakdown of democracy. All of

the parties of the social democratic left, which remained by far the largest of the working class parties in every country, maintained a commitment to democracy.
8. In Stephens (1989) and Stephens and Kümmel (2002) I show that this generalization can be extended to all other countries in Western, Central, and Eastern Europe.
9. See Rueschemeyer, Stephens, and Stephens (1992: 111–14) and Stephens (1995: 173–80) for further evidence on this point.
10. Students of the welfare state may be surprised at the inclusion of Britain, New Zealand, and Australia in this group of generous welfare states as of 1950. It is the infrequent periods of labor government in the subsequent three decades which arrested welfare state development.

References

Amenta, E. 1998. *Bold Relief: Institutional Politics and the Origin of Modern American Social Policy*. Princeton: Princeton University Press.

Bradley, D., E. Huber, S. Moller, F. Nielsen, and J. D. Stephens. 2003. 'Distribution and Redistribution in Post-Industrial Democracies.' *World Politics*, 55, 193–228.

Castles, F. G. 1985. *The Working Class and Welfare*. Sydney: Allen and Unwin.

Collier R. B. 1999. *Paths Toward Democracy: The Working Class and Elites in Western Europe and South America*. New York: Cambridge University Press.

Ertman, T. 1998. 'Democracy and Dictatorship in Interwar Western Europe Revisited'. *World Politics,* 50, 475–505.

Esping-Andersen, G. 1990. *The Three Worlds of Welfare Capitalism*. Princeton: Princeton University Press.

Esping-Andersen, G. and W. Korpi. 1984. 'Social Policy as Class Politics in Post-War Capitalism: Scandinavia, Austria, and Germany', in John Goldthorpe (ed.), *Order and Conflict in Contemporary Capitalism: Studies in the Political Economy of Western European Nations*. Oxford: Clarendon Press, pp. 179–208.

Hagtvet, B. 1980. 'The Theory of Mass Society and the Collapse of the Weimar Republic: A Re-examination', in S. Ugelvik Larsen, B. Hagtvet and J. P. Myklebust (eds), *Who Were the Fascists? Social Roots of European Fascism*. Bergen: Universitetsforlaget, pp. 66–117.

Hicks, A. 1999. *Social Democracy and Welfare Capitalism: A Century of Income Security Policies*. Ithaca: Cornell University Press.

Hicks, A. and J. Misra. 1993. 'Political Resources and the Growth of Welfare in Affluent Capitalist Democracies, 1960–82.' *American Journal of Sociology*, 99, 668–710.

Huber, E. and J. D. Stephens. 1999. 'The Bourgeoisie and Democracy: Historical and Contemporary Perspectives from Europe and Latin America', *Social Research*, 66, 759–88.

Huber, E. and J. D. Stephens 2001. *Development and Crisis of the Welfare State: Parties and Policies in Global Markets*. University of Chicago Press.

Huber, E., F. Nielsen, J. Pribble, and J. D. Stephens. 2004. 'Social Spending and Inequality in Latin America and the Caribbean'. Paper delivered at the meetings of the Society for the Advancement of Socio-Economics, Washington, DC, 8–11 July.

Huber E., C. Ragin, and J. D. Stephens. 1993. 'Social Democracy, Christian Democracy, Constitutional Structure and the Welfare State', *American Journal of Sociology*, 99, 711–49.

Huber, E., D. Rueschemeyer and J. D. Stephens. 1993. 'The Impact of Economic Development on Democracy', *Journal of Economic Perspectives*, 7, 71–85.

Huber, E., D. Rueschemeyer and J. D. Stephens 1997. 'The Paradoxes of Contemporary Democracy: Formal, Participatory, and Social Dimensions.' *Comparative Politics*, 29, 323–42.

Immergut, E. 1992. *The Political Construction of Interests: National Health Insurance Politics in Switzerland, France and Sweden, 1930–1970*. New York: Cambridge University Press.

Katzenstein, P. 1985. *Small States in World Markets: Industrial Policy in Europe*. Ithaca, NY: Cornell University Press.

Korpi, W. 1983. *The Democratic Class Struggle*. London: Routledge & Kegan Paul.

Korpi, W. and M. Shalev. 1979. 'Strikes, Industrial Relations and Class Conflict in Capitalist Societies.' *British Journal of Sociology*, 30, 164–87.

Mackie, T. T. and R. Rose. 1974. *The International Almanac of Electoral History*. London: Macmillan Press Ltd.

Maioni, A. 1998. *Explaining Differences in Welfare State Development: A Comparative Study of Health Insurance in Canada and the United States*. Princeton: Princeton University Press

Moore, B. 1966. *The Social Origins of Dictatorship and Democracy*. Boston: Beacon.

Ragin, C. 1987. *The Comparative Method: Moving Beyond Qualitative and Quantitative Strategies*. Berkeley: University of California Press.

Rueschemeyer, D., E. Huber Stephens, and J. D. Stephens. 1992. *Capitalist Development and Democracy*. Chicago: University of Chicago Press.

Stephens, J. D. 1979. *The Transition from Capitalism to Socialism*. Urbana: University of Illinois Press.

Stephens, J. D. 1989. 'Democratic Transition and Breakdown in Western Europe, 1870–1939: A Test of the Moore Thesis', *American Journal of Sociology*, 94, 1019–77.

Stephens J. D. 1995. 'The German Path to Modern Authoritarianism: Germany, Britain and Sweden Compared', in H. E. Chehabi and Alfred Stepan, *Politics, Society, and Democracy; Comparative Studies: Essays in Honor of Juan Linz*. Boulder: Westview Press, pp. 161–81.

Stephens, J. D. and G. Kümmel. 2002. 'Social Structural Dynamics', in Dirk Berg-Schlosser and Jeremy Mitchell (eds), *Crisis, Compromise, Collapse, Volume II, Authoritarianism and Democracy in Europe 1919–39: Comparative Analyses*. Basingstoke: Palgrave – now Palgrave Macmillan, pp. 39–63.

Swank, D. 2002. *Global Capital, Political Institutions, and Policy Change in Developed Welfare States*. New York: Cambridge University Press.

Therborn, G. 1977. 'The Rule of Capital and the Rise of Democracy', *New Left Review* 103, 3–41.

van Kersbergen, K. 1995. *Social Capitalism*. London: Routledge.

Wilensky, H. 1981. 'Leftism, Catholicism, and Democratic Corporatism', in Peter Flora and Arnold Heidenheimer (eds), *The Development of the Welfare State in Europe and America*. New Brunswick, NJ: Transaction Press, pp. 314–78.

Wilensky, H. 2002. *Rich Democracies*. Berkeley: University of California Press.

3

Democratization and Social Policy Development in Japan

Toshimitsu Shinkawa

This chapter aims to clarify the trajectory of democratization and social policy development in Japan and interactions between them since the beginning of its modernization in the late nineteenth century. Since Japan experienced a regime shift, following the end of the Second World War, its prewar and postwar periods are going to be treated separately.

The basic assumptions of this chapter are as follows. Organized labour provides a most powerful locomotive to promote both democratization and social policy development (the thesis of power resource mobilization). Increased political influence of organized labour can bring about the introduction of universal manhood suffrage and a fully-fledged welfare state, as witnessed in Western Europe. The democratic framework itself may work for the expansion of social policy through party competition for power. Welfare expansion is generally popular so that politicians compete to claim credit for it. Social policy in turn may promote democratization, if its development is based on the principle of social citizenship. Guaranteed minimum livelihood as a right makes mature and independent citizens necessary for the smooth functioning of democracy.

The role of state bureaucracy is also a focal point. Bureaucratic initiatives are comprehensible in terms of the statist thesis. Scholars who privilege the bureaucracy as an explanation for welfare development take the state as an actor independent of societal forces. Granted that the state can be an independent actor, it should be noted that state bureaucrats usually perceive the problem to be dealt with by receiving signals from society. The democratic process that opens to various societal interests is, thus, relevant to policy development even in the context of statism.

Decision making is further defined by historical contingencies and institutional legacies. It is all but impossible to predict how and when a policy window opens, since numerous factors are intricately interwoven. We can detect historical conjunctures only in retrospect. In short, historical conjunctures cannot be treated theoretically in a deductive fashion. Once a programme is established, however, we can predict that it tends to develop its own logic and network of interests, which are resistant to change. Especially when policy change imposes tangible burdens upon specific groups, it tends to be minimal and marginal (Weaver 1986; Shinkawa 2005). Such unpopular policies would be extremely difficult to attain in democratic politics, where politicians seek re-election. Policy change can be accomplished only when politics provide compensation, or an all-party consensus is formed.

Prewar Japan

Social policy development

The first social policy in the modernizing Japan appeared in 1874 with the introduction of the Relief Regulation (Jukkyu Kisoku). It adopted a residual approach by stipulating that poor relief be fundamentally provided through mutual aids, with a special emphasis on family ties. The state was to provide aid to foundlings and orphans less than 13 years old or extremely poor individuals living alone or with families aged below 15 or above 70 years, who are unable to work due to aging, sickness, and disabilities. Annual relief outlays under the Relief Regulation amounted to less than one per cent of government expenditures through the 1890s (Kinzley 1991: 8). The marginality of the programme reflected uneasiness among government leaders as regards public relief. Since poverty was caused by personal failings, they believed, the government should not provide too overly generous assistance, which would facilitate idleness and work disincentives among paupers. In contrast to the poor relief law in Britain, the Relief Regulation excluded the working poor completely from its coverage.

To protect employees from injuries, sickness, and disabilities, the government and business leaders encouraged the establishment of mutual aid societies. Between 1890 and 1904, 26 mutual aid societies were established in the private sector. The number rose to 97 between 1905 and 1911 and 263 between 1912 and 1917, respectively. In the pubic sector, six mutual aid societies were founded before 1911. Eight were added between 1911 and 1925. Such societies were organized not voluntarily by employees, but under employers' initiatives. Mutual aid societies were financed out of employees' contributions and employers' subsidies. Business and political elites regarded the mutual aid society as a means by which to promote firm loyalty among employees, maintain labour–management harmony, prevent employees from organizing themselves and acting collectively. A prominent business leader, Sanji Muto, president of a major textile company of the time, contended that relief should be provided in such a fashion that employees would appreciate generosity and paternity of their employers (Shibata 1998: 123).

Paternalism worked well at least during the initial stage of industrialization, when light industry (most notably textiles) was the locomotive of the Japanese economy. In textiles, the principal workers were young females, typically recruited from rural areas. They normally stayed in the labour market for a short period (several years) before getting married. Most of them lived in factory-run dormitories, isolated from the outside world. Thus they were kept under employers' surveillance all the time and had no chance to organize their interests.

With the outbreak of the First World War, heavy industry started to replace light industry as the locomotive of the Japanese economy. Male workers outnumbered female workers in 1914. Japanese heavy industry rode on an upward trend during the period of the First World War, due to the devastated European economy. The expansion of heavy industry caused a shortage of skilled labour, in the face of which large firms in shipbuilding and iron and steel introduced various techniques to secure stable supplies of skilled labour. So-called lifetime employment, seniority-based wages, and firm specific welfare were introduced around this period.

Retirement allowances in particular became a core of firm-specific welfare as the Japanese economy suffered a prolonged recession in the 1920s, following the end of the First World War. The recession encouraged emerging labour unions to call for the institution of government-sponsored unemployment insurance. Both the government (except for the Social Bureau of the Home Ministry) and the majority of business leaders rejected the idea of unemployment insurance due to the fear that such a programme might be viewed as creating a right for labour and strengthen the sense of class solidarity at the expense of firm loyalty. Instead, they opted for a revision of the 1911 Factory Law. The 1922 revision of the Factory Law (enforced in 1926) required management to give a dismissed employee the equivalent of their fortnightly wages. This hardly constituted a satisfactory response from the standpoint of labour's demand for unemployment insurance, but it did contribute to a reconfirmation of long-standing links between employment and welfare.

Firm-based retirement allowances developed, first as a means of securing skilled labour, and then as a substitute for unemployment insurance. The provision of retirement allowance, however, was not compulsory. Employees in smaller companies tended to receive less generous payments – or nothing at all. As of 1926, 89 per cent of Japan's establishments with 1,000 employees or more had retirement allowance schemes, while only one per cent of those with fewer than 50 employees did. Larger firms with 200 employees or more provided a lump sum dismissal fee equal to between 542 and 714 days wages for employees with 20–25 years service, while smaller firms paid less than half that amount. Retirement allowance was seen as a gratuity from the employer, rather than as a right of the employed. Thus, when an employee left the job of his own volition, he would receive only half the amount given to one who was dismissed. Allowances might not be paid at all when the employee quit 'against the will of the employer,' moved to a rival company, or started competing businesses (Shinkawa and Pempel 1996: 287–90).

Eventually, the government made retirement allowance compulsory among firms with a certain number of employees in the 1936 law. In the original bill, establishments with ten or more employees were obliged to introduce retirement allowance schemes. In the face of strong opposition from employers (the Association of the National Industrial Organizations in particular), however, the government narrowed its coverage to those with 50 or more employees.

The recession in the aftermath of the First World War heightened the necessity of providing public assistance as well as of protecting employees. The Relief Regulation was replaced with the Relief Law, passed in 1929 and coming into effect in 1932. The Relief Law kept poor relief still residual as the Minister of Home Affairs explicitly stated its aim as a means of complementing the functions of the family and mutual aid as well as of removing anxiety over national livelihood, in an attempt to counter the rise of radicalism. In spite of the unchanged residual approach, however, the new legislation substantially broadened the range of relief (Shibata 1998: 137–140). Consequently, the government spent 5.7 times more for poor relief in 1932 than in the previous year. The numbers of those relieved jumped from 18,118 in 1931 to 157,564 in 1932 (Okamoto 1991: 24 and 34).

The prolonged recession of the 1920s encouraged employees to raise voices for unemployment insurance, but the mainstream of elites in the government and business rejected the introduction of unemployment insurance with a fear that it may facilitate solidarity among workers and calls for labour rights. A response to the workers' demand was the introduction of retirement allowance plans in individual companies, as mentioned above. In addition to the revision of the Factory Law, the government responded by providing public works for the relief of the unemployed. To protect those hired for public works, working with low wages under poor working conditions without the coverage of the Factory Law or the Mine Law, the government offered compensation for work injuries and introduced the Workers' Compensation Act in 1931.

The passage of the Health Insurance (HI) Bill in 1922 was also considered as a substitute for unemployment insurance. The Minister of Agriculture and Commerce defended his bill by stressing the function of promoting labour productivity and conciliation between labour and capital. The enacted Health Insurance covered only manual workers. Compulsory coverage was limited to workers in establishments under the regulation of the Mine Law or the Factory Law. Establishments with fewer than ten employees were exempt from this regulation. Establishments with 300 employees or more were able to organize their own health insurance associations. The voluntary coverage of their families included in the initial plan was ruled out. The Health Insurance Act was expected to come into effect in April 1924, but postponed until January 1927, mainly as a result of the devastating Kanto earthquake of 1925.

Further developments in health care were brought about by the escalation of Japan's military invasion of China, which required the provision of able-bodied men. In the end, the Ministry of Health and Welfare (MHW) was created in response to the military request in 1938. Soon after its initiation, the MHW submitted three health-related bills to the Diet: the National Health Insurance (NHI) Bill, the Clerks' Health Insurance (CHI) Bill, and the Seamen's Insurance Bill. The NHI was introduced by establishing health insurance societies in municipalities, with the aim of maintaining health and order in economically damaged agrarian areas. Voluntary as it was, it could potentially cover tens of millions of people. The revision of 1942 enabled governors to order the establishment of health-insurance associations. The system provided a firm basis of health insurance for all in the postwar period.

The CHI was to cover white-collar workers excluded from the HI scheme. Compulsory coverage was applied to establishments with ten or more employees. Family members were able to join on a voluntary basis. Correspondingly, the HI was revised to allow family members to join the programme voluntarily. In 1941 the CHI was merged with the HI. The Sailors' Insurance was drafted but not submitted to the Diet, when the HI was enacted. In 1939, however, the increased importance of marine transportation in terms of national security made the government perceive the necessity of securing the number of marine workers. Noteworthy in the Seamen's Insurance was that the programme also offered pensions, which was not provided for general workers until the Workers' Pension Law was passed in 1941.

The Workers' Pension Plan was a manual workers' programme and excluded female workers and clerks. A member was entitled to receive 25 per cent of the average pensionable income after 20 years of contributions. The Plan was rearranged in 1944 into the Employees' Pension Plan by stretching the coverage to female workers and clerks. Besides, tiny establishments between five and nine employees were covered compulsorily.[1]

Democratization in prewar Japan

(a) *Party politics*

The political regime of prewar Japan was far from an ideal case of democracy. The Meiji Restoration in 1867 restored the emperor to political power. By placing the emperor at the top of the government, the Meiji elites, who smashed the Tokugawa Shogunate, gained legitimacy and popular support for the new regime and successfully established a centralized state, by which to pursue 'a rich country and a strong army'. The Meiji oligarchs suppressed the Movement for Freedom and Popular Rights as a challenge to their rule, but they committed themselves from the outset to the idea of a western constitution providing a representative assembly. Enlightened on western experiences, the Meiji oligarchs believed that a constitution was a prerequisite for modernization and industrialization. Besides, constitutional rule was considered necessary to negotiate the revision of the unequal treaties with the western powers.

The Meiji Constitution was promulgated in 1889 as the emperor's gift to his subjects (people). It stipulated that sovereignty resides in the person of the emperor. The authority and power of the oligarchy relied upon the myth of imperial sovereignty. The imperial Diet was introduced accordingly in the subsequent year. The Diet was defined merely as a supporting organ of the emperor. The Lower House members were elected by a limited number of landlords and property owners. Its power was shared equally with the appointed House of Peers, which counterbalanced the House of Representatives. The Privy Council further limited the power of the Lower House. The Privy Council composed of 26 venerable senior statesmen (the oligarchs) exercised a supervisory role over the constitution and the state.

Political influence of the Lower House was constitutionally quite limited, but its presence became increasingly important in real political life since industrialization contributed to an increased number of urban voters and reinforced voices for political rights and social protection. The elder statesmen initially ignored such voices and advocated the idea of 'cabinet beyond political partisanship' (*chozen naikaku*) to serve the emperor and his polity. They, however, gradually came to perceive the importance of party politics in legitimizing government policies and formed a close affiliation with a party named Seiyukai by allotting ministerial posts to its members. Eventually in 1918, the elder statesmen asked the Seiyukai leader, Hara Kei,[2] to form a government.

The Seiyukai-based government was the first authentic party-led government in Japanese political history. Meanwhile, anti-Seiyukai forces formed Kenseikai, which was relatively free from the control of elder statesmen. Kenseikai grew large enough to compete with Seiyukai for power by the mid-1920s.[3] The years 1924–1932 witnessed an era of party politics, which is referred to as the 'Taisho democracy', during which the two parties alternatively formed government.

When the military challenged the legitimacy of party politics in the early 1930s, the party government had no means by which to control the military. The Meiji Constitution provided no clauses to subordinate the military to the civilian authorities. The military enjoyed independence and privileges as a body directly belonging to the emperor. The military virtually made decisions freely within its own sphere and, in addition, could intervene in civil governmental and political affairs by not providing army and/or navy ministers for a cabinet or withdrawing the minister(s) from a cabinet.

> By the support of a strategy of nationalistic propaganda campaign, by the intimidation and assassination of leading opponents, and by the use of a popular and successful program of foreign expansion, the military was able to displace the parties completely and seize the dominant position in the governing coalition during the years 1936–45.
>
> (Richardson and Flanagan 1984: 14)

(b) Power resource mobilization of labour

Paternalism was a major feature of social policy in prewar Japan, as seen in the previous section. Government and business leaders were generally negative on the expansion of public welfare on the grounds that it would turn workers into idlers. Employees' welfare was expected to be provided by employers as a gift. When young female workers living in isolated dormitories were the absolute majority in the labour market, employers' paternalistic posture worked effectively to conciliate workers and prevent their collective actions. As a shift from light to heavy industry resulted in an increased number of male workers, however, paternalism became challenged by collective actions calling for wage increases, improved working conditions, and the introduction of social insurance.

Between 1897 and 1899, the first three representative labour unions (the Iron and Steel Workers' Union, the Japan Railway Workers' Union, and the Print Workers' Union) were organized. The year 1907 witnessed the largest number of strikes in the Meiji period, counting 57 with 9,855 people involved. During the Taisho period (1912–1926), the number of strikes decreased after a peak of 495 in 1919, but went up again well over 900 in 1924, as Table 3.1 shows. The number of labour unions also increased to 469, holding 2,228,278 workers, in the same year.

The growth of labour and socialist movements, however, was severely restrained by the Police Peace Law (PPL) enacted in 1900. Article 17 of the PPL outlawed the use of violence, intimidation, and public slander in strikes, as well as prohibited the act of 'instigating' or 'inciting' others to strike, join unions, or engage in collective bargaining. According to the PPL, the Social

Table 3.1 Labor unions and industrial strikes, 1914–1929

	Unions	*Union Members*	*Strikes*	
			Incidents	*Participants*
1914			50	7,904
1915			64	7,852
1916			108	8,413
1917			398	57,309
1918	107		417	66,457
1919	187		497	63,137
1920	273		282	36,371
1921	300	193,442	246	58,225
1922	389	137,381	250	41,503
1923	432	125,551	270	36,225
1924	469	228,278	933	94,047
1925	457	254,262	816	89,387
1926	488	284,729	1,260	127,262
1927	505	309,493	1,202	103,350
1928	501	308,900	1,021	101,893
1929	630	330,985	1,420	172,144

Source: Shibata 1998: 125.

Democratic Party formed in 1901 was ordered to dissolve on the very day of its birth. In spite of the police's frequent interference and suppression, the government and employers were unable to eradicate labour unions and socialist forces completely. The expansion of the industrial (male) labor force during the First World War, nationwide rice riots of 1918, and the incidence of the Russian Revolution combined to facilitate the growth of labour unions and socialist forces.

Yuaikai (the Friendly Association) was established in 1912 with an anti-communist, social democratic stance explicitly taken. Yuaikai was rearranged in 1919 into the Great Japan Federation of Labour and the Friendly Society (Dai Nihon Rodo Sodomei-Yuaikai), which was renamed the Japan General Federation of Labour (Sodomei) in 1921. Yuaikai/Sodomei called for free labour union activities, legislation on minimum wages and work hours, and the implementation of labour insurance, among others. The leadership of Yuaikai/Sodomei was in the hands of social democratic leaders, such as Matsuoka Komakichi, Nishio Suehiro, and Suzuki Bunji, who stood up against the communists or anti-capitalist forces. Sodomei leaders focused on establishing labour's rights and improving workers' living standards through cooperation with government and business leaders.

Employers flatly rejected Sodomei's requests at first. Their posture changed when the leftist splinter group kicked out of Sodomei organized the Japan Council of Labor Unions (Nihon Rodo Kumiai Hyogikai) in 1925 by holding 32 unions. Hyogikai was ordered to dissolve in 1928 and, immediately following its dissolution, the Japan National Federation of Labour Unions (Nihon Rodo Kumiai Zenkoku Kyogikai) replaced it in December 1928 without the permission and authorization of the government. The Japan Communist Party organized in 1922 also developed underground activities. The rise of the leftist/communist movement changed the atmosphere among business leaders. Sodomei came to be regarded as the lesser evil. In the mid-1920s some companies even concluded collective agreements with Sodomei.

Sodomei leaders were rather paternalistic, in spite of their belief in fairness and equality. In December 1926, the socialist intellectual Aso Hisashi, who considered Sodomei too rightist, led 6,000 workers out of the federation to form the 'centrist' Federation of Japanese Labour Unions (Nihon Rodo Kumiai Domei). In August 1929, Sodomei expelled an Osaka-based faction representing 5,000 workers on the grounds that it had harshly criticized Sodomei's support of the ILO and its opposition to allying with leftist labour organizations. Meanwhile, Sodomei successfully formed the Council to Promote Labour Legislation (Rodo Rippo Sokushin Iinkai) in collaboration with the Governmental Workers, the Seamen's Union, the Maritime Officers' Association, and the Cooperationist League of Naval Labour Unions. The five federations combined to represent approximately 190,000 of the 309,000 organized workers. The 'right-wing' labour unions maintained their hegemony in prewar Japan. The Social Bureau of Home Ministry estimated that over 80 per cent of all union activists belonged to 'right-wing' unions. The number of trade unions increased steadily throughout the 1920s. The unionization rate reached its peak in 1931, with 7.9 per cent of the industrial labor force being organized.

As the military invasion in China developed in the 1930s, however, the relatively liberal atmosphere created during the Taisho period disappeared and the labour movement was more severely restricted and suppressed by the Peace Preservation Law introduced in 1925, coupled with universal manhood suffrage. The legality and legitimacy the labour movement gradually obtained was flatly denied in the late 1930s.

The first attack on the labour movement came from the army. In September 1936, the army ordered all workers in its arsenals to withdraw from unions. The army's denial of unions had a spill-over effect on business in general. The employers followed the army's policy and refused to accept the presence of unions. The Social Bureau of the Home Ministry opposed the army's policy at first. In the face of the acceleration of dispute activity, however, it changed its stance from the protection of labour rights to the regulation of unions on the basis of 'familialism and a beautiful custom of Japan'. The Social Bureau was separated from the Home Ministry and upgraded to a fully-fledged welfare ministry, the Ministry of Health and Welfare (MHW), on 1 January 1938. The MHW was expected to maintain peace and social harmony through social policy, following the military course, rather than to protect social or labour rights. In the end, the MHW promoted the Industrial Patriotic Movement. Unions were replaced with plant-level industrial patriotic units. After the passage of the National General Mobilization Law in March 1938, all independent workers' organizations were eradicated (Garon 1987: 208–18).

Interaction between democratization and social policy development

In prewar Japan, trade unions and socialist parties had never been strong enough to promote democratization or social policy development. Poor social policy development can be explained by weak class mobilization, according to the power resource theory (Korpi 1978; Korpi and Shalev 1979; Huber and Stephens 2001). Yet, labour disputes and strikes often led by socialist activists urged the power elite to perceive the necessity of dealing with 'social problems'.

The state bureaucracy played a major role in social legislation, as state-centric scholars argue (Heclo 1974; Evans *et al.* 1985). Two streams can be distinguished among bureaucrats. One is paternalistic, inclining towards the Prussian-type and the other is liberal-oriented, granting citizenship rights. The former includes the mainstream of the state elites. The Ministry of Agriculture and Commerce was representative of the paternalistic advocates of social legislation. Senior bureaucrats in the Ministry of Agriculture and Commerce, who were enlightened on European experiences, committed to the passage of the Factory law in 1911 with the conviction that social protection of industrial workers was an inevitable 'world trend'.

'The Factory Law imposed minimum health and safety standards in factories employing fifteen or more workers, as well as in any other enterprise engaged in dangerous or unhealthy work. It also established a special factory inspectorate within the Ministry of Agriculture and Commerce. One important provision made employers liable in the case of job-related injuries. The minimum age of employment was set at twelve. With regard to women and youths under fifteen, the . . . law generally established a twelve-hour day, in addition to prohibiting night work' (Garon 1987: 28–29). The Ministry of Agriculture and Commerce was, however, not necessarily pro-labour. It initiated the law in spite of objections from business leaders because it believed that some degree of labour protection would improve productivity and prevent a rise of the socialist movement.

The Social Bureau of the Home Ministry established in 1920 attracted young reform-oriented bureaucrats and proposed a liberal idea of labour union law, accepting labour's rights to act collectively and strike. Their attempts to develop a liberal social policy rarely bore fruit due to the opposition of the paternalistic bureaucrats. However, the emergence of party politics, or democratization in the 1920s, opened a policy window to liberal bureaucrats. As described above, Seiyukai and Kenseikai competed for power. Of the two, Kenseikai was more liberal-oriented. The difference of the two parties as regards social policy was explicit on the issue of the Factory Law. Seiyukai had opposed the introduction of the Factory Law, delayed its implementation, and limited the coverage after its passage. As late as 1916 a leading member of Seiyukai spoke out against the enforcement of the Factory Law:

> Relations between owner and employee in our country are quite different from those in the West. We have no laws now, yet isn't it true that relations here are conducted in the spirit of friendship? Is it wise to enforce an unnecessary law and thereby destroy these beautiful friendly relations by using legal language to guide relations between employee and employer in a forcible and explicit fashion?
>
> (Garon 1987: 36)

Kenseikai was supportive of social legislation. In 1910 Kenseikai vigorously advocated the government-submitted factory bill. Some of Kenseikai's leaders were invited to fill some posts in the Ohkuma cabinet. They authorized funds to enforce the long-postponed Factory Law in 1916. Kenseikai in opposition submitted bills to the Diet on health insurance and unemployment insurance, respectively in 1920 and 1921. Liberal-mindedness was brought into Kenseikai by ex-Kokuminto members as well as ex-Home Ministry bureaucrats. The increased influence of Kenseikai in the Diet worked in favour of reformist bureaucrats in the Social Bureau of the Home Ministry.

Even the conservative Seiyukai played a critical role in modifying strict regulations on labour union activity, when it formed its own cabinet for the first time in 1918, in spite of its negative attitudes towards the idea of labour union law and social entitlements. Home Minister Tokonami Takejiro and his staff reinterpreted the 'instigation and incitement' clause in Article 17 of the PPL in such a way as to promote patronized enterprise-based 'vertical unions' while checking the growth of horizontally organized (class-based) unions. To maintain and promote harmony between employer and employee, Tokonami sponsored the creation of a semi-governmental organization in 1919. Kyochokai (the Harmonization Society) was designed to educate workers in the spirit of cooperation and self-restraint, thereby precluding the need for horizontal trade unions.

Shibusawa Eiichi, who took the lead in creating Kyochokai in the business circle, held a far-sighted view as regards the role of Kyochokai. Unlike the conservative Seiyukai leaders, Shibusawa realized the positive role of independent labor unions and kept good relations with the Yuaikai/Sodomei leaders (he was one of Yuaikai's advisors). He agreed with Tokonami that Kyochokai should instil cooperative attitudes in both worker and management, but contended that Kyochokai should study social problems and provide informal conciliation independently before strikes would take place. During the democratic period of the 1920s, Kyochokai was inclined towards Shibusawa's vision (cf. Umeda, Takahashi, and Yokozeki 2004; Kinzley 1991).

Generally, Kenseikai, the Social Bureau of the Home Ministry, Kyochokai, and Sodomei advocated the idea of labour union law, the revision of the Factory Law, and the enforcement of health insurance. Kenseikai and reformist bureaucrats in the Home Ministry Social Bureau collaborated to accomplish liberal reforms. A Kenseikai-centred coalition government formed in 1925 enacted the Universal Male Suffrage Law, which enfranchised nearly all males aged 25 years or older.[4] The law came only six and seven years after the enactment of truly equal and universal male enfranchisement in Weimar Germany and Great Britain respectively. It expanded the electorate from 3,288,000 in the 1924 election to 12,409,000 at the time of the general election of 1928.

It should be noted, however, that the Kenseikai government introduced the notorious Peace Preservation Law simultaneously with the Universal Male Suffrage Law. That was a compensation for the conservatives. The Kenseikai Cabinet and the Home Ministry wanted to restrict its target to the communists, but their attempt eventually failed as the Peace Preservation Law came to be abused by the Special Police to arrest practically anyone who stood against the military dominance later in the 1930s.

A prominent Kenseikai leader, Wakatsuki Reijiro, contributed a great deal as home minister (1924–26) to the advance of the Social Bureau's liberal voice in the formulation of labour policy. He removed pro-Seiyukai officials from major posts. The most critical was the change of the Social Bureau's director, who had stifled his subordinates' recommendations for a labour union law and the repeal of Article 17. Completing his preferred personnel deployment,

Wakatsuki ordered to formulate a legislative package based on the Social Bureau's draft labour union bill, labour disputes conciliation bill and proposed repeal of Article 17.

The original labour union bill was drafted by the Social Bureau and discussed in the Investigative Commission in 1925. The bill was quite liberal because it guaranteed the validity of collective agreements, levying fines against employers who arbitrarily dismissed or refused to hire union members, and exempting unions from liability for dispute-incurred damages. The Investigative Commission, where conservative officials were dominant, however, revised the bill so that legal recognition would be confined to craft and industrial unions, anti-union employment practices would be invalidated with no penalties imposed on guilty employers, and government would be able to dissolve disruptive labour unions. The revised bill was submitted to the Diet in February 1926.[5] The revised version satisfied neither labour nor capital. It was too conservative for labour, and yet too liberal for capital. With no back-up from societal forces, the revised union bill was tabled and eventually scrapped in the committee in March 1927, due to Seikyukai's all-out opposition.

As for the labour disputes conciliation bill, the Kenseikai government successfully obtained the support of Seiyuhonto (a splinter of the Seiyukai) in the 1926 Diet session and overcame the opposition of Seiyukai. Other liberal measures taken by the Kenseikai government included the repeal of Article 17 (and supplementary Article 30) of the PPL and the enforcement of the long-frozen 1922 Health Insurance Law. To implement the health insurance policy, the Health Insurance Division was created within the Social Bureau. Finally, it should be noted that the Kenseikai government overcame opposition in the conservative Privy Council and enforced the 1923 revision of the Faculty Law (Yasuda 1994; Garon 1987).

It can be concluded that democratization and social policy development in prewar Japan were certainly interacted. Unlike Western Europe, however, the labour movement and socialist forces were not strong enough to directly promote democratization or social policy expansion. Yet they provided a critical condition for urging government and business leaders to perceive the 'trends of the world' (inevitable development of democracy and social protection). Some elder statesmen sponsored party formation and tried to control the Diet through their affiliated parties. Political parties, however, gradually became independent and opened the era of party-led government in the 1920s. Liberal-minded bureaucrats were the first to realize the necessity of social legislation departing from paternalism. They were never predominant within government, but played critical roles in introducing social measures during the era of the Kenseikai-centred government.

However, such democratic and social policy development in prewar Japan was limited by constitutional constraints. Sovereignty resided not in the hands of the people but in the person of the Emperor. The fatal defect of the Constitution was that it had no civilian control of the military. Therefore, civic governments had no means by which to deal with the military challenge. A short period of liberalism and democracy ended due to the abuse of the military prerogative.

Postwar Japan

The Occupation Period (1945–1951)

The Allied/US Occupation was the sole independent variable that explains the overhaul of Japan after the end of the Second World War until Japan's independence was allowed in 1952. The initial goals of the Supreme Commander of Allied Powers (SCAP) were democratization and demilitarization. The SCAP ordered the hesitant Japanese government to pass a new Constitution based on the draft made by the young New Dealers. According to the new Constitution, the emperor, deprived of sovereignty and divinity, stays only as a symbol of national unity. Popular sovereignty is explicitly stated. Article 9 of the Constitution declares that 'the Japanese people permanently renounce war as a sovereign right of the nation' and that 'land, sea and air forces, as well as other war potential, will never be maintained'. The Privy Council was abolished and the House of Peers was rearranged to the elected Upper House.

The new Constitution includes not only the right to collective bargaining, full employment, free choice of residence and occupation, academic freedom, sexual equality but also the right to maintain the minimum standard of wholesome and cultured living, not to mention a bill of rights that protects life, liberty, the pursuit of happiness, and the freedom of thought, religion, assembly, and petition (Richardson and Flanagan 1984: 35). In addition to civil rights, the Japanese Constitution explicitly protects political and social right citizenships.

The first general (Lower House) election through universal suffrage was conducted in 1946. The conservatives won the election, but the rise of the socialists attracted public attention. In the second general election of 1947, the Japan Socialist Party (JSP) obtained plurality and formed a centre-left coalition government. The SCAP welcomed the emergence of a JSP-led government as a positive sign indicating a sound growth of democracy in Japan. The locomotive pushing the JSP upwards was the mobilization of workers and ex-tenant farmers, who obtained the right to vote, thanks to the Occupation's democratization strategy.

The SCAP considered that independent farmers and workers would form the core of democratic citizens. In prewar Japan, tenants were the majority of farmers. Approximately 70 per cent of the farmers rented part or all of the land they cultivated. They barely supported their daily lives and committed themselves to revolts against landowners on occasions, thereby causing social disturbances. The Occupation conducted a radical land reform to transform discontented and unhappy tenants into self-confident independent small farmers. Landlords were forced to sell their holdings exceeding three cho (seven and one-half acres) to the tenants through the government. High rates of inflation made landlords give away their properties for practically nothing and thus severely eroded their economic bases. By 1950, more than 60 per cent of farmers owned the land they tilled.

In the process of the land reform, the socialist-led Japan Farmers' Union (JFU) acted for tenants and extended support among them. The JFU gained 250,000 members in a couple of months after its foundation in 1946. The number expanded to 2.5 million by the end of 1948. In the 1947 election, 31 of 143 seats gained by the JSP were occupied by the JFU representatives and seven by JFU affiliates. In total, 69 socialist Lower House members came from agrarian districts (Calder 1988: 250–3).

The rising organized labour, along with the newly formed class of independent farmers, contributed to the success of the socialists at the initial stage of the postwar period. The new Constitution guaranteed labour's right to organize and bargain collectively and required that standards for wages, hours, rest, and other working conditions be set by law. The government accordingly enacted the Labor Union Law by the end of 1945, the Labour Relations Law in the following year, and the Labor Standards Law in 1947. The liberal labour policy facilitated the proliferation of labour unions. Over 500 unions had been founded by the end of 1945, which held 38 million members in total. Two years later, the number of trade unions jumped up to 28,000, with 62.6 million members. The unionization rate reached the peak of 55 per cent in 1949, the highest ever in Japanese labour union history.

The socialist experiment in Japan, however, did not last long. The JSP-centred coalition government collapsed in less than a year due to political scandals involving the top leaders of the JSP. Structurally, more serious was a deepening schism between left-wing and right-wing factions within the JSP, which made the party unable to unify itself to underpin the coalition government. With few achievements, the socialists stepped down from power in 1948. Disappointed farmers withdrew support from the JSP and became an entrenched conservative constituency through various policies providing subsidies later in the 1950s.

Schism and confrontation within organized labour also contributed to the failure of the socialists. As conflicts between labour and management escalated, radical actions led by the communists gained widespread support among the rank and file. The communists and their allies occupied the leadership of the largest confederation of industrial unions (Sanbetsu) and took a confrontational stance with the government and employers, thereby rejecting class settlement for economic reconstruction. Therefore, even if the JSP had been unified, it would have been all but impossible to adopt a long-term strategy of social democracy, given the split of labour and the predominance of the communists in the labour movement.

The course not only of democratization but also of social policy was set by the Occupation. To rescue paupers and war victims, the SCAP issued the Relief and Welfare Plan in December 1945 and, accordingly, the Japanese government adopted a plan of poor relief in emergency. The SCAP, dissatisfied with the government plan, issued another memorandum as regards public assistance, based on which the Japanese government enacted the Livelihood Protection Law, which came into effect in October 1946 (revised in 1950). The SCAP was concerned with poverty and scarcity of fundamentals, including food and housing, which might cause social instability and disturbances. The Livelihood Protection Law advanced far ahead of the prewar Relief Law in admitting the obligation of the state to provide those in need with minimum daily life security on an equal and fair basis.

The new legislation, however, did not grant the right of those in need to request protection to the government. Relief was regarded as 'reflexive benefit,' which meant that those in need had no right to request relief but receive benefit reflexively as a result of welfare provided by the government. Thus, the government is responsible to provide a national minimum, but its obligation does not accompany the right of those in need to request protection. The idea of 'reflexive benefit' became an authorized interpretation of Article 25 of the Constitution stipulating a citizen's right to maintain the minimum standards of wholesome and cultured living, when the Supreme Court made the judgment on the Asahi case to the effect that 'individuals could not sue to compensate for inadequate welfare allowances, although the state has the responsibility to provide benefits that are "realistic"' (Anderson 1993: 94).[6]

The government instituted the Social Insurance Investigation Commission (SIIC) in March 1946 to discuss social problems and envision a future plan. The report released by SIIC in December 1946 included the recommendation of an unemployment insurance scheme and the improvement of the social insurance programmes established in the war period. The first social insurance scheme introduced in postwar Japan was the Workers' Compensation Law enacted in April 1947, with the aim of securing a compensation for injuries at the workplace prescribed in the Labor Standards Law. In November of the same year, the Unemployment Insurance Law was passed. As seen above, labour unions had called for both labour union legislation and the introduction of unemployment insurance for years, but never succeeded in the prewar period. It was clearly an effect of democratization during the Occupation period that facilitated their enactment.

Major features of the welfare regime in postwar Japan

During the Occupation period, the SIIC, the Wandel Committee (a visiting committee of the American experts led by William H. Wandel), and Social Security Systems Board (instituted according to a recommendation of the Wandel Committee) publicized ideas and visions of social security in the future. Their proposals differed considerably from one another, but they had one thing in common: they shared the perception that constructing a unified comprehensive system was desirable and of necessity. Yet the government did not follow such a line. It showed no serious interest in overcoming fragmentation in the social security system caused by patchwork efforts in the prewar period.

It can be argued that the government had little time for the construction of a unified comprehensive welfare state for a while after the end of the Second World War. The government, however, did not make a move towards it, even after the economy got on a right track and the Economic White Paper stated the postwar period was over in the mid-1950s. Accordingly, social security developed within the framework of occupationally divided programmes, furthering the fragmentation of the system. This chapter contends that democratic politics, together with historical contingencies and path dependence, contributed to the fragmentation of the social security system in postwar Japan. Welfare bureaucrats and social policy experts held ideas for an integrated social security system, but obtained no opportunities to embody their ideas in a situation where politicians regarded social policy as nothing more than a measure of gaining support in elections. Politicians looked for prompt policy effects with no grand design of long-term welfare state building.

In terms of major social security provisions, such as pension and health care, the Japanese welfare regime is defined as a system of 'welfare through work', borrowing Goodin's (2001) words. Pension and health insurance schemes are occupationally divided. Public sector employees, private sector employees, and the self-employed belong to different schemes. Mutual aid plans provided for public sector employees are divided largely between central government and local government employees. In addition to such occupational distinctions, private sector employees are treated differently by firm size. Large firms with 500 or more employees are allowed to opt out of the earnings-related part of public pension (the Employees' Pension Insurance, abbreviated hereafter as the EPI) and establish their own Employees' Pension Fund (EPF). In other words, a large firm with a certain number of employees can substitute its specific pension for the earnings-related part of the EPI. Smaller firms are also allowed to jointly form an EPF, but required more employees. When a group of business-affiliated firms establish an EPF, it must hold at least 800 employees in total. In the case of a local group of firms, 3,000 employees are required. EPFs enjoy preferential tax treatment. An EPF is not taxed unless the fund goes over 2.7 times the substitute benefits.

In the case of health insurance, large firms are allowed to establish their own health insurance associations, while employees in smaller businesses belong to the government-managed scheme. A health insurance association in surpluses provides more generous benefits and services than the government-managed scheme. The self-employed and those not covered by employees' insurance schemes join the National Pension Insurance (NPI) and National Health Insurance (NHI), which provide minimum levels of protection. In 1985 the NPI was merged with flat-rate parts of employees' pension schemes. In the integrated Basic Pension, however, employees and the self-employed are treated differently. They pay different amounts of contributions in different ways.[7] The Basic Pension is, after all, made for financial transfers (called 'fiscal adjustment') across different schemes.

Thus, social security provision in Japan reflects status differentials in the labour market, as do most conservative welfare states. Family-based benefits in Japanese social security are also typical for the conservative regime, especially among Southern European countries. Japan's welfare regime defined in terms of social security provision is undoubtedly based on the conservative principle. However, a couple of deviances from the conservative type are confirmed in Japan's welfare regime. Its social security provision is less generous than conservative welfare states in continental Europe, such as France and Germany. France and Germany guarantee over 70 per cent of income replacement in their pension schemes, while Japan provides less than 60 per cent of the average salary of the time. The recently passed revision makes pension benefits below 50 per cent of the average salary in the future. Thus, while its principle is definitely conservative, Japan is closer to liberal welfare states in terms of generosity in social security provision.

Another deviance from the conservative type, which leads Japan closer to the liberal type, is the proliferation of corporate welfare or firm-specific welfare, including retirement allowances and pensions, housing provisions, and savings and loans programmes. Firm-specific welfare is a reflection of less generosity in public welfare provision. Corporate welfare complements public welfare. Of the most significant among company welfare provisions is retirement payment/pension. Retirement allowances expanded in the 1950s broadly among businesses of various sizes due to the introduction of generous tax treatment in 1952, which allowed companies to claim lump-sum retirement payments as non-taxable expenses.

The 1962 tax code revision realized corporate pension with preferential tax treatment. A company with 15 or more employees can establish a tax-qualified pension programme based on a contract with a life insurance company or a trust bank. Like the EPF, the tax-qualified pension fund is basically non-taxable, although it must pay a special corporation tax instead. In addition to helping firms level off their annual expenses for retirement allowances through non-taxable pension funds, the tax-qualified pension also smoothens replacement of more expensive and less productive older employees with cheaper and more productive younger entries and provide reliable resources for capital formation in general. Company-specific welfare, including the EPF and tax-qualified pension, fosters a general spirit of mutuality among employees and a sense of loyalty to their companies, thereby helping to maintain labour-management harmony (Shinkawa and Pempel 1996: 300).

Japan's welfare regime features occupationally divided public welfare and well-developed corporate welfare. The latter is certainly a common feature of the liberal welfare regime, but it is misleading, however, if Japan's case is regarded as identical with that of the US. In the US, a company provides employees with fringe benefits according to their achievements, credentials and expertise through individual contracts. On the other hand, a Japanese company provides (provided at least until recently) a package of welfare on a collective basis. What an employee can receive depends largely on the length of his/her employed period, rather than his/her merits. In other words, corporate welfare in Japan is also provided collectively in a conservative fashion.

Social policy determinants in the expansion era

Japan has been ranked bottom or near bottom in the ratio of social security expenditure to GDP among OECD member countries, along with the United States. 'Laggardness' of the Japanese welfare state is well explained by the power mobilization thesis; that is, Japan failed to establish a generous welfare state due to weak labour and leftist forces. The socialists had never been back in power until 1993. Moreover, since the Marxists and pro-Marxists became hegemonic within the party after the failure of the centre-left coalition government in 1947–48, the JSP was far from an earnest promoter of the welfare state.[8] They occasionally called for improvements in social security, but basically regarded the welfare state as a device of capitalism for its survival (Shinkawa 1999). The Marxist-dominated JSP had stayed as the largest opposition by gathering support from anti-conservative, liberal pacifist groups of people, but never been a realistic alternative to the LDP government.

In addition to ideological rigidity, the decline and containment of the labour movement was a cause behind the stagnancy of the JSP. The unionization rate fell to a third of the workforce in the 1950s and has not recovered since. The Occupation changed its liberal policy to a hard-line policy (the so-called 'reverse course') against the Communists and their allies as a result of the radicalization of the labour movement and increased tensions between East and West.

The economic recession following the end of the Korean War facilitated business streamlining, which inevitably led to a decrease in the number of labour unions. Anti-capitalist union activists were the first to be fired. The unionization ratio subsequently dropped sharply.

Organized labour in Japan suffered not only low unionization density, but also ideological divisions. The largest national confederation called 'Sohyo', which was founded in 1950 as a unified front of anti-communist moderate labour unions, soon radicalized itself and developed a class-oriented movement, which confronted the communist movement, on the basis of Marxist doctrine. Sohyo underpinned the leftist stance of the JSP. Sohyo's deviation from the course of social democratic class settlement led moderate unions to pursue the possibility of organizing a different national confederation. The second largest confederation, 'Domei', and IMF-JC (International Metal Federation-Japan Council) were established in the early 1960s. The split within organized labour further weakened Domei's political influence.

Weak power mobilization and splits in organized labour and leftist forces explain the laggardness of Japanese welfare provision, but to explain individual policy development and the aforementioned features of Japan's social security system, party competition and interest group politics in the context of democratization must be taken into account. As mentioned above, the NPI was proposed by the LDP to obtain support in the national election, in spite of the ironical fact that farmers (the major target of the NPI) responded negatively to it because they did not like the idea of paying contributions (Campbell 1992: chapter 3).

Mutual aid pension schemes were newly instituted in the 1950s for private-school teachers and clerks, and employees in pseudo-public corporations in agriculture, forestry, and fishery. They called for their own mutual aid plans by contending that their work was equivalent to that of public sector employees. They were unhappy with low standards of benefits in the Employees' Pension Plan at that time, which reached barely one-third of their counterparts in Mutual-Aid Pension Plans.

More significant than partisan politics and interest group politics in forming the private–public mix and the fragmented public welfare system are historical contingencies and path dependence. The development of corporate welfare took place due to Japan's defeat in the Second World War. Enterprise welfare was a substitute for public welfare, which the government was unable to provide due to fiscal tightness for a while after the end of the Second World War. Once it was established, corporate welfare defined the subsequent development of public welfare. Given the dominance of corporate welfare provision, the establishment of the universal welfare state was all but impossible. Even the improvement of EPP benefits within the ongoing system was rejected by employers in the 1950s. Consequently, mutual aid plans proliferated, as mentioned above.

The private–public mix fits well the assumption of the Japanese-style labour management. Given lifetime employment and seniority-based wages, what matters in the provision of corporate welfare is the length of the employment period. A sense of loyalty and belonging to the company is reinforced by the fact that what he/she receives varies according to the size of his/her company and how long he/she has served. Company-based labour unions had no reason to fight management as long as employment is secured and wages and welfare are provided on a seniority basis.

It will be quite misleading, however, to conclude that such welfare arrangements were accepted by workers without problems. The 1950s witnessed fierce class confrontation in Japan. The class-oriented Sohyo attempted to strengthen ties of workers across enterprises and encourage industrial organizations. To prevent Sohyo's challenge, contain and divide organized labour along enterprise lines, employers exerted both 'hard' and 'soft' measures. Company-specific welfare was employed to make a counter-attack against the leftist labour movement calling for class-based unionism, promote firm loyalty among employees, and contain trade unions along company lines (Shinkawa 1999, 2000).

The Employees' Pension Funds (EPFs) were enacted in 1966 as a compromise hammered out between welfare bureaucrats and employers. By the late 1950s, the Japan Employers' Association (JEA) started to call for preferential tax treatment for company specific pension plans. By shifting lump-sum retirement payments to pension payments, the JEA aimed at levelling off annual costs for retirement payments. Welfare bureaucrats were negative on the idea, fearing that a new scheme would provide another barrier to improving EPI benefits. The JEA's proposal of a tax-qualified pension in November 1961 provided a way out. In the proposal, the JEA accepted increases in EPI benefits on the condition that a firm is entitled to opt out of EPI's earnings-related part and establish its own employees' pension fund. With the consent of the MHW, a tax-qualified pension was introduced in 1962. Due to labour's fierce opposition the establishment of the EPF scheme was delayed until 1966. In the same year, the model monthly benefit of the EPI was raised from 3,500 yen to 10,000 yen, or 40 per cent of the then average wage (Campbell 1992: 89).

The transformation of the Japanese-style welfare regime

Japan made a critical move towards a more comprehensive welfare state in the early 1970s. The government carried out a series of welfare expansion programmes in a short period of time, including pension benefit raises (e.g., a model pension benefit of the EPI was set at 60 per cent of the average wage), improvements in health care insurance (e.g., the coverage rate of employees' family members was raised from 50 per cent to 70 per cent and reimbursement for expensive medical treatment was introduced), and the provision of child allowances. The expanded social welfare was developed by the LDP government as compensation through which to co-opt opponents of the production-first policy (cf. Calder 1988; Shinkawa 1993).

If social welfare expansion had lasted for a substantial period of time, a major feature of the Japanese-style welfare regime would have disappeared. Unfortunately, however, as soon as a severe recession hit Japan in 1973, the idea of welfare cutbacks emerged within as well as outside of government to alleviate financial burdens. The political leadership, however, made no move towards welfare retrenchment and let financial deficits grow in the late 1970s. Welfare cutbacks are politically risky, especially when the ruling party does not enjoy a stable majority in the Diet (the LDP barely maintained a majority in the Upper House of the Diet in the late 1970s).

A policy window opened for a review of public welfare when the LDP won a comfortable majority both in the Lower and Upper Houses in the 1980 double election. The LDP government successfully gained popular support by proposing the idea of administrative reform to reconstruct public finance without tax increases. Administrative reform, in turn, legitimized welfare cutbacks. The government abolished free medical care for the aged in 1982, introduced co-payment in employees' health insurance schemes, and tightened the relationship between contribution and benefit in the 1985 pension reform. The most significant in a series of welfare retrenchments was the establishment of fiscal adjustment across different schemes. On the abolition of free medical care for the aged, health insurance associations agreed to equalize fiscal burdens to a certain degree by contributing to a financial pool for elderly medical care. The Basic Pension was created to save the NPI from deficits through fiscal transfers. Meanwhile, the importance of company welfare as a complement to public welfare was reconfirmed and reinforced. Corporate welfare was frequently praised as the core of Japanese-style welfare (Shinkawa 1993: ch. 4).

The heightened importance of corporate welfare corresponded to the rearrangement of Japanese-style labour management in the 1980s. The experience of the two oil crises in the 1970s urged Japanese firms to pursue more efficient labour management. Redundant manpower was redeployed, dispatched, or transferred to subsidiaries, but rarely dismissed. By holding redundant employees within a group of subsidiaries or affiliated businesses (the so-called intermediate labour market), Japanese firms maintained the practice of lifetime employment. As long as employment was secured, labour unions collaborated with the management to trim the number of workers in regular employment. Consequently, Japanese-style labour management was rearranged peacefully in such a way as to shrink the core of employment and enlarge the periphery composed of employees in smaller businesses, temporary workers, and part-time workers. That is, the dualist structure of the labor market was reinforced (Shinkawa 1993: ch. 7).

The rearrangement of Japanese-style labour management into its upgraded version in the 1980s paralleled the decline of the leftist labour movement. Since the defeat of Sohyo in the 1975 spring offensive for a demand of higher wage raises by the unified front formed by the government, employers' organizations, and moderate trade unions, the leftist labour movement has been in decline. Moderate trade unions obtained hegemony and initiated the unification of labour movements. Private sector unions got together first and, in 1989, a national peak confederation named 'Rengo' was founded by bringing private sector and public sector labour unions together (Shinkawa 1999, 2001). Thus, the moderate leadership in organized labour successfully upgraded Japanese-style labour management.

Towards a liberal welfare regime?

Japan's ageing ratio of 14 per cent caught up with Western Europe in 1994. Japan entered the stage of the aged society according to the UN's definition. More noteworthy, however, is that Japan spent only 24 years to go from 7 to 14 per cent, whereas it took France 117 years. The country with the shortest transition in Western Europe, Germany, still spent 44 years to move from 7 to 14 per cent. Furthermore, Japan's ageing is projected to last until more than a third of its population become aged over 65 over in 2050. Against this backdrop, various measures have been introduced to absorb impacts of population ageing upon society.

The LDP government introduced a consumption tax in 1989 with the words that the increased revenue would be used mainly to cope with the ageing population. Subsequently the government released a plan to increase the number of facilities for the elderly as well as manpower for elderly care. Eventually, in April 2000, the programme of public care for the elderly came into effect. It is compulsory for those at the age of 40 and over to contribute to the programme. Increases in financial burden are seen also in health insurance and pension. The rate of co-payment was raised in 1999 to 30 percent of medical treatment costs. When co-payment was introduced in 1984, its rate was set at 10 percent. The rate trippled in only fifteen years.

The most serious problem Japan faces today is the sustainability of public pensions. Since the basic principle of its finance is pay-as-you-go, younger generations most severely suffer from population ageing. To balance burdens among different generations, the government raised pension entitlement ages in 1994 and 1999. In addition, the government raised contribution rates and reduced levels of benefits almost every five years in actuarial recalculation. Repeated retrenchments, however, not only failed to guarantee the sustainability of public pension, but also undermined its credibility. Table 3.2 shows the variation of trust in public pension along generational lines. It clearly indicates the correlation between the age and the degree of trust. The younger a generation is, the less it trusts public pension.[9]

To erase widespread anxieties about sustainability and regain credibility, the government conducted the 2004 pension reform. The major changes included in it are as follows. The contribution rate would be raised gradually from the current 13.58 per cent of annual income to 18.30 per cent by 2017 and kept at that level ever afterwards. Benefit levels would vary according to changes in demographic and economic factors, including life expectancy, the fertility rate, interest rates, and prices, and not on the basis of political decisions. In short, the pension system is to shift from defined benefits (DB) to defined contributions (DC).

Table 3.2 Trust in public pensions

Generation	*Trust (%)*	*Distrust (%)*
20+	32	67
30+	27	72
40+	46	54
50+	58	41
60+	68	30
70+	71	22
Average	51	47

Source: *Asahi Shinbun*, 21 June 2003.

In the 1980s, corporate welfare was expected to expand to complement retrenched public welfare. Such an optimistic view was no longer maintained in the 1990s, as the Japanese economy suffered a serous trouble. The central issue over corporate welfare in the 1990s was not expansion but curtailment. Many firms attempted to alleviate financial burdens incurred by corporate pension schemes. The number of qualified pensions went down to 73,600 in March 2002, after reaching a peak of 92,5000 in 1993. The number of EPFs reached a peak in 1996 and then started to decline. Since the first dissolution of an EPF was permitted in 1994, the number of dissolved EPFs has increased annually. Between 1996 and 2001, approximately 150 funds were dissolved and the total number of EPFs decreased to 1,737 in 2002. Consequently, the total number of employees covered by corporate pension schemes (including both qualified pension and EPFs) declined from 22.89 million in 1996 to 20.04 million in March 2002.

To overhaul the corporate pension system, the government conducted a comprehensive reform in 2001. Under the new regulation, firms are more freely able to dissolve EPFs. Tax-qualified pensions will be replaced by new schemes, including a DC plan or the Japanese version of 401 (k). Since new DB schemes request heavier financial responsibility on the management side, more employers are expected to go for the DC scheme (Shinkawa 2005). The 2001 corporate pension reforms corresponded to labour market deregulation.

In the face of globalization and prolonged recession, Japan's major firms decided to depart from the traditional Japanese-style labour management. The Japan Employers' Association (JEA) released a watershed report in 1995, according to which conventional lifetime employment based on seniority is limited to those who are expected to be executives in the future. High-skilled labour or professionals are hired on a contract basis. Most workers, including professionals and general clerks, are employed on a contract basis to maintain flexible employment. Following such a change in the management strategy, the government deregulated the labour market in the late 1990s through a series of revisions in labour legislation. The clauses of female protection in the labour law were erased to realize equal treatment between men and women. Restrictions on labour dispatching business was removed. Flex-time can be applied more broadly and freely than before (Shinkawa 1999: 220–2).

The overhaul of corporate pensions in 2001 was a readjustment to the deregulation of the labour market in the late 1990s. Corporate pensions based on lifelong employment became outdated by that time. The new system is designed to deal with flexible employment or the high rate of labour turnover. The DC scheme is perfect for flexible employment, though it cannot encourage firm loyalty as strongly as the conventional DB plans; nor can it be perfect for income security after retirement.

In conclusion, Japan steered for the liberal welfare regime in the 1990s by dismantling the traditional labour management and welfare provisions. The process was gradual rather than drastic. Since cuts in welfare are obviously unpopular, the government tried to reduce their effects. Together with the policy of decrementalism, phase-in periods are usually introduced in welfare restraints. Phase-in periods make it difficult to trace back the effects to responsible actors when welfare retrenchment starts. Attempts at lowering visibility of decision makers as well as policy are defined by democratic procedures. Politicians who seek re-election try to avoid blame for welfare cutbacks.

The neoliberal strategy also reflects the decline of the leftist forces. The JSP changed its name to the Social Democratic Party in 1996, but became a tiny, politically ineffective party as a result of the defection of most of its members to the newly formed Democratic Party. The Democratic Party adopts a centrist stance and quite a few members are inclining towards the ideas of neoliberalism and small government, rather than the social democratic idea. Organized labour is in consistent decline. Rengo has found no effective measures by which to stop the constant decline of the unionization ratio since 1975. The recent figure of the unionization rate fails to maintain the 20 per cent line. Rengo supports the Democratic Party but fails to penetrate effectively its leadership and establish as close a relationship as the Sohyo did with the JSP. The leadership of the Democratic Party keeps Rengo at arm's length and cautiously avoids commitment to it. In short, no counterweight forces to neoliberal welfare reform can be found in the current political scene in Japan.

Concluding remarks

Organized labour provides an explanation for both democratization and social policy; the increased political influence of organized labour prompts the government to introduce universal suffrage and expand social welfare, as witnessed in some West European nations. Organized labour in Japan, however, has never been strong enough to form a major locomotive of democratization or social policy development.

In prewar Japan, progressive bureaucrats took the lead in promoting social policy development. They came to realize the importance and necessity of social policy by perceiving the 'social problems' caused by tenants and industrial workers and by learning experiences in Western Europe. Progressive bureaucrats were not predominant within the state, but gained a chance to reflect its ideas in policy making in the era of the Taisho democracy, during which party-led governments operated. Kenseikai in particular supported the expansion of social protection and helped the progressive bureaucrats go for liberal social legislation. Thus, democratization facilitated social policy development, although democracy in prewar Japan was severely constrained by the Meiji Constitution. On the other hand, the repercussions of social policy development on democratization can hardly be properly assessed because the Taisho democracy was too short-lived to let social policy affect national livelihood.

The US Occupation established the basic framework of democracy and social policy in postwar Japan. The liberal constitution was drafted by the young New Dealers and forced upon the conservative Japanese government. Labour legislation set industrial workers free. The land reform made small independent farmers the majority in agriculture. The mobilization of industrial workers and independent farmers contributed to the emergence of the centre–left coalition government in 1947, which symbolized the success of democratic reforms in spite of its disastrous end.

During the period of social policy development, the most important facilitator was party politics. Social policy was employed as a means to mobilize popular support in elections. Democratization, reflected in party competition for power, contributed to social policy development. Such democratic politics, however, paid little attention to the long term goal of systematic welfare development. Against the wish of welfare bureaucrats and experts to build a universal welfare state, the LDP governments opted for short-sighted improvements in social security, thereby furthering fragmentation, which would cause fiscal vulnerability and risk the sustainability of the social security system over the long run.

Bureaucracy-initiated social policy retrenchments since the mid-1980s are also comprehensible in the context of democracy. As Kent Weaver suggests, politicians do not want to risk their political life by committing themselves to unpopular policies. When they have to do so, they will try to lower the visibility of policy effects on themselves in democratic politics (Weaver 1986; Shinkawa 2005). In a democratic political system, politicians and political parties compete to gain popular support. They claim credit in the expansion of social security, while trying to avoid blame in social policy retrenchment. Their behavior is thus defined by the context of democratic politics.

Finally, it should be noted that the transformation of the Japanese-style welfare regime reflects the changes in industrial relations. Corporate welfare based on lifelong employment is now outdated and regarded as a cause of rigidity in the labour market. A portable type of corporate welfare becomes popular, given the higher rate of turnover. Social security programmes are retrenched to reduce labour costs, which would otherwise explode as population ageing accelerates. Welfare retrenchment has been carried out gradually, incrementally, and steadily. Unified labour has failed to counterbalance the neoliberal reforms. Its shrinking power base or the consistently decreasing union density further reduces its political influence.

Notes

1. Historical description in this section was based mainly on Yokoyama and Tada (1991) and Yoshiwara and Wada (1999).

2. Japanese names are placed in the original order. The family name comes first.
3. Both the seiyukai and the Keinseikai were rearranged and renamed several times. Fore convenience and simplicity, however, these changes are ignored throughout the chapter.
4. To be precise, the Universal Male Suffrage Law passed the Diet, based on an all-party consensus. Challenging the legitimacy of the oligarch government following the assassination of PM Hara Takashi in 1921, the anti-oligarchy alliance proposed the idea of universal male suffrage in the 1924 election.
5. Although the bill was far less progressive than the Social Bureau's initial draft, it was still a great advance in several respects. First, it exempted unions from any liability for damages caused during disputes. Second, the permission of government was not necessary to organize a union. All a new union had to do was report its formation to the authorities. Third, it prohibited yellow-dog contracts that forced workers to agree not to join unions. Finally, it recognized all currently active unions and federations.
6. On August 8, 1957, Asahi Shigeru took his claim to court, claiming that the monthly welfare benefit of 600 yen he received was not enough to guarantee his constitutional right to a minimum standard of wholesome living. The Tokyo District Court supported the petitioner's claim in 1960, but the Supreme Court overruled its decision (Anderson 1993: 94).
7. Contributions are automatically deducted from their paychecks in the case of employees, while payments of the self-employed depend on the will to do so.
8. The JSP changed its name to the Social Democratic Party (SDP) in January 1996 and tried to follow a path towards the 'western-style' welfare state. The SDP, however, fell into a minor party in the election of fall 1996 after the majority of its Diet members joined a newly-formed centrist party named the 'Democratic Party'.
9. A widely circulated discourse since the late 1990s is that future generations can receive less than the total amounts of their payments whereas the balance is quite favorable to current beneficiaries. According to an intergenerational calculation, a model couple of 1940 (composed of a male breadwinner born in 1940, working between the ages of 20 and 60, and living the average span of life, and a two-year younger spouse) gain 2.68 times the total amount of payments, while the model couple of 1980 gain 0.73 times, and the couple of 2000 gain 0.61 times (Nishizawa 2003, p. 33).

References

Japanese

Asahi Shinbun. 2003. June, 21.

Nishizawa, K. 2003. *Nenkin Daikaikaku (Great Pension Reform)*. Tokyo: Nihon Keizai Shinbunsha.

Okamoto, T. 1991. 'Kyuhin Seido no Hensen (The Transformation of Poor Relief Programs)', in K. Yokoyama and H. Tada (eds), *Nihon Shakai Hosho no Rekishi (The History of Social Security in Japan)*. Tokyo: Gakubunsha, pp. 20–41.

Shibata, Y. 1998. *Nihon no Shakaihosho (Social Security of Japan)*. Tokyo: Shin-nihon Shuppansha.

Shinkawa, T. 1993. *Nihon-gata Fukushi no Seiji Keizaigaku (The Political Economy of Japanese-Style Welfare)*. Tokyo: San-ichi Shobo.

Shinkawa, T. 1997. 'Nihon: Nihongata Fukushi no Shuen? (Japan: The End of the Japanese-Style Welfare?)', in N. Okazawa and T. Miyamoto (eds), *Hikaku Fukushi Kokka-ron (Comparative Welfare States)*. Kyoto: Horitsu Bunkasha, pp. 154–75.

Shinkawa, T. 1999. *Sengo Nihon Seiji to Shakai Minshu-shugi (Social Democracy in Postwar Japan)*. Kyoto: Horitsu Bunka-sha.

Shinkawa, T. 2001. Sengo Shakai Hosho Seisaku no Katei to Kozo (The Development and Structures of Social Security Programmes in Postwar Japan). *Kikan Shakai Hosho* 37 (1)4–16.

Shinkawa, T. 2003. 'Nihon niokeru Fukushikokka no Atarashii Seiji (The New Politics of the Welfare State in Japan)', in I. Takagi *et al.* (eds), *Gurobaruka to Seiji no Inobeshon (Globalization and the Innovation of Politics)*. Kyoto: Minerva, pp. 214–31.

Tanaka, K. 2000. *Kindai Nihon no Fukushi Jissen to Kokumin Togo (Welfare Policy and National Integration in Modern Japan)*. Kyoto: Horitsu Bunkasha.

Umeda, T., H. Takahashi, and I. Yokozeki. 2004 *Kyochokai no Kenkyu (A Study of Kyochokai)*. Tokyo: Kashiwa Shobo.

Yasuda, H. 1994 *Taisho Demokurashi Shiron (The History of Taisho Democracy)*. Tokyo: Azekura Shobo.

Yokoyama, K. and H. Tada (eds). 1991. *Nihon Shakaihosho no Rekishi (The History of Social Security in Japan)*. Tokyo: Gakubunsha.

Yoshiwara, K. and M. Wada. 1999. *Nihon Iryo Hoken Seidoshi (The Institutional History of Medical Insurance in Japan)*. Tokyo: Toyo Keizai Shinposha.

English

Anderson, S. J. 1993. *Welfare Policy and Politics in Japan*. New York: Paragon House.

Calder, K. 1988. *Crisis and Compensation*. Princeton: Princeton University Press.

Campbell, J. C. 1992. *How Policies Change: The Japanese Government and the Aging Society*. Princeton, NJ: Princeton University Press.

Esping-Andersen, G. 1990. *The Three Worlds of Welfare Capitalism*. Princeton: Princeton University Press.

Esping-Andersen, G. 1997. 'Hybrid or Unique? The Distinctiveness of the Japanese Welfare State', *Journal of European Social Policy* 7(3), 179–89.

Evans, B. P., D. Rueschemeyer and T. Skocpol. 1985. *Bringing the State Back In*. Princeton, NJ: Princeton University Press.

Garon, S. 1987. *The State and Labor in Modern Japan*. Berkeley, CA: University of California Press.

Goodin, R. E. 2001. 'Work and Welfare: Towards a Post-productivist Welfare Regime'. *British Journal of Political Science* 31, 13–39.

Gordon, A. 1991. *Labor and Imperial Democracy in Prewar Japan*. Berkeley, CA: University of California Press.

Heclo, H. 1974. *Modern Social Politics in Britain and Sweden*. New Haven: Yale University Press.

Huber, E. and J. D. Stephens. 2001. *Development and Crisis of the Welfare State*. Chicago: University Press of Chicago.

Kinzley, W. D. 1991. *Industrial Harmony in Modern Japan*. London: Routledge.

Korpi, W. 1978. *The Working Class in Welfare Capitalism*. London: Routledge and Kegan Paul.

Korpi, W. and M. Shalev. 1979. 'Strikes, Industrial Relations and Class Conflict in Capitalist Societies', *British Journal of Sociology* 30, 164–87.

Pierson, P. 1994. *Dismantling the Welfare State*. Cambridge: Cambridge University Press.

Pierson, P. 1996. 'The New Politics of the Welfare State', *World Politics* 48 (January), 143–79.

Pierson, P. (ed.). 2001. *The New Politics of the Welfare State.* Oxford: Oxford University Press.

Richardson, B. M. and S. C. Flanagan. 1984. *Politics in Japan.* Boston: Little, Brown and Company.

Shinkawa, T. 2000. 'Failed Realignment and Policy Changes of the SDPJ', in Hideo Otake (ed.), *Power Shuffles and Policy Processes: Coalition Government in Japan in the 1990s.* Tokyo: Japan Center for International Exchange, pp. 152–82.

Shinkawa, T. 2005 'The Politics of Pension Reform in Japan: Institutional Legacies, Credit-claiming, and Blame Avoidance', in G. Bonoli and T. Shinkawa (eds), *Ageing and Pension Reform Around the World: Evidence from Eleven Countries.* London: Edward Elgar, pp. 157–81.

Shinkawa, T. and T. J. Pempel. 1996. 'Occupational Welfare and the Japanese Experience', in M. Shalev (ed.), *The Privatization of Social Policy?* London: Macmillan, pp. 280–326.

Skocpol, T. 1985. 'Bringing the State Back In: Strategies of Analysis in Current Research', in P. Evans *et al.* (eds), *Bringing the State Back In*, Cambridge: Cambridge University Press, pp. 3–37.

Weaver, R. K. 1986. 'The Politics of Blame Avoidance', *Journal of Public Policy* 6(4), 371–98.

4
Democratization and Social Policy in Southern Europe: From Expansion to 'Recalibration'

Maurizio Ferrera

Introduction

The core understanding of the expression 'Southern Europe' is geographical. In its broad sense, this notion denotes the lands stretching from the Iberian Peninsula to the Bosphorus, including the largest islands of the Mediterranean Sea, from the Balearics to Cyprus. In a narrower sense, however, the expression is mainly used to designate the four largest countries located within this broad area: Portugal, Spain, Italy and Greece. In the social science debate of the last three or four decades, these countries have tended to be treated as a distinct 'region' or cluster, sharing not only geographical, but also other, substantive traits. In this debate, the notion of Southern Europe has a richer, politico-economic connotation, which invites and facilitates intra-regional comparisons (Gunther, Diamandouros and Puhle 1995).

Looked at from a long-term perspective, each of the four countries included in the narrow notion of Southern Europe has witnessed, at different times, periods of power and splendour in European history. All of them entered, however, the epoch of modernity in a state of socioeconomic and political decline (Malefakis 1995). Throughout the nineteenth century, their economies remained characterized by backward agriculture and marked underdevelopment, especially in certain areas (the 'Souths of the South'). In social relations, patron–client networks survived for a much longer time than in other, early modernizing European countries (Eisenstadt and Roninger, 1984). Industrial take-offs were delayed and had to overcome severe structural disadvantages (such as the paucity of natural resources and difficult communications). When economic modernization gained momentum, at the turn between the nineteenth and twentieth centuries, its 'compressed' timing and its internal variegation (sectoral and territorial) exacerbated social conflict, promoting working-class radicalization and 'maximalist' militancy both within industrial workers and the peasantry. Especially in Italy and Spain, the period 1980–1920 witnessed very turbulent labour relations, which left a legacy of ideological polarization and offered fertile grounds for the rooting of communist movements and doctrines. The factious and polarized nature of civil society remained a typical trait of Southern Europe well into the 1970s.

Political modernization was also far from smooth and easy. During the nineteenth century, the road to liberalism, first, and mass democracy later was rough and constantly challenged from both the right and the radical left. The twentieth century witnessed long authoritarian spells: two decades of Fascism in Italy, four decades of Francoism in Spain, half a century of dictatorship in Portugal under Salazar and Caetano and recurring periods of autocratic rule in Greece. The same period also witnessed moments of acute social and political conflict, culminating in civil wars (in Spain and Greece)[1] or 'revolutions' (in Portugal). The long authoritarian spells and the episodes of war-like internal conflict left a deep mark in the politics of Southern European countries.

After the Second World War, Portugal, Spain, Italy and Greece found themselves at their socioeconomic and political nadir: deep economic problems (with the partial exception of Portugal), marked social impoverishment, overt political polarization in Italy and Greece and severe political repression in Spain and Portugal. In the subsequent quarter century, however, a process of rapid and – again – highly compressed change took place, which led to the emergence of a 'new' Southern Europe by the end of the 1970s (Morlino 1998; Pridham 1984). This change affected the economic, the social, the cultural and the political dimensions at the same time and allowed the four countries to rapidly catch up with the rest of Western Europe. Italy was the first country to leap forward, with an early consolidation of the new democratic regime and an economic 'miracle' that more than doubled average per capita income between the 1950s and the 1970s, transforming this country into one of the biggest and most prosperous economies of the world. In the other three countries, economic development proceeded at a lower pace, disturbed by military concerns (in Portugal and Greece) and persisting protectionism. But change did take place: during the 1960s and early 1970s both the Iberian countries and Greece became increasingly richer, more open and modern – also in the wake of the spread of compulsory education, growing urbanization and the intensification of external contacts through tourism and the mass media. With the demise of the authoritarian regimes in the mid-1970s and the return of democracy, Southern Europe became 'new' from its Atlantic shores to the Aegean Sea.

The 1980s and 1990s witnessed an acceleration of modernization dynamics (Bermeo 2000), partly promoted and supported by European Community (EC) membership (Ferrera and Gualmini 2004; Guillén, Alvarez and Adao Silva 2001; Sotiropoulos 2004). The economy continued to grow and its internal structure rapidly changed, substantially attenuating historical dualisms and backwardness. Social relations have gradually 'civilized' and levels of political legitimacy and systemic loyalty have 'normalized' (Morlino and Montero 1995; Morlino 1998). Portugal, Spain, Italy and

Greece are now full members of the group of rich and stable democracies. At the beginning of the new millennium, Southern Europe has lost much of its 'peripheral' character: indeed, some areas and some aspects of South European societies can today offer 'models' and 'benchmarks' to other societies – in Europe as well as in other regions of the world.

On top of a common floor of substantive and 'developmental' traits, there are of course big differences between the four countries: Southern Europe is not a 'region' or a 'family of nations' in the same sense as the Nordic area, for example. We agree however with Gunther, Diamandouros and Puhle (1995) in suggesting that there is sufficient evidence of similarities and shared experiences at the socioeconomic and political levels for undertaking fruitful comparative analyses across the four countries.

Resting on this methodological assumption, this chapter will offer a comparative discussion of welfare state developments in Portugal, Spain Italy and Greece since the end of the Second World War. The idea that Southern Europe forms a distinct cluster not only in general socioeconomic, cultural and political terms, but also as regards the welfare state in particular started to be an object of debate in the early 1990s (Castles 1993; Leibfried 1992; Ferrera 1996; Petmesidou 1996). But this idea could not be pursued based on the literature of the 1970s and 1980s. On the one hand, past research on the political economy of Southern Europe had largely neglected the social dimension; on the other hand, the mainstream comparative welfare state literature had not traditionally included Southern Europe (with the partial exception of Italy) within its samples of observation. Starting from the early 1990s, the social protection systems of the new Southern Europe have become, however, an increasingly investigated object of research, largely confirming the presence of common characteristics (for example, Rhodes 1997). Building on this literature, this chapter will try to pinpoint the main features and trajectories of development of the welfare state in the four countries, identify the contextual factors that can be called into question for explaining such traits and trajectories, and discuss the present problems and future prospects of social policy in this area of Europe.

The chapter is organized in four sections. The first section will offer a brief historical reconstruction of welfare state developments from the early origins up to the late 1980s. Then we discuss the politics of welfare state expansion and the role played by social policy in consolidating and legitimizing the new democratic regimes. Next we will illustrate the adjustment process of the 1990s, aimed both at responding to inherited problems and at modernizing social protection, also in the wake of European integration. The final section will draw some conclusions.

Welfare state formation in Southern Europe: an overview

The early origins of South European social insurance date back to the first two decades of the twentieth century, prior to the advent of authoritarianism.

Italy was the pioneer in this field, introducing compulsory work injury insurance as early as 1898. The 'big bang' occurred in 1919, when the Nitti government passed a law establishing compulsory insurance for old age, invalidity and unemployment. Greece introduced (limited) insurance against work injuries in 1915. Portugal and Spain also made their first steps towards social insurance in 1919.

During Fascism, Italy consolidated the schemes established in 1919, experimented with sickness insurance (which was made compulsory at the end of the Second World War) and introduced new family benefits and services. The period between the 1950s and the 1970s witnessed several important ameliorative reforms, especially in the field of pensions, which put in place a highly articulated social protection system.

The building blocks of the Greek social insurance system were posed in 1934, with the establishment of compulsory pension and sickness schemes. The system was extended and improved on various occasions between the 1950s and 1970s. But the big wave of expansive reforms came after the return of democracy and especially in the 1980s. Pensions were a central concern of Greek social reformism during the expansionary phase.

In Portugal, compulsory social insurance was introduced under Salazar's *Estado Novo*, in 1935. The reach of these early compulsory schemes remained relatively circumscribed, despite the reforms of the 1960s. After the revolution of 1974, a rapid expansionary phase began, which eventually put in place a modern system of social protection covering the whole population.

In Spain, the actual introduction of compulsory insurance was delayed by the turbulent events of the First Republic and the Civil War. While work injury insurance was introduced in 1932, compulsory sickness insurance was only implemented in 1942 and compulsory pension insurance in 1947, both under Franco's regime. In the 1960s and early 1970s, during the *desarrollismo* (a growth-oriented phase of economic policy), the regime also promoted some expansion of social insurance. But as in Portugal and Greece, the big wave of reforms came only after the transition to democracy. As we shall see, in these three countries welfare state reform and expansion played an important role in the rapid legitimation of the new democratic regime.

Even if its timing was different in each of the four South European countries, the path followed by social insurance displayed a number of similar traits in all of them. To begin with, social insurance co-evolved with a segmented labour market (and a context which I have elsewhere called 'weak fordism': Ferrera 2005) and thus acquired its own degree of internal polarization: generous entitlements for core/regular workers, modest benefits for the peripheral/irregulars, and only meagre crumbs (if anything at all) for those workers who were unable to establish a formal contact with the regular labour market. In addition to this, in its expansionary phase, South European social insurance over-privileged the risk of old age (at least in terms of legal formulas) and reserved only a marginal role for family benefits

(Ferrera 1996). In line with the conservative-corporatist welfare regime tradition, it also privileged transfers over services and promoted the proliferation of differentiated schemes, tied to occupational status. Institutional fragmentation reached impressive levels in Italy and especially in Greece. It has to be noted, however, that the link with the Bismarckian tradition was broken in the field of health care (Guillen 2002). All four countries established national health services during the 1970s and 1980s: a rather infrequent, but very significant instance of 'path shift', which has worked to smoothen the profile of the welfare state edifice and has contributed to upgrading the allocative and distributive efficiency of social expenditure in these countries.

The institutional growth of social insurance reflected itself in expenditure trends. In particular, the fifteen-year period 1975–1990 witnessed a marked increase of social transfers in all countries, but especially in Greece (8.1 percentage points, up to 15.2 per cent of GDP) and in Spain (6.4 percentage points, up to 15.9 per cent). The lion's share of this quantitative growth was absorbed by pensions. In only one decade (1980–1990) these benefits grew by 94 per cent in real terms in Greece, by 33 per cent in Italy, by 27 per cent in Portugal and by 23 per cent in Spain. Family benefits on the contrary stagnated in Italy and Portugal, declined in Spain and grew only modestly in Greece.[2]

The dark spot of the expansion during the *Trente Glorieuses* was the social assistance sector. This was the weakest front of achievement for our four countries – at least up to the late 1980s (Matsaganis *et al.* 2003). The South European 'safety net' evolved slowly, through a sequence of fragmented and mainly categorical additions (such as orphans, widows, disabled, and the poor elderly) with disparate rules and differentiated benefit amounts, with a low (if not altogether lacking) degree of integration between cash benefits and services and with wide holes in the overall fabric of public provision. As a consequence of this, poverty levels have traditionally remained very high in Southern Europe. Many poor households were (and still largely are) ineligible for social assistance because they failed to fulfil the narrow conditions set out by the various categorical programmes. Needless to say, those affected by this syndrome included the largest groups of outsiders: the long-term unemployed, the new entrants into the labour markets, the irregulars and underground workers and – increasingly – immigrants. As has been shown by recent scholarship, the marginal role of social assistance within South European systems of social protection is explained by three main causes: the role of the family (Moreno 2004; Naldini 2003), the incidence of the irregular and underground economy and low administrative capacities (Ferrera 2005).

The politics of welfare state expansion and its role in regime consolidation

As illustrated by a vast literature, the expansion of social insurance coverage and the improvement of its benefits have played an important role in stabilizing European democracies since the Second World War.[3] On the one hand, welfare state programmes have strengthened citizens' loyalty to national institutions, enhancing the latter's 'bottom-up' legitimacy; on the other hand, such programmes have operated as 'anchors' that political institutions have cast towards the various groups of civil society, thus securing their allegiance through the provision of material advantages – a top-down process of consensus building and socio-political stabilization (Morlino 1998). The literature on the democratization of Southern Europe has already highlighted the importance, in general, of social policy for easing and smoothening the transition and especially for the consolidation of the new democratic regimes (Gunther, Diamandouros and Puhle 1995; Diamandouros and Gunther 2001; Morlino 1998). In this section we will identify some of the main forms and mechanisms through which the link between social policy and democratic consolidation has manifested itself in the four countries. Given the different mode and timing of the Italian regime change with respect to the other three, we will first deal with this case. We will then deal with Greece – which shares some common traits with Italy in terms of welfare politics – and finally with the two Iberian countries.

Italy

Democracy returned to Italy in 1946, after a national referendum which established the Italian Republic and the national elections for the Constitutional Assembly. The new Republican Constitution entered into force in 1948. In the same year, after a heated campaign, the elections consigned the national executive to the Democrazia Cristiana (Christian Democracy or DC), which had defeated a Popular Front comprising both Communists and Socialists. Between the late 1940s and the 1980s Italy's party system was characterized as a form of 'polarized pluralism' (Sartori 1976, 1982), displaying not only high fragmentation (many parties), but also a wide ideological distance between left and right. Ideological polarization made the legitimation of the new democratic regime a rather difficult and slow process. The centre of the political spectrum was occupied by the DC, which presented itself as a watchdog of western-style liberal democracy and market capitalism. The left pole was occupied by the largest communist party of the western world, the Partito Comunista d'Italia (PCI), while the right pole was occupied by a fairly strong neo-fascist party, the Movimento Sociale Italiano (MSI). Both the PCI and the MSI were anti-system parties, i.e. they explicitly aimed at altering in fundamental ways the country's political and economic regime. In this setting, electoral competition followed a distinct tri-polar and centrifugal logic. All three poles had an interest in playing on the pro-system vs anti-system dimension. Sitting in the middle, the DC had an interest in expanding its votes both towards the left and towards the right, trying to capture all potentially pro-system voters. The other two poles had in their turn an interest in capturing all anti-system voters located around the extremes (lest splinter parties emerge), by means of various strategies of issue radicalization and social mobilization. Squeezed between the DC and the PCI, the socialist party (Partito Socialista Italiano: PSI) oscillated between pro-system and anti-system stances during the 1950s, but opted for the former at the beginning of the 1960s, negotiating an organic alliance with the DC and forming the first *Centro-sinistra* (centre-left) government in 1962.

Already during the 1950s, the DC centred its strategy of electoral expansion and regime legitimation on an extensive use of public sector resources. As many scholars of the Italian party system have underlined, the DC (especially in the period 1950–1970) can largely be seen as a 'mass patronage party', inclined to seek consensus via a web of political exchange relationships, which developed especially in the South of the country (La Palombara 1964; Di Palma 1977; Hine 1993). The proliferation of social insurance schemes for various occupational categories (often micro-categories) can be seen as one side – the most visible – of mass patronage practices. There was, however, a second, less explicit side of such practices, which rested on individualized forms of political exchange. In order to gain votes, the DC provided its 'clients' with individual benefits in a number of ways: for instance granting them job opportunities in the public sector or assisting them in obtaining a subsidy from the welfare bureaucracy. The 'control' of the exchange on the side of the party mainly occurred through the system of preference votes, in ways which were not necessarily illegal (Ancisi, 1976). The extended area of *sottogoverno* (that is, the various spoils represented by state enterprises, public agencies of various sorts, social security funds and so on) were the main *loci* of these particularistic exchanges, and welfare benefits their privileged currency.

The micro-clientelistic use of the welfare state for electoral purposes was implemented in two ways (Ferrera 1986 and 1996: 1) through the partisan penetration of the welfare administration – not only the upper end of the administrative echelon, but especially the lower end, i.e. the points of actual benefit delivery; (2) through the bypassing of the welfare administration via the creation of ad hoc bodies (e.g. 'political commissions') entrusted with discretionary powers with respect, again, to the provision of individual benefits.

Agricultural sectors in the background *Mezzogiorno* (Italy's South) were the preferred (though not the sole) grounds of operation of such a clientelistic market. In these sectors, state subsidization was often the only opportunity to gain income and unemployed or underemployed (that is, underground or peripheral) workers were well prepared to 'sell' their votes to political entrepreneurs capable of supplying some sort of income, especially an invalidity pension. The growth of invalidity pensions in Italy during the 1960s was really spectacular, especially in the South. Their number almost trebled between the 1960s and 1971 and came to overtake the number of old age pensions in 1972. It was only in 1984 that a restrictive reform was finally introduced, with a view to preventing abuses.

It would obviously be misleading and exaggerated to interpret Italy's welfare state developments between the 1950s and the 1980s solely in terms of clientelism. Important sectors of this country's welfare state operated according to modern, universalistic criteria. In the education, health care and social service sectors innovative reforms were passed in the 1960s and 1970s (for example, the establishment of a British-style National Health Service in 1978), which significantly contributed to modernizing the political culture and social behaviour and to substantially improving living conditions. As a matter of fact, with the launch of the *Centro Sinistra* – the alliance between the DC and the PSI – a very ambitious project was elaborated, aimed at replacing the prevailing mode of regime legitimation and consensus building, based on mass patronage practices, with a new mode resting on universalistic inclusion – and partly inspired by the Scandinavian models. The project was especially ambitious in the field of pensions: but it failed to materialize, largely owing to the electoral logic of polarized pluralism. Instead of a Swedish-style pensions system, a law passed in 1969 introduced a reform which was 'universalist' only in the sense that all the participants in the political process that led to it got some spoils. The real winners were the PCI and the CGIL, which obtained the introduction for all employees of one of the most generous pension formulas ever introduced in Europe, including the option to retire after 35 years of insurance regardless of age (the infamous – with hindsight – seniority pensions). Even if excluded from the government, the PCI had demonstrated its massive 'blackmail potential' *vis-à-vis* the social and economic policy choices of the government, thanks to its power to mobilize workers in the electoral and industrial conflict arenas. Politically, the 1969 pension reform inaugurated a new phase of all-inclusive spoils-sharing systems, extended to the PCI and to the trade unions (which gained an important role in the actual management of the pension funds, including grassroots decisions about disability pension applications: the political machine described above). Institutionally, the reform created a true 'labyrinth' of different occupational funds, with different regulations. These funds continued to remain easily permeable to partisan manipulations and mass patronage practices. Financially, the reform created a spending engine that over the course of two decades brought pension expenditure up from 6.9 per cent of GDP in 1970 to 11.8 per cent in 1990 (1992 = 12.8 per cent).[4] Though clearly effective in terms of consensus building, the Italian pension system – and the welfare state more generally – had embarked upon a path of financial unsustainability, that was only abandoned – with socially painful reforms – in the course of the 1990s.

Greece

As in Italy, also in Greece the welfare state has been widely used for purposes of consensus building via clientelistic practices. The clientelistic manipulation of social policy had already been inaugurated in the prewar period, during which many influential social groups (especially the urban free professions) were able to set up highly advantageous and state subsidized social protection funds (Liakos 1997). The Second World War, the occupation and the civil war exacerbated the country's social and political divisions, generating a climate of marked ideological polarization (Diamandouros 1994). Ruling elites continued to use social policies (and especially occupational pension insurance funds) as particularistic 'anchors' for the selective inclusion of groups (such as farmers) that were seen as crucial for political stability. A military regime took over in 1967 and the authoritarian spell lasted until 1974. The return of democracy ushered in a period of rapid welfare state expansion (Matsaganis 2005).

In 1981, the Socialist party (Panellinio Sosialistiko Kinima: PASOK) rose to power in the wake of a 're-aligning' election, which saw the emergence of a new social bloc consisting of employees (blue and white collar), pensioners, the petit bourgeoisie (independent farmers, artisans and shopkeepers) and the new middle classes (public sector employees, the liberal professions) (Sotiropoulos 2004). PASOK's social policy during the 1980s closely reflected the interests of this new social bloc. One of the first measures of the new government was to raise the statutory minimum wage by 40 per cent, with a corresponding increase in all the various 'social minima' that were indexed to it. Immediately afterwards, agricultural pensions were doubled and extended to women, while in 1982 a means-tested social pension was introduced for those with insufficient contributions and incomes below a certain threshold. Such redistributive policies had a high political and symbolic visibility: they were in fact presented – and largely perceived – as a 'just reward' for social groups that had been excluded from the rapid economic progress of the 1960s and had been hit hardest by the high inflation of the 1970s. PASOK's programme included an ambitious reform of health care along universalistic lines, aimed at offering good medical coverage to the whole population. In 1983, a 'National Health Service' was officially created, based on a wide network of local health care centres: also this reform had high symbolic visibility, at least on paper.

PASOK's social reforms did open the gates of the welfare system to formerly excluded or under-protected social categories, thus bringing them closer to state institutions and enhancing their loyalty to the democratic regime. However, such reforms fell prey to traditional modes of consensus building and – as in Italy – they set the welfare state on a dangerous course towards financial bankruptcy.

Although for the Greek case the formation of *Mezzogiorno*-style 'political machines' for the individualized exchange of social benefits for votes is not documented, most commentators agree that traditional patronage practices survived and indeed proliferated after the return of democracy and under PASOK rule.[5] This is especially true for invalidity pensions, which soared in the mid-1980s, often as a result of local committees taking a 'broad view' on applications that failed to meet strict medical requirements (Matsaganis 2005). In Greece, mass patronage took more explicitly the form of selective (often micro-selective) legal advantages to various components of the new social bloc that formed with the 1981 election. A strong 'advocacy coalition' of insiders (economically and politically) made sure that the massive expansion of public resources for social policy would produce 'concentrated benefits' for each constituent of such coalition, at widely distributed or even hidden costs for the Greek economy: in the early 1990s, public debt had soared to 125 per cent, with a political syndrome sharing many common traits that were experienced by Italy in the same period.

Portugal

The Portuguese transition to democracy was very different from that of the other three South European countries. The authoritarian regime collapsed suddenly on April 25, 1974, with a *coup détat* accomplished by the Movement of the Armed Forces (MFA) led by General Antonio de Spinola. In 1976, a new Constitution was adopted, establishing representative institutions, but under the tutelage of a Revolutionary Council comprising top military cadres. This body was eliminated in 1982, through a Constitutional revision which marked the end of the transition and the beginning of a new phase of fully fledged representative democracy (Bruneau and MacLeod 1986).

The period between the revolution of April 1974 and the 1982 Constitutional revision witnessed a veritable 'big bang' in terms of social policy developments. In 1974 and 1975, minimum pensions were doubled and a ceiling was posed on higher benefits; non-contributory benefits were introduced for old age and disability; unemployment subsidies were introduced for all wage-earners and the coverage gaps of agricultural labourers were filled. The 1976 Constitution included two articles (nos 63 and 64) offering extremely ambitious and universal guarantees in the fields of social insurance, health care and social assistance. In 1979, the National Health Service was legislated into existence. By 1980, social spending had almost doubled compared to 1970. This rapid expansionary phase can partly be explained as a reaction to the social conservatism of the Caetano regime: at the Revolution's eve, the Portuguese welfare state was indeed in a state of marked underdevelopment. But the 'big bang' was also the result of high levels of political turbulence, rapid and intense social mobilization, ideological maximalism, and organizational and financial chaos. The Revolution opened the gates of the state and prompted a rapid process of institutional disarticulation and fiscal profligacy. It is also true, however, that given the economic crisis following the Revolution, the extension and improvement of social benefits provided an economic safety net serving the important purposes of basic social integration – an essential condition for the successful completion of democratic consolidation.

After the 1983 general elections, a new political coalition called *Bloco Central* rose to power, bringing together the centre-left Socialist Party (PS) and the centre-right Social Democratic Party (PSD). The two fundamental (and interconnected) objectives of the new government were economic and fiscal stabilization, on the one hand, and EC accession on the other hand. A new policy of budgetary austerity was inaugurated, which lasted until 1986, when Portugal was finally admitted into the EC.[6] During this period, the level of social expenditure per capita fell slightly. But social policy remained at the core of Portuguese politics and continued to serve important legitimation functions in at least two ways. In the first place, the *Bloco* government maintained the momentum of welfare state building in institutional terms: in 1984 a comprehensive Basic Law for social security was passed, which re-designed in a more rational and orderly fashion the whole system, creating three distinct spheres: contributory schemes, non-contributory schemes and 'social action' programmes (i.e. social assistance and services). In the second place, the government made explicit efforts to involve the trade unions in economic and social policy making, experimenting with forms of neo-corporatist concertation (Mozzicafreddo 1997). In 1984, a Permanent Council for Social Dialogue was set up, in which all social partners were given a seat. The Communist trade union (CGTP) initially refused to occupy its place – a refusal which slowed down the institutionalization of the new body and its effectiveness in terms of policy making and consensus building. But the creation of the Council and the first rounds of social dialogue did help in legitimizing the austerity package of the *Bloco* executives. The first tripartite social pacts between the government, the unions and the employers were signed in 1986.

After EC accession, a new expansionary phase began, also in the wake of the inflow of cohesion funds from Brussels. It is estimated that the latter gave an impulse to economic growth equal to an average of 2.6 per cent per year between 1989 and 1993 (1.5 per cent in Spain). In 1989, the percentage of fixed gross capital formation due to the structural funds was equal to 7.7 per cent (2.9 per cent in Spain) (EC 1993). Between 1986 and 1995 (Cavaco Silva's government: the epoch of *cavaquismo*) social expenditure per capita grew from 32.4 per cent of the EU average to 47.6 per cent.

As this brief outline shows, Portuguese developments followed a rather different trajectory to those of either Italy or Greece. The transition originated initially a syndrome of 'hyperinflation' of new social entitlements, in a context of high ideological radicalization and fiscal irresponsibility. After 1982, an almost specular syndrome of 'containment' developed itself, which cooled down popular expectations and demands for social protection and posed the basis for a new and more balanced *reprise* after EC accession. Although the literature has highlighted the occurrence of patronage and spoil-sharing practices within Portugal's public sector on the side of political parties and local notables (Lopes 1997), these practices do not seem to have affected specifically the welfare state as in Italy and in Greece. Moreover, contrary to the latter two countries, Portugal was able to enter the 'Maastricht decade' in a much better shape from the fiscal point of view: not a bad performance, given the unpromising post-revolutionary start.

Spain

Spain's democratic transition during the 1970s proceeded smoothly and steadily, without the outbreak of major social or political turbulences. The authoritarian regime came to an end with the death of Franco in November 1975. During the first half of the 1970s, Franco had already made some steps towards forms of socio-economic pluralism – by, for example, allowing for the establishment of informal collective bargaining in industrial relations. The transition to representative democracy was characterized by a highly consensual style and rested on a number of political and social 'pacts' that defined the basic institutional framework of the new democratic regime through widespread and open negotiation. The new Constitution was adopted in 1978. Its text explicitly mentioned a number of universal social rights and recognized significant powers to the autonomous communities in health care and social assistance.

Gradualism and consensualism characterized also the institutional reform of the welfare system and its politics. Social insurance had been broadly reorganized in 1972 and in 1974 the pension system had been substantially improved. Both reforms had been accompanied by a relatively broad debate. With the advent of democracy, this debate rapidly widened in terms of participants and articulated itself in terms of diagnoses and proposals. In 1976 and 1977, there was a proliferation of publications on social protection. While the general orientation of this new phase of debate was towards expansion and improvement – in order to 'catch up with Europe' – a number of different positions emerged on various issues: e.g. universalism vs professionalism, centre–periphery relations, public versus private management etc. (Guillén 1992 and 1996).

The unions and the parties of the left were strongly in favour of a rapid expansion and universalization of social protection, along Scandinavian lines.[7] The employers and right-wing parties advocated an incorporation of private initiative in the management of the system and insisted on the need to streamline public finances and the tax system as a precondition for any concrete reform. The government – controlled by the centrist UCD party – kept social policy high on its agenda, but was both cautious and vague in formulating actual proposals. The Moncloa pact of 1977 did include the amelioration of social insurance and the consolidation of a progressive tax system among its policy priorities but it also promised to keep employer contributions under control. Consensus building in the field of social protection was painstakingly low during the transition also owing to the demands of self-determination (especially in fiscal and welfare affairs) on the side of the 'historical nationalities' and the difficult negotiations on the relationships between the central state and the autonomous communities.

Debating, negotiating and 'pacting' did not result in significant departures from the institutional status quo inherited by Francoism. In turn, the economic crisis of the late 1970s posed additional constraints on reformist ambitions. A major organizational reform was, however, adopted in 1978. The old Institute for Social Provision (INP) created by Franco was dismantled and four separate institutes were set up in its place: INSALUD for health care,

INSS for pensions and other temporary cash transfers, INSERSO for social services and INEM for unemployment benefits and policies. The establishment of the latter institute was particularly important from a symbolic point of view, given the mounting employment problems in the country. The social partners were programmatically included in the governance of the new bodies. In 1981, the National Employment Agreement (ANE) strengthened union participation in the management of social security institutions.

Despite institutional continuity, the 1975–1982 period witnessed a significant quantitative expansion of social benefits. According to Guillén (1992: 130),

> the number of pensioners rose by 31.6% between 1976 and 1982, while the contributors only increased by 0.04%. Such a high increase was only partly due to the expansion in the amount of retirement pensions (16.5%); the upward trend in disability pensions was much more significant, amounting to an increase of 42.2 %. The latter figure may be explained by the use of disability pensions as a substitute for unemployment insurance.

In 1981, social expenditure was one and a half higher than in 1975 (Guillén 1996).

In 1982, a new phase began for the Spanish welfare state. The Partido Socialista Obrero Español (PSOE) won an absolute majority at the elections and then won again in 1986 and in 1989, governing for 14 consecutive years. It thus gained the opportunity of implementing its modernizing and universalizing ambitions in social protection. But the economic context did not favour expansionist reforms – at least initially. Though in a better shape than its Portuguese counterpart, the Spanish economy was in crisis – as regards both production and employment – and the new government had to adopt an austerity approach, also with a view to joining the EC. In 1983–84, a number of measures (such as temporary contracts) were introduced with the aim of flexibilizing the labour market, and in 1985 a restrictive reform was passed in the field of pensions. These provisions posed an end to the 'historical brotherhood' between the Unión General de Trabajadores (UGT) and the PSOE, and to neo-corporatist pacts.

The second half of the 1980s witnessed a change of climate and a wave of expansionist reforms. The economy improved and EC accession brought a significant inflow of cohesion funds. During their second legislative term, the Socialists could thus implement much of their modernizing and universalizing project. In 1986, the National Health Service was established. Between 1988 and 1991, some measures improved pensions (including the introduction of non-contributory benefits), family allowances and unemployment subsidies. Powers in the field of social services and assistance were devolved to regional governments, prompting a process of decentralized innovations and improvements (Moreno 2001). Even though labour market conditions continued to be rather problematic (due to high unemployment rates), the second half of the 1980s and the early 1990s were the heyday of the post-authoritarian welfare state: a sort of belated and compressed 'golden' phase, in which Spanish GDP per capita grew from 69.7 per cent of the EU average in 1985 to 79.8 per cent in 1993, and social spending per capita grew from 54.3 per cent of the EU average to 66.2 per cent (Guillén *et al.* 2001).

There can be little doubt about the role which social protection played in sustaining Spain's democratic transition and consolidation and in the overall modernization of this country between the death of Franco and the early 1990s. As in Portugal (albeit with different timing), social pacts were important instruments for both consensus building and policy making. Initially very contentious, the issue of the division of powers between the central government and the meso-governments – especially those of the historical nationalities, such as Catalonia or the Basque Country – gradually found a viable settlement, allowing all actors to keep a slice of the social protection pie and thus to take advantage of its legitimacy-generating potential.

It must be noted that the rapid and massive expansion of social benefits has produced also in Spain some incentives (and offered material resources) for the formation of clientelistic channels of consensus building and political exchange, especially in agriculture and in the less developed regions. During the 1980s, patronage-based circuits developed for the delivery of subsidies in exchange for deferent votes, involving party and union notables at the local levels (Cazorla 1992, 1994). Though on a much smaller scale than in Italy, the 'spectre of neo-clientelism' (Perez Diaz 1994) made its appearance during the Spanish *dix glorieuses* (i.e. the 1980s), building on a historical residue of cultural and institutional predispositions. In the course of the 1990s, the opportunities for patronage practices linked to the design of specific programmes were gradually closed, in the context of an overall financial and institutional adjustment of the Spanish welfare state that started after 1993.

Welfare state recalibration in Southern Europe

In the wake of the developmental trajectory illustrated in the previous sections, South European social protection entered the 1990s in a state of still-incomplete institutional maturation and laden with internal imbalances, which both were functional and distributive in nature. Social transfer systems displayed an institutional bias in favour of old-age protection, to the detriment of other life-course risks (and typically of the needs linked to family and 'care' needs, as well as active labour market policies). From a distributive viewpoint, Southern welfare was in turn characterized by peaks of generosity (at least in terms of legal formulas) for certain occupational groups ('core' industrial employees and civil servants) and gaps of protection for certain others (e.g. irregular workers, workers located in small enterprises, workless households in general). 'Insiders' and 'outsiders' were still separated by a sharp divide in terms of guarantees and opportunities – in some cases with a middling group of semi-peripheral workers bouncing between the inside and the outside (Moreno 2000; Perez Diaz and Rodriguez 1994). The black economy was still very extended in these countries, posing serious efficiency and equity problems. Public services were rather unevenly distributed and, in some cases, insufficient and/or inefficient. It must be noted that the 'calibration' problems of Southern Europe were aggravated by pronounced territorial disparities – with the south of the South displaying a situation of cumulative disadvantage.

The most natural and politically simplest way out of this syndrome would have been to complete the developmental parabola, gradually ironing out the internal imbalances with more institutional and quantitative growth. But this option was made more difficult in the early 1990s by exogenous constraints (especially the prospect of EMU). In 1993 – when the Maastricht Treaty came into force, envisaging a GDP/deficit ratio of 3 per cent as a maximum by 1998 – the public deficit was 7.1 per cent in Portugal, 7.3 per cent in Spain, 9.5 per cent in Italy and 16.3 per cent in Greece (EU average = 6 per cent). South European countries were thus forced to tread on the politically perilous grounds of internal restructuring: less generous benefits for insiders in order to cut down debts and deficits and also – to the extent that budgetary constraints allowed – in order to finance new benefits and services for the outsiders. Southern Europe is definitely the geo-social context for which the metaphor of 'recalibration' – recently suggested by the literature (Ferrera, Hemerijck and Rhodes 2000; Ferrera and Hemerijck 2003)[8] – seems most appropriate. To a large extent this is also the context where this metaphor has served as an explicit reference point for policy reform: both per se and in connection with the wider goal of 'catching up' with the other member states – perceived, precisely, as possessing a more balanced and solid array of social programmes (Guillén, Alvarez and Adao é Silva 2001; Guillen and Matsaganis 2000).

Given the starting conditions, promoting the recalibration of Southern welfare has not been an easy operation. The inherent difficulty of this operation has been aggravated not only by EMU's *marche forcé* and the increasing winds of 'globalization' but also by a particularly adverse demography. South European populations (especially those of Italy and Spain) are ageing at one of the fastest speeds in the world. Yet, despite such difficulties a rather ambitious agenda was pursued in the four countries during the last decade, centred on the following ingredients: attenuation of generous guarantees for historically privileged occupational groups, accompanied by an improvement of minimum or 'social' benefits; introduction and consolidation of the so-called safety net, especially through means-tested minimum income schemes; the expansion and amelioration of family benefits and social services – with explicit attention to gender equality and equity issues; measures against the black economy and tax evasion; the reform of labour market legislation with a view to promoting de-segmentation and modification of unemployment insurance benefits. Another distinctive element of South European recalibration has been politico-institutional: additional competencies have been assigned to regions and local governments (especially in the fields of health and social services and especially in Spain and Italy) and novel *concertation* approaches have been experimented with (at the national, but also sub-national levels: e.g. territorial pacts), promoting the involvement of social actors in the process of policy formulation and the formation of mixed partnerships in processes of policy implementation (Rhodes 2003)

Italy can be regarded as an almost emblematic case of multidimensional recalibration since the early 1990s (Ferrera and Gualmini 2000). Functionally, this country strove to halt the expansion of its hypertrophic pension system, with a view to 'restoring to health' its battered public budget in the new post-Maastricht framework and, at the sametime, to make room for some upgrading in the underdeveloped areas of family policy and social assistance. Pensions were reformed in 1992 and then again in 1995, 1997 and 2004. The so-called Dini reform of 1995 completely changed the pension formula, linking it closely to contributions in a quasi-actuarial fashion. This reform was reached through a compromise between the Dini government and the trade unions, who actively contributed to outlining the technical contents of the law. If we exclude the brief parenthesis of the first Berlusconi government (1994), the 1990s were characterized by close *concertation* between the various governments and the unions, with two official social pacts signed in 1993 and 1998 (Ferrera and Gualmini 2004). Between 1998 and 2000, family benefits were improved and a broad reform of social services and assistance was passed by the Amato government in 2000, establishing an 'integrated system of social services and interventions' and introducing – among other things – a minimum income guarantee against extreme poverty.[9]

From a distributive point of view, the reforms of the 1990s worked in the direction of leveling off social rights and obligations (e.g. contributory rates) across the various occupational groups. Within the pension system, for example, the privilege enjoyed by civil servants to retire after only 20 years of service regardless of age (which had created a mass of 'baby pensioners' since the 1960s) was phased out by the 1995 and 1997 reforms; on the other hand, pension rights were accorded to atypical workers, and lower pensions were repeatedly upgraded – most recently through the 2004 reform passed by the Berlusconi government.[10]

The reforms of the 1990s have sculptured a new organizational profile to the Italian welfare state – especially in the field of pensions, health care, active labour market policies, social services and assistance. Between 1997 and 2001, substantial powers were transferred from the central government to the regions (and from these to the municipalities). While creating numerous problems of implementation and giving rise to new risks of inter-territorial inequities, this process of quasi-federalization of important sectors of Italy's social protection system constitutes a far-reaching experiment in politico-institutional recalibration.

Finally, this sequence of reforms was accompanied by the appearance of a novel discourse on the current state and future prospects of the Italian social protection system. This new discourse contained an articulated diagnosis of the traditional imbalances of the status quo and put forward a range of possible courses of remedial action, explicitly building on various notions of 'social equity', 'inter-generational justice', 'gender equality', 'productive efficiency', 'economic compatibilities', 'subsidiarity' (vertical and horizontal) and so on. The ideas that the Italian welfare state ought to give 'more to children, less to fathers' (Rossi 1997), that it should be aimed less at 'indemnifying' than at 'promoting' people's opportunities, and that more autonomy should be given to the local level became the object of a dense calendar of public discussions and events (from TV shows to party congresses). Measured against an historical background of harsh ideological confrontations between opposing visions of the world ('communism' vs 'capitalism'), the new argumentative climate of the late 1990s can be undoubtedly taken as a clear indicator of a significant 'normative' recalibration, that is a process of collective redefinition of the nature and role of Italy's *stato sociale* in a changed economic context – especially in the wake of European integration.

European integration played a prominent role in prompting recalibrating reforms also in the Iberian countries (Guillén, Alvarez and Adao é Silva 2001). In their effort to join EMU by 1998, both Portugal and Spain engaged in restrictive pension reforms. Like Italy, however, they also proceeded during the 1990s to improve minimum benefits: in the field of old age, of family allowances and of the basic safety net. As regards the latter, in Spain all the regions introduced their own RMI schemes, embarking on a path originally opened by the Basque country in 1989 (Arriba and Moreno 2005). Portugal introduced in turn a pilot national minimum income scheme in 1996, which was generalized in 1997 (Capucha *et al.* 2005).

In Spain, the 1997 pension reform was the result of a broad process of negotiation and consensus building. The process started with the preparation of an articulated report on social insurance reform in 1995, which was accepted by the main political parties with the 'Toledo Pact' and then adopted by Parliament. The report envisaged a clearer separation of contributory and non-contributory benefits, as a result of which universal health and social services as well as means-tested social assistance were to be fully financed out of general taxation, while a reserve fund was to be set up within the contributory regime to strengthen its future viability. The provisions of the Toledo Pact were agreed upon by the social partners in the course of 1996 and in 1997 the pension reform was finally adopted.

During the 1990s, Spain – like Italy – witnessed a thoroughgoing process of decentralization of competencies in health care and social services from the central government to the regions. But the major challenge that this country had to confront during that decade was labour market reform, in order to reduce the remarkably high levels of unemployment. Several measures were introduced with this objective in mind by the Socialist government up to 1996 and by the Conservatives thereafter: the introduction of flexible forms of contract, the rationalization of unemployment benefits, new programmes and incentives to reconcile family responsibility and work (and thus gender equality), various activation measures, and a broad reform of employment services. Compared to Italy, Spain has made more progress in terms of labour market de-segmentation: in 1997 and again in 2001, labour laws were changed, relaxing the protection of 'core' employees and improving both the social security rights of irregular/temporary workers and their opportunities to access the regular labour market. These reforms were introduced by the new conservative government that was voted into office in 1996. Though initially opposed to the reforms, the unions adopted a negotiational rather than an antagonistic stance: they were aware of the weakness of the Left, which was affected by internal divisions and by the corruption scandals of the time (Gutierrez and Guillén 2000). As a result of these new labour policies, Spain's employment performance has undoubtedly improved: unemployment fell from 24 per cent in 1994 to 13 per cent in 2001.[11]

In contrast to Spain (and many other European countries), Portugal's employment performance remained remarkably good. In 1999, this country registered one of the highest employment rates in the EU (including a surprisingly high female employment rate of 59 per cent) and an unemployment rate of only 4.5 per cent. While the superior employment performance of the Portuguese labour market in the European context is connected with certain characteristics of this country's economic structure and political history,[12] its low unemployment rates during the 1990s are instead linked to specific policy choices – especially with the advent of the new Socialist government in 1995. The modernization of social protection was a prime objective of the new government, which placed particular emphasis on active labor market measures and, more generally, social inclusion policy (Cabral Villaverde 2000; Guillén, Alvarez and Adao é Silva 2001). Unemployment insurance was broadly reformed, occupational training and insertion programmes were expanded and specific incentives were deployed in order to promote a 'social market for employment', based on insertion enterprises and local initiatives targeted on the most vulnerable groups of workers. In 1996, an innovative 'social pact for solidarity' was signed between the government and the associations of municipalities, charities and mutualities, with a view to mobilizing local potentials for employment creation. In the wake of this pact, a national scheme of guaranteed minimum income was introduced in 1997 – the first of this kind to be introduced in Southern Europe (Capucha *et al.* 2005). With its explicit reference – in official policy statements and public debates – to the principles of solidarity, social inclusion, but also to the fight against frauds and abuses on the one hand (especially in the field of sick pay) and to the need to rationalize pension protection, on the other, the Portuguese reforms of the 1990s can be interpreted as an interesting case of normative redefinition of the tasks and priorities of this country's social policy.

While Italy and the Iberian countries have clearly made significant steps in recalibrating their welfare systems, Greece has definitely lagged behind

(Guillén and Matsaganis 2000). The 1990s did witness in this country some movements towards reform in many sectors and a gradual reorientation of the overall discourse on social policy, reflecting the new EU guidelines and recommendations. But the pace of institutional innovation has been very slow. The hyper-fragmented character of Greek society and its mechanism of interest representation have posed insurmountable obstacles to the formation of adequate social and political consensus about reforms: as noted by Petmesidou and Mossialos, in comparison to the other South European countries, no platform of social concertation for reform emerged in Greece during the 1990s, owing to the weakness of state institutions, on the one hand, and to the extended veto powers held by a great number of sectional interests (Petmesidou and Mossialos 2005). The government did intervene more than once on the pension front, with a view to recalibrating an internally polarized and financially unsustainable system. But none of these interventions has been able to effectively tackle the roots of the Greek pension crisis (Matsaganis 2004): pension expenditure projections for Greece are the gloomiest in the whole of the EU. On the other hand, the efforts to strengthen the safety net, with a view to filling its relatively wide coverage gaps, have not resulted in any substantial reform (Matsaganis 2005). Most of the items on the Greek-specific recalibration agenda still remain to be implemented.

Conclusions

As stated in the introduction, during the second half of the twentieth century, the four nations of Southern Europe gradually 'caught up' with the more advanced European countries and are now fully part of the group of rich and stable democracies. Italy pioneered developments, consolidating the new, post-Fascist democratic regime by the end of the 1940s and then inaugurating in the 1950s a process of rapid economic growth, accompanied by an equally rapid expansion of the welfare state. In Portugal, Spain and Greece, democracy consolidated in the late 1970s and the process of welfare state expansion took off later and in a highly compressed period of time. Total social expenditure as a percentage of GDP is still somewhat lower than the EU average in all four countries: but the distance has been declining gradually.

Welfare state building has followed a distinct path in Southern Europe, characterized by 'weak fordism', 'dualistic social insurance' and 'faulty and fragmented safety nets'. From a political point of view, welfare state expansion has undoubtedly played an important role in 'anchoring' the democratic regime, in fostering increasing levels of legitimacy and civic cohesion. In certain historical moments, policy sectors and territorial areas, social benefits have, however, fallen prey to forms of clientelistic manipulations and have at times prompted dynamics of fiscal irresponsibility.

The 1990s witnessed in all four countries substantial efforts to streamline and further modernize the welfare state, under the increasingly constraining spurs of European integration. Through various institutional reforms – often directly negotiated with the social partners – the South European welfare states have embarked upon a process of incisive recalibration of their policy instruments and budgets, with a view to achieving more efficient and equitable labour markets, more sustainable and internally more homogeneous social insurance systems and a more effective and inclusive safety net.

To what extent are South European developments and recent innovations relevant for other regions of the world? A debate has recently started on the potential relevance of the experience of Portugal, Spain, Italy and Greece for Eastern and in particular South Eastern European countries (Sotiropoulos 2005). Southern Europe is not used to considering itself as a social policy 'model': but, as the third section of this chapter has suggested, some promising lights have started to glow in the South during the last 15 years. And besides, everything is relative, including social policy models. For Eastern European reformers in search for ideas and inspiration, the Greek, Italian and Iberian experiences are the most obvious and probably most promising point of reference.

Notes

1. To some extent, Italy also experienced a quasi-civil war during 1943–1945: according to some historians, the *Resistenza* was at the same time a war of liberation (against the Nazis), a civil war (fascists vs anti-fascists) and a class war (proletarians vs the bourgeoisie): cf. Pavone (1994).
2. OECD (2004).
3. For a literature survey, cf. Myles and Quadagno 2002.
4. Ministero del Tesoro (1981), Ministero del Lavoro e della Previdenza Sociale (2000).
5. Cf the references quoted in chapter 1, note 12 and especially Petmesidou, 1991 and Mavrogordatos, 1997.
6. In 1985 the *Bloco Central* fell apart and a new minority executive led by the PSD leader Cavaco Silva was formed. The PSD won an absolute majority in 1987 and then ruled until 1995.
7. The Communist party and the *Comisiones Obreras* (the Communist trade union) were, however, more in favour of reforms that immediately improved the position of workers, rather than all citizens.
8. This notion refers to institutional reforms deliberately aimed at shifting the weight and emphasis among the various instruments and objectives of social policy, with a view to better responding to new risks and to adequately cover the most vulnerable social groups, while scaling down the most generous benefits for insider groups.
9. The new scheme is called *reddito minimo d'inserimento*-RMI (minimum insertion income) and is largely modelled on the French RMI analogue. The Italian scheme was introduced in 1998 as a pilot experiment in a number of local municipalities and was subsequently extended to a larger sample in 2000. The Berlusconi government has announced that the scheme will not be generalized and seems to be

oriented towards the establishment of a non-binding framework of regional minimum income schemes (Sacchi and Bastagli 2005).

10. Welfare state reform ranked high in the electoral program of the center-left *Unione* coalition, led again by Prodi which won the 2006 elections. The new government aims at remodulating Berlusconi's pension reform, at upgrading family benefits and at reforming unemployment insurance.
11. In 2004 a new socialist government took office, led by Zapatero. This government has embarked upon an ambitious agenda of social and welfare state modernization, introducing a host of important reforms: increase of minimum pensions and of the minimum wage; a new national sysetm for long term care; various measures to support young people and women; a package of measures to fight labour market precariousness and to support the incomes of the unemployed; incisive reforms of the civil code and of family law.
12. As a consequence of the colonial wars, which kept large numbers of men away from home serving as soldiers, Portuguese women were used to participating in the labour market already in the 1960s and 1970s. In the mid 1970s, at the collapse of the authoritarian regime, the female employment rate was 48.2 per cent (EU average = 44.5 per cent; Spain = 31.5 per cent; Italy = 30.7 per cent; Greece = 33.6 per cent). Female employment was (and still largely is) concentrated in agriculture (which absorbed in 1999 more than 15 per cent of total female employment), traditional industrial sectors (e.g. textiles, often resorting to forms of subcontracted home work) and domestic services (data taken from EC 1999).

References

Ancisi, A. 1976. *La cattura del voto.* Milano: Angeli.

Arriba, A. and L. Moreno. 2005. 'Spain: Poverty, Social Exclusion and Safety Nets'. In Ferrera, 2005.

Bermeo, N. ed. 2000. *Unemployment in Southern Europe: Coping with the Consequences.* London: Frank Cass.

Bruneau, T. C. and A. MacLeod. 1986. *Politics in Contemporary Portugal: Parties and the Consolidation of Democracy.* Boulder, CO: Lynne Rienner Publishers.

Cabral Villaverde, M. 2000. 'Unemployment and the Political Economy of the Portuguese Labor Market', in N. Bermeo (ed.), *Unemployment in Southern Europe: Coping with the Consequences* London: Frank Cass, pp. 165–93.

Castles, F. 1993. 'Social Security in Southern Europe: a Comparative Overview'. Paper presented at the Sub-Committee on Southern Europe of the Social Science Research Council, September, University of Bielefeld.

Cazorla, J. 1992. 'Del Clientelismo tradicional al clientelismo de partido: evolucion y carateristicas'. Barcelona, Institut de Ciencies politiques I Socials, WP no. 55.

Cazorla, J. 1994. 'Del clientelismo de partido en Espana ante la opinión publica'. Barcelona, Institut de Ciencias politiques i Socials, WP no. 86.

Capucha, L., Bomba, T., Fernández, R. and Matos, G. 2005. 'Portugal: a Virtuous Path Towards Minimum Income?', in M. Ferrera (ed.), *Welfare State Reform In Southern Europe: Fighting Poverty and Social Exclusion in Italy, Spain, Portugal and Greece* London: Routledge, pp. 204–65.

Diamandouros, N. 1994. 'Cultural Dualism and Political Change in Post-Authoritarian Greece'. Madrid, Juan March Institute, working paper.

Diamandouros, N. and T. Gunther (eds). 2001. *Parties, Politics and Democracy in Southern Europe*. Baltimore: The Johns Hopkins University Press.

Di Palma, G. 1977. *Surviving without Governing: The Italian Parties in Parliament*. Berkeley: Berkeley University Press.

Eisenstadt, S. and L. Roninger. 1984. *Patrons, Clients and Friends*. Cambridge: Cambridge University Press.

European Commission (EC). 1993. *Fourth Annual Report on the Impact of the Structural Funds*, COM (93). Brussels: European Commission.

European Commission (EC). 1999. *Employment in Europe*. Brussels: European Commission.

Ferrera, M. 1986. 'Italy', in P. Flora (ed.). *Growth to Limits: The European Welfare States Since World War II*, vol. 2. Berlin/New York: De Gruyter, pp. 385–499.

Ferrera, M. 1996. 'The Southern Model of Welfare in Social Europe.' In *Journal of European Social Policy*, 6(1), 17–37.

Ferrera, M. (ed.) 2005. *Welfare State Reform In Southern Europe: Fighting Poverty and Social Exclusion in Italy, Spain, Portugal and Greece*. London: Routledge.

Ferrera, M. and E. Gualmini. 2000. 'Italy: Rescue from Without?', in F. Scharpf and V. Schmidt (eds), *Welfare and Work in the Open Economy*, 2 vols. Oxford: Oxford University Press.

Ferrera, M. and A. Hemerijck 2003. 'Recalibrating European Welfare Regimes', in J. Zeitlin and D. Trubeck (eds), *Governing Work and Welfare in a New Economy: European and American Experiments*. Oxford: Oxford University Press, pp. 88–128.

Ferrera, M. and E Gualmini. 2004. *Rescue by Europe? Social and Labour Market Reforms from Maastricht to Berlusconi*. Amsterdam: Amsterdam University Press.

Ferrera, M., A. Hemerijck and M. Rhodes. 2000. 'The Future of Social Europe: Recasting Work and Welfare in the New Economy'. Report prepared for the Portuguese Presidency of the EU, Oeiras, Celta Editora, 2000.

Guillén, A. M. 1992. 'Social Policy in Spain: From Dictatorship to Democracy, 1939–1982', in S. Ferge and J.E. Kolberg (eds), *Social Policy in a Changing Europe*. Boulder, Westview, pp. 119–42.

Guillén, A. M. 1997. 'Welfare State Development in Spain: A Historical and Explanatory Approach', In *'Comparing Social Welfare Systems in Southern Europe'*, MIRE – Florence Conference, vol. 3. Paris: MIRE, pp. 67–92.

Guillén, A. M. 1996. 'Citizenship and Social Policy in Democratic Spain: the Reformulation of the Francoist Welfare State. In *South European Politics and Society*. 1(2), 253–71.

Guillén, A. 2002. 'The Politics of Universalisation: Establishing National Health Services in Southern Europe.' *West European Politics*, 25(4), 49–68.

Guillén, A. M. and M. Matsaganis. 2000. 'Testing the social dumping hypothesis in Southern Europe', *Journal of European Social Policy*, 10(2), 120–45.

Guillén, A. M., S. Alvarez and P. Adao é Silva. 2001. 'Redesigning the Spanish and Portuguese Welfare States: the Impact of Accession into the European Union'. Working paper. Harvard, MA: Center for European Studies, Harvard University.

Gunther, R., P. N. Diamandouros and H. J. Puhle (eds). 1995. *The Politics of Democratic Consolidation: Southern Europe in Comparative Perspective*. Baltimore: The Johns Hopkins University Press.

Gutierrez, R. and A. M. Guillén. 2000. 'Protecting the Long-Term Unemployed.' In *European Societies*, 2, 195–216.

Hine, D. 1993. *Governing Italy*. Oxford: Clarendon Press.

La Palombara, J. 1964. *Interest Groups in Italian Politics*. Princeton: Princeton University Press.

Leibfried, S. 1992. 'Towards a European Welfare State? On Integrating Poverty Regimes into the European Community', in Z. Ferge and J.E. Kolberg (eds), *Social Policy in a Changing Europe*. Capus, Campus and Westview, pp. 245–79.
Liakos, A. 1997. 'Welfare Policy in Greece (1909–1940): From the Private Needs to the Social Question', in *Comparing Social Welfare Systems in Southern Europe*, MIRE – Florence Conference, vol. 3. Paris: MIRE, pp. 93–108.
Lopes, F. 1997. 'Partisanship and Political Clientelism in Portugal (1983–1993).' In *South European Politics and Society*, 2(3), 27–51.
Malefakis, N. 1995. 'The Political and Socioeconomic Contours of Southern European History', in R. Gunther, P.N. Diamandouros and H.J. Puhle (eds), *The Politics of Democratic Consolidation: Southern Europe in Comparative Perspective*. Baltimore: The Johns Hopkins University Press, pp. 33–76.
Matsaganis, M. 2004. 'A Tale of Recurrent Policy Failure? Tackling Retirement Pensions in Greece', WP no 4, Unit of Research on European Governance (URGE), Fondazione Colegio carlo Alberto, Moncalieri, Torino.
Matsaganis, M. 2005. 'Greece: Fighting with Hands Tied Behind the Back', in M. Ferrera (ed.), *Welfare State Reform in Southern Europe: Fighting Poverty and Social Exclusion in Italy, Spain, Portugal and Greece*. London: Routledge, pp. 33–83.
Matsaganis, M., L. Capucha, M. Ferrera and L. Moreno. 2003. 'Mending Nets in the South: Anti-Poverty Policies in Greece, Italy, Portugal and Spain', *Social Policy and Administration*, 37(6), 639–55.
Mavrogordatos, G. T. 1997. 'From Traditional Clientelism to Machine Politics: The Impact of PASOK on Populism in Greece.' *South European Politics and Society*, 2(3), 1–26.
Ministero del Tesoro. 1981. *La spesa previdenziale e i suoi effetti sulla finanza pubblica*. Roma: Istituto poligrafico e Zecca dello stato.
Ministero del Lavoro e della Previdenza Sociale. 2000. *Gli andamenti finanziari del sistema pensionistico obbligatorio*. Rome: NVSP.
Moreno L. 2000. 'The Spanish Development of Southern Welfare', in S. Khunle (ed.). *Survival of the Welfare State*. London: Routledge, pp. 146–65.
Moreno, L. 2001. *The Federalization of Spain*. London: Frank Cass.
Moreno, L. 2004. 'Spain's Transition to New Risks: A Farewell to 'Superwomen'', in P. Taylor-Gooby (ed.), *New Risks and New Welfare in Europe*. Oxford: Oxford University Press, pp. 133–56.
Morlino, L. 1998. *Democracy Between Consolidation and Crisis*. Oxford: Oxford University Press.
Morlino, L. and J R. Montero. 1995. 'Legitimacy and Democracy in Southern Europe', in R. Gunther, P.N. Diamandouros and H.J. Puhle (eds), *The Politics of Democratic Consolidation: Southern Europe in Comparative Perspective*. Baltimore: The Johns Hopkins University Press, pp. 231–60.
Mozzicafreddo, J. 1997. *Estado Providencia e Cidadania em Portugal*. Oeiras: Celta Editora.
Myles. J. and J. Quadagno. 2002. 'Political Theories of the Welfare State', *Social Service Review*, March issue, 34–57.
Naldini, M. 2003. *The Family in the Mediterranean Welfare State*. London: Frank Cass.
OECD. 2004. *Social Protection Expenditure and Receipts: 1980–2001*. Paris : OECD.
Pavone, C. 1994. *Una guerra civile*. Turin: Bollati e Boringhieri.
Perez Diaz, V. 1994. 'El espectro del neoclientelismo', *El Pais*, 15 June, pp. 15–16.
Perez Diaz, V. and J. Rodriguez. 1994. 'Inertial Choices: Spanish Human Resources Policies and Practices', in *Analistas Socio-Politicos Research Paper 2b*, Madrid.
Petmesidou, M. 1991. 'Statism, Social Policy And The Middle Classes in Greece', *Journal of European Social Policy*, 1(1), 31–48.

Petmesidou, M. 1996. 'Social Protection in Southern Europe: Trends and Problems', *Journal of Area Studies*, 9, 95–125.

Petmesidou, M. 2000. 'Social Protection in Greece in the Nineties: Reforming the "Weak" Welfare State', in A. Mitsos and E. Mossialos (eds). *Contemporary Greece and Europe*. Aldershot: Ashgate, pp. 303–30.

Petmesidou, M. and E. Mossialos. 2005. *Social Policy Developments in Greece*. London: Ashgate.

Pridham, G. (ed.). 1984. *The New Mediterranean Democracies*. London: Frank Cass.

Rhodes, M. (ed.). 1997. *Southern European Welfare States: Between Crisis and Reform*. London: Frank Cass.

Rhodes, M. 2003. 'National "Pacts" and EU Governance in Social Policy and the Labour Market', in J. Zeitlin and D. Trubeck (eds), *Governing Work and Welfare in a New Economy: European and American Experiments*. Oxford: Oxford University Press, pp. 129–57.

Rossi, N. 1997. *Piú ai figli, meno ai padri*. Bologna : Il Mulino.

Sacchi, S. and F. Bastagli. 2005. 'Italy: Striving Uphill but Stopping Halfway', in M. Ferrera (ed.), *Welfare State Reform in Southern Europe: Fighting Poverty and Social Exclusion in Italy, Spain, Portugal and Greece*. London: Routledge, pp. 83–141.

Sartori, G. 1976. *Parties and Party Systems: A Framework for Analysis*. New York: Cambridge University Press.

Sartori, G. 1982. *Teoria dei partiti e caso italiano*. Milano: SugarCo.

Sotiropoulos, D.A. 2004. 'The EU's Impact on the Greek Welfare State: Europeanization on Paper?', *Journal of European Social Policy*, 14(3), 267–84.

Sotiropoulos, D.A. 2005. 'Poverty and the Safety Net in Eastern and South Eastern Europe in the Post-Communist Era'. In M. Ferrera (ed.), *Welfare State Reform in Southern Europe: Fighting Poverty and Social Exclusion in Italy, Spain, Portugal and Greece*. London: Routledge, pp. 266–96.

5
Democratization and Social Policy in East Central Europe

Terry Cox

Introduction

The experience of East Central Europe since the fall of the communist regimes in 1989 raises many questions for the debate about the historical relationship between capitalism, democracy and changes in social policy. These countries, comprising Poland, the Czech Republic, Slovakia, Hungary and Slovenia, have proceeded further down the path of transition towards both capitalism and liberal democracy than most other former communist countries. They have been among the quickest to reorient their economies and political systems to the West; their economies experienced shorter post-communist recessions and earlier recoveries in the mid-1990s; and they have been part of the first wave of entrants from Eastern Europe into the European Union (Blazyca 2003). They have also attempted more radical changes in aspects of social policy than most of their former communist neighbours.

At first sight, therefore, the evidence seems to suggest a supportive and contingent relationship between capitalism, democracy and social welfare systems in East Central Europe along the lines identified in the history of Western Europe.[1] However, on closer examination there are several significant differences. These stem mainly from the legacy of communist rule that had already created its own different kinds of industrial economy and welfare state. Under communist rule, the administration of both economy and society was integrated within the same overall bureaucratic structures of government under the supervision of the ruling communist party, and on the whole, welfare provision was subordinated to the wider aims of expanding production. The concepts of democracy and civil rights were understood in terms of the obligations of the state to provide for the welfare of citizens and to administer it. Rights to paid employment and welfare were given a higher priority than rights to freedom of individual expression or electoral choice. Social welfare was provided by the state, either through state-owned workplaces, or through trade unions that were also incorporated into the state.

In this context, capitalist development in East Central Europe is not creating an industrial economy, but is restructuring an existing developed economy along capitalist lines. Consequently, capitalism is not creating the conditions for democratization in the form of the emergence of civil society and a labour movement based on a mass party and trade unions, but requires instead their extrication from the ruling party-state structures of the communist period. Social policy reform is not concerned with the development of a redistributive social welfare system in response to pressures from civil society or the labour movement, but instead with the separation of social policy from economic policy, the extrication of social welfare provision from the workplace and economic institutions, and the reconsideration of how to reduce the role of the state in welfare provision. Finally, all these developments are taking place in the context of the same global trends that are currently affecting western countries, including economic liberalization, the decline of party and trade union membership levels, and the marketization of welfare provision. More specifically, policy makers in East Central Europe during the 1990s have also been concerned to ensure that both democratization and welfare reform met the requirements for the EU membership to which they aspired.

The economic and welfare changes sought by the post-communist governments of the region have been radical and caused considerable pain to large sections of their citizens. During the first half of the 1990s nearly all the countries of East Central Europe experienced a decline in the per capita income of the population, with only Slovenia experiencing a rise in average incomes during this period (Milanovich 1998: 34). Declines in output and per capita income gave rise to increasing income inequality and poverty. Between 1987 and 1998 income inequality rose throughout the region, ranging from the Czech Republic where Gini coefficients for per capita income rose from 0.19 to 0.25, to Poland where there was a corresponding increase from 0.28 to 0.30 (World Bank 2002: 9).[2] At the lower end of the income range growing numbers of people fell into poverty. According to World Bank figures, by the late 1990s the proportion of households that fell below the poverty line of US$4.30 per day ranged from 0.7 per cent in Slovenia and 0.8 per cent in the Czech Republic, to 8.6 per cent in Slovakia, and 15.4 per cent in Hungary and 18.4 per cent in Poland (World Bank 2000: 35).[3]

A particularly important factor connected to poverty was employment status. There was a rapid growth in registered unemployment in most of East Central Europe in the early 1990s. By 1993, it seemed to have reached a peak of between 12.1 per cent of the labour force in Hungary and 16.4 per cent in Poland, and then to be in decline. (The exception was the Czech Republic where it remained under 5 per cent until 1997.) However, during the late 1990s, and into the new century, it began to rise again in each country except for Hungary. In 2001, it ranged between 18.5 per cent in Slovakia and 11.0 per cent in the Czech Republic and Slovenia, but was only 6.0 per cent in Hungary. Within the overall figures, there were rapid increases in youth unemployment, and significant differences in levels of unemployment between different regions within countries. Long-term unemployment of over a year was particularly significant since it usually involved not only loss of earned income but also loss of unemployment benefits (Milanovich 1998: 94–5; Cox 2003).

Moreover, a specific feature of the new kinds of poverty that have emerged in some countries in Central and Eastern Europe, is poverty in the working population. Vulnerable groups include farm workers, industrial manual workers in the declining formerly state-owned heavy industries, and low skilled clerical workers who formerly worked in the lower levels of the communist state bureaucracies. For people in this situation, their income from a main job is clearly inadequate to meet their subsistence needs. The 2001 New Europe Barometer (NEB) survey found that only 34 per cent of employed people in the ten EU candidate countries (i.e., including the Baltic States as well as Central and Eastern Europe) report that 'they earn enough to buy what they need'. For the majority of the population, economic transformation has resulted in people achieving subsistence through a range of different kinds of work, including growing their own food and various kinds of unregistered casual work in the 'grey economy' (Rose 2002a: 13–15).

During the early 1990s, there was considerable concern among the new political elites that the adverse effects of economic transition such as those described above would provoke widespread protests and the growth of significant popular opposition to the post-communist reforms. In the event, however, although there were protests against liberal economic reforms, they did not give rise to political destabilization or a return of more authoritarian regimes. As Ekiert and Kubik have shown, East Central Europe 'experienced no massive and violent rebellions against the economic reforms, despite the deep economic recession', and that 'the magnitude of protest... was lower than in established democracies in Western Europe' (1998: 578). Most protests, whether strikes or street demonstrations, were organized by established political parties or trade unions and were used as part of a wider repertoire of methods of exerting influence on government and other political authorities.

This fits with opinion poll evidence that suggests that although there was a decline in approval for the market economy during the 1990s, a significant proportion of the population were prepared to accept some deterioration in their standards of living in the interests of transforming the economy (European Commission 1994; European Commission 1998; European Commission 2002: 12–16). Moreover, although negative experiences of the new economic order gave rise to widespread nostalgia for aspects of life under communist rule, this did not equate with political support for a return to the old regime. On balance, there remained greater support, or at least acceptance, of the current political and economic institutions than there was for their replacement by any alternative (Rose 2002b: 11–12). As Mason and Kluegel have found, a majority of people surveyed in the region 'supported the principles of capitalism, but were disappointed in the outcomes'. To some extent they reflected peoples' personal experiences of the recession and growing problems of unemployment, poverty and inequality, but 'the perceived fairness of the economic order' they suggest, is 'critical in advancing public support for capitalism and the values of market justice' (Mason and Kluegel 2000: 239–40, 253).

The last-mentioned point highlights an important factor for understanding the significance of both democratization and social policy reform in securing the legitimacy of the economic transformation and the political system that brought it about. If Kluegel and Mason are right that fairness is an important criterion in peoples' evaluations of governments and their policies then it could be suggested that it was because of the increased accountability and openness of the new democratic forms of government and a social policy that provided some degree of social protection that economic transformation was legitimized. On the other hand, both democracy and social policy reform entailed dangers for the new political elites. In the new economic environment, the reformed social welfare system had to take account of market criteria of success and could not rely so much on state subsidies. Changes in this direction, however, risked creating a significant section of the population whose welfare was impaired as a result of the changes. At the same time, improved democratic accountability provided better channels through which opposition and protest could be expressed. Both democracy and social policy were subject, therefore, to contradictory influences, resulting in complex patterns of change. In the following two sections, the changes will be assessed for each in turn.

Democratization

In the years immediately following the end of communist rule in 1989, the countries of East Central Europe all introduced reforms to establish a liberal democratic political system. These included an enhanced legislative role for parliaments, improved accountability of executives to parliaments, the introduction of competitive multi-party and multi-candidate elections, strengthening the role of the constitutional court, and provision in the constitution for freedom of speech, expression and assembly. There is now a broad consensus among international agencies and political scientists that, in terms of both the rights enjoyed by citizens and the workings of the main political institutions, the countries of East Central Europe are now established democracies.[4] For many commentators, however, doubts remain about the relation between state and civil society. An essential feature of the extension of democratization and its consolidation beyond its minimal, procedural level involves the opening up of the political sphere to participation by citizens (Ágh 1998). This involves two main features of a democratic polity that enable the effective participation of citizens in politics. First, viable competing political parties should ensure the aggregation and channeling of influence over decision makers, and secondly other institutions should provide social groups with the means to influence decisions makers and press their claims more directly than in the processed and amalgamated forms of party programmes (Dawisha and Parrott 1997). If democratization in the societies of East Central Europe is assessed by these considerations, the picture, according to most observers, is one of a weak development, still short of full democratic consolidation.

Political parties

In relation to the role of political parties, all the countries of East Central Europe have developed systems of competing parties that are effectively organized to mobilize voters, compete in parliamentary elections, form parliamentary caucuses and provide the basis for the forming of governments. However, the general consensus in research literature on the new party systems in the region is that parties have weak links with the wider electorate, and even with their rank and file members (Kaase and Klingemann 1994: 139; Lewis 2003: 167). According to Ilonszki, this is because parties were not formed on the basis of the main cleavages in society but were created by political elites. As a result, in the case of Hungary for example, party programmes do not set out clear policies for the electorate and, in any case, parties change their policy position during the electoral cycle (Ilonszki 1998). In Poland, according to Szczerbiak, parties do not aim to appeal to clearly defined social interests but try to draw support from 'loose electoral constituencies', either by stressing their greater competence or trustworthiness, or by appealing across social divisions 'on the basis of moral-cultural issues' (Szczerbiak 2001: 149). At the same time, voters tend to choose which party to support on the basis of their estimation of the party leaders, or the position of parties in terms of historical cleavage lines between communist successors and anti-communists, rather than in relation to the parties' positions on policy issues. For example, in Poland, according to Bielasiak and Blunck, economic issues are only significant in deciding electoral choice between liberal parties and those of either the left or the right, but are not important in deciding between the socialists and the Solidarity/moderate right parties (2002: 574, 580). Similarly, in Hungary, Todosoijevic (2005: 123) has found that 'specific issues... are weakly related to vote choice'. Although none of these studies focuses specifically on parties' social policies, or electoral appeal on the basis of social policy issues, the clear implication is that in this policy area, as in all others, political parties are not playing any significant role in the aggregation and channelling of citizens' views or interests in the making of social policy.

Interest representation

A similar picture emerges from the literature on interest groups. Although there is some evidence of effective interest representation, the general consensus of research on East Central Europe suggests a weak civil society with poorly developed links with policy makers. On the one hand, evidence from Hungary suggests that interest group leaders claim effective interest representation in influencing governments to change aspects of draft legislation, or to introduce items onto the policy agenda (Cox and Vass 2000). In Slovenia research by Fink Hafner has found that although, compared with Western Europe, there is relatively little interest group activity aimed at policy makers, there is significant activity in some policy areas including agriculture, employment, health care and education, and in the representation of retired people and people with disabilities. Much of the lobbying done by groups in these areas is aimed at parliament rather than the executive (Fink Hafner 1997: 116–18, 120). On the other hand, according to Howard, comparative data shows that in general 'post-communist civil society is distinctively weak, characterised by low levels of organisational membership and participation by ordinary citizens' (2003: 1). This is supported by the essays edited by Rueschmeyer, Rueschmeyer and Wittrock, which show that 'both participation in politics and involvement in various kinds of civic organizations are not strongly developed. And the articulation of collective interests is rather inchoate, probably because it is still in the process of formation' (1998: 266–7). Moreover, the problems extend to trade unions, including those that were 'successor organisations of those existing under communist rule, despite their inherited advantages of an existing mass membership, organisational structures and extensive property'. Although accurate figures are difficult to come by, Crowley and Ost have estimated that during the 1990s, union density declined to around one-third of the workforce in the Czech Republic, Hungary and Poland, and to around two-fifths in Slovakia (2001: 220).

Various reasons have been suggested for the political weakness of interest representation. For trade unions, these include changes in the structure of the economy and patterns of ownership as well as a lack of concern for active recruitment among union leaders (Crowley and Ost 2001: 221). More generally, Howard places the problems in the context of post-communist legacies that produce an aversion to membership in collective organizations, the persistence of private networks that developed under the communist regimes, and the demoralization of citizens in the post-communist period (Howard 2003). For Ágh, a further factor is that after 1989 civil society had effectively been demobilized as a result of the development of political parties. The problem, he argues, has been the dominance of political society over civil society, or more specifically, its 'overparliamentarization' and 'overparticization'. Within the main 'site' of democratization, the parliament, 'the chief actors of democratic transition are the parties'. They have monopolized the political scene and have contributed to a weak set of links to the wider civil society (Ágh 1998: 22).

Social dialogue

In contrast to the general picture of a weakly developed independent civil society, a very distinctive feature of the societies of East Central Europe has been the establishment of tripartite organizations. These represent an attempt to set up formal mechanisms for the state to consult some of the major social interests in society, and an opportunity for social groups to attempt to influence policy makers before legislation was passed through parliament. They were adopted in all countries in the region, in Hungary as the Interest Reconciliation Council (IRC) and in Czechoslovakia as Council of Social and Economic Agreement in 1990, and in Poland as the Tripartite Commission for Social and Economic Affairs and in Slovenia as Economic and Social Council in 1994. In each case these councils comprised trade unions and employers' organizations alongside government, and had responsibilities for consultation on economic and social issues and commenting on proposed legislation in these areas. In addition, in Slovenia the Council was given the right to put forward proposals and opinions for policy or legislation on social, economic and employment policy to the government, parliament and the State Council. In Hungary, the IRC was given the responsibility for determining the national minimum wage as well as making recommendations for average annual wage increases. In Czechoslovakia, and subsequently in the Czech and Slovak Republics, and in Slovenia, the Councils were responsible for negotiating an annual General Agreement to determine guidelines for the different sectors of the economy.

Opinions vary considerably on how to interpret the significance of tripartite councils and the inclination to attempt social pacts in post-communist East Central Europe. For some writers, these developments suggest the possible beginnings of a distinctively East Central European pattern of democratic consolidation. For example, Myant *et al.* (2000: 737) have seen tripartism in the Czech and Slovak Republics as a possible resolution to the problems identified by Ágh as 'over-particization', suggesting that tripartite bodies might be able to exert enough pressure on parties to concede a role in policy making to civil society organisations.

In practice, however, and despite the more proactive role of the Slovenian council in initiating legislation, the tripartite councils have faced similar problems in each country in that they have had neither the power nor the constitutional authority to insist that governments should keep agreements or heed the council's advice, especially when compelling economic considerations led them to prefer different options instead (Luksic 1997; Fink Hafner 1997; Vodovnik 1999; Myant *et al.* 2000: 727; Pankow 1996).[5] The Councils have also been vulnerable to government intervention to reform or further limit their powers. Although some socialist-led governments, such as in Hungary in 1994–5, have sought to extend social dialogue by negotiating a tripartite social pact on important areas of policy, such ambitions have ended in failure. Conservative and economically liberal governments have been less sympathetic to social dialogue. Slovenian coalition governments of the early 1990s resisted the setting up of a tripartite organization despite attempts by the Ministry of Labour and the trade unions. In the Czech Republic, the conservative Klaus government showed little sympathy for negotiated social agreements and set up a new council in 1995, under the title of Council for the Dialogue of Social Partners, with a reduced role. In Hungary, the 1998–2002 conservative Fidesz-led government sought to limit the influence of the trade unions and replaced the IRC by a series of separate councils for different policy areas, involving a wider range of interest groups (Lado and Toth 2000; Cox and Vass 2000: 1098–1108; Gallai 2001; Hethy 1999).

Bearing such limitations in mind, David Ost has taken a more critical view of East Central European tripartism, describing it as only 'illusory corporatism'. Tripartism, he argues, was primarily 'a way of providing societal support for the government to reform the economy as it wished'. It allowed political elites to share responsibility for the social consequences of economic change while also enhancing their reputation for supporting social dialogue in the eyes of the EU. In the unions, it provided a more stable and cooperative social partner than groups more directly focused on problem issues such as poverty or unemployment. In this context, the participation of the unions in tripartite bodies reveals their political weakness rather than their strength. 'Instead of leading to concertation and concrete material benefits, East European tripartism has legitimised the marginalisation of labour' and offers only 'symbolic inclusion in return for acceptance of a weakening of labour and a radical decline of the welfare state' (Ost 2000: 507–9). As far as democratization is concerned, therefore, the implication of Ost's analysis is that, far from providing an education in democratic values and practices, tripartism has been anti-democratic in bolstering the interests and dominance of new political elites.

For Bela Greskovits, East Central European tripartism should be seen as part of an incomplete form of democracy. In the context of a deepening recession and growing social unrest during the early 1990s, the political elite opted for a limited compromise with unions and employers' associations, allowing them some role in social dialogue, while excluding other interest groups such as the anti-poverty protest movement (1998: 174). Greskovits suggests the issue of democratic consolidation should not be seen in terms of a stark opposite between full consolidation and breakdown but as comprising a range of possibilities, including an incomplete form of 'dual democracy', which is 'based on an alliance between the governing elite and a strategic minority of the opposition. The purpose is to exclude "the majority of the remaining social actors by disarticulating and neutralizing their capacity for collective action"' (Greskovits 1998: 174). In the case of East Central Europe, tripartism can be seen as an example of such incomplete or 'dual' democracy. 'By including trade unions and business associations, the traditional social partners, in the negotiations, consultative policy approaches involved only a portion of an organized civil society in the policy discourse, while excluding numerous social groups with relatively little political weight' (Greskovits 1998: 171–2).

Social policy in the 1990s

The post-communist economic transformation created a complex situation for the making of social policy. On the one hand, it required the restructuring and scaling down of many aspects of the welfare system inherited from the communist regimes. On the other hand, social policy had to serve the aim of ameliorating some of the worst social consequences of the introduction of the market economy. The social policy agenda therefore comprised both new policies to deal with new problems such as unemployment and the changing character of poverty as well as measures to restructure the welfare system inherited from the old regime, such as existing health care, old age and disability pension arrangements.

New measures relating to unemployment and poverty

While the creation of unemployment was seen as an inevitable consequence of the transition, governments took two kinds of measures in the early 1990s: on the one hand to restrict increases in unemployment as far as possible, especially in the rate of officially registered unemployment; and on the other hand, to provide income support for those who did register as unemployed. The main measures to restrict the growth of unemployment were the creation of employment offices to help people find employment and receive new training, and schemes to promote self-employment and small business development.

In order to alleviate some of the consequences of unemployment, all countries in the region introduced income-related unemployment benefit schemes quite early in the transition period. In Hungary, this occurred under the reform communist government as early as 1988, followed by Poland in 1989, Czechoslovakia in 1990 and Slovenia in 1991. To begin with, the provisions of the schemes were relatively generous, reflecting concerns that unemployment could provoke serious discontent. Benefits were set at over 60 per cent of the previous wage in Hungary and Slovenia and began at 70 per cent in Poland, reducing by stages to 40 per cent after a year. After the break-up of Czechoslovakia, the rates were 60 per cent in Slovakia and 50 per cent in the Czech Republic. The time periods over which these benefits were available also varied. To begin with, they were offered for an unlimited period in Hungary, for up to 24 months (depending on the past employment record) in Slovenia and Poland, up to 12 months in Slovakia and six months in the Czech Republic. However, governments soon found these levels very difficult to sustain as unemployment rates rose – as a result both the level and duration of benefits were cut back. For example, the maximum duration of unemployment benefits was cut to 12 months in Hungary, and also reduced by half in Slovakia and the Czech Republic towards the end of 1991, and Poland introduced a flat-rate benefit of 36 per cent of the average wage in 1992 (Boeri 2000; Kramer 1997: 94; Svetlik 1992: 60–1).

In more informal ways, all governments in the region also hoped to encourage a reduction in the size of the workforce – for example, by encouraging women to stay at home or encouraging people to retire early. Particularly important, as a short-term measure in the early 1990s, was the early retirement of workers who would have probably remained in their jobs under the old regime by relaxation of the regulations on both old age and disability pensions. Large numbers of workers in their fifties and sixties were offered early retirement deals in order to facilitate the restructuring of enterprises on more market-oriented lines while limiting the effect on rising unemployment rates. Others were offered retirement on disability pensions. As a result, East Central Europe has some of the highest proportions in the world of the population on disability pensions: for example, 10 per cent in the Czech Republic and 17 per cent in Poland. The advantage of such moves for the governments was that it produced lower figures for unemployment than would have been the case otherwise, and softened the political impact of the decline in employment brought about by the transition. However, it had the distinct disadvantage of further increasing the costs of welfare provision to the state on top of the growing cost of providing unemployment benefit.

Alongside new policies to deal with unemployment, all governments in the region also sought to expand social assistance payments to alleviate poverty during the initial years of the transition. In each case, the new provisions set out a range of different grounds on which people might be eligible for support, expanded the numbers of local offices to administer the system, and in general gave local welfare workers quite large discretionary authority to decide on whether applicants qualified for assistance. To begin with, many liberal reformers had expected the large increase in social assistance claims would be a short-lived episode in the early stages of the transition and that the expansion of the market economy would rapidly create new jobs and sources of income for those who had been displaced by the economic restructuring. They were soon to be disappointed, however, as numbers continued to rise. The situation became more serious as a consequence of decisions to restrict the duration of the unemployment benefit entitlements. For the growing numbers of long-term unemployment, there was no alternative to applying instead for social assistance. Between 1990 and 1993, the numbers of applications for assistance doubled in Hungary and trebled in Poland (Kramer 1997: 100–1). The press reported many cases of local offices becoming overwhelmed.

Reform of the communist welfare system

As part of the dismantling of the former regime's centralized management system, each country in the region sought to encourage local authorities and charities to develop the provision of welfare support to expand the provision of poverty relief and to replace the facilities being closed down by employers in response to new market disciplines. Otherwise, their goal was to adapt other elements of the welfare system inherited from the old regime, to decentralize the management of existing health care, old age and disability pension arrangements and, where they had been financed directly from the state budget, separate its social funds from the state budget. In each country, employer and employee representatives were involved in the administration of the funds, and in Hungary each was placed under the administration of a self-governing board of representatives from employers and trade unions, where, to begin with, the union representatives were chosen by nationwide elections of the whole electorate. During the 1990s, elements of competition in health insurance were introduced in most countries with the founding of private funds or the establishment of competing public funds. In the Czech Republic, competition between public and private funds was introduced in 1993 and by 1995 more than 20 different funds were in operation. Similar trends were evident in the other countries of the region. In Slovakia, ten funds were operating by 1998. Alongside these developments, private general practitioner practices were also approved and increased in number during the 1990s.

Perhaps the main social policy problem facing governments in the 1990s, however, was the growing cost of the pensions system. The inherited system was based on a 'pay as you go' arrangement in which the pensions of the older generation were funded from taxes paid by the current generation of workers. This method of financing pensions came under increasing criticism from economic reformers who argued that it provided a disincentive to company expansion and job creation. Given conditions of almost full employment under communist rule, the system was designed to provide universal coverage for the whole workforce. From a strictly economic point of view, the system was also costly in other ways. In some countries in the region, the retirement age was relatively low. Although it was 65 for men and 60 for women in Poland, it was set at 60 for men and 55 for women in Hungary and the Czech Republic. Between twenty and twenty-five years of work experience was required to qualify for a full pension, but this was often waived for particular categories of employees, including miners and others working in hazardous occupations and also some professional groups.

During the early 1990s, partly as a result of the use of the pensions system to keep unemployment rates down, there were significant increases in the numbers of pensioners and in state expenditure on pensions. In Slovenia, the number of contributors per pensioner fell from 2.3 in 1990 to 1.7 in 1993. Expenditure on pensions rose from 10.9 per cent of GDP in 1991 to 14.1 per cent in 1993 (Muller 2002). Hungary, Poland and the Czech Republic also experienced similar trends. The numbers of pensioners (in millions) rose in each country between 1989 and 1994, from 6 to 8.7 in Poland, from 1.9 to 2.9 in Hungary, and from 2.9 to 3.1 in the Czech Republic. During the same period expenditure on pensions increased as a percentage of GDP, from 7.9 to 15.5 in Poland, from 9.9 to 10.8 in Hungary and from 8.3 to 9.0 in the Czech Repulic. Meanwhile, the number of workers (in millions) whose incomes contibuted to the schemes was falling: from 14.5 to 12.7 in Poland, from 4.4 to 3.7 in Hungary, and from 5.6 to 5.0 in the Czech Republic (Kramer 1997: 59). In the medium term, such an imbalance and such a growth of state expenditure would not be sustainable. Even without the extra burdens placed on it as a consequence of the transition, the existing system of funding had already become more problematic as a result of the 'ageing of the population' and the declining birth rate – features the countries of East Central Europe shared with most other industrialized countries. As a result of both these long-term trends and the adaptations of the early 1990s, the pension systems of all countries in the region became increasingly problematic. In several cases they experienced large annual deficits and the trend has been for them to absorb increasingly higher proportions of GDP (Kramer 1997: 82–5).

During the first half of the 1990s, however, no significant major reforms were introduced. To some extent this reflected the lower priority given to social policy by the liberal reformers in government and among their advisors who saw social problems primarily in terms of the unavoidable consequences of necessary economic reforms. Social policy, in this view, was there to provide a safety net to avoid the worst aspects of the threat to some peoples' standards of living. However, there were also more explicitly political concerns that resulted in the lack of activity in reforming social security and welfare systems and this concerned the fear that further market reforms in the social policy field would give rise to serious political opposition to the whole transition strategy. By the mid-1990s, however, the focus of social policy debates turned to the reform of the pensions system on market lines. A number of factors influenced this shift in the policy agenda. As well as the economic problems discussed above, policy makers were becoming increasingly concerned about demographic pressures resulting from the 'ageing of the population'. In particular, the debate was shaped by neoliberal economic ideas and the way they were promoted by international institutions including the World Bank and the International Monetary Fund. This influence was either directly in the character of the reforms that were introduced, or indirectly in the way reforms represented a reaction against neoliberal ideas.

By the mid-1990s, a 'new pension orthodoxy' had emerged in international debates on social policy, promoted especially by the publication in 1994 of the World Bank report *Averting the Old Age Crisis* (World Bank 1994). According to the 'new orthodoxy', the 'pay as you go' system becomes prohibitively expensive as the age balance in society shifts towards older age groups. Instead, they argue, governments should opt for an approach that provides pension protection to workers more directly according to their own contributions to a pension scheme. On retirement, workers then receive a pension reflecting their own contributions and the interest or profit gained on them through investment. This approach translates into a policy that usually farms out pension provision to a number of private companies that hold and invest workers' contributions (Fultz 2003: 2–3).

It was this approach that formed the advice offered to governments in East Central Europe by the World Bank during the 1990s, in the form of specific country reports and visits by working parties of World Bank advisors. In general, the solution proposed by the World Bank was for a pension system in which the existing 'pay as you go' schemes were scaled back to allow for the expansion of one or two further elements (usually known as 'pillars') based on the second approach described above. Thus, the new pensions systems envisaged the following three elements:

1. A state-funded component on a 'pay as you go' basis aimed at providing a basic pension income above the poverty line.
2. A privately funded component, preferably compulsory.
3. A voluntary privately funded insurance component (World Bank 1996: 82–3; Deacon and Hulse 1997).

In practice, however, the reform of pensions systems proceeded in quite different ways in each country in the region. All five countries passed laws authorizing voluntary private pension funds to provide supplementary coverage to those who opt for it (third pillar), but then took different courses in relation to the first and second pillars. On the one hand, Hungary and Poland adopted systems during the 1990s along the general lines proposed by the World Bank. They scaled down the 'pay as you go' social insurance system (first pillar) and introduced a mandatory second pillar of commercially managed personal pensions. Slovakia moved at a slower pace, but also explored proposals along the same lines. On the other hand, the Czech Republic and Slovenia debated such changes but decided not to introduce them.

By the mid-1990s, in both Hungary and Poland, there was widespread dissatisfaction with the existing pension system and in both countries the piecemeal changes introduced in the first half of the decade had only added to the feeling that they were inefficient and unfair. This provoked much debate. Although a majority could agree that reform was needed, there was much less agreement on what form any new system should take. In the end, while both countries introduced a new mandatory second pillar of private pension schemes, they have differed in their approach to reforming the first-pillar defined benefit schemes. While Hungary only made changes in detail and reduced its share of the pension system as a whole, Poland introduced more substantial changes in the way benefits reflect the individual employee's own contributions from income.

In both countries, World Bank advice and support were important in the drafting of the reform legislation. In Hungary, the Ministry of Finance was then able to guide the legislation through its various stages with little serious resistance from within government. In Poland, however, a debate developed between the Ministry of Finance, favouring a three-pillar system along the lines advised by the World Bank, and the Ministry of Labour and Social Policy which supported a rationalization of the existing 'pay as you go' system alongside voluntary individual pensions. The conflict was only resolved in favour of the three-pillar system when a separate office of Plenipotentiary for Social Security Reform was created within the Prime Minister's Office. In both countries, potential opposition from trade unions was defused by undertaking extensive consultations and reaching compromise deals with them, either on amendments to detailed aspects of the pension reform, or in the case of Hungary, on separate issues (concerning their representation on the boards administering social funds) on which they were in debate with the government. The passage of the legislation was further helped in both countries by favourable public opinion polls (Nelson 2001; Hausner 2001).

Meanwhile in the Czech Republic and Slovenia, by the mid-1990s the existing pension systems were also attracting much criticism and proposals for new second-pillar schemes were also put forward there. However, the outcome of the debates in both countries was to reform the first-pillar 'pay as you go' schemes instead of introducing a second pillar, and also to authorize a (third-pillar) voluntary private pension scheme. In order to make the first pillar more cost-effective, changes included a gradual increase in the age of retirement, a tightening of the eligibility rules and the abolition of occupational privileges within the system. In Slovenia, further changes were introduced to impose penalties for early retirement and bonuses for delayed retirement. In both of these countries, World Bank experts provided advice for reform along neoliberal lines and there was support within each country from liberal and conservative parties in parliament, as well as from financial interests in society more widely. However, in these cases, alternative international advice from EU Phare Programme experts had a higher profile and trade unions mounted more vociferous campaigns against the introduction of a mandatory second pillar, including the organization of large street demonstrations (Macha 2002; Muller 2002; Stanovnik 2002).

In many ways, the pensions reforms of the 1990s should be seen as only a stage on a long-term process of the restructuring of social policy that is likely to continue for many years to come. On the question of pension reform, debate still continues: in the Czech Republic and Slovenia there remains a body of opinion in favour of a more radical reform of the existing arrangement; in Hungary and Poland meanwhile the new pensions systems have met with a range of criticisms. According to Augustinovics *et al.* (2002), the main problems with the reformed Hungarian system are that the formula for awarding pension benefits in the first pillar is unclear and individual contribution records are unavailable, the system remains excessively redistributive so that higher earners are discontent with their benefits levels, and, most fundamentally, that the growing costs of the system brought on by the changing demographic balance were not seriously addressed by the reform and therefore remain a problem for the future. According to Chlon-Dominczak (2002), the new system in Poland will result in a decline in pension levels as a proportion of wages (the wage replacement rate), raising the prospect of an increase in poverty among pensioners. Meanwhile, other areas of social policy, including health and education, are also likely to come under increased scrutiny. In all these, governments are under pressure to introduce reforms. However, they are also aware of the potentially divisive nature of the measures they seek to adopt, but lack effective links with civil society in order to predict the impact of their reforms and the likely reaction of different sections of society to them.

Thus, a number of different factors can be identified that explain the different experiences and outcomes of social policy reform in each of the countries of East Central Europe. Clearly, the role of international organizations has been very important as a source of ideas, both in defining the nature of the problem to be solved by social policy change and in offering a package of policy solutions. However, as can be seen from the examples of the four countries of East Central Europe where there has been a clear outcome to debates over pensions reform, the influence of the international agencies that have been the main advocates of neoliberal policies, and in particular the World Bank, was not sufficient in itself to bring about changes of the kind that they support. They were only able to exert an influence where they had the support of influential local policy actors within the national governments, and in particular in the Ministry of Finance. In Hungary and Poland, where the Finance Ministry was a major supporter of the second pillar of mandatory individual insurance schemes, they worked closely with the World Bank in devising the new policy. However, in the Czech Republic and Slovenia, where the Finance Ministries were less committed to the new policy orthodoxy, and where other policy actors such as the Ministry of Labour were more active, the second-pillar proposals were put forward but not adopted. In these cases the World Bank proved less influential and indeed, other international influences with different ideas, such as the European Union's Phare programme and the ILO played a more influential role.

The question of which internal policy actors had greater influence was in turn related to the economic context within which the policy debate took place. It is no coincidence that the two countries that were able to remain sceptical about the new orthodoxy on pensions policy and to reject the idea of a mandatory personal pension strand were the two strongest in terms of many indicators of economic performance. According to World Bank classifications, the Czech Republic is 'an upper-middle income, less indebted country' while Slovenia is a 'high income country' (Muller 2002: 117). On the other hand, Hungary and Poland were in a more vulnerable situation because of their relatively higher levels of debt. In these circumstances, it can be argued, governments will be more open to policy advice from international agencies such as the World Bank and the IMF, whether they are directly indebted to them, or simply because they believe such compliance would signal that they are developing sound economic policies that will attract future investors (Muller 2002: 130–1).

However, none of these influences operated in a social vacuum. Since 1989, the whole question of the direction of economic transformation had been a highly politicized issue and governments were aware of the need to adopt policies that won popular support, or at least to influence that support in favour of their chosen policies. This meant that they had to take account of a number of channels through which the support or opposition of society in general would make itself felt, and this, in turn, brings us back to the question of the relation between social policy and democracy.

Democracy and social policy

The influence of democracy on social policy

On the basis of the foregoing discussion it can be seen that the somewhat piecemeal character of welfare reform and a process of democratization based on a weak development of links between state and civil society stand in a complex relation to each other. In particular, the most obvious channels through which democratic debate on policy issues could be conducted seem to have been largely inactive. As noted above in the section on democratization, links between parties and interest groups, and with the wider electorate, all seem very weak; evidence suggests that the party programmes of the main parties do not set out clear policies on social policy issues and parties tend to change their policy positions between elections; and voters tend not to give priority to policy issues in making their choice of party. Although single-issue parties representing pensioners were formed, and had some impact in the Czech Republic, they did not exert a major influence on the outcomes of the reform legislation. However, in securing the passage of their social policy reforms, democratic politics have been a significant aspect of the policy process in two main ways: first, in responding to public opinion; and secondly in engaging in social dialogue with various interest groups in society.

(i) Public opinion. The need to take public opinion into account and to subject themselves periodically to the judgement of the electorate has had some influence in general on both the timing and content of social policy reforms. This is especially significant if we bear in mind the findings of Kluegel and Mason above that citizens in East Central Europe typically judge the performance of their governments in terms of concepts of general fairness and social justice as well as in relation to their own interests as consumers or employees. While it is difficult to trace the effect of this in any precise way, it seems reasonable to suggest that the introduction of new forms of unemployment benefit and poverty relief in the early 1990s, the (mis)use of the regulations governing early retirement and disability pensions to reduce the numbers of the registered unemployed, and the decision to postpone consideration of subjecting pensions policy to the rigours of market forces in all countries in the early 1990s, and in the Czech Republic and Slovenia throughout the 1990s, were all responses to what politicians assumed public opinion might be.

On pensions policy, public opinion has also had a more direct influence on policy outcomes. In terms of social policy making, regular polling material was available in all countries in the region on public attitudes to the existing pensions system and to the proposed reforms. Moreover, from the narratives above, it is clear that public opinion was one of the key variables explaining different outcomes to pension reform debates in each country. In Poland and Hungary, where market-oriented pension reforms succeeded, public opinion was highly critical of existing arrangements and at least tolerant of the proposed reforms. In the Czech Republic and Slovenia, however, where a mandatory individual insurance scheme was rejected, public opinion was more satisfied with existing arrangements and opposed to the reform proposals.

(ii) Interest group politics and social dialogue. As noted above, trade unions played a significant role in social policy debates in all countries in the region. In Slovenia and the Czech Republic, their ability to organize popular demonstrations and mount a sustained campaign played an important part in the defeat of proposals to introduce three-pillar pensions systems. In Hungary and Poland, where they did not mount such sustained campaigns they were nevertheless important policy actors whose support or compliance the government had to secure. Lobbying and pressure brought to bear by other, smaller interest groups also had some small influence on policy making, especially in Hungary and Slovenia. Furthermore, if institutions for social dialogue are also taken as an aspect of democracy, representing interest-based constituencies instead of territorial constituencies, then here again the discussions and consultations that took place within such bodies can be seen as examples of democracy affecting the outcomes of particular policy debates. For example, in both Poland and Hungary the path of pension reform legislation was cleared at a point where it had become deadlocked through the agency of the tripartite council or its subcommittees.

However, it should also be noted that there are no obvious examples of either interest group lobbying or tripartite consultation as a major factor in the initiation of policy changes. In all cases where they have had an effective impact it has been as a response to elite initiatives or external influences. Where interest groups and movements have attempted to initiate policy change from outside the formal channels of consultation, for example the anti-poverty movements in Hungary in the early 1990s, they have not gained an effective voice. Even social partner organizations such as trade unions have not been very effective in initiating reforms or new legislation. For example, although the Solidarity union confederation in Poland put forward its own reform package on pensions, they were not successful in having it adopted. Furthermore, interest groups and the partner organizations in formal social dialogue have not successfully converted the pressure they have exerted into effective social pacts and agreements that have had a consistent impact on social policy making. Although governments are willing to consult them and discuss policy with them they have not accepted them as regular partners in the making of social policy. Where agreements have been reached, such as the Czechoslovak agreement of 1991, or later less ambitious agreements in Slovakia and Slovenia, governments have not kept to them when faced with economic problems that they gave priority over social welfare issues.

In Hungary, where a socialist government began its term of office with a strong commitment to a social pact in 1994, economic pressures led the government to take harsh economic measures that unions found impossible to agree with, thus ending any possibility of achieving the social pact.

The influence of social policy on democratization

To a lesser extent, it can also be suggested that the politics of social policy has had a small impact on the development of democratic politics in East Central Europe. At the very least social welfare reforms have not served to undermine democratization in East Central Europe. Although there were fears in the early 1990s that welfare issues and declining living standards would cause widespread opposition and popular resistance to the post-communist reforms in general, this outcome did not take place anywhere in the region. In some ways welfare concerns have even reinforced democratization. While social policy issues did not influence the initial establishment of the constitutions and institutions of parliamentary democracy, their influence can be seen in the interest governments have shown in all countries in the region in exploring social pacts and agreements, even if they have not been very successful in binding social partners to the terms of the agreements. More successfully, social welfare issues have been an important stimulus to the formation and continuing relevance of tripartite councils to enable consultation, dialogue and even sometimes participation in policy making.

Although some of the neoliberal politicians who came to power in the early 1990s were not sympathetic to the idea of social dialogue, they either came to accept the idea later in response to economic crisis and/or popular discontent, or they were replaced by other politicians who were more sympathetic to tripartite consultations. This occurred most dramatically in Hungary in 1990 when demonstrations and blockades by taxi drivers and transport workers over rising fuel prices convinced the Antal government to change its mind about tripartism and revive the Interest Reconciliation Council, which then proved to be a successful forum for solving the dispute. Occurring as it did, at the beginning of the 'transition' period, it also seems reasonable to suggest that this development was influential on the thinking of governments in other countries in the region in convincing them of the benefits of formal institutions for social dialogue. While social democratic parties and trade unions have tended to be more enthusiastic about tripartite councils, the opinions of conservatives had softened by 1994 in Slovenia and by 1997 in the Czech Republic as they recognised their usefulness as a means of bringing opposing interests together to reach compromises. Of course, conservative parties remain more suspicious of tripartite arrangements, often seeing them as undemocratic cosy relations through which former communist successor elites in government, unions and employers' organizations renew their old networks and ensure their own common interests are served. Such was the thinking behind the conservative FIDESz government's reforms of 2000 in Hungary that replaced the Interest Reconciliation Council by a series of separate councils for social dialogue in different policy areas. Even here, however, they did not try and return to the idea of governing without institutions of social dialogue altogether as conservative governments of the early 1990s had done.

From the experience of the decade and a half since the end of communist rule in East Central Europe, a rather brief period in comparative historical terms, the conclusion so far seems to be that democracy and social policy change have had a complex and contingent relationship. While the institutions and rules of the game of a liberal democracy are now well embedded in East Central Europe, and more recently reinforced by EU membership, effective links between state and civil society remain weakly developed. This is the case both with party development and with the patterns and mechanisms of interest representation and social dialogue. This is a problem in all areas of policy making, but perhaps it is most acute in relation to social policy. It is on these policy issues that governments have to strike a fine balance between, on the one hand, restructuring the provision of welfare and support for social development for citizens whose living standards have been lowered as a result of economic transformation, and, on the other hand, the wider requirements to operate a system of welfare provision that conforms to the market-oriented criteria of the emerging capitalist economy. The effective management of the dilemmas experienced by governments in striking such a balance would be much improved if they had access to reliable information on the interests and attitudes of the citizens affected by these changes. However, it is precisely in these aspects of the channelling of information and the aggregation of interests between state and society that the new democracies of East Central Europe are at their least developed. The relation between democracy and social policy will therefore remain central in the further stages of East Central Europe's post-communist development as they gradually unfold.

Notes

1. See Stephens chapter 2 in this volume.
2. Gini coefficients measure the degree of income inequality, in this case between individuals, on a scale ranging from the hypothetical extremes of 0, representing perfect equality, to 1, representing the complete monopolization of all income by one person.
3. For further discussion of the range of groups experiencing poverty see (Milanovich 1998: 101–7; World Bank 2000a: 68–90). For the methods used to calculate the incidence of poverty see (World Bank 2000a: 370).
4. For example, the Freedom House ratings classify them all as 'electoral democracies' (Karatnycky 2002), while the European Commission (2001) have recognized them as 'established democracies'. See Pridham 2003 for further details and discussion.
5. Uniquely in Slovenia, in addition to the tripartite council, the second chamber of the parliament is based on the representation of interest groupings as well as territorial constituencies. The forty-member State Council consists of 22 seats representing local

communities, four each for employers and trade unions, two for farmers' organizations, and one each for a range of professions and occupational interests, including the social services, medicine, and education. The State Council can require the main legislative chamber of parliament to reconsider a bill it has already passed and if the bill fails to win a two-thirds majority it fails.

References

Ágh, A. 1998. *The Politics of Central Europe*. London: Sage.

Augustinovics, M., R. Gal, A. Matits, M. Levente, A. Simonovits, and J. Stahl. 2002. 'The Hungarian Pension System Before and After the 1998 Reform', in E. Fultz (ed.), *Pension Reform in Central and Eastern Europe*, volume 1. Budapest: ILO, pp. 25–94.

Bielasiak, J. and D. Blunck. 2002. 'Past and Present in Transitional Voting: Electoral Choices in Post-Communist Poland', *Party Politics*, 8(5), 563–85.

Blazyca, G. 2003. 'Managing Transition Economies', in S. White, J. Batt and P. Lewis (eds), *Developments in Central and East European Politics 3*. Basingstoke: Palgrave – now Palgrave Macmillan.

Boeri, T. 2000. *Structural Change, Welfare Systems and Labour Reallocation: Lessons From the Transition of Formerly Planned Economies*. Oxford: Oxford University Press.

Chlon-Dominczak, A. 2002. 'The Polish Pension Reform of 1999', in E. Fultz (ed.), *Pension Reform in Central and Eastern Europe*, vol. 1. Budapest: ILO, pp. 95–198.

Cox, T. 2003. 'Changing Societies: Class and Inequality in Central and Eastern Europe', in S. White, J. Batt and P. Lewis (eds), *Developments in Central and East European Politics 3*. Basingstoke: Palgrave – now Palgrave Macmillan, pp. 234–52.

Cox, T. and B. Mason. 1999. *Social and Economic Transformation in East Central Europe*. Cheltenham: Edward Elgar.

Cox, T. and L. Vass. 2000. 'Government–Interest Group Relations in Hungarian Politics Since 1989.' *Europe–Asia Studies*, 52(6), 1095–114.

Crowley, S. and D. Ost (eds). 2001. *Worker After Workers' States: Labour and Politics in Postcommunist Eastern Europe*. Lanham: Rowman and Littlefield.

Dawisha, K. and B. Parrott. 1997. *The Consolidation of Democracy in East-Central Europe*. Cambridge: Cambridge University Press.

Deacon, B. and M. Hulse. 1997. 'The Making of Post-Communist Social Policy: The Role of International Agencies.' *Journal of Social Policy*, 26, 43–62.

EBRD. 1996. *Transition Report*. London: EBRD.

Ekiert, G. and J. Kubiak. 1998. 'Contentious Politics in New Democracies.' *World Politics*, 50(4), 547–81.

European Commission (EC). 1994. *Central and Eastern Eurobarometer Survey*. Brussels: European Commission.

European Commission (EC). 1998. *Central and Eastern Eurobarometer Survey*. Brussels: European Commission.

European Commission (EC). 2001. *Enlargement: 2001 Regular Reports on Progress Towards Accession*. Brussels: European Commission.

European Commission (EC). 2002. *Candidate Countries Eurobarometer 2001*. Brussels: European Commission.

Fink Hafner, D. 1997. 'Interest Organisations in the Policy Making Process', in D. Fink Hafner and J. Robbins (eds), *Making a New Nation: The Formation of Slovenia*. Dartmouth: Aldershot, pp. 114–34.

Fultz, E. 2003. *Recent Trends in Pension Reform and Implementation in the EU Accession Countries*. Budapest: ILO.

Gallai, S. 2001. *European Social Dialogue*. Budapest: Budapest Economics.
Greskovits, B. 1998. *The Political Economy of Protest and Patience*. Budapest: CEU Press.
Hethy, L. 1999. 'Tripartism and Industrial Relations in Hungary', in G. Casale (ed.), *Social Dialogue in Central and Eastern Europe*. Budapest: ILO, pp. 180–201.
Hausner, J. 2001. 'Security Through Diversity: Conditions for Successful Reform of the Pension System in Poland', in J. Kornai, S. Haggard and R. Kaufman (eds), *Reforming the State: Fiscal and Welfare Reform in Post-Socialist Countries*. Cambridge: Cambridge University Press, pp. 210–34.
Howard, M. 2003. *The Weakness of Civil Society in Post-Communist Europe*. Cambridge: Cambridge University Press.
Ilonszki, G. 1998. 'Representation Deficit in a New Democracy', *Communist and Post-Communist Studies*, 31(2), 157–70.
Kaase, M. and H-D. Klingemann. 1994. 'The Cumbersome Way to Partisan Orientations in a New Democracy', in M. Jennings and T. Mann (eds), *Elections at Home and Abroad*. Ann Arbor: University of Michigan Press, 123–56.
Karatnycky, A. 2002. 'The 2001 Freedom House Survey', *Journal of Democracy*, 13(1), 99–112.
Kluegel, J. and D. Mason. 2004. 'Fairness Matters: Social Justice and Political Legitimacy in Post-Communist Europe.' *Europe–Asia Studies*, 56(6), 813–34.
Kramer, M. 1997. 'Social Protection Policies and Safety Nets in East Central Europe: Dilemmas of the Postcommunist Transformation', in E. Kapstein and M. Mandelbaum (eds), *Sustaining the Transition: the Social Safety Net in Postcommunist Europe*. New York: Council on Foreign Relations, pp. 46–123.
Lado, M. and A. Toth. 2000. *The Fate of Tripartism in Hungary*. Budapest: National Labour Centre.
Lewis, P. 2003. 'Political Parties', in S. White, J. Batt and P. Lewis (eds), *Developments in Central and East European Politics 3*. Basingstoke: Palgrave – now Palgrave Macmillan, pp. 153–72.
Luksic, I. 1997. 'Changing Patterns of Social Partnership', in D. Fink Hafner and J. Robbins (eds), *Making a New Nation: The Formation of Slovenia*. Dartmouth: Aldershot, pp. 106–13.
Macha, M. 2002. 'The Political Economy of Pension Reform in the Czech Republic', in E. Fultz (ed.), *Pension Reform in Central and Eastern Europe*, vol. 2. Budapest: ILO, pp. 75–112.
Machalikova, A. 1999. 'Tripartism in the Slovak Republic', in G. Casale (ed.), *Social Dialogue in Central and Eastern Europe*. Budapest: ILO, pp. 288–304.
Malova, D. 1997. 'The Development of Interest Representation in Slovakia After 1989', in S. Szomolanyi and J. Gould (eds), *Slovakia: Problems of Democratic Consolidation*. Bratislava, pp. 93–128.
Mason, D. and J. Kluegel. 2000. *Marketing Democracy: Changing Opinion About Inequality and Politics in East Central Europe*. Oxford: Rowman and Littlefield.
Milanovich, B. 1998. *Income, Inequality and Poverty during the Transition from Planned to Market Economy*. Washington: The World Bank.
Muller, K. 2002. 'Between State and Market: Czech and Slovene Pension Reform in Comparison', in E. Fultz (ed.), *Pension Reform in Central and Eastern Europe*, vol. 2. Budapest: ILO, pp. 113–38.
Myant, M., B. Slocock and S. Smith. 2000. 'Tripartism in the Czech and Slovak Republics', *Europe Asia Studies*, 52(4), 723–39.
Nelson, J. 2001. 'The Politics of Pension and Health Care Reforms in Hungary and Poland', in J. Kornai, S. Haggard and R. Kaufman (eds), *Reforming the State: Fiscal and*

Welfare Reform in Post-Socialist Countries. Cambridge: Cambridge University Press, pp. 235–66.
Ost, D. 2000. 'Illusory Corporatism: Tripartism in the Service of Neoliberalism', *Politics and Society*, 28(4), 503–30.
Pankow, I. 1996. 'The Main Actors on the Political Scene in Poland', in A. Agh and G. Ilonszki (eds), *Parliaments and Organised Interests: the Second Steps*. Budapest: Hungarian Centre for Democracy Studies, pp. 130–47.
Pridham, G. 2003. 'Democratisation in Central and Eastern Europe: A Comparative Perspective', in S. White, J. Batt and P. Lewis (eds), *Developments in Central and East European Politics 3*. Basingstoke: Palgrave – now Palgrave Macmillan, pp. 269–89.
Rose, R. 2002a. 'A Bottom Up Evaluation of Enlargement Countries: New Europe Barometer 1', *Studies in Public Policy*. No. 364. Glasgow: Centre for Public Policy.
Rose, R. 2002b. 'Advancing Into Europe: Contrasting Goals of Post-Communist Countries.' Unpublished paper. Glasgow: Centre for the Study of Public Policy.
Rueschmeyer, D., M. Rueschmeyer and B. Wittrock (eds). 1998. *Participation and Democracy East and West: Comparisons and Interpretations*. New York: Sharpe.
Stanovnik, T. 2002. 'The Political Economy of Pension Reform in Slovenia', in E. Fultz (ed.), *Pension Reform in Central and Eastern Europe,* vol. 2. Budapest: ILO, pp. 19–74.
Svetlik, I. 1992. *Social Policy in Slovenia*. Aldershot: Avebury.
Szczerbiak, A. 2001. *Poles Together? The Emergence and Development of Political Parties in Postcommunist Poland*. Budapest: CEU Press.
Todosijevic, B. 2005. 'Issues and Party Preferences in Hungary', *Party Politics*, 11(1), 109–26.
Vovodnik, Z. 1999. 'Tripartism and Industrial Relations in Slovenia', in G. Casale (ed.), *Social Dialogue in Central and Eastern Europe*. Budapest: ILO, pp. 305–18.
World Bank. 1994. *Averting the Old Age Crisis*. Washington DC: World Bank.
World Bank. 1996. *World Development Report 1996: From Plan to Market*. Oxford: Oxford University Press.
World Bank. 2000. *Making Transition Work for Everyone: Poverty and Inequality in Europe and Central Asia*. Washington DC: World Bank.
World Bank. 2002. *Transition, The First Ten Years: Analysis and Lessons for Eastern Europe and the Former Soviet Union*. Washington DC: World Bank.

6

The Latin American Social States: Critical Junctures and Critical Choices*

Fernando Filgueira

Introduction

Latin America's social states are inextricably linked to the development of modern states and bureaucracies, the emergence of a new development model and mass politics with democratic interludes. Democracy has not been irrelevant in the construction of social states, although it has been a weaker building block of the region's welfare regimes than state expansion and import substitution industrialization (ISI). Both country-specific analyses and cross-national evidence suggest that the formal rules of democracy and the quality and level of political incorporation have played important roles. There is no correlation between democracy and welfare when the effect of stable democratic rule (that is years of uninterrupted democratic rule) between the 1950s and 1990s on social state size (social expenditure over GDP) are considered.

The finding that supports the democracy-welfare hypothesis in Latin America is a peculiar one. In countries where democracy took hold or survived for relatively long periods between the 1950s and 1970s, social spending 30 years later is higher than would be expected given the GDPs of such countries. In contrast, where democracy was weak or non-existent between the 1950s and 1970s, social spending underperforms, again 30 years later, when measured in terms of the GDPs of such countries. Such a finding is no proof of a relationship between democracy and social state development. Both the data and the number cases suggest caution. Yet this is indeed a curious pattern, and no easy alternative explanation seems obvious. The hypothesis that best fits the data pattern here is that the relationship between democracy and welfare expansion is strongly path-dependent. When major developmental

* This is a revised and edited version of a previous paper cominnsioned by UNRISD. I wish to thank the insightful comments of Yusuf Bangura, Jorge Papadópulos and Federico Tobar. I also wish to acknowledge, beyond the appropriate references and quotes, the inspiration, analyses and data that came from the studies of Carmelo Mesa-Lago and Evelyne Huber. Errors, remain, of course, my responsibility.

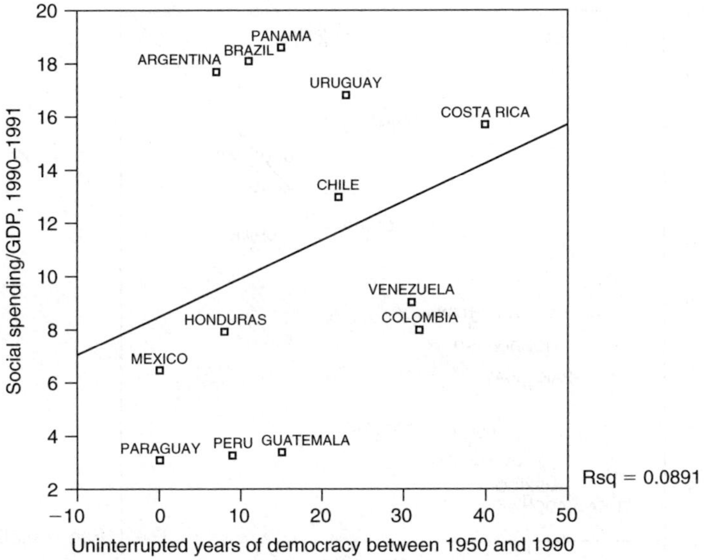

Figure 6.1 Social spending as part of GDP in Latin American countries plotted against number of years in a uninterupted period of democracy, 1950–1990
Source: Author on the basis of data from Przeworski *et al.* 2000; UNDP 2001; and CEPAL 2000, 2001, 2002.

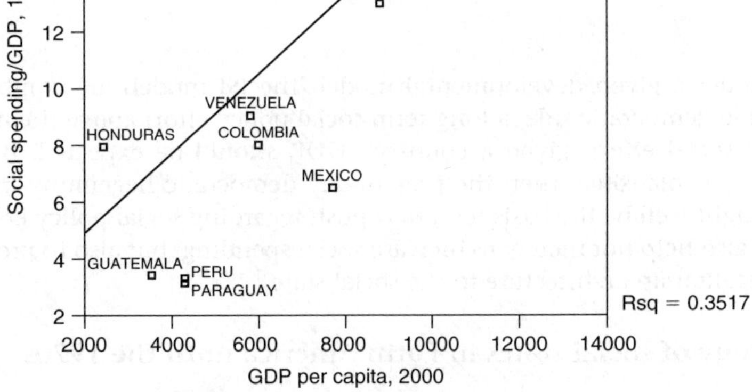

Figure 6.2 Social spending/GDP, 1990–1991 plotted against GDP per capita 2000
Source: Author on the basis of data from Przeworski *et al.* 2000; UNDP 2001; and CEPAL 2000, 2001, 2002.

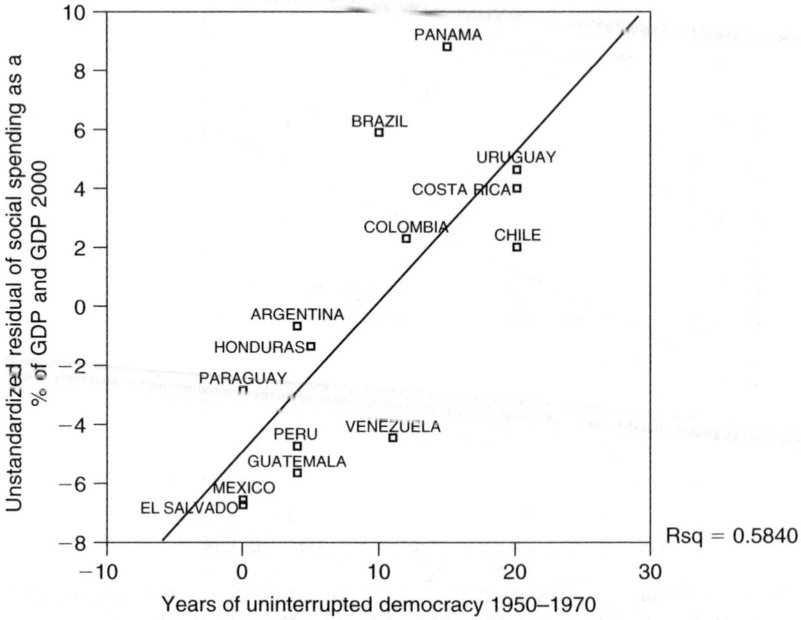

Figure 6.3 Relation between years of uninterrupted democracy between 1950 and 1970 and the unstandardised residual of social spending over GDP and GDP per capita, 2000

Note: The measure of democracy is based on the classification of Przeworski *et al.* (2000) considering uninterrupted years of democracy (considers lapses of six or more years and adds them for the period considered). A measure that only considers years of democracy (even if it is one or two isolated years) does not yield significantly different results, but some countries with very bad records of democracy rank above some good ones, like the comparison of Guatemala and Chile. Uninterrupted democracy suggests that democracy did not only last, but overcame some sort of crises.

Source: Author on the basis of data from Przeworski *et al.* 2000; UNDP 2001; and CEPAL 2000–2001, 2001–2002.

surges under a given developmental model (the ISI model) are combined with stable democratic rule, a long-term social policy effort above the mean expected social effort, given a country's GDP, should be expected. If this hypothesis is plausible, then the present-day democratic hegemony in the region might well be the basis for a new push regarding social policy efforts. It might also help not merely to increase social spending, but also to provide a more egalitarian architecture to the social state.[1]

A typology of social states in Latin America until the 1970s

In order to compare the Latin American social states, a typology rather than a classification based on a continuum is required. Furthermore, the explanation

Table 6.1 Selected variables on social policy effort for types of social states, circa 1970*

	% covered by social security in EAP	*% covered by social security in total population*	*Social expenditure as % GDP*	*% of children under one year vaccinated against tuberculosis*	*Primary education gross enrollment rates*	*Secondary education gross enrollment rates*
Stratified universalism	83.3	67.93	15.63	96	108	47.33
Dual	50.2	27.55	8.65	73	93	24
Exclusionary	16.3	9.2	2.75	37.5	80.33	18

Sources: Mesa-Lago 1991; World Bank 1994; Miranda 1994; and Cominetti 1994. *Unweighted averages.
Stratfied universalism: Uruguay, Chile and Argentina; *Dual*: Mexico and Brazil; *Exclusionary*: Guatemala, Salvador, Nicaragua, Honduras, Bolivia.

for differences in the development of national social states will be path-dependent or structural rather than linear. In other words, structural variables and historical sequences rather than singular temporal starting points and levels of maturity inform the analysis. The fundamental indicators to be considered will be: coverage (i.e., to some extent 'how it is spent'), expenditure (i.e. 'how much is spent') and its sector distribution and levels of services given (i.e. an additional approximation of 'how it is spent'). We therefore analyze inclusiveness as well as expenditure. Our interest is on 'how' as an issue of sector distribution and population coverage, and on a second level, as it relates to decommodification. Three distinct types of social states can be identified (see Table 6.1). Argentina, Uruguay, and Chile (and also, although only in the 1980s, Costa Rica) offered universal or near-universal coverage regarding social security for the economically active population, as well as primary education and basic health services to all – or almost all – citizens. With the exception of education, the social states of these Southern Cone countries are marked by a strong pattern of stratification. Brazil and Mexico (together with Venezuela, Panama and, to a lesser extent, Colombia) can be characterized as dual social states. A large portion of the population was covered by social services and income maintenance schemes (also in a strongly stratified manner), and another very large part remained outside the state protection system. Finally, countries such as El Salvador, Honduras, Bolivia, Ecuador and Guatemala (to a lesser extent) can be termed exlusionary social states, where a small and privileged part of the population had access to social protection. The development of these different systems of social protection had an important impact on variables relating to social welfare as can be seen in Table 6.2. The argument that these differences can be explained by their GDP per capita levels does not withstand a simple empirical test. As can be seen in Figure 6.4, the unstandardized residuals between GDP and social development

Table 6.2 Selected social development indicators for types of social states, circa 1970*

	% of households below the poverty line	*% of households below the indigence line*	*Illiteracy rate*	*Infant mortality*	*Life expectancy at birth*
Stratified universalism	11.67	3.67	9.53	50	67.07
Dual	41.5	18.5	29.7	77.5	61.25
Exclusionary	62.5	31.33	40.4	112	54.08

Sources: ECLAC 1995; ECLAC 1980. *Unweighted averages.

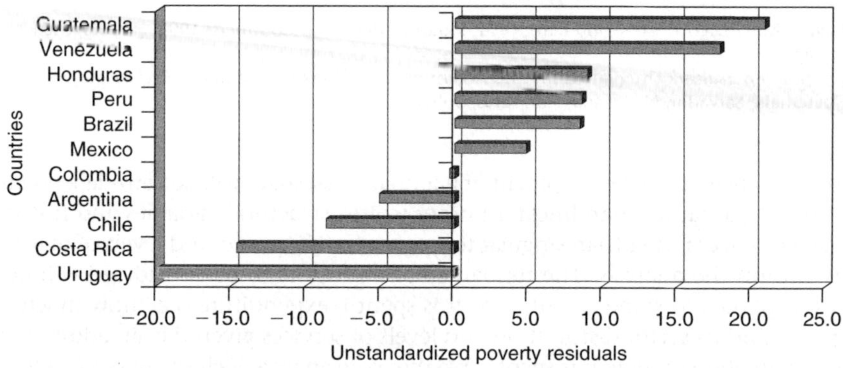

Figure 6.4 Unstandardized poverty residuals from the regression between GDP per capita and % of households below the poverty line, 1970
Source: ECLAC 1994.

(measured through households below the poverty line) shows a clear pattern where universalistic, dual and exclusionary countries present an almost perfect fit with the hypothesis presented above.

The differences in the paths to social state formation lay in the political economy and politics of the different groups of countries. For the purpose of this analysis I will leave aside the exclusionary cases. This is due both to reasons of space and to the fact that most of these countries do not in reality have a social state or a state for that matter until the 1970s, but rather a 'coercive apparatus servicing the privileged'.[2] We focus on the dynamics of the stratified universal and dual social state regimes.

The political economy and politics of social states in Latin America

In Argentina and Uruguay, ISI was based on the export of primary goods, especially cattle, which had low labour demand and high international profitability.

These were the first two countries in the region to experiment with mass politics and democracy. Early social state formation is highly correlated with early democratic experiments. Argentina and Uruguay experienced democratic rule as early as the 1910s and 1920s and were the first countries to develop mass systems of basic education, some attempts at public health and social security schemes. Indeed, the Yrigoyenista and Batllista years of the 1920s witnessed not only an important expansion of the vote and mobilization of the middle and working classes, but also the first clear-cut pro-labour bills, and the expansion of public education, which started in the late nineteenth century. Chile had to build its social state on a much tougher structural terrain than Argentina and Uruguay. It may seem a paradox that in Chile it was a military leader, Ibañez, who came to power in a coup d'état, who would establish the basis of Chile's social state.

Even though Argentina's experiment with democracy ended in the 1930s, only to become a stable democracy again in the 1980s, the country never ceased to be a nation of mass politics. Despite almost 15 years of authoritarianism, the trade unions remained important actors and, with industrialization, grew even more powerful. In the early 1940s, the government made strong and ultimately successful attempts to co-opt the trade union movement. The ministry of labour of the military regime (Peron) that started in 1943 created a corporatist alliance between workers, a new movement/party and the state. Between 1946 and 1955, Peronismo co-opted what were already important and powerful trade unions. With this alliance and the return to electoral mass politics, the Peronist government reformed the labour code, granted family allowances, established a minimum wage, provided accident insurance, and placed restrictions on the dismissal of workers. It also financed the health programmes, known as Obras Sociales, and expanded public health and social security. The authoritarian period of the 1930s and early 1940s did not end the process of social state expansion. Instead, it shifted what seemed like a pluralist route to a modern social state, with left-wing autonomous trade unions, into a corporatist route.

After a short period of semi-authoritarian rule in the 1930s, Uruguay returned to mass democracy in 1938 and the country remained democratic until 1973. The Colorados led the expansion of the social state, which was verging on universal coverage as early as the late 1960s. In the early 1940s, two bills were instrumental in the construction of Uruguay's social state and democracy. Before the Catholic-leaning parties in Europe did it, the Union Civica in Uruguay proposed and got passed a bill for flat rate universal family allowances. Also before the success of the socialists and social democrats of Europe, the Socialist Party in Uruguay was able to pass a law creating tripartite wage councils that granted state recognition and virtual monopoly of workers' representatives of the left wing trade unions. Both bills relied on the support and encouragement of the Colorado government.

The answer to the paradox of the radically distinct political trajectories of Argentina and Uruguay after the 1930s, having had such similar trajectories in the early twentieth century, might rest at least partially on the logics driving their social states in the late 1930s and in the 1940s. Uruguay never ceased to base its social state on parliamentary processes and the pressures of left-leaning trade unions; by contrast, Argentina adopted a vertical, corporatist arrangement in the expansion of its social state. Yet, either through corporatist arrangements and the dynamics of electoral politics and military interludes, as in the case of Argentina, or stable democracy, as in the case of Uruguay, the social states of these countries continued to expand.

The Chilean case is more complicated. While it is also a country that had an important import substitution model, it was based on mining and an export-oriented agrarian economy, which was more diversified and had a higher labour force demand. Yet mining based on modern forms of labour–capital relations allowed the emergence of a strong left-wing trade union movement. Chile, like the other cases, also experienced important rural–urban migration. By the 1900s, important trade unions from Santiago and Valparaiso developed and defended the well-being of members through strikes and social mobilization. As in Uruguay and Argentina, the first groups to be incorporated into the social protection system were professionals and public employees. Using revenues from foreign trade, state elites developed the first programmes of social service provision, (education and, to a lesser extent, health) and social security. Mining workers that were strongly unionized, and urban workers allied to left-wing political parties in the urban centres, were able to exert enough pressure for incorporation into the systems of social protection and services.

The importance of left-wing political parties, the Christian Democratic Party, and Congress in Chilean politics cannot be overstated regarding the expansion of the social state. While formally, right-wing parties governed for much of the period between the 1940s and early 1960s, the importance of centre Catholic-leaning parties and left-wing populist and programmatic parties (and especially their flexibility regarding their parliamentary alliances), helps to promote an understanding of the expansion of the Chilean social state.

By 1970, the Chilean social security system consisted of more than 100 institutions and programmes that covered old age, disability, death, unemployment (only some), sickness and health. Political coalitions, as well as the pluralist and institutionalized nature of the game, reflected a vibrant democracy by any standard in Latin America. Parties came together to provide a robust universal educational system, and bargained to expand a stratified but universal and, by many standards, generous social security and health care system.

Yet, for all their advances, these countries were not welfare states because they lacked the ideas and political basis to construct a framework of social citizenship that went beyond equalizing opportunities and providing insurance-based schemes for sickness, old age and disability. They also lacked the economic and labour market characteristics that allowed continental European states to become true welfare regimes. At cradle they looked pretty much like a welfare state; close to the grave too; but between cradle and grave, only economic citizenship and its link to political citizenship guaranteed some form of stratified social citizenship.

However, Chile, Argentina and Uruguay represent the closest cases that resembled in the 1970s the welfare regimes of continental Europe in the 1960s. Elites that did not depend on the coercive control of labour and that had developed into a political professional class, partly autonomous from the landowning elites, are critical in explaining the early appearance of education, primary health care and the creation of stratified, yet close to universal social security schemes in these countries. Mass politics and especially inclusionary mass democratic politics (democratic in the case of Uruguay, limited democracy in the case of Chile, populist and corporatist in the case of Argentina) were not as effective in the rest of Latin America compared to the Southern Cone states and account for the variation in social expenditures and coverage.

There were variations in the form of the social states, but not the depth of the social states. Chile and Uruguay advanced their social agenda and the social incorporation of the popular sectors by combining clientelism and broader agendas fueled by electoral competition. Argentina advanced its social agenda through vertical corporatism and broad policies enacted as power changed hands between the military, the radical party and the builder of the social state – the Peronist movement. These cases show that early democratic experiments, even when restricted, are critical in predicting early social state origins. Yet in the 1930s these three countries became authoritarian, with radically different effects on social policy development. In Uruguay, authoritarianism did not dramatically alter the game of politics and of social state building. In Argentina, authoritarianism brought it to a halt and then allowed for the creation of an unstable, but critical corporatist arrangement that would push for the expansion of the social state. In Chile, the dictatorship of the 1930s broke the impasse that the conservative elites had imposed on the country, by limiting the role of Congress and expanding the vote. This opened the way for the real origins of the Chilean social state and an expanded presidential democray with a vibrant parliament.

In all three countries the return to democracy, or at least to mass electoral politics, would become the building block for the expansion of benefits, services and protections, and in some cases for the 'massification of privilege'. In no country was an organized and powerful labour party with a trade union constituency the leader of the social state-building process. But while in Uruguay the space for trade union influence was granted through parliamentary representation and wage councils at the sector level, in Chile it was through political coalitions and lobbying within parties that this was achieved; and in Argentina, a populist movement either co-opted or repressed the trade unions to build a vertical corporatist arrangement. In all three cases, democracy and elections increased the power of these sectors between the 1940s and 1970s and helped fuel and finance the social states.

Where the origins of the social state was the product of congressional debates, autonomous trade unions and non ideological catch-all parties as in Uruguay, democracy was most stable; when the genetic code was that of an electorally restrictive political system with an institutionalized Congress, lobbying type trade unions and wide-ranging coalitional politics on the left and centre, democracy was slow but stable. Finally, when the political genetic code was the result of an aborted pluralist route recreated and rechanelled in a tense pact between the military, a populist movement, organized workers and elites, where mostly the second and third actors built the social states and the first and last controlled its limits, the result was a very unstable political system with many but also short periods of attempted democracy.

As the 1970s approached, these three countries, pioneers in import substitution industrialization and the formation of social states, confronted systemic crises that affected their economies, societies and political regimes. Chile and Uruguay in 1973 and Argentina in 1976 would see their democratic regimes destroyed. On this occasion the military regimes that emerged would attempt to reshape the developmental model from the state-centred approach to market-oriented economies. In the field of welfare development, only Chile would move radically in the market-oriented direction. Argentina and Uruguay would financially neglect and at the same time try to put some order into the old social states; and would later move more moderately than Chile to the new liberal creed on social policies.

Costa Rica as a particular marriage of democracy and universalism?

Costa Rica stands out amongst Central American countries because of its democratic stability, relative egalitarianism, GDP per capita and its social state. Indeed, for many analysts (Huber 1996; Fleury 2001) Costa Rica belongs in a class of its own:[3] the closest case to a universalistic, egalitarian social state; or, even more, an embryonic social democratic welfare state. It is also a country that has remained export-oriented in combination with import substitution, and that based its rural production not on coerced and semi-coerced labour, not on militaristic oligarchic regimes, but on a pattern of land distribution and a form of economic relation that was closer to the farmer model than to the traditional landed elite model in Latin America (yet for many analysts, this last farmer-type feature is largely exaggerated, making the Costa Rican case even more exceptional in terms of its democratic stability and robust social state).

With the Figueras revolution in the 1940s and the suppression of the Armed Forces, Costa Rica would initiate a path that was unique in Latin America. Between 1950 and 1980, it experienced an uninterrupted period of democracy, stable growth rates, and increasing social performance. The social protection system established in Costa Rica in this period was not at first sight so different from those of universalistic stratification as can be documented by the 19 different special and privileged regimes of social protection. Yet a closer look would reveal a completely different picture of the Costa Rican social state. First, and maybe most importantly, the Costa Rican state made as axis of its social policy the expansion of education and primary health care. While the other universalistic countries chose to cover their citizens from top to bottom and tended to add vertically more privileges to the already covered population, Costa Rica rapidly expanded health and education to most of its population. The fact that trade unions have always been weak, and for a long time two catch-all parties dominated the electoral arena, might help to explain these broad-based policy options. It is also true that state unionization was always higher than private sector unionization. The advantages in protection for state employees are in some way a direct consequence of this. Costa Ricans like to think of themselves as living in a middle-class country. The bureaucracy and independent professionals are 'middle class'; the old *bananero* (mostly foreign) and *cafetalero* elites also exist. But there is indeed a wide group of people that are neither poor nor middle class, including not just urban workers but also small propertied classes and even workers in the rural areas. These groups are the backbone of something resembling, though not completely meeting, the standards of an egalitarian universalistic social state of basic protection.

Regarding pensions, once again a closer look shows a remarkable pattern. In Costa Rica, between 25 and 30 per cent of the population receives non-contributory social assistance pensions. The 1970s saw the most important push for social state expansion, and once again coverage of basic income and health care, as well as education access were the major aims of the governments. Costa Rican society is not a mobilized society in the same sense as Argentina, Chile and Uruguay. Largely rural and weakly organized along capital–labour lines, social-based solidarity organizations of workers tend to interact with political parties and political leaders. The absence of strong lobbies (with the exception perhaps of teachers and doctors) has left room for elites who wish to gain popular support to move towards more universalistic goals right from the start. Closely contested elections and high levels of electoral participation combined with a relatively autonomous professional state and political elite are the backbone of the Costa Rican social state.

As Costa Rica's development model faced the crises of the 1980s, a trend towards targeted liberal-type social policies dominated the 1980s governments. Yet by 1994, the Figueres administration would revamp universal social services and attempt to articulate the new small targeted programmes with the fundamental institutions of social protection of the Costa Rican social state. By 1997, health care was covering close to 90 per cent of the population, and pensions, including non-contributory social assistance pensions reached almost 82 per cent of the elderly (Mesa-Lago 1999). Yet as defined by contributions of the working population, coverage in 1997 was around

50 per cent (Muller 2003). The positive gap between coverage of the population and contributions highlights the importance of non-contributory social protection in Costa Rica.

A catch-all party system in a stable democratic environment and the absence of powerful lobbies on the state and the parties, combined with thirty-odd years of relative economic growth, contributed to the creation of perhaps the rarest jewel in Latin America's social states. Costa Rica stands today as one of the most socially advanced countries in the continent, and does so with a GDP per capita that is still substantially smaller than those of Chile, Argentina and Uruguay. It is also true that Costa Rica lacked any form of unemployment insurance and that non-contributory social pensions only amounted to half the basic insurance pension (Mesa-Lago 1999). Still, for a country that in the 1940s was overwhelmingly agrarian and lacked almost any form of social protection and services (with the exception of education) what has been achieved is a considerable achievement. It is also unthinkable to speak of Costa Rican democracy without considering the role that has been played by the social state. Through education first and health care and social security later, the Costa Rican state rests on solid grounds of basic social citizenship. The allegiance of Costa Ricans to democracy is not naïve; it is based on the proven conviction that elites, elections and society can find middle grounds in the construction of a mixed economy with social protection as a major building block.

Perhaps no other case is as clear as that of Costa Rica in explaining the relevance of democracy in pushing social state expansion. This country is a relative latecomer to modern social policy; it was between the 1940s and the 1970s, a period of unprecedented democratic stability, that it developed and institutionalized its social state. A coffee-based and fruit-based export economy in the 1930s, it had few structural factors that would predict a robust social state. Without the Figueres revolution, the suppression of the armed forces, and the creation of a stable two-party system that compete for the popular vote, it is hard to even imagine how this small Central American country could boast today of what some define as the only egalitarian Latin American social state.

Dual regimes: Brazil and Mexico[4]

In Brazil and Mexico, the frailty, short duration and lack of intensity of electorally competitive democratic regimes allowed for the development of dual forms of incorporation, with increasing differences between the power of the rural and urban sectors, backward and advanced areas, and formal and informal labour. Unlike stratified universalism countries, the social state moderates the social segmentation only in those sectors that are incorporated into the modern econmy. However, the protection systems accentuate social differences between urban advanced sectors on the one hand, and non-protected rural, traditional and urban informal sectors on the other. Furthermore, one of the main features and challenges of these systems is a direct legacy from a peculiar form of statecraft (Malloy 1985) these countries pursued. Unlike the universalistic countries, the state was not merely an instrument that contending elites used as a basis of competition for popular support and market regulation. The state was the realm where a previously patrimonial, traditional and status-based political and social order found its ultimate expression and refuge from the more meritocratic logic of modern markets, thus creating a state apparatus less bent on redistribution for popular support and more oriented towards redistribution for elite accommodation and popular control. The wages and pensions of state officials were indeed extremely high in these regimes, far higher than those of Chile, Argentina and Uruguay, when compared to the private sector. Still today, in Brazil, approximately one million pension beneficiaries from the state take up a similar amount of money as 14 million pension beneficiaries from the private sector. Also, as Heredia (2002) points out, the Mexican state is unique not so much because of its size but because of the relative share of the wages of state employees (45 per cent) in total public expenditure. This is the highest by far in Latin America, whilst in terms of the relative number of state employees *vis-à-vis* the total working population, Mexico ranks about average in Latin America.

Despite their commonalities, the data on social indicators in Mexico and Brazil present important differences. Mexico clearly outperforms Brazil in the 1970s in all of the social aspects considered above. The most important reason behind such differences cannot be placed on social spending. As a matter of fact, Brazil spent more by the late 1970s and early 1980s than Mexico did. Three differences help us understand dissimilar social outcomes. The first is the overall pattern of inequality, which was much more entrenched in Brazil than in Mexico, especially in the rural areas, where the latter had an agrarian reform based on a revolutionary movement and armed peasant struggle. The second is the fact that social spending in Mexico concentrated more on health care and education than it did in Brazil, where the emphasis was on the pension system. Finally, in Mexico, even though the rural population and its corporatist organizations were a weaker partner in the populist pact, they were a major building block of the ruling PRI structures. As Brachet-Márquez (2004) points out, Mexico starting in the 1920s, and thereafter with Cardenismo, incorporated to a larger extent than other dualist social states the peasantry and poor rural population as not merely 'issues' but also subjects. In contrast, Brazil was, as Draibe (2004) puts it, maybe the quintessential 'industrially biased' developmental social state. By such she means a social state that centred on regulating industrial relations between labour and capital and providing protection only for labour that was engaged in formal production activities (and of course public employees). This industrial bias anchored in labour-capital relations also helps explain why Brazil had such emphasis on social security, leaving education and health care neglected for a long time.

Thus mass politics and institutions help us explain a major variation within similar countries: they were essentially dual regimes, yet in Mexico an urban peasant revolution and a party that explicitly and really integrated the peasants' organizations into the populist party, stands in stark contrast to the almost cosmetic creation of a national party in Brazil (the PSB) that was essentially a new name for the traditional 'coronelismo' practices of the landed elites. The effects of such differences were the 'industrialist bias' of Varguismo and the 'limited space', but space nevertheless, for rural-oriented social policies, especially in health and education in the Mexican case.

Crisis of the old model and neoliberalism

The economic and social critique of import substitution industrialization

In January 1990, the Institute for International Economics published Williamson's 'The Progress of Policy Reform in Latin America', in which he advanced the notion of a 'Washington Consensus': a set of policy prescriptions advocated by multilateral institutions and US authorities regarding the development process in Latin America. Williamson's contribution did not ask why reform took place or why reform followed certain recipes. His concern was simpler: Did reforms take place? Yet, behind such a narrow concern rests a formidable faith – namely, that those were the right reforms. Part of this faith is based on an additional belief: the absolute conviction regarding the ills of the previous model of import substitution industrialization. It was argued that trade barriers had a detrimental effect on Latin America's natural comparative advantage; and internal regulations and oversized and inefficient bureaucracies inhibited the role of the market in allocating resources efficiently, and contributed to the region's chronic fiscal deficits and inflation-prone economies. More sophisticated political economy approaches argued that they created rentier behaviour, inhibiting capitalist development. According to this critique, the state subsidized elites from rents extracted from international trade taxes. It protected the market space and share of industries through tariffs, legal monopolies, tax exemptions, credits and subsidies. Trade unions asked for higher benefits and wages that were promptly granted for political reasons, as well as to minimize labour conflicts. In turn, the costs of these benefits were passed on to consumers in the form of higher prices. Capitalists and labour unions had no incentive to support strategies that increased productivity or share the costs and benefits of innovations since they had an easier way to maintain profits and gain wage increases. This state of affairs was defined by Evans (1979) as the creation of an anti-Schumpeterian triangle, where protected workers, protected entrepreneurs and the state elites and employees engaged in rentier games driven by a political logic rather than by the driving force of competition and innovation.

The complement of the economic critique is the widely held view that Latin America's abominable pattern of inequality is also due, at least in part, to this import substitution model. The social critique can also be framed in what Evans termed the 'anti-Schumpeterian triangle' of State, Urban Labour and Industrial Elites. The Import Substitution Model redistributes income within this triangle, but in the process deprives other social sectors of protection and benefits. In the first place, it clearly hurts landed elites that have to part with some of their profits in order to finance subsidies and also have to accept an exchange rate that lowers the competitiveness of their products. This group, in contrast to the industrial elites protected from outside competition, is a price taker in the market and thus cannot pass its losses to the consumer or buyer. Secondly, rural labour and small agrarian propertied classes lose. In this model, the burden of countries' development rests with the tradable sector, which in most of the region was based on a couple of agrarian staples. Small and medium-sized proprietors who sell their product to larger export conglomerates are the weakest link and thus will be passed on part of this burden. In addition, elites pass onto rural labour their costs in the Import Substitution Model through the impact that rentier groups' behaviour and low investment have on agrarian labour, wages and employment. Informal urban labour is not protected in the Import Substitution Model. It constitutes the surplus labour the model could not incorporate, given the rate of industrial development and state employment. While it does not benefit from the protection and subsidies that both formal labour and entrepreneurs enjoy, informal labour is affected by the increases in prices generated by this model. The end result is that these societies end up dual, with a small, protected domestic modern sector and a large unprotected rural and informal urban popular sector.

A central error in the overall critique of the social aspects of the Import Substitution Model is that it does not take into consideration important variations within the region. In effect, not all countries developed the social side of the Import Substitution Model equally. In other words, the size of the anti-Schumpeterian triangle varied widely within Latin America. While the Import Substitution Model critique might very well be valid for cases in which the triangle reached less than a third of the population, it is less appropriate in cases in which it reached more than half of it, and clearly without merit as we move to the few cases in which most of the population benefited from transfers from the landed elites and the export sector to the urban protected sectors. While dual social realities represent the end result of a good part of Latin America, Central America ended up not dual but exclusionary, precisely because the ISI model was weakly advanced, not because of its strength. Finally, the Southern Cone countries ended up not dual but rather universalistic, though they did end up highly stratified in their system of social benefits and protection. Both cases of dualism and universalistic stratification played a central role not simply in protecting their population but also in building democratic and semi-democratic regimes. The political process of incorporation of the popular sectors and the middle classes is to a large extent the social process of incorporation of these sectors into education first and social security and health care later.

Yet a part of the social critique of ISI makes perfect sense. The social states were inefficient, though, for some of them, not necessarily ineffective, in giving basic protection to their citizens. Highly stratified social insurance schemes based on contributions from wages, health care for the middle classes also based on stratified differentiated systems of compulsory and voluntary insurance, and the absence of a strong tax base to support non-contributory health care and education, made for inefficient, deficit-prone and stratified social protection systems. However, the road to reform was not self-evident. Latin America opted both in its new economic model as well as in its new social protection system overwhelmingly for neoliberal solutions. This choice challenges the quality and sustainability of the region's democratic processes in terms of fiscal stress, narrowly understood elite self interest, avoidance of immediate domestic political costs by parties and party leaders, and weakness of a broad-based political movement from below.

Agenda, reality and politics of social reform after the 1980s

Both international and internal forces pushed for social policy reform. In the eyes of those who criticized the old model, the content of such a reform should be able to avoid the problems and inefficiencies of traditional social policies. In order to do so, certain basic features of what the new social policy system should look like slowly took shape in the minds and documents of market-oriented social reformers: targeted social policies, decentralized administration and decision making, private providers both for profit and not for profit, and a shift from supply-based to demand-based social policies. The menu for reforms is today a matter of debate, but it truly represented a new 'Washington Consensus' in the 1980s and especially in the early to late 1990s. Such an agenda was different in its liberal stress and accomplishments, depending on countries' realities and politics as well as policy sector-specific configurations. Since they carry the basic blueprints of broader social state reform, the analysis will concentrate on social security reforms in the 1990s.[5]

A peculiar liberal route of reform: social spending and social security

If the 1980s were characterized by an impasse, a process of restructuring by default, decreasing social spending, adoption of emergency funds strategies and absence of structural social state reform, the 1990s would imply a definite structural shift with an articulated liberal agenda. The 1990s were also times of expanding social spending and of persistent corporatism. On average, for 17 Latin American countries, public social spending went from US$350 per capita to US$550 per capita. ECLAC's analysis shows that the reasons behind this important increase in social spending are not due solely to GDP growth or to an overall expansion of state spending. A large part of the new money for social policy came from an increased fiscal priority of social policies.

What may even be more important, after 1997 when growth slowed down and led to a reduction of total state expenditures, social spending continued to crawl upwards until 1999. The deepening of the regional economic crises brought social spending to a halt in some countries, but continued to move slowly upwards in others. On the whole as a percentage of GDP, the 1990s showed a robust recovery of social spending (see Table 6.3). This also translated into better per capita expenditures, even in amplified form, since 1990–1997 was a period of GDP growth in Latin America.

If in the 1980s, democracy was unable to prevent the fall of social spending, in the 1990s, partially aided by the economy, social spending recovered vigorously. A large part of this increase went to health care and education, allowing for a significant expansion of these services. In the analysis that follows, health care will be considered as a close sibling of social security reform. In many countries, the lion's share in this rapid increase in social spending went precisely to social security, not just to finance old obligations, but also to cover the costs of structural transformations.

The 1990s defined Latin America as a world laboratory on pension reform. After the pioneering reform of 1981 in Chile, little had happened for the rest of the decade besides some relevant parametric reforms in Uruguay and Argentina. Yet in the 1990s, the liberal agenda came into the region with a vengeance. If we count Nicaragua and the Dominican Republic, which have legislated though not yet implemented reform, 11 countries introduced compulsory individual capitalization funds administered by private firms or by private and parastatal entities.[6] There are three central new and powerful

Table 6.3 Social expenditure as a percentage of GDP for Latin American countries

	1990–1992 (%)	*1992–1994 (%)*	*1994–1997 (%)*	*1997–1999 (%)*
Argentina	8.0	9.0	−6.0	4.0
Brazil	−2.0	13.0	−2.0	7.0
Chile	5.0	0.0	6.0	11.0
Colombia	18.0	22.0	33.0	−2.0
Costa Rica	−3.0	5.0	6.0	−1.0
Honduras	8.0	−9.0	−6.0	3.0
Mexico	25.0	9.0	−3.0	7.0
Nicaragua	−2.0	19.0	−13.0	15.0
Panama	5.0	2.0	6.0	−7.0
Paraguay	10.0	13.0	14.0	−7.0
Peru	45.0	21.0	5.0	11.0
Uruguay	12.0	7.0	3.0	9.0
Venezuela	−1.0	−15.0	9.0	4.0
Non-weighted average	16.8	7.4	4.0	4.2

Source: CEPAL, Panorama Social de América Latina, 2000–2001.

actors to be considered when the causes behind social security reform in Latin America in the late 1980s and throughout the 1990s are analysed: local and international financial interests, multilateral agencies, and democratically appointed techno-political elites with a strong representation of economists. In addition, there are traditional actors that operate and interact with these new players: trade unions and beneficiaries from the old programmes of the social state. And there is a stage where these players made their moves: with the exception of Chile (and to a certain extent, Peru) major reforms were carried out in democratizing or democratic and fiscally constrained yet not fiscally bankrupt contexts and with credit lines for certain types of reforms and social policy innovations. Such a stage and such players led to a peculiar mix of reforms. On the one hand, previous privileges were partly maintained, while future beneficiaries entered a more market-based, rather than occupationally- and status-based social security system. Privatization along the lines of liberal regimes combined with the persistence of Bismarckian and many times dualist models were sought as the predominant routes of reform. In cases where structural reforms did not take place, two major strategies were considered with dissimilar results depending on the countries: parametric reforms and homogenization reforms.

Countries that sought liberal lines of reform belong to the three different types of social states that had developed between the 1930s and 1970s. Indeed, what is most surprising in these reform trends is that countries facing widely different challenges in their social protection systems leaned towards the private solution (Mesa-Lago 2004; Muller 2003). Yet it is also true that, with the exception of Chile, the two other universalistic stratified countries and Costa Rica, all under democratic regimes, assumed the mildest forms of privatization of social security. Among the dualist countries, only Mexico moved to a private system and it did so much more radically than the universalistic countries, closing down the old system under the PRI administration. Brazil, under a democracy and with the constitutionalist movement of 1988, did not seriously at any point consider privatization. Peru, under the 'constitutional dictatorship' of Fujimori, and a legacy of a peculiar and truncated case of dualism, moved to the private system but maintained the old system, with minor parametric reforms as a competitor. Yet, by increasing contributions in the old public tier, Peru provided central incentives for people to move to the private option. Furthermore, all new contributors enter directly into the private system. In short, the public system today is being closed down, with less than 5 per cent of all contributors. Finally, those exclusionary countries that moved towards privatized social security systems, Bolivia and El Salvador, did so radically, closing down or phasing out the previous pay-as-you-go systems.

Yet this transformation of social security systems was less liberal than one could assume at first sight. Most countries did not include in these reforms some special privileged groups from the past. Table 6.4, based on Mesa Lago's

Table 6.4 Latin American social protection in comparison

	PAYG tier	*Role of private tier*	*Remaining privileged systems*	*Social assistance*
Uruguay	Remains	Second tier	Armed forces, bank employees, notaries, state university	Yes
Argentina	Remains	Second tier	Elected officials, judiciary, diplomats, provincial civil servants, independent professionals	Yes
Costa Rica	Remains	Second tier	Judiciary and teachers	Yes
Chile	Closed down	Substitutive	Armed forces	Yes
Mexico	Closed down	Substitutive*	Civil servants (federal, state and municipal), oil company workers	No
Colombia	Competes	Competes	Most of the public sector, elected officials, oil company workers, teachers	No
Peru	Competes	Competes	State employees (phasing out)	No
El Salvador	Phased out	Substitutive	Armed forces	No
Bolivia	Closed down	Substitutive	Armed forces go to new system but with privileges	No

Sources: Mesa-Lago 1999, 2004; Muller 2003.
*Protection for Sickness and Death was not privatized.

thorough and keen evaluation of the reforms, combines information of the shift to liberal systems in Latin America and the remaining legacies that each system kept from the times of privilege. Many countries did not also incorporate what is today a standard instrument of liberal regimes for dealing with those that do not reach the qualifications to be granted a pension: a non-contributory means-tested social assistance pension. Some of the countries that adopted liberal models do offer a state guarantee that if the contributor does not reach an adequate contribution and thus pension value, the state will provide the difference up to a basic pension. Yet this is different from social assistance non-contributory pensions, since for eligibility some years of work and contributions are still required. No democracy, with the exception of Costa Rica and Uruguay, dealt with the issue of non-contributory protection as a major issue of the reform, yet all the democratizing or democratic regimes honoured old-time beneficiaries and lobbies, leaving them out of the reform or buying with additional privileges their non-opposition.

Why didn't the liberal reform hailed as a better deal for future beneficiaries include those who control, run and/or have the coercive means of control of the state? The question is of course rhetorical. Under the liberal regimes they would lose part or all of their previous privileges. These privileges include, in most cases, better replacement rates, earlier ages of retirement and broader coverage of personal and family risks that are covered by state resources beyond contributions or by private state-endowed tariffs for services (independent professionals). Another question, which might give us some clue about the politics of social security reform, is why did all countries incorporate, albeit to differing degrees, private capitalization funds, even when they previously operated different social state regimes? Part of the answer rests on the major political force behind these processes of privatization: the multilateral lending agencies.

It is indeed true that the universalistic countries shared a common problem of chronic deficit and an active population-to-pensioners population ratio that made it hard to sustain a pay-as-you-go (PAYG) system into the future. It is also true that this situation had led the universalistic countries to finance social security only partly from contributions. In Argentina and Uruguay, prior to the reform, almost half of all social security revenues came from general taxes, not from contributions. Technically, this allowed for three basic solutions: individual capitalization funds, collective capitalization funds, or a shift to a general tax-based financed social security system. Both the second and third choice allows for intra-generational distribution of rent and risks, the former does not (Huber, 1996). The choice was always for the former. Only the universalistic countries, with the exception of Chile, allowed for a redistributional dimension in the form of PAYG systems. Besides the multilateral lending agencies (MLAs), the reasons for such a choice lays additionally in three major players: domestic and international financial capital, old privileged groups in the previous social security system, and neoclassic trained economists in the Ministries of Finance, Central Banks and Economics.

The influence of the Chilean example and of the World Bank publication *Averting the Old Age Crisis* cannot be sufficiently stated. But there were also concrete pressures from the MLA for countries to push this type of reform. For political elites, this allowed for an easy way out of their social security crises. Loans would help cover the costs of transition, which is simply another way of saying that they would subsidize the phasing out of the old systems, while the promise of better pensions could be made with a time frame for contrasting such claims well ahead of their periods in office (Kay 1999). In Argentina and Uruguay, the increasing organization and actions of the retired people's movement placed mounting fiscal pressure on an already bankrupt system. These constituencies tended to struggle for better pensions within the old stratified social security system. The Left usually aligned themselves with these movements as did the trade unions. Government on the other hand and their political parties increasingly looked at the MLAs both for financial and technical support.

While in most countries either the crises of social security or fiscal and economic crises helped set the stage for reform, the driving force behind such reforms came from domestic economic elites and international financial agencies. The Bank Association of Argentina had made a proposal for privatization as early as 1992, and the IADB and the World Bank had also explicitly pushed for privatization – Chilean style. In the agreement of 1992 with the IMF, the need and commitment of the Argentinean government for privatization was explicitly stated (Muller 2003). In Uruguay, a consultancy from the IADB drafted in 1993 a document indicating that parametric reforms would not be sufficient to deal with the crises of social security. Increasingly, the political arena in Uruguay became divided, with one side composed of the Left, the trade union movement and the retired people's movement defending the old system, and the governments trying to find a way out of the crises (Filgueira and Moraes 1999). In 1995, a team of experts with a US$3.8 million loan promise from the IADB and a team of government experts worked for three months, isolated from the political process, came up with the proposal that was finally approved.

Democracy helped moderate and at the same time keep the privileges of old beneficiaries in the systems of Argentina and Uruguay. The case of Costa Rica shows a different pattern. Even though it needed reform and assistance from the MLAs, Costa Rica also developed wide-ranging negotiations with social and political actors at the same time that it pushed for reforms that would increase coverage. The end result is a liberal reform with egalitarian undertones (Martinez and Mesa-Lago 2003). Of the 19 privileged systems for pensions of the past only two remain: teachers and the judiciary, and the non-contributory pensions remain as a major pillar of the system (Mesa-Lago 2004). In the case of Peru, the need for recognition by the MLAs made Fujimori a staunch defender of structural reforms, where social security was one component. Once again, the economists, the MLAs and the political need of the executive guaranteed a rapid reform – the first to be carried out in Latin America after the Chilean reform. After the coup by Fujimori in 1992, the stage was set for reform. Yet after publishing the draft of the reform law, serious opposition from the beneficiaries of the old models and from the trade unions limited the reform proposal and ended up maintaining the old system parallel to the new one. Yet a number of incentives implied that by 2001 the public system was bankrupt and small. Currently, Peru is steadily moving towards a purely private system (Muller 2003). Bolivia's path to reform was marked by the open opposition of trade unions and left-wing parties and by the support of the business and financial community. The programme of reform was also linked to a broader privatization plan (capitalization plan in the words of the reformers) and once again relied on the financial and technical support of the World Bank and the technical support of Chilean experts. Once again, this reform met with the opposition of trade unions and retired people. In its Capitalization Programme Adjustment Credit, the World Bank made future loans conditional on structural pension reform. In 1997, the law was passed and, despite constitutional complaints by beneficiaries, has so far remained in place (Muller 2003).

In Mexico, the crises of 1994 opened the road for wide-ranging attempts at structural reform. The idea behind pension privatization was not simply to deal with a system that was approaching fiscal problems, but more to open opportunities for investment and capital markets. The proposal by the Zedillo government of 1994 did not face the opposition of the workers' confederation, but did have to confront both opposition parties and the very vocal trade union of the Mexican Institute of Social Security. Yet the support of entrepreneurs that saw their contributions diminished and the support of the MLAs tilted the balance and allowed for the law to be approved. Alongside capitalization, this was an important parametric reform that made eligibility much harder by drastically increasing the needed years of contribution. Finally, it must also be noted that in the case of Mexico, together with this privatization reform, the old emergency fund strategies of the 1980s persisted and enhanced their aims and population coverage. Pronasol would turn into Progresa, and then into the Fox government programme Oportunidades. This programme targets the poor and transfers rents in exchange for school attendance and health check-ups for mothers and children in this population. At present, it is one of the most important social programmes in the country with a coverage of 4.6 million poor households.

Given this brief description of the politics and major features of social security reform in the countries that introduced liberal reforms, some patterns are worth mentioning.

- All reforms counted on the technical and financial support of MLAs. In some countries conditionality was a major instrument pushing reforms.
- All countries faced fiscal or economic crises, some located within the social security system, some beyond it.
- In all countries the business community was either an open supporter or a sympathizer of the reforms. Consistently, in most countries, entrepreneurs' contributions either disappeared or were clearly diminished as a basis for financing social security.
- With the exception of Mexico, where there is not a clear opposition from trade unions, labour opposed these reforms, as did old beneficiaries. Most beneficiaries from the old models were able to see their entitlements honoured and in some cases kept their old systems squarely in place.

- No alternative proposal to the liberal model was either made or gained adequate visibility. The Left, trade unions and beneficiaries defended the old model and pressured for increased resources.
- The non-contributory social assistance pensions were rarely a major issue in the reform proposals. Clearly no party or social movement pushed forward or at least was able to place that area of reform at the centre of the agenda.
- Indeed, the mottos of reform were about fiscal and economic efficiency and equity concerns (understood as getting out what you put in), not about coverage and equality.

Democracy and politics played a definite role in these reforms, but did so in a rather perverse fashion. The old state constituencies of the ISI model were usually able to hang on to a large part of their privileges, especially where they were either a part of the powerful old lobbies or a large electoral constituency, while private workers were moved to the capitalization funds. The absence of representative parties and of ideologies that looked at social policy as a matter of social inclusion rather than poverty alleviation, left the historically and newly excluded sectors either without institutionalized forms of protection or with only very weak forms of protection. On the other hand, the need for democratic governments to balance their budgets and have a positive credit line with MLAs led them to support structural adjustment packages that included the newly privatized creed on social security. By shifting from a PAYG system to private capitalization systems and by getting financial backup in the form of credit to finance the old deficit-prone system, political elites with debt bought time well beyond their times in office (Kay 2000). The fiscal costs of present-day reforms will only be known in the future when countries have to pay their debts with MLAs and when the new capitalization private systems start to pay their pensions. These costs have indeed been pushed well into the future.

Regarding social costs, most models built to predict the effect of these reforms on future social situations of the elderly suggest that both coverage and equality will suffer. A simple table on the percentage of population covered by one- or two-tiered models clearly points to the deficit in coverage that these systems will have to face in the future. Will the state eventually confront this coming crisis with some form of flat-rate non-contributory social assistance pension for all? The fact that today most of these regimes are democracies suggests that this might well be a possibility, since many will reach old age without adequate social security protection. If this happens, then the road may be open for a more egalitarian and inclusionary social security system. Uruguay, Costa Rica and, to a lesser extent, Argentina are best positioned to attempt such a shift. They kept their PAYG systems and have some form of social assistance non-contributory pensions. If such an outcome becomes the first integrated pillar with collective capitalization funds or with flat-rate benefits (be they means-tested or universal) financed

Table 6.5 Coverage before and after structural social security reforms measured by percentage of the population making contributions to social security

	Coverage by actual contributions before reform	*Affiliates considering all tiers after reform (2002)*	*Coverage by actual contribution considering all tiers after reform (2002)*
Chile	64	111	58
Argentina	50	69	24
Uruguay	73	77	60
Costa Rica	53	65	48
Mexico	37	72	30
Colombia	32	59	24
Bolivia	12	23	11
El Salvador	26	40	19
Peru	31	28	11

Source: Mesa-Lago 2004.

out of general taxes, then basic universal income protection might be closer than what the last twenty years of reform might lead us to expect. Oddly, Chile, the most liberal of all regimes, might also be moving in that direction. The fact that only 50 per cent of the population currently contributes to the private system leaves a large number of people without protection at old age. In addition, Chile, Brazil, Uruguay, Argentina and Costa Rica also have some form of rent guarantee for the working population with children (Mexico's Oportunidades also has developed such a system); and Argentina has also developed a form of unemployment insurance with the plan 'Jefes y Jefas'.

Brazil: on the road from dual to basic inclusionary universalism?

The Brazilian dictatorship of 1964 inherited a stratified dual regime based on the ISI model. In contrast to the authoritarian regimes of the Southern Cone, the Brazilian government did not pursue neoliberal reforms, but rather deepened the ISI model. In doing so, and with a certain degree of success, Brazil continued to modernize its social structure, and with it diminish its dual, though by no means stratified, nature. Yet, by 1970 almost 30 per cent of the urban population and most of the rural population had no form of protection. But the military regime, besides pushing the ISI agenda, did two things that would start to redefine the spirit, if not the reality, of its social state. First, between 1966 and 1976 the state unified and standardized a good part of the social security system under the authority of the Ministry of Social Insurance and Social Assistance. While this did not imply a suppression of benefits, it did take the old corporations out of the management of the system. Secondly, it pushed for the expansion of coverage of the non-organized population, especially rural workers, by creating a rural pensions fund (FUNRURAL), with no contributions from rural workers, and by also expanding health care to the previously uninsured urban population and part of the rural sectors (Fleury 2001). Despite the fact that resources were not enough to turn these initiatives immediately into major transformations in terms of coverage, they generated three positive developments: they set the stage for the social policies of democratic governments to come; they fuelled the health movement (*Sanitarista* movement), with doctors and medical personnel classified as civil servants in the new social protection systems; and they later contributed even during the authoritarian period to an important expansion in coverage of the rural population, thus helping the process of politicization and mobilization of the rural base (Santos 1979). Maybe, the most important aspect of FUNRURAL is its departure from the notion of social citizenship based on formal wage employment. In doing so, Brazil made a major leap towards the possibility of a basic inclusionary universalistic system.

The democratic transition of Brazil brought with it an effervescence of organizations, some from the old ISI model, but many from the new constituencies and the historically excluded. The constitution of 1988 would for the first time recognize social rights as inherent citizenship rights – a direct product of a broad alliance between opposition parties and the new social movements that emerged with democratization. Yet, together with it came new democratic pressures from the powerful old beneficiaries of the social security system. While the social security law defined three universal pillars based on health, social insurance and social assistance, a large part of the social protection system was still going to cover the more than one million retirees of the privileged state structures in a differentiated system. Also the very letter of the law recognized two different principles, one of citizenship and the other of insurance. Most of the income transfers remained in the area of social security while social assistance would grow, but at a moderate rate. It was in the area of health care that the most radical transformation took place, creating the Unified Health System (Sistema Unico de Saude) granting free, universal access to all Brazilians. The *Sanitarista* movement started in academia and, with the support of a part of the medical corporation, became the leaders of a wide political movement pushing to turn the letter of the constitution into effective public policy.

Yet Brazil tends to write its laws ahead of its resource base and resource commitments, and thus real access and quality many times suffer the consequences. The popular phrase 'paper citizenship' that many Brazilians use, illustrates the point. Still, coming from a dual and stratified system, Brazil has made important progress towards a more egalitarian basic inclusionary system (Draibe 2002).[7] Only after the old corporations that formed the basis of the ISI model of social protection had been attacked by the military, and only after a new set of parties, one with technocratic social democratic leanings (PMDB) and another with constituencies from the old workers of the ISI model and the historically excluded (PT), did the politics of social protection shift from narrow corporatism – not to liberal privatization, but to embryonic, basic inclusionary universalism.

Social policy and democratization in Latin America

The universalistic, dualist and exclusionary models are no longer adequate to explain current social policy trends. New models have instead emerged in the region. Chile stands alone as a universalistic liberal residual regime that has attempted steps towards a less inegalitarian social protection system. Costa Rica and Brazil seem to be making strides towards a basic protection inclusionary regime with stratification at the top. But these countries are still a long way to go, given previous privileges and the scarcity of quality broad coverage in non-contributory social services and social pensions. After their liberal turn and retaining both the PAYG systems and the social assistance pensions, Uruguay might also move in that direction. Mexico stands at the crossroads with a model that seems to have two purposes: efficiency and fiscal responsibility with limited coverage for the present population, and targeted integrated programmes for the poor, aiming more at breaking the inter-generational transfer of poverty than at combating poverty (Brachet-Márquez 2004). Yet in the case of Mexico, Argentina and Uruguay, there is also the need to address the issue of special privileges from the old systems.

The future of the social state in Latin America will, hopefully, be the history of its future democratic struggles. Never has the region known such a hegemony of democracy and such an expansion of basic political incorporation measured in terms of clean, regular and free elections where all or most of the adult population votes. In this single fact rests, perhaps, the biggest hope for social citizenship in Latin America. Also, the recent backlash to neoliberal reforms and the electoral victory of Left-leaning political parties in large parts of the region, suggest that there is new room for manouvre. But as the last 20 to 30 years of social policy crises and reforms have shown (1970s–1990s), such a future might well be impaired by the constraints posed by global capitalism, the beliefs and interests of its financial gatekeepers, the defence of patrimonial privileges of the middle classes, and by the frailty of Latin America's tax systems and their political basis of support. Yet, there is room for moderate optimism. After almost two decades of the wrong medicine for the old social states, political realities and technical possibilities are coming together and might shape a renewed and better road for the creation of true welfare regimes. There is, of course, the possibility of a distinctly more pessimistic outcome: the increasing disappearance of the state not just as provider of social protections, but its disappearance as a basic provider of public goods in general (security, basic services, justice systems, public infrastructure, and so on). In its place, a sort of neo-feudal order might remerge with market solutions for the rich, retreating but still regressive corporatism for a shrinking middle class, and a large excluded mass of population without any form of basic quality state protection.

Structural conditions and political actors, both national and transnational, will be key in defining the future routes of the Latin American states. For the optimistic road to triumph, it is necessary that elite-based and popular-based political parties reach a historical compromise. Both elite parties and popular-based parties may have to redefine their roles regarding their old and new constituencies. Indeed, one of the major problems facing the political systems of Latin America is that parties leaning left and parties leaning right tend to privilege the representation of the constituencies from the old developmental model rather than the new constituencies that emerged from the breakdown of the Import Substitution Model and the emergence of the new export-oriented model. However, change is not only needed at the domestic level. Change is also needed at the transnational level – a drastic humbling of the MLAs to make them aware of their responsibility and future action after twenty years of misguided developmental projects. Neither social emergency funds, nor fiscally restrictive budgets, nor defensive and regressive corporatism, nor private and market-oriented solutions to social protection have been adequate for the immense challenge of incorporation that lies ahead for the Latin American states and people.

Notes

1. Latin America does not have a welfare state. This assertion is true on two counts. First, no social policy system in Latin America can truly be considered a welfare state system; secondly, if we would consider their social policy systems as something resembling a welfare state, we would have to speak about at least three different types of welfare states. Since I choose not to label them as welfare states, I will refer to the system of social policies and social protection as Social States. Latin America has, indeed, social states, if by such we mean those aspects and actions that the state develops in the form of policies concerned with transfers, subsidies and services that resemble a social safety net and a set of redistributive transfers and services.
2. For an overview of these cases see Filgueira (1998, 2004).
3. Fleury pairs it with Cuba, which is not considered in my analyses.
4. The cases of Colombia, Venezuela and Panama could also be classified under the dual types, yet I lack systematic historical and statistical evidence for a proper analysis. The case of Peru is analyzed in my previous paper as a peculiar form of dualism.
5. For a discussion of the 1980s social policy reforms see my previous paper, the basis of this chapter.
6. Chile did it as we said in 1981, Peru in 1993, Argentina in 1994, Uruguay in 1996, Mexico, El Salvador and Bolivia in 1997 and Costa Rica in 2001.
7. The passing of the Organic Law of Social Assistance and the creation of 'bolsa familia' of a pension for poor families that joins the old age social assistance pensions are also steps in the same direction. The recent reform of social security, limiting and in some cases suppressing the privileges of the old state insurance systems advances towards the same goal.

References

Avelino, G. 1997. 'Democratización y Gasto Social en América Latina, 1980s–1990s', in Andrés Perez Baltodano (ed.), *Globalización, Ciudadanía y política social en America Latina: tensiones y contradicciones*. Caracas: Nueva Sociedad, pp. 97–122.

Brachet-Márquez, V. 2004. 'Nacimiento, auge y transformación del Estado benefactor mexicano (1823–2000)'. UNRISD Project, Social Policy in a Development Context.

CEPAL. 1994. *Panorama Social de América Latina*. Santiago de Chile: CEPAL.

CEPAL. 1995. *Panorama Social de América Latina*. Santiago de Chile: CEPAL.

CEPAL. 2000–2001. *Panorama Social de América Latina*. Santiago de Chile: CEPAL.

CEPAL. 2001–2002. *Panorama Social de América Latina*. Santiago de Chile: CEPAL.

Cominetti, R. 1994. 'Gasto Social y Ajuste Fiscal en América Latina', in Serie *Reformas de Política Pública*, 20. Santiago de Chile: CEPAL.

Deacon, B. 1994. 'Global Institutions, Social Policy and Social Development'. Working paper for the United Nations Summit on Social Development. Leeds, UK: United Nations Research Institute for Social Development.

Draibe, S. M. 2004. 'The Brazilian Developmental Welfare State: Rise Decline and Perspectives.' Working Paper, UNRISD Development Project, Social Policy in a Development Context.

Draibe, S. M. 2002. 'Social policies in the Nineties', in R. Baumann (ed.), *Brazil in the 1990s – An Economy in Transition*. Houndmills, UK: Palgrave Publishers (St Antony's Series).

Esping-Andersen, G. 1990. *The Three Worlds of Welfare Capitalism*. Princeton: Princeton University Press.

Esping-Andersen, G. 1994. 'Welfare States and the Economy', in Smelser and Swedberg (eds), *The Handbook of Economic Sociology*. Princeton: Princeton University Press.

Evans, P. 1979. *Dependent Development: The Alliance of Multinational, State, and Local Capital in Brazil*. Princeton, NJ: Princeton University Press.

Filgueira, C. and F. Filgueira. 2002. 'Models of Welfare and Models of Capitalism: the Limits of Transferability', in Evelyne Huber (ed.), *Welfare Regimes and State Reform in Developing Countries*. University Park, PA: Penn State Press.

Filgueira, F. 1998. 'El nuevo modelo de prestaciones sociales en América Latina: residualismo, eficiencia y ciudadanía estratificada', in Brian Roberts (ed.), *Ciudadanía y Política Sociales*. San José de Costa Rica: FLACSO/SSRC.

Filgueira, F. 1997. 'La nueva arena de las políticas sociales: vectores internacionales y mediación doméstica en la reforma del sector social en América Latina', in Andrés Perez Baltodano (ed.), *Globalización, Ciudadanía y política social en América Latina: tensiones y contradicciones*. Caracas: Nueva Sociedad.

Filgueira, F. and Moraes, J. A. 1999. 'The Political Economy of Institutional Reform in Uruguay: Enabling Conditions, Strategic Devices and Sector Specific Configurations'. *Working Paper Series*. Washington: BID.

Filgueira, F. and Papadópulos, J. 1997. 'Putting Conservatism to Good Use? Neoliberal Transformations in Uruguay', in D. A. Chalmers, C. M. Vilas, K. Hite, S. B. Martin, K. Piester and M. Segarra (eds), *The New Politics of Inequality in Latin America: Rethinking Representation in Latin America*. Oxford: Oxford University Press.

Fleury, S. 1999. 'Reforma del Estado en América Latina. Hacia donde?' *Nueva Sociedad*, 160, 58–80.

Fleury, S. 2001. 'Universal, Dual or Plural? Health Care Models and Issues in Latin America', in C. G. Molina and J. Núñez del Arco (eds), *Health Services in Latin America And Asia*. Washington DC: IADB.

Heredia, B. 2002. *La Economía política de la creación de servicios civiles de carrera: la experiencia de México*. Mexico D.F.: CIDE.
Huber, E. 1994. 'Social Policy in Latin America: Welfare State Aspirations, Crisis and Prospects'. Mimeo. University of North Carolina.
Huber, E. 1996. 'Options for Social Policy in Latin America: Neoliberal vs Social Democratic Models'. In G. Esping-Andersen (ed.), *Welfare States in Transition: National Adaptations in Global Economics*. London: Sage and UNRISD.
Kay, S. 2000. 'The Politics of Postponement: Political Incentives and the Sequencing of Social Security Reforms in Argentina and Uruguay'. Working Paper, Research Department. Federal Research Bank of Atlanta.
Malloy, J. 1985. 'Statecraft and Social Security Policy and Crisis: A Comparison of Latin America and the United States', in C. Mesa-Lago (ed.), *The Crisis of Social Security and Health Care*. Pittsburgh: University of Pittsburgh Press.
Martinez, J. and C. Mesa-Lago. 2003. *Reformas inconclusas: salud y pensiones en Costa Rica*. San José de Costa Rica: Friedrich Ebert Stiftung.
Mesa-Lago, C. 1991. 'Social Security in Latin America', in IADB, *Economic and Social Progress in Latin America*. 1991 Report. Washington: IADB.
Mesa-Lago, C. 1999. *Old-Age Security and Health Care for the Poor in Latin America and the Caribbean*. Conference on Social Protection and Poverty. Washington: IADB.
Mesa-Lago, C. 2004. *Las reformas de pensiones en América Latina y su impacto en los principios de la seguridad social. Serie Financiamiento del desarrollo* no. 144. CEPAL.
Miranda, R. E. 1994. 'Cobertura, Eficiencia y Equidad en el Area de Salud en América Latina. Problemas y Propuestas de Solución'. In *Serie Políticas Sociales*, no. 5. Santiago de Chile: CEPAL.
Muller, K. 2003. *Privatizing Old Age Security: Latin America and Eastern Europe Compared*. Cheltelham: Edwarg Elga Publishers.
Przeworski, A., M. Alvarez, J. A. Cheibub, and F. Limongi. 2000. *Democracy and Development: Political Institutions and Well-Being in the World, 1950–1990*. Cambridge: Cambridge University Press.
Rueschemeyer D., J. D. Stephens and E. H. Stephens. 1992. *Capitalist Development and Democracy*. Chicago: University of Chicago Press.
Santos, W. G. dos. 1979. *Cidadania e justiça*. Rio de Janeiro: Editora Campus.
United Nations Development Programme. 2001. *Human Development Report 2001*. New York: Oxford University Press.
Williamson, J. (ed.). 1990. *Latin American Adjustment: How Much Has Happened?* Washington DC: Institute for International Economics.
World Bank. 1994. *World Development Report, 1994*. Washington DC: World Bank.
Wurgaft, J. 1993. *Fondos de Inversión Social: América Latina*. Santiago de Chile: PREALC/OIT.

7
Democracy and Well-Being in India*

Neera Chandhoke

Introduction

What *is* the relationship between democracy and well-being? Is the relationship an essential one? Or is it random and contingent? There are perhaps no clear answers to these questions for if there was ever a time when theorists assumed that democracy ensures welfare, that time seems to have long passed. After all, authoritarian regimes in, say, Singapore have managed to assure the people some modicum of social and economic well-being. This is something that theorists in the business of conceptualizing democracy have had to confront with some degree of discomfort. It is even more disconcerting to find that *political* democracy can coexist quite easily with high levels of social and economic *inequality* and *repression*.

Take India: on the one hand, the country holds an enviable record in institutionalizing democracy vide constitutionalism, a rule of law, civil and political liberties, a free press, a vibrant civil society and regularly held elections. But even as India satisfies all the conditions that permit it to claim the label of democracy with some justification, a majority of the people continue to suffer from unimaginable hardship, with the most vulnerable at tremendous risk in matters of both lives and livelihoods.

It is true that the decade of the 1990s, which heralded the onset of economic reforms, did see a decline in poverty figures.[1] In 1973–74, 55 per cent of India's population fell below the poverty line; this was reduced to 36 per cent in 1993–94, to further fall to 26 per cent of one billion people in 1999–2000. In absolute terms, the number of poor people declined from 323 million in 1983 to 260 million in 1999–2000 (PC 2002a). The fall in poverty figures has been accompanied by a great deal of improvement in the basic parameters of human development. According to the 2003–2004 Report of the Ministry of Health

*I would like to thank Thomas Pogge, Rohini Nayyar John Harriss, Niraja G. Jayal, Praveen Priyadarshi and Yusuf Bangura for their helpful comments on an earlier draft of this paper. Thanks to Komal and Ravi Ranjan for help with the data.

and Family Welfare, infant mortality has declined significantly, from 110 deaths per 1,000 live births in 1981 to 66 deaths per 1,000 live births in 2001. Correspondingly, life expectancy has increased from 54 years in 1981 to 64.6 years in 2000 (Annual Report 2003–04). According to the 2001 Census, the literacy rate for the population above the age of seven stands at 65.38 per cent, compared to 52.21 per cent in 1991 (Census 2001).

Four factors need to be noted in this connection. Firstly, poverty is unevenly spread across regions, with Uttar Pradesh, Bihar, Madhya Pradesh, West Bengal, and Orissa accounting for 69 per cent of the poor in 1999–2000 (PC 2002b). Equally striking are rural–urban disparities: 75 per cent of the 260 million poor live in rural areas with no access to land, productive resources or employment. Whereas the literacy rate in urban areas is 80.3 per cent, the corresponding literacy rate for rural areas is only 59.4 per cent. Secondly, different states have differing records of human development. Whereas Kerala has a literacy rate of 92 per cent, which is comparable to that of Vietnam, Bihar – a backward state – has a literacy rate of only 47.5 per cent. Thirdly, human development may not be explained by economic development. Although the sex ratio according to the 2001 Census has improved slightly for the country in the decade of the 1990s, and is now 933 women per 1,000 men compared to 927 women per 1,000 men in the 1991 census, the situation has actually worsened in Himachal Pradesh, Gujarat, Haryana, Punjab, and Delhi – states that rank high on the scale of economic development. Fourthly, we find a contradiction in human development indicators within states. Take Himachal Pradesh, at the very time the state has witnessed a dramatic expansion of literacy levels, the sex ratio in the state has declined from 976 females per 1,000 males in 1991 to 970 per 1,000 males in 2001, problematizing thereof the postulated link between literacy and women's status.

In sum, not only do a quarter of the world's poor live in India. The number of illiterates, school drop-outs, people suffering from communicable diseases and infant, child and maternal deaths account for a staggering proportion of the respective world totals. More troublesome is the fact that the country has high numbers of hungry people despite the existence of huge buffer stocks of food. It is clear that political democracy has simply not been accompanied by the institutionalization of economic and social democracy.

Does it then follow that given a choice between *more* democracy and *more* well-being, democrats should opt for more well-being? Arguably democracy is *always* preferable to authoritarianism for one basic reason: the possession and exercise of basic rights *enables* citizens to mobilize and press the state to deliver on the promises embedded in the Constitution and in policy pronouncements. Mobilization results in enhanced participation, and participation *deepens* democracy because it helps realize the prime legitimacy claim of the concept – that of popular sovereignty. In effect, the peculiar virtue of Indian democracy, howsoever formal and minimal our *avatar* of democracy may be, is that it is premised on the recognition of, the grant of, and the codification of basic rights: the right to freedom of expression, of assembly, of association, and more significantly the *root* right to demand other rights. This alone allots to democracy an intrinsic value, which outweighs greater well-being delivered by non-democratic regimes.

The argument in this chapter is that whereas the codification of Directive Principles of State Policy in part four of the Indian Constitution has *motivated* the enactment of social policy, the codification of fundamental rights in part three of the Constitution has *inspired and empowered* collective action for the implementation of the said Principles. In turn, collective action serves to connect entitlements, policy, and well-being via the expansion of the vocabulary and the conceptual repertoire of rights. The basic argument is that whereas the compulsions of political democracy facilitate the enactment of social policies, social democracy can be established only when civil society mobilizes for the effective implementation of these policies. But civil society interventions have their own limits. What these limits are forms the last section of this chapter.

Structures of social opportunities

The juxtaposition of political freedom and social and economic unfreedom in India is cause for some regret. For as far back as the 1920s, the leaders of the freedom movement had realized that political freedom is incomplete unless it is accompanied by social and economic freedom and vice versa. Consequently, they had conceptualized an integrated agenda of political, civil, social, cultural, and economic rights in the 1928 Nehru Constitutional Draft and in the Karachi Resolution on Fundamental Rights adopted by the Indian National Congress in 1931. The Constituent Assembly, however, split this integrated agenda into two autonomous units. Whereas political, civil, and cultural rights in part three of the Constitution are backed by legal sanction, social and economic rights, which are placed in part four under the title of Directive Principles of State Policy, are *not* backed by such sanction. The cost of implementing positive rights was considered far too prohibitive. Consequently, the Directive Principles of State Policy are intended as general guidelines for legislatures and governments even though Dr Ambedkar, the president of the Constituent Assembly, assured members that 'whoever captures power will not be free to do what he likes with it. In the exercise of it, he will have to respect these Instruments of Instructions, which are called Directive Principles. He cannot ignore them. He may not have to answer for their breach in a court of law. But he will certainly have to answer for them before the electorate at election time' (in Rao, 1968: 329).

In pursuance of the general objectives of establishing a social order based on social and economic justice, the Directive Principles urge the state to assure the people of India a cluster of social goods that meet basic needs on the one hand, and ensure a life of dignity for the ordinary individual on the other. Towards this end, the Government of India has enacted several policies,[2] which aim to

Table 7.1 Total Expenditure of central and state governments on social services

Years	*1986–87*	*1995–96*	*2004–05*
As percentage of total expenditure			
Social Services	18.9	21.6	19.3
Education	8.6	10.7	9.4
Health	4.5	4.7	4.4
Others	5.7	6.3	5.4
As percentage of expenditure on social services			
Education	45.6	49.4	48.8
Health	24.1	21.6	23.0
Others	30.3	29.0	28.2

Source: Adapted from 2005 Budget, Chapter 10, http:/indiabudget.nic.in.

(a) satisfy basic needs and generate social protection and (b) engender income and employment. Whereas the first set of policies is geared towards providing *all* people with basic goods essential for leading a life of dignity, other schemes are targeted towards raising the purchasing power of the poorer sections.

Basic needs and social protection

Food security

Since the Bengal famine of the 1940s, the Government of India has concentrated on establishing food security by (i) achieving self-sufficiency in food grains; and (ii) building buffer stocks of food grains, particularly rice and wheat. The government obtains food grains from direct producers through the fixing of procurement prices/minimum support prices, by announcing support prices at sowing time, and by agreeing to buy all the food grains offered for sale at this price.[3] Today, procurement stands at 20 per cent of food grain production. This has resulted in surplus buffer stocks that by 1 January 2004 stood at 24.4 million tonnes.

However, despite the fact that food grain production went up from 175 million tonnes in the 1980s to 206 million tonnes in the 1990s, per capita availability of food grains has declined, mainly because the poor lack purchasing power. After the food shortages of the 1960s the government had instituted a public distribution system (PDS), which supplied food grains, edible oil, and kerosene at subsidized prices to households. In time, it was found that the PDS benefited the non-poor more than the poor and that it was biased towards urban areas. Therefore, it was converted into a targeted public distribution system in 1997. Households below the poverty line (BPL) are able to buy 20 kilograms of subsidized food grains per month through a network of 400,000 Fair Price Shops. The identification of beneficiaries is based on state-wide poverty estimates of the Planning Commission. According to the Ministry of Food and Civil Supplies, against a total ceiling of 6.52 crore[4] BPL families in the country as per poverty estimates of the Planning Commission for 1993–94, state governments have issued more than 8 crore ration cards per BPL family. Correspondingly, the food subsidy has jumped from Rs 2,450 crore in 1990–91 to Rs 25,160 crore in 2003–04 (The Hindu 2004a).

The PDS is supplemented by other nutrition-related schemes. Under the Antodya Anna Yojana, 25 kg of food grains is provided to destitutes at low rates. This covers more than 1.5 crores of citizens. The Annapurna Scheme introduced in April 2000 provides free food grains to senior citizens below the poverty line. And food-for-work programmes aim to provide food security.

The country has not been able, however, to realize food security for poor households. For one, it was found that large amounts of food grains under PDS are diverted to the market. The diversion rate is 64 per cent in Bihar and Assam, 100 per cent in Nagaland and 69 per cent in Punjab. Secondly, most states do not have either funds or adequate infrastructure to deliver food grains to BPL families. Thirdly, the off-take from the central pool by state governments is much lower than allotted quotas. Fourthly, the poor do not have the resources to buy their quota of food grains. Fifthly, the quality of food grains is abysmal, a fact that is exacerbated by poor storage conditions. Above all, weak monitoring, lack of transparency and accountability, and sale of food grains at higher prices than those fixed by the government, have combined to create an unprecedented crisis of food security (PC 2000).

Nutritional security

The scheme of providing midday meals for primary schoolchildren is meant to ensure nutritional security. The government of Tamil Nadu – where the scheme had been originally introduced in 1925 – had adopted the programme in 1957. In 1995, the Ministry of Human Resources conceptualized a fully funded and centrally sponsored scheme of midday meals. The objective of the programme is to supplement the nutrition of primary school-going children and through this to improve school enrolment, retention, and attendance. Six states began to provide cooked meals to schoolchildren and in 2001 a Supreme Court Order made it obligatory for each government, and government-funded school to provide cooked food to primary schoolchildren. Some states have extended the scheme to class X children. By 2001, 105.1 million children were being served midday meals in 576 districts.

Evaluations of the scheme have found that the quality of food served to the children is poor, that proper data on enrolments on the basis of which food grains are made available is not forthcoming, that transport to transfer food grains to states is not at hand, and that in some states lack of funds prevent meaningful implementation of the scheme. But on the whole, the programme has resulted in increased recruitment of schoolchildren and ensured attendance. The Integrated Child Development Services provides food supplements to pre-school children, pregnant women, and lactating mothers in the country. However, the reported coverage is only between 15 to 20 per cent of the targeted population. There has been no significant decline in maternal under-nutrition and half of the children below the age of five years continue to be severely malnourished.

Education

Article 45 of the Indian Constitution stipulates that the state shall endeavour to provide within a period of ten years free and compulsory education for children until age 14.[5] The National Policy of Education 1986, which was revised in 1992, provided momentum to the task and has been attended by some success. The Census of India defines literacy rates as the proportion of literates to the total population above the age of seven years. By these standards, at independence, literacy stood at merely 18.3 per cent for the age group five years and above. Literacy rose to 43.6 per cent in 1981, to 52.21 per cent in 1991, to rise further to 65.4 per cent in 2001. From 1991 to 2000, illiteracy declined by 32 million in absolute terms. Of this figure, 75.85 per cent of males are literate and 54.16 per cent of women are literate. Significantly, in rural areas the literacy rate increased from 36 per cent in 1981 to 59 per cent in 2001. This is despite the fact that public spending on education has not increased appreciably since 1986 (see Table 7.1).

The goal of universalizing elementary education has been achieved through the establishment of government or government-aided primary schools. By 1993, 94 per cent of the total rural population was served by primary schools; and from 1950 to 1990 the number of schools increased by more than three times. The number of upper primary schools increased 15 times in the same period. This expansion of the school system was accompanied by the provision of midday meals, free uniforms, textbooks, and scholarships in order to increase recruitment and prevent drop-outs.

The elementary educational system has been strengthened from time to time by the launch of special campaigns such as 'Operation Blackboard' to upgrade infrastructure, train teachers, and improve the environment. In 2000–01 the Government of India launched the Sarva Shiksha Abihiyan or the 'movement for education for all' to provide elementary education to children in the age group 6–14, in partnership with state governments, local governments and communities. The school system has been decentralized to enable community participation. As reports show, this has led to improved performances, motivated community-owned education, and bridged gender and social disparities to some extent. The District Elementary Education Plan, which is supported by international agencies, was launched in 1994. The plan is based on assessments of specific needs of each habitat, particularly in the field of Early Child Care and Education (ECCE).

From 1986 onwards, the Government of India initiated several schemes to bring more than half the children in the age group 6–14 who are outside the school system within the ambit of education. This has been done by setting up a parallel stream of non-formal education, through opening literacy classes, and through establishing World Bank-sponsored District Primary Education Programmes (DPEP). Under the DPEP, 21,000 new alternative schools have been established and 10,000 ECCE clusters have been set up. However, initiatives to introduce parallel streams of cheap, but low-quality education for poor children have come under considerable fire from educationists and activists. For instead of strengthening existing government and government-aided school systems, these schemes provide for contracting of often under-qualified youths at low salaries to teach children for nine months, thus compromising the quality of education itself.

Adults above the age group of 15–35 are provided functional literacy through the National Literacy Mission, which was established in May 1988 in 561 districts and administered by local communities and self-government bodies. The purpose is to achieve literacy for 75 per cent of the population by 2005, which, it is expected, will lead to increased productivity, improvement in health care, and the betterment of social life. More importantly, elementary education is compulsory in 14 states and four Union Territories. In 2001, the Central government passed the 93rd Constitutional Amendment Bill, subsequently adopted as the 86th Constitutional Amendment Bill, which grants the fundamental right to free and compulsory education.

The right to education, however, makes little sense unless the school system, characterized as it is by high rates of drop-outs, teacher absenteeism, low levels of learning, low participation, particularly among girls, and lack of infrastructure and qualitative aspects of education such as teacher training, educational curricula, equipments, and training material, is restructured. It has been estimated that more children drop out of school for these reasons rather than those of poverty. Families would rather incur debt and send their children to expensive private schools.

Considering that of 200 million children in the age group 6–14 years, 42 million children *do not* attend school, the National Human Development Report 2001 concluded that 'India's educational development is a mixed bag of remarkable successes and glaring gaps. In the post-independence period, the pace of educational development was unprecedented by any standards. At the same time policy and public intervention in the provision of educational services was not adequately focused, or even misplaced, to the extent that even after 50 years of planned effort in the sector, nearly one-third of the population or close to 300 million people in the age group 7 years and above are illiterate' (Planning Commission 2002a: 51). Literacy rates have improved in Rajasthan, Orissa, and Madhya Pradesh in the 1990s, and Himachal Pradesh is a success story because by the end of the 1990s, 98 per cent of children were going to school. But literacy rates continue to be modest in Uttar Pradesh and Bihar.

Health

In 1946, on the eve of independence, the Bhore Committee had suggested a detailed and comprehensive plan for health security. If the report had been implemented effectively, the private sector in health would have been rendered irrelevant, and the level of health services in the country would have reached three-fifths that of Britain during the Second World War. The most significant suggestion of the Bhore committee was that the focus of health policy should be preventive rather than curative through the provision of nutrition, safe drinking water, sanitation, hygiene, education, the institutionalization of an extensive public health system, such as immunization programmes and clinics, and community health centres staffed by trained medical personnel and para-health workers. All this requires a great deal of public investment, yet the Government of India invests only 0.9 per cent of GDP on health.

In fact, there is an odd schism between financial outlays and the provisions of a health system. The public health system consists of a three-tiered layer of primary health centres, sub-centres, and community centres providing multi-functional outpatient facilities. The number of centres is in direct proportion to the number of people being served, with special provisions being made for hill and tribal areas. The Government has also initiated and implemented several disease-control programmes and immunization schemes, some of which have shown remarkable successes. Under the Central Government Health Scheme, health care is provided to government employees, pensioners, and public officials living in big cities. The global debate on health strategy, the signing of the Alma Ata declaration of 'Health for All' by 2000, and the recommendations of various specialized bodies, have resulted in the enunciation of a comprehensive, integrated, approach to health care in the form of the National Health Policy in 1983. The 2002 National Health Policy aims to achieve basic standards of good health among the population through national public health programmes, the extension of infrastructure, medical education, research, enhanced role of stakeholders such as NGOs, enforcement of quality standards in food and drugs, and women's health. It is also not as if India has made no progress in the past several decades in the field of health. There have been no reported cases of smallpox since 1985, of guinea worm disease since 1996; and of plague since 1969. Cholera epidemics and related deaths have become more infrequent. In 1950, cholera cases numbered 1,76,307 with 86,997 deaths, by 2001 the total reported cases of cholera were 5,000 (Deodhar 2001). The incidence of measles, polio, whooping cough, and tetanus is lower than before. And the proportion of children without immunization declined from 30 to 14 per cent between 1992/93 and 1998/9.

Yet, the presence of both communicable and non-communicable diseases casts a heavy miasma over every prospect of well-being. Infant mortality rates still have to be reduced to less than 60 per 1,000 live births, which was the expressed goal of the 1983 health policy. Maternal mortality rates continue to be 540 per 100,000 live births annually (UNDP 2004). The main causes of mortality in the age group 0–5 are common diseases, which can be easily avoided, such as lower respiratory tract infection, diarrhoeal diseases, perinatal causes and vaccine preventable diseases. Communicable diseases like viral encephalitis, meningococcal meningitis, rabies kala azhar, dengue fever and tuberculosis have escaped control. Epidemics of food poisoning, infectious hepatitis, typhoid fever, measles, tetanus, and pneumonia regularly appear to bedevil the health scenario. It is estimated that about 15 million people suffer from tuberculosis, and that 2.2 million are added to this figure every year (Misra *et al.* 2003). The emergence of AIDS has begun to affect national and regional epidemiological profiles and priorities, and leprosy cases constitute a major part of the world's cases of leprosy.

The picture is not even across the country. For instance, Kerala has made progress on all health indicators, whereas Bihar, Uttar Pradesh, and parts of Madhya Pradesh and Rajasthan show tremendous vulnerability on this front. The rural sector is most vulnerable to malnourishment and disease. What is also worrying is the massive social inequity between income groups across all regions of the country. A study has shown that the richest 20 per cent enjoy three times their share of the public subsidy for health compared to the poorest quintile, and that 20 per cent of the population which belongs to the poorest section of society has more than double the mortality rates, fertility rates and levels of under-nutrition of the richest 20 per cent of the population (Misra *et al.* 2003).

The malaise of the health scene in India is conceivably due to the interaction of a number of factors. Firstly, there has been no legislation to make health a right. Secondly, the health system is heavily bureaucratized and marked by erosion, corruption, inadequate infrastructure, and the non-availability of medicines. Thirdly, whereas the Government of India has concentrated massive resources in specific disease eradication campaigns, such as the massive pulse polio immunization campaign initiated in 1995, this has been at the cost of other programmes that aim to annihilate common ailments such as diarrhoea and dysentery. Even though dysentery and diarrhoea along with acute respiratory infections leading to pneumonia happen to be the main killers of children below the age of five, these are not even seen as diseases by the government. Fourthly, universal programmes of immunization have failed to establish efficient epidemiological surveillance services for controllable diseases. And fifthly, health policy in India has concentrated more on curative measures than on preventive measures. It is, therefore, not surprising that with the onset of liberalization in the 1990s, the profit-driven and curative-centred private sector in health has expanded enormously, putting effective health care outside the reach of many citizens.

Above all, public investment and expenditure in health has declined. From the Fourth Five Year Plan onwards, budgetary provisions for health shrank drastically, reaching a new low in the first decade of the twenty-first century though the WHO has recommended that a minimum of 5 per cent of GDP should be allotted to health care. India has one of the lowest health budgets in the world, and plan allocation for the year 2003–04 has been pegged at 2002–03 levels, that is Rs 1,500 crore, leading to reduced allocations for various priority programmes (Ministry of Health and Family Welfare Annual Report 2003–04: 1). Health is a state issue and states are expected to contribute to a major part of the finances allotted to the sector, but the budgetary allocation of state governments has shown a consistent decline over the years. The general neglect of preventive health care and the increasing push towards the involvement of the private sector in the delivery of health services highlights a dramatic reduction in the level of public commitment to health.

Social protection

The *National Social Assistance Programme* launched in 1995 has three components: the National Old Age Pension Scheme, the National Family Benefit Scheme (NFBS), and the Janani Suraksha Yojana (JSY). The schemes are sponsored by the central government in order to ensure minimum standards of social assistance over and above the assistance provided by state governments. The National Old Age Pension Scheme is a tax-financed scheme that provides floor-level income assistance of Rs 75 per month to very poor persons over 65 years of age. The NFBS gives Rs 10,000 to BPL families in event of the death of the breadwinner, and JSY is a maternity benefit scheme, which benefits women from BPL familes for the first two live births. The Janshree Bima Yojana, which has been launched through state insurance companies, is a group insurance scheme that does not require premiums to be paid by workers. It covers contingencies in cases of natural/accidental deaths and partial or total permanent disability due to accident for people below the poverty line. The Krishi Shramik Samajak Suraksha Yojana 2001, which is a group insurance scheme for agricultural landless labour, provides for pension, insurance and money-back schemes. The beneficiaries contribute Rs 1 per day and the government contributes Rs 2 per day to the scheme. In addition, public initiatives launched by, for instance the Self-Employed Women's Association (SEWA) provides social security through the setting up of cooperatives.

The finance minister has announced a new universal health insurance scheme for the poor, a special group insurance scheme at a low premium, and the setting up of a Rural Health Mission, in the 2005 budget. The limited coverage of the clearly insufficient social security programme is largely due to resource constraints. For instance, against a target of 8.71 million beneficiaries for old age pensions in 1999–2000, only five million people were provided assistance from central funds (PC 2002b). On the whole, the majority of the working people have little or no social protection.

The *Employees Provident Fund Scheme* is a publicly managed, contributory, and mandatory scheme to ensure that employed workers save some percentage of their wages. But compliance mechanisms are ineffective and the accounting methods are unreliable. In 2004, the Unorganized Sector Workers Social Security Scheme, which was launched on a pilot basis in 50 districts, provides old age pension, personal accident insurance, and medical insurance for workers drawing not more than Rs 6,500 per month. Workers give a single contribution of Rs 50 per month with the government's contribution assessed on a relative basis. The scheme is implemented through the Employees Provident Fund Organization.

In addition, the government has set up five welfare funds for specific sectors of unorganized workers. Resources are raised outside the employer–employee relationship on a non-contributory basis, and the delivery of welfare services does not have any link to individual contributions. The cess collected from the employers and manufacturers of particular commodities go towards these funds. Some state governments such as West Bengal have introduced state-assisted provident funds for unorganized workers. However, the coverage under all these programmes is a little more than 10 million out of 370 million workers in the unorganized sector.

Poverty alleviation

Income generation schemes

Since the 1970s, the Government of India has enacted several anti-poverty programmes to provide self-employment to BPL families through the extension of bank credit and subsidies. On 1 April 1999, a self-employment programme called the Swaranjayanti Gram Swarozgar Yojana (SGSY), or the rural self-employment plan, was merged with the existing Integrated Rural Development Programme [IRDP] and several sub-schemes. The programme, which is credit-driven, encourages the development of micro-enterprises through the formation of self-help groups, the extension of credit and subsidies to groups, capacity building, selection of activity clusters, infrastructural development, and access to technology and markets. The Tenth Plan seeks to enhance SGSY by focussing on social mobilization and group formation in the first phase, thrift and credit augmented by a revolving fund in the second phase, and access to credit from micro-finance institutions in the third phase. The plan stipulates that 50 per cent of self-help groups must be formed exclusively by women, and that 50 per cent of the benefits should flow to the Scheduled Castes/Tribes. Some provision has been made for the disabled (PC 2002b).

However, the Tenth Plan estimates that the implementation of SGSY between 1999 and 2002 has been hampered because intermediate organizations lack the requisite skills to mobilize people into self-help groups, and because they have failed to establish linkages with NGOs that could have facilitated this process. This resulted in lower releases of funds from the central government as well as lower mobilization of credit. Consequently, only one-third of the target of credit allocation could be achieved, and the coverage was considerably lower than the 2.2 million who benefited under IRDP during the Eighth Plan period every year.

Wage generation schemes

In December 2004, the long-awaited National Rural Employment Guarantee Bill was introduced in the lower house of Parliament. By this Act, India joins 30 countries that grant the constitutional right to work to their citizens. However, it is important to note that the Act does not grant a *generic* right to work because it promises only 100 days of employment per year to adult members of poor rural households. If an eligible applicant is not provided employment within 15 days of receipt of his application, s/he shall be entitled to a daily unemployment allowance, the rate of which shall be specified by the state government. The wage rates will be fixed by the Central Government. The Act further provides for the establishment of a Central Employment Guarantee Council at the Central Government level, and State Employment Guarantee Councils in states where the legislation is applicable. The councils will be responsible for the review, the monitoring, and the effective implementation of the scheme. A National Employment Guarantee Fund at the Central level and a State Employment Guarantee Fund at the State level will take care of the funds required for the scheme. In the 2005 budget speech, the Finance Minister announced that food-for-work programmes, which have been introduced in 150 districts, will be converted into the National Rural Employment Guarantee Scheme. He also announced a substantial increase in allocations for the programme, from Rs 4,020 crores in the current year to Rs 11,000 crores alongside promises of additional funds.

The Act is significant since rural unemployment has increased over the decade of the 1990s. According to the National Sample Survey data 1999–2000, unemployment rates are as high as 7.2 per cent for rural males in the workforce and 7 per cent for rural women (Vijay Shankar and Reddy 2004). Since the unemployed constitute the single largest group among the rural poor, there is urgent need that they be assured work. Employment will be offered on asset-enhancing works, such as public works, afforestation, irrigation facilities, ponds, road connectivity, wasteland development, and regeneration of degraded lands. This is important because although almost 79 per cent of agricultural labour owns land, environmental degradation has rendered landholdings unproductive, forcing thereby thousands of poor families to seek work. Assured work on asset-creating public works will lead to infrastructural development as well as to greater productivity, because land will be now protected against drought and floods. This will necessarily result in an improvement of both labour absorbing capacities of small farms and profitability of farming activities. Peasants will consequently move out of state-sponsored employment schemes and back to their own land.

The development of infrastructure and enhanced productivity will not only lead to a reduction in rural poverty, but also lessen migration to other parts of the country, both rural and urban. More importantly, wages will serve to generate demand for rural goods and services, even as the construction of roads will facilitate the reach of rural markets benefiting thus the rural economy. The development of infrastructure may well boost private investment, and generate secondary employment. Finally, assured employment at minimum wages will ensure that people have the opportunity to participate in other social sector programmes, such as the provision of midday meals in schools. And if people are encouraged to participate in the selection of sites for work, in the making of cost estimates, and in the fixing of wages, this will result in an enhancement of popular participation.

The selective initiation of the Act in 330 districts ensures that the cost of guaranteeing employment will not be more than 2 per cent of the GDP. The size of investment will inevitably fall in time because the need of families to work outside their land will decline over the years. Correspondingly, the programme by assuring Rs 6,000 per year to each rural household will result in 75 per cent of the rural poor rising above the poverty line (*The Hindu* 2004b).

The introduction of the Act followed a period of sustained campaign by several civil society groups. Yet social activists are not happy with the Act for several reasons: it will be introduced only in a few districts; it will replace food-for-work schemes; and it will be confined to only one adult member of BPL households. Moreover, the guarantee of employment will be expanded to other parts of the country only if the experiment proves successful in 150 districts.

Earlier employment schemes – the Jawahar Rojgar Yojana, the National Rural Employment Programme, the Rural Landless Employment Guarantee Scheme, and the Employment Assurance Scheme – which were merged into a single wage payment scheme, the Sampoorna Gramin Rozgar Yojana in 2001 – and the 1979 Employment Guarantee Scheme for rural areas and C class municipal councils in Maharashtra have produced mixed results. However, unorganized casual labour has unionized to demand stipulated minimum wages and better implementation of projects. In addition, although the scheme may not have reduced poverty, it has worked well for the poorest of the poor, for only this section of the population opts for often back-breaking work on asset-creating jobs. Furthermore, some rural infrastructure has been created and village self-government bodies that administer these schemes have been strengthened. The right to work has also been put on the political agenda.

On the other hand, these programmes have not generated adequate employment for several reasons: indiscriminate universalization of the programme led to the neglect of poor areas; benefits were cornered by the non-poor; allocations were based on fixed criteria that did not distinguish between needs; and resources were spread thinly over the country. Even in poorer regions, employment was provided for only 31 days, works were not labour-intensive, and implementation was marked by massive corruption in the form of fictitious muster rolls and bogus employment records. A review of earlier wage employment schemes in the Ninth Plan showed a considerable reduction of both allocation and employment generation. Allocations for wage employment declined in the Ninth Plan to only 88 per cent of what they were in the Eighth Plan (PC 2002b). And only 15 per cent of the people who sought work in a village panchayat were actually given employment under JRY (Tenth Plan 2002: 296). These problems were compounded by rising costs of creating jobs. In 1999, when the JRY was revamped as the Jawahar Gram Samridhi Yojana, the programme was mainly meant to create rural infrastructure, with employment generation being a secondary objective. Above all, village panchayats, which administered the scheme, received inadequate funds. Consequently, the schemes generated lower mandays of employment each successive year. Unemployment continues to stalk the lives of the rural poor. Therefore, unless serious attempts are made to correct existing flaws, the current avatar of an employment guarantee scheme may not be effective.

Assessing social policy

Although the Government of India has enacted a number of policies that target in particular the rural poor, it is precisely this section of the population that remains vulnerable to all kinds of insecurities. Four reasons can be cited for the failure of the Indian state to implement social goals laid down in part four of the Constitution. Firstly, there are huge gaps between policy and implementation, between policy and financial outlays, and between policy and the needs of the people. Secondly, the enactment of social policy has been somewhat incoherent, characterized as it is by overlaps between policies, periodic recasting of existing policies in new forms, and, in particular, the employment of these measures as political tools that address constituencies and forge vote banks. Thirdly, policies meant for the poor have been indiscriminately generalized, benefited often the non-poor, and been attended by mismanagement, corruption, and tardy implementation. Fourthly, though the provision of social goods falls more or less within the provenance of state governments, the Planning Commission through the Five Year Plans determines strategy, priority, and allocation of resources. However, since the planning process 'was initiated without altering initial structural inequities, the distribution of benefits of economic growth has not been egalitarian' (Prabhu and Sudarshan 2002: 4–5).

An ex-civil servant who is extensively involved in monitoring government-sponsored social programmes is more blunt on this front: 'even as the new development state in India has steadily amassed functions, and vastly extended financial powers often in the name of the poor, its capacity to deliver has declined over the years. This is due to rising indiscipline and a growing belief, widely shared among the political and bureaucratic elite, that the state is an arena where public office is to be used for private ends' (Saxena 2004: 49). The definitive statement on the incapacity of the Indian state to deliver social goods effectively has been made by Drèze and Sen. They conclude that despite some notable successes, India's overall success in promoting social opportunities has been quite limited. The intensities of many basic deprivations have been considerably reduced, but there is nevertheless a long way to go in ensuring anything like acceptable living conditions for all citizens (Drèze and Sen 2002).

This conclusion is supported by the findings of the 2004 ILO report on 'Economic Security for a Better World'. The report commends India for maintaining high growth in the past two decades, but also comments adversely on the country's record of social security. India is ranked 74 out of 90 countries on the economic security index constructed by the ILO; the index is constructed on seven indicators – income, work, representation, job, employment protection, labour market, and skill reproduction. On income security India ranks 94th out of 96 countries, only above Congo and Sierra Leone, both with a recent record of civil war. The report concludes that anti-poverty programmes have failed to reach the poor, that the poor are often unaware of the benefits they are eligible for, and that they are less likely to receive benefits than the non-poor. More importantly, the take-up rate of social assistance programmes is very low (ILO 2004). These findings beg the following question: Why has economic growth *not* been accompanied by the distribution of benefits especially to the poor?

Structural barriers to well-being

Land ownership

Axiomatically, social policy does not function in a vacuum; it is constrained or enabled by the distribution of resources and the structure of the labour market. Ownership of resources/income dictates access to social opportunities. To put it sharply, in a highly iniquitous society like India, social policy can prove effective only if it addresses the structural roots of inequality. For instance, the prevalence of deep poverty in the rural areas, where today around 60 per cent of the population lives and works, requires at the very least a radical restructuring of land relations. However, the conceptualization and administration of land reforms in India have suffered from serious shortcomings. Though intermediaries were abolished and land was transferred to the tenants vide a series of legislations, not only were land reforms confined to 40 per cent of the cultivated area, they suffered both from flawed conceptualization and sluggish and ineffective implementation. Administered by often-recalcitrant bureaucrats, land reforms failed to transfer land to the tiller, correct inbalances in the structure of land relations, provide security to tenants, and secure implementation of land ceiling laws. More significantly, land reforms slowed down because the issue of compensation to erstwhile landowners was bogged down in massive litigation.

By the 1990s, land reform was set on the backburner, for the subdivision and fragmentation of land weakened the case for a lowering of the land ceiling.

This was despite the fact that inadequate tenancy reforms had resulted in concealed tenancy, thereby denying to the tenants security of tenure and rent regulation. Further massive alienation of land from tribal communities that live off the produce of the land reduced many to penury. The decade also heralded the liberalization of land laws to further corporate farming, in sharp contrast to the post-independence period when considerations of equity and social justice governed land reforms. Therefore, whereas by the end of the Eighth Five Year Plan (1992–1997) 52 lakh acres out of a ceiling surplus of 75 lakh acres were distributed among 5.5 million beneficiaries, the position remained unchanged at the end of the Ninth Five Year Plan 1997–2002 (PC 2002b). The net result is that in major parts of the country the poorest of the poor, mainly belonging to the Scheduled Castes, have been unable to access land, productive assets, and skills.

Poverty

From 1950 to 1970 poverty figures fluctuated between 45 and 60 per cent of the population. Poverty began to decline from the 1970s onwards, partly because of economic growth in primary and tertiary sectors and mainly because of the initiation of the green revolution, which raised productivity (Dyson *et al.* 2004).[6] Yet by 2000, three-quarters of the rural poor were unable to access the minimal consumption basket that defines the poverty line. What is more disquieting are regional inbalances when it comes to poverty: in Madhya Pradesh and Orissa the numbers of those in absolute poverty went up between 1993 and 2000, although poverty fell somewhat in other states in the same period. Secondly, states containing larger proportions of the poor are also marked by low human development indicators, slower economic growth and higher population growth. Thirdly, poverty is much higher among the landless and among the marginal farmers whose small landholdings have been rendered unproductive because of environmental degradation and the vagaries of the monsoon. Above all, half of India's 206 million Scheduled Castes/Tribes belong to the category of the absolute poor (NCAER 1996), with no access to employment and minimum wages because they lack educational skills. In sum, the ability of social policy to address deep problems of poverty is limited because it has *not* addressed the issue of redistribution.

Labour markets

Considering that the contribution of agriculture to GDP had fallen from 50 per cent to 25 per cent by the beginning of this decade, the labour market in rural areas is marked by near zero elasticity of employment. Even if agricultural productivity rises dramatically in the next ten years it will not be able to absorb much rural labour. That is why towns and cities witness streams of migrants in search of gainful employment. Here they join thousands of workers who are already employed as casual, contract, and sub-contract labour in the informal economy. 90 to 93 per cent of the working population of about 39.7 crores is in the unorganized sector: 62 per cent of unorganized workers are in agriculture, 11 per cent in industry and 27 per cent in the service sector. Of the 10 per cent of workers employed in the formal sector, 6 per cent have jobs in the public sector. But even here the onset of economic reforms has led to a decline in employment opportunities.

Patterns of unemployment

Even as employment experienced a steady growth of around 2 per cent per annum from 1960 to 1990, and GDP grew by about 3.5 per cent, the labour force grew at the rate of 2.5 per cent per annum. Consequently the magnitude of unemployment increased from 6.5 million in 1961 to 16 million in 1990, and the rate of unemployment rose from 3.6 per cent to around 5 per cent of the labour force over the same period. In the first two years of the decade of the 1990s, the rate of employment growth declined to 1.5 per cent to further fall to 1.07 per cent in the period 1993–2000, with the informal sector absorbing much of the workforce (Dyson *et al.* 2004). The growth rate of rural employment, however, was only 0.5 per cent during the same period. Although the growth of GDP accelerated to 6.5 per cent by the end of the 1990s from 3.4 per cent in 1990–92, the increase failed to generate employment (Papola and Sharma 2004). This is mainly due to the low capacity of agriculture to absorb the workforce and job losses in the public sector. The Tenth Five Year Plan intends to introduce ten million jobs by the end of 2007. However, a study undertaken by the Planning Commission concludes that unemployment will grow from 9.2 per cent at the beginning of the Plan to 11 per cent of the total workforce by the end of the Plan. In effect, 45 million people are going to be unemployed on the assumption of a 6.5 per cent average GDP growth rate in the rest of the plan period (The Economic Times 2004). The economy is doing well, but this is not matched by commensurate growth in economic opportunities, leading to the phenomenon of jobless growth.

Historical evidence suggests that structural barriers to welfarism *can* be neutralized if political agents, such as parties and trade unions, mobilize citizens on social issues. Trade unions have, however, failed to address problems of poverty and ill-being because they represent a bare 7–10 per cent of workers in the organized sector, and lend themselves to the charge of being a labour aristocracy. More importantly, major unions are affiliated to political parties and are bound by the respective mandates of parties.

In 1999, issues of governance came onto political agendas when the Bharatiya Janata Party-led National Democratic Alliance drafted a 'National Agenda of Governance' to guide policies. In the State Assembly elections of December 2003 and the General Elections of 2004 'governance' was catapulted into the political limelight. But governance was reduced to the slogan of 'roads, electricity, and water', delivery of services and construction of infrastructure, leaving poverty, ill-health, illiteracy, and unemployment intact.

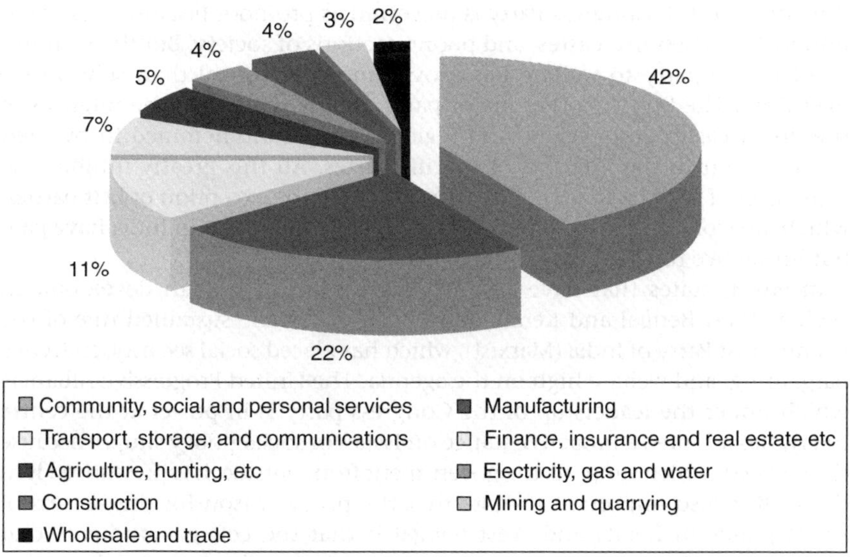

Figure 7.1 Employment by sector, 2005

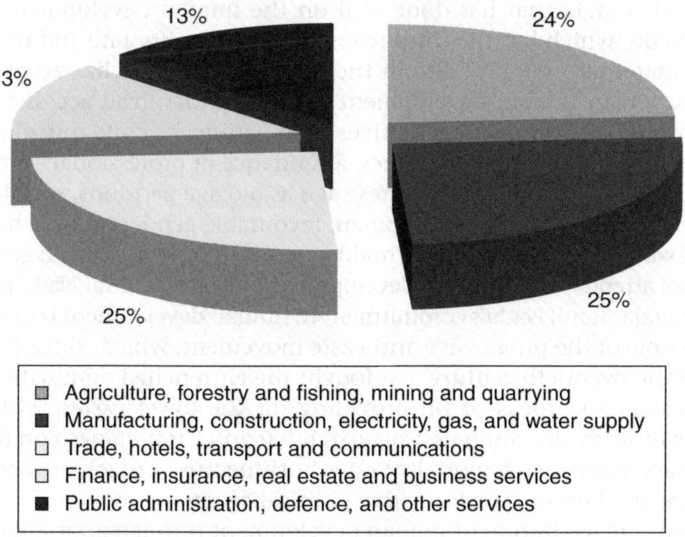

Figure 7.2 Sector-wise contribution to GDP, 2005
Source: adapted from Government of India. Economic Survey of India 2004–05
Political Actors and Well-being.

It is true that the Congress Party is perceived as pro-poor because it caters to minorities, scheduled castes, and poorer sections of society. But the commitment of the party to welfare has proved more rhetorical than substantive over time. The BJP, the other major party, clearly represents the interests of the upper castes and classes. And regional parties are hemmed in by their commitment to the interests of specific castes. All this greatly inhibits the legislation of social welfare policies. In sum, with the exception of Left parties, which are working class and peasant based, political parties in India have paid but lip service to well-being.

In effect, states that have attained high levels of human development, such as West Bengal and Kerala, have been under the sustained rule of the Communist Party of India (Marxist), which has placed social security, collective bargaining, and welfare high on the agenda. The United Progressive Alliance, which under the leadership of the Congress party is in power at the centre today, has adopted a proactive stance on issues of social policy simply because the CPI (M), which supports the government from outside, has pressurized it to do so. It is also important to note that the prime reason for the success of social policy in Kerala and West Bengal is that the Left governments that have governed those states for a long period have effectively implemented land reforms. Contrast this with Jammu and Kashmir: though Sheikh Abdullah had launched a dramatic programme of land reform from 1948 onwards, equalization of land holdings has not been followed by the enactment of appropriate social policies in the state.

The other state that has done well on the human development front is Tamil Nadu, which has the third lowest child mortality rate and the second lowest maternal mortality rate in the country. The state has accomplished a revolution in human development through widespread access to health care, sustained government initiatives in providing for child nutrition, wide-ranging immunization programmes, attendance of professionals at the birth of children, social security measures such as old age pensions, social support to widows, improved status of women, favourable gender ratios, a high presence of women in the workforce, midday meals in schools, and no gender bias in school attendance. On social development indicators, Tamil Nadu ranks just below Kerala. Tamil Nadu's commitment to human development is in the main an outcome of the progressive anti-caste movement, which, since the beginning of the twentieth century, has fought the entrenched domination of the upper castes and focussed on providing for the lower castes, which have been historically discriminated against. Bihar and Uttar Pradesh on the other hand have high infant mortality rates both because of lack of social infrastructure and lack of transformative political agents.

In sum, the realization of human development through appropriate social policies requires three preconditions. Firstly, the political parties, and by implication the government, should be committed to the well-being of the people. Secondly, Kerala has done better than West Bengal on the human development front because it has a competitive party system. Thirdly, Kerala has also done better than West Bengal because a number of social movements, notably the Kerala Sastra Sahitya Parishad, have mobilized popular opinion on social issues, as did the anti-caste movement in Tamil Nadu in an earlier time.

Civil society and well-being

Given that political parties and trade unions have been reluctant to take up the issue of social and economic democracy in a sustained manner, the only way that governments can be compelled to implement social policy is through civil society activism. The grant of civil and political rights has enabled civil society groups in India to demand that the state undertake appropriate action to realize the objectives laid down in the Directive Principles. Ever since independence, groups have mobilized for social and economic justice and tenaciously fought somewhat entrenched systems of domination: the peasants' movement, the movement for land rights, the women's movement, the anti-caste movement, the environmental movement, the movement against displacement on account of large projects, and the radical armed struggle being fought by Maoist groups – the Naxalite movement. Most of these movements, embedded as they are in a strong redistributive ethos, have asked for a radical restructuring of power relations.

Since the late 1990s, however, a qualitatively different series of campaigns have appeared on the political scene. Five of these campaigns – the campaigns for the right to food, the right to education, the right to health, the right to work, and the right to information – are of some interest because they have catapulted issues of serious concern into the limelight. Spearheaded mainly by social activists and NGOs, these campaigns have demanded that the provisions of part four of the Constitution be *upgraded* to the status of part three of the Constitution, or that social and economic rights be given the same status as political and civil rights. Some of these campaigns have fetched notable results, for instance the Right to Information Bill was introduced in Parliament in December 2004 as a response to the campaign for the right to information. Nine state governments have already enacted the Right to Information Bill. This is of some consequence because the right to information constitutes the bedrock of democracy, ensuring awareness of what is due to citizens, popular participation, and accountability.

The campaign for the right to education, which has mobilized around the Eighty Sixth Amendment that makes elementary education a fundamental right, has demanded that the scope of the Act be widened to cover Early Childhood Care and Education in the age group 0–6 years, that children over the age of 14 be included in the new system, and that anomalies in the system of parallel education be removed. Whereas the campaign for the right to health focuses on strengthening the health system and making health a fundamental right, the right to food has insisted that entitlement to food is a basic right. In fact, the right to food campaign has achieved notable success, because in response to a writ petition filed by the Peoples Union of Civil Liberties in 2001, the Supreme Court has adopted a proactive stance on the matter. In a series of interim orders the Court has instructed the central and the state governments to streamline the PDS and other nutrition-related schemes, to introduce midday meals in schools, and to strengthen provision of nutrition to children below six years of age and to lactating mothers. In time, the campaign for food rights developed into the campaign for the right to work.

The right to food campaign

In August 2004, newspaper reports on 15 starvation deaths in Baran district of Rajasthan in July of the same year (*The Hindu* 2004c) served to draw attention to the paradox of the Indian political system. The country's stocks of food grains are far in excess of the normal buffer norms of food security. And yet, in the same period reports of starvation deaths, hunger, and generalized malnutrition have appeared regularly on the front pages of newspapers.[7] The National Nutrition Monitoring Bureau has reported that although the percentage of children affected by malnutrition declined from 56.2 per cent in 1990–91, to 47.7 per cent in 2000–01, nearly half of children in the rural areas suffer from malnourishment, which has been identified as the single largest cause of child mortality (Radhakrishnan 2002). The extent of malnourishment among adults, particularly pregnant women and lactating mothers, is no better.

It was in response to this paradox that in 2001 the Rajasthan-based *Akal Sangarsh Samiti* – an all-state network of 60 grass roots organizations – launched a sit-in in Jaipur, the capital of Rajasthan. The immediate provocation for the sit-in was the inability/unwillingness of the state government to redress unfavourable conditions caused by severe drought in the state. The state government, pleading a lack of funds, vacillated on the issue of continuing relief works beyond the minimum period, in the process violating its own 1962 famine code; on the issue of picking up the full quota of food grains that had been allotted to it from the central pool; and on the issue of expanding the constituency for PDS. On 16 April 2001, the People's Union for Civil Liberties (PUCL) Rajasthan filed a writ petition before the Supreme Court, citing the Government of India, the Food Corporation of India, and six state governments as respondents. The list of respondents was enlarged in time to cover the governments of all States and Union Territories, and the issues raised by the writ petition – the provision of relief works during drought and the utilization of surplus food stocks to feed starving people – were expanded to that of chronic hunger (PUCL 2004).

The issues raised by the writ petition, including the view that the right to food is an integral part of the right to life guaranteed by Article 21 of the Constitution, were serious enough to warrant a proactive stance by the Supreme Court. The Court ruled that it was of utmost importance that food be provided to vulnerable sections (PUCL 2004). In a series of interim orders in 2001, the Court directed the central and state governments to ensure that hardship was reduced through the provision of food, that various modalities that assure this be strengthened, that nutrition-related schemes be implemented in full, that government and government-funded schools provide cooked midday meals to schoolchildren, and that institutional arrangements to deliver food to target groups be fortified.

The public hearings held by the Court on the petition bred two consequences: firstly, they gave rise to the campaign for the right to food, which is an informal alliance of organizations and individuals committed to the right to be free from hunger and from under-nourishment. Secondly, on 15 August 2001 the prime minister announced that his government would initiate a massive programme of employment generation via the *Sampoorna Grameen Rozgar Yojana*. This was followed by a Central Government order streamlining the PDS. Several state governments conforming to the orders of the Supreme Court introduced midday meals in primary schools, and updated and improved other food-related programmes.

The campaign for the right to food realized fairly early on that assured employment is an essential precondition for food security for it liberates people from dependence on outside agencies for the satisfaction of their basic needs. The demand for this right (distinct from the demand for food-for-work programmes) has not raised a new entitlement onto policy agendas. As discussed above, several employment-generating schemes have been introduced in the country, but have failed to generate either meaningful employment or generate purchasing power. The current bill can thus be but a transitional measure, leading, in the long run, to a fuller right to work.

Conclusion

The preconditions that enable a transition to social democracy are (i) a competitive party system, (ii) political parties (and thereby government) and trade unions that are committed to social welfare, and (iii) civil society activism that presses social issues onto the policy agenda. The experience of India, however, suggests that *one* more precondition is required to translate policy into practice: a proactive judiciary. It is instructive to note in this context that most of the campaigns mentioned above have succeeded in accomplishing their objectives only when the Court has intervened on their behalf with the state. This is particularly evident in the case of the right to food campaign. In response to the writ petition filed by the PUCL in 2001, in a series of interim orders the Court directed the Central and State governments to ensure nutritional security. Above all, the Court ruled that the right to food directly emanates from Article 21 of the Constitution, which protects the right to life, and from Article 47 of the Directive Principles of State Policy, which, *inter alia* provides that the state shall regard the raising of the level of nutrition and the standard of living of its people and the improvement of public health as among its primary duties. The Court has in effect accorded legal backing to the right to food.

In May 2002, the Supreme Court ruled that village self-government bodies shall frame employment generation proposals in accordance with the *Sampoorna Gramin Rozgar Yojana*. And earlier in 1993, the Supreme Court in the case of Unnikrishna J.P versus State of Andhra Pradesh had ruled that although the right to education is not stated expressly as a fundamental right, it is implicit in and flows from the right to life guaranteed under Article 21. The court further declared that the Directive Principles of State Policy form the fundamental feature and social conscience of the constitution and the provisions of parts III and IV are supplementary and complementary to each other. Fundamental rights, ruled the court, are means to ensure the goals laid down in part IV and must be construed in light of the Directive Principles.

Though court interventions have helped campaigns to achieve their goals, the need for the Court to intervene illustrates the paradox of civil society mobilization. In much of the literature, it is assumed that civil society groups have the capacity to address the state and to oblige the latter to heed demands made by these groups. However, the Indian state has proved more responsive to court injunctions, compelling more and more groups to appeal to judicial activism. In part, the court has adopted a proactive stance because the agenda of contemporary civil society mobilization is self-limiting and confined to the framework of the Constitution. But social movements that demand a radical restructuring of power relations in the country have just not fetched the required response from the judiciary. This is most evident in the case of the Narmada Bachao Andolan (NBA), a movement that has concentrated on the plight of the thousands of people who have been displaced by the building of the gigantic Sardar Sarovar Project on the river Narmada in Western India. The project, consisting of 30 large, 135 medium and 3,000 small dams, has displaced more than 44,000 families in three states. In 1994, the NBA had approached the court and asked it to order the government to stop construction of the dam. In October 2000, however, the court permitted the raising of the height of the SSP to 90 metres. The ruling not only resulted in the displacement of more families, it also mounted a serious setback to one of the most spectacular movements that had challenged both iniquitous development planning and the power of the state to deal with its people as it wills (Chandhoke 2003).

Contemporary campaigns concentrate on specific issues and leave the *big* story untouched – the huge inequalities of resources in the country, for instance. These campaigns just do not dream the large and expansive dreams that were dreamt of by earlier generations of social activists – restructuring existing structures of power and forging new and equitable structures of social relations. These campaigns would rather ensure that the state delivers what it has promised in theory, that policy be implemented effectively, that local authorities be made accountable, that the functioning of the government be made public and transparent, that midday meals be provided to children in primary schools, that the poor get jobs for at least 100 days a year, and that children are brought into school. All this may not ensure a transition from formal to egalitarian democracy. But the quality of life for the ordinary Indian just may improve somewhat until substantive democracy is realised.

Notes

1. Scholars, however, disagree sharply on the methodology of estimating poverty. See the special issue on poverty reduction in *Economic and Political Weekly*, January 2004.
2. Though much of social welfare falls within the provenance of State Governments, in the subsequent section I deal only with Central Government Schemes for reasons of space.
3. The two crop insurance schemes, National Agricultural Insurance Scheme and the Farm Income Insurance Scheme, have proved largely ineffective.
4. A crore is equal to 10 million.
5. This has been originally conceptualized as a fundamental right, but deliberations in the Constituent Assembly reduced education to a Directive Principle of State Policy.
6. Dyson *et al.* (2004) calculate that there are 300 million people in India below the poverty line.
7. There is a fine line of distinction between hunger and malnutrition, whereas the former can be assuaged by the consumption of cereals, the latter requires also non-cereal foods, safe drinking water, and sanitation.

References

Chandhoke. N. 2003. *The Conceits of Civil Society*. Delhi: Oxford University Press.

Deodhar, N.S. 2001. *Health Situation in India: 2001*. Delhi: Voluntary Health Association of India.

Drèze, J. and A. Sen. 2002. *India: Development and Participation*. Delhi: Oxford University Press.

Dyson T., R. Cassen and L. Visaria. 2004. *Twenty-first Century India: Population, Economy, Human Development, and the Environment*. Delhi: Oxford University Press.

Economic and Political Weekly. 2004. 'Poverty Reduction in 1990s: Towards a Better Understanding', Special issue, 38(4), 296–412.

Economic Times. 2004. Delhi Edition, 21 November.

Government of India. 2002. *Census of India*. http:/censusindia.nic.in. Accessed in August 2005.

Government of India. 2005. *Economic Survey of India 2005–2006*, http:/indiabudget.nic.in. Accessed on 20 June 2005.

Government of India. 2005. *Budget 2005*. Chapter 10, http:/indiabudget.nic.in. Accessed in August 2005.

Hindu. 2004a. Delhi Edition, 18 September.

Hindu. 2004b. Delhi Edition, 21 August.

Hindu. 2004c. Delhi Edition, 11 August.

International Labour Organisation (ILO). 2004. *Economic Security for a Better World.* Geneva: ILO.
Ministry of Health and Family Welfare. *Annual Report 2003–04.* Delhi: Government of India.
Misra, R., Chatterjee and S. Rao. 2003. *India Health Report.* Delhi: Oxford University Press.
National Council of Applied Economic Research (NCAER). 1996. *Human Development Profile of India: Inter-State and Inter-Group Differentials.* Delhi: NCAER.
Papola, T. S. and A. N. Sharma. 2004. "Labour: Down and Out?", *Seminar,* May, 19–23.
Planning Commission. 2000. *Mid Term Appraisal of Ninth Five Year Plan 1997–2002.* Extracts. Delhi: Government of India.
Planning Commission (PC). 2002a. *National Human Development Report 2001.* Delhi: Government of India.
Planning Commission (PC). 2002b. *Tenth Five Year Plan 2002–2007, volume 2, Sectoral Policies and Programmes.* Delhi: Government of India.
Prabhu, S. and R. Sudarshan. (eds). 2002. *Reforming India's Social Sector: Poverty, Nutrition, Health and Education.* Delhi: Social Science Press.
PUCL. 2004. *Legal Action For The Right To Food: Supreme Court Orders and Related Documents.* Mumbai: Support Group of the Right to Food.
Radhakrishnan, R. 2002. 'Food and Nutrition Security', in Kirit S. Parikh and R. Radhakrishnan (eds), *India Development Report.* Delhi: Oxford University Press.
Rao, S. B. 1968. *The Framing of India's Constitution.* Delhi: Indian Institute of Public Administration.
Saxena, N. C. 2004. 'Improving Service Delivery', *Seminar.* Special issue on 'New Priorities', September, pp. 49–53.
UNDP. 2004. *Human Development Report 2004.* Oxford: Oxford University Press.
Vijay Shankar, P. and C. R. Reddy. 2004. 'Ensuring Employment Guarantee,' *Seminar,* Special Issue on 'New Priorities', September, 24–28.

8
Democracy and Social Policy in Botswana

Keitseope Nthomang

Introduction

Since independence in 1966, Botswana has attempted to strike a balance between its social, economic and political development agendas. Economically, the focus has been on attaining financial viability and economic growth. This is expected to enable the government to provide and deliver tangible public goods and services. Political development, on the other hand, could be regarded as the accountability of central government to the people through the electoral process, legal recourse, the separation of powers and transparency. Both of these developments ultimately provide the basis for framing and implementing social policy. However, in practice, the effectiveness of social policies varies considerably, depending on the extent to which the economic and political dimensions are truly democratized. Given the possible contradictory outcomes of political and economic transformations, this situation of uncertainty poses challenges for social policy to improve human well being while promoting economic growth and democracy.

This chapter will assess the extent to which democracy provides a basis for effective social policy development in Botswana. The first section discusses the evolution of Botswana's economy and its impact on the labour market. Then we address the evolution of social expenditure. A closer look at the development of social welfare programmes is undertaken, including an examination of the statutory framework for the protection of social rights. This is followed by a brief overview of the evolution of Botswana's democracy, that pays particular attention to the forces that sustain it and the extent to which democracy provides the basis for effective social policies. The final part of the chapter draws conclusions and highlights the challenges inherent in the development of effective social policies and democratization processes.

Evolution of Botswana's economy and labour market

Botswana is a landlocked country, situated north of South Africa with a population of 1.7 million, making it one of the most sparsely populated nations in the world. It is a non-racial country and maintains freedom of the press and association, and affords all citizens equal rights. All these are enshrined in the constitution, which also provides for a unicameral legislature. Members of the National Assembly are directly elected from the constituencies and themselves elect additional specially elected members and a speaker of the National Assembly. The presidential candidate of the party that wins the majority of seats in parliament becomes president.

At independence, Botswana was one of the poorest countries in the world, with a per capita GNP of about US$50 per annum. However, since then, the Gross Domestic Product (GDP) per capita increased ninefold between 1966 and 1995/96, from P375 to P3,475. Nominal GDP increased from P228 million in 1974/75 to P25,759 million in 1999/2000. When expressed in 1999/2000 constant prices, the increase during the period was 9.1 per cent per year, rising from P2,881 million to P25,759 million (GoB/UNDP 2002).

Until recently, Botswana has been the fastest-growing economy in the world. In the post-independence period, Botswana's average growth rate was around 13 per cent (Hope 1996). Birdsall, *et al.* (1995), quoting the World Bank, put Botswana's average annual growth rate, in per capita GNP, at 8.4 per cent for the 25-year period between 1965 and 1990. During this period, Botswana's average annual growth rate per capita GNP exceeded that of the then high-performing East Asian economies. In 1998, Botswana achieved a per capita GNP of US$5,796 (CEPR 2002). The exceptional performance and transformation from severe poverty have been described by some as a 'miracle' (Harvey 1992) or a success story in sub-Saharan Africa (Siddiqi 1999).

However, in the early 1990s, Botswana's economy began to slow down. The rate of economic growth declined from 6.5 per cent in 1991/92 to a modest 0.3 per cent per annum in 1992/93. Matsheka and Botlhomilwe (2000) attributed this mainly to the effects of the global recession, which resulted in the contraction of the key sectors of mining and construction. In 1999, Botswana experienced yet another economic boom. The growth rate was around 8.3 per cent, in contrast to the 3 per cent experienced in 1993/94. This was due to strong expansion of the mining and general government sectors that increased at 9.5 per cent and 11.0 per cent respectively in 1997/98. The manufacturing sector grew at 4.7 per cent and was forecast to grow at a faster rate and be a source of economic diversification and employment.

The other positive changes in macroeconomic conditions include an emerging tourism sector and commercialization of livestock, rapid growth in formal employment in public, parastatal and private sectors, high foreign reserves and less government intervention in the running of the economy, leading to greater involvement in development activities by the private and parastatal sectors.

Botswana is currently classified as an upper-middle-income country. In recent decades its economy has shifted from dependence on agriculture and finance (42.7 and 20.1 per cent respectively in 1966) to mining and government services (33.8 and 17.1 per cent respectively in 1994/95). The share of agriculture to GDP in 1966 stood at 73 per cent and represented the largest single contributing sector. Thirty-five years later, in 2001, the agricultural sector's share has fallen dramatically–from 73 per cent to a mere 2.6 per cent. Currently, mining constitutes the leading sector, rising to 52 per cent of GDP in 1988/89. The mining sector registers an average of 4.3 per cent growth with a value added of P8,389 million in 1999/2000. The thrust of Botswana's development strategy is exploiting the country's mineral wealth and investing the proceeds in social development initiatives. However, social development has meant substantial spending on social services such as education, health and water but less spending on social welfare provision. In fact, Botswana's rapid growth has had very little impact on improving people's welfare.

Formal sector employment

The labour market represents a key arena for socioeconomic empowerment. At independence, formal sector employment was estimated at about 25,000. It has grown tremendously over the years. Table 8.1 shows employment in the formal sector for selected years.

A key feature of the employment situation in Botswana is the slow growth rate of the private sector. As indicated in Table 8.1, total formal sector employment increased from 231,324 in 1994 to 264,355 in 2000, showing an increase of 14.3 per cent during the six-year period, and accounting for 46 per cent of formal employment. However, during the same period, the private sector created an additional 7,089 jobs, implying an increase of only 5.2 per cent; while employment in central and local government and parastatals grew by 29.4 per cent, 22.1 per cent and 24.8 per cent, respectively. Available statistics

Table 8.1 Formal sector employment in Botswana 1994–2000

Economic sector/years	*1994*	*1995*	*1996*	*1997*	*1998*	*1999*	*2000*	*% changing 1994–2000*
Central government	66,438	69,425	70,077	71,448	81,799	84,856	85,690	29.4
Local government	15,433	15,921	16,341	16,555	18,217	19,073	18,847	22.1
Parastatals	13,222	13,420	13,718	13,787	13,608	15,522	16,498	24.8
Private sector	136,231	132,621	133,980	135,760	125,877	137,615	143,320	5.2
Total (all sectors)	231,324	231,387	234,116	237,550	239,501	257,066	264,355	14.3

Source: Bank of Botswana 2001.

show that total employment has increased by 5.4 per cent per annum since 1998. The growth rate was above the growth of the labour force, which suggests that unemployment is falling. Despite its economic importance, the mining sector accounts for only 3.5 per cent of the labour force, while informal sector employment accounts for between 10–15 per cent.

Informal sector employment

The Central Statistics Office (CSO) (2003: 6) provides a working definition of the informal sector in Botswana as comprising enterprises not registered as companies or with professional associations, employing no more than five employees, maintaining no formal accounts and having no fixed location of operation, expenditure not easily distinguishable from household expenditure, hiring casual employees, being temporary or in the owner's home. The contribution of the informal sector to household income is so significant that, in some instances, it exceeds that of the formal sector. In terms of employment creation, it is acknowledged that the informal sector makes a significant contribution to the economy. For example, according to the 1995/96 Labor Force Survey and the 2000 Multi Indicators Survey, total employment opportunities in the economy grew from 345,400 in 1996 to 483,400 in 2000, an average annual growth rate of 8 per cent. Much of that employment growth was due to increases in employment opportunities in the informal sector, which, as may be inferred from these figures, was about 226,000.

Employment and unemployment

Botswana's spectacular growth in the first three decades after independence did not translate well in terms of employment creation. Figures presented in the UNDP-Human Development Report (2005) paint a bleak scenario. Whereas real GDP grew by 45 per cent between 1991 and 1999, formal sector employment increased by only 13 per cent, and was in 1999 estimated at 257,066. This represents an average annual increase of 1.6 per cent compared to 5 per cent for GDP. However, between 1997 and 2001, formal sector employment grew at a rate of 4.9 per cent per annum, before declining to 1.8 per cent between 1999 and 2002. The report also notes that more than one in six job-seekers could not find a job in 2000. The 1995/96 Labor Force Survey shows that 182,703 of the total labour force (or 34.6 per cent) were unemployed. Of these, 48 per cent (or 88,175) were discouraged job-seekers. Current unofficial estimates suggest a 40 per cent unemployment rate. This figure includes mainly the youth aged 15–24 estimated at approximately 37 per cent, and is almost double the adult unemployed. In addition, this includes most people without regular income, such as farm labourers, domestic workers and peasant farmers (GoB/UNDP 2002). It should be noted that most people in Botswana tend to equate employment with a formal wage. An individual is deemed unemployed even if s/he is self-employed. Unemployment is a serious problem, despite high rates of economic growth.

It is important to note that there is no national social security scheme covering all workers and non-workers and the existing social safety nets are inadequate. Notwithstanding, most people survive on remittances and transfers from working family members. While it is often argued that the extended family system in Botswana is weak, it remains functional and has in most cases subsidized inadequate or non-existent government social provision.

The development of workers' unions

Section 13(1) of the constitution guarantees protection of freedom of assembly and association and accords every Motswana the right to form or belong to trade unions or other associations for the protection of their interests (Constitution of Botswana 1966). However, Mogalakwe (1995) argues that the labour relations in Botswana must be located within the context of the state policy of economic growth and development. According to the government, wage restraint and industrial peace would lead to political stability, which is presumed to be a prerequisite for economic development. A plethora of labour laws was introduced, such as the Trade Unions and Employer's Organization Act (1984) amended in 2004, and the Trade Disputes Act (2004). However, these were unduly restrictive and anti-labour as they sought to exercise control over labour organizations. These restrictions prevent trade unions from organizing in ways they believe are most effective. They have implications for the development of effective social policy, which requires a strong labour movement.

The first trade unions started operating in Botswana in the early 1970s with the establishment of the Botswana Trade Union and Education Centre. This was later to become the Botswana Federation of Trade Unions (BFTU). According to the information compiled by the Registrar of Trade Unions and Employers Organizations (Mogalakwe 1995), there were 26 workers' unions in January 1996, with a total trade union membership of 66,886. As a percentage of the total labour force, this represented a low union density. However, it is important to note that this number does not include permanent and pensionable public sector employees estimated at about 80,000, who are not unionized but belong to the Botswana Civil Service Association. Further, it should be noted that until recently (2004), public sector employees were barred by law from forming and participating in unions. They could only form associations. Thus, political activism by government employees is discouraged. The current union membership numbers are not known due to the unavailability of data, but they are expected to have grown substantially.

The labour movement is largely apolitical. The BFTU has not formed an alliance with any political party, including the ruling party. In fact, its members and officials are allowed to join parties of their choice. The overarching objective of the BFTU is to build a non-partisan, politically neutral labour movement, whose primary responsibility is to fight for the interests of its members. In this regard, the BFTU has remained independent of the government and will not explicitly support any political party, but will only encourage them to support the cause of labour. However, lack of a clear ideological position has made it difficult for the unions to influence government policy except in an advisory capacity, where unions work with the government to advocate for the implementation of policies that promote the interest of their members. The government never feels compelled to advance the interests of labour to any considerable degree, since trade unions do not have a direct influence on the outcome of general elections. The government allows participation in and contribution of the labour movement to government policies but only on matters relating to labour and employment. The weakness of the labour movement allows government to dominate the social policy agenda.

In terms of membership density, trade unions can be divided into two groups: in-house and industrial. In-house unions refer to those operating within formal organizational structures. These have a relatively high rate of unionization as the recruitment process targets all eligible employees. Perceived benefits such as negotiated better pay packages and representation in terms of disciplinary hearings are usually the motivation for membership. With industrial unions, the rate of unionization is relatively lower, mainly because most employees appear to be ignorant of the importance of unionization beyond the fact that they campaign for higher wages. Further, most people are not aware that they do not have to be an employee in order to belong to a union.

A study conducted by the Friedrich Ebert Stiftung (2003) concluded that, due to lack of capacity in both individual trade unions and the BFTU, there are no statistics to show the rate of unionization in the different workplaces. However, the rate of unionization among women is very low across the different age groups, compared with that of their male counterparts. The report concluded that, overall, the level of unionization in Botswana is still very low, with the informal sector virtually unorganized and hence un-unionized. Despite the existence of BFTU, the labour movement remains weak, fragmented, and uncoordinated, and therefore has very little or no impact on social policy. This has been attributed to problems of financial resources, lack of qualified personnel and restrictive legislation. Trade unions seem to be overly concerned about wages and salary issues and less about broader welfare policy issues.

Evolution of social policy

Although there was some attempt by the colonial administration to provide welfare in Bechuanaland (Hedenquist 1992), the evolution of social expenditure in Botswana is directly linked to the country's economic growth. Immediately after independence, the political leaders of the country made a deliberate decision to invest in mining and other productive sectors of the economy and vowed to re-invest the returns in social development. Thus, Botswana has relied on mineral revenue to finance both human and physical

Table 8.2 Selected demographic indicators

	1971	*1981*	*1991*	*Estimates 2001*
Total population (thousands)	596.9	941	1,327	1,694
Life expectancy at birth (per 1,000)	55.5	56.2	65,2	68.0
Total fertility rate (per 1,000)	6.5	7.1	4.23	3.83
Crude birth rate (per 1,000)	45.3	48.7	39.3	32.1
Crude death rate (per 1,000)	13.7	13.9	11.5	6.6

Sources: Ministry of Finance and Development Planning 1997; 1991.
Note: Estimates for 2001 were obtained from Central Statistics Office: Populations Projections 1991–2021 (Gaborone, April, 1997). Estimate of life expectancy for 2001 were made in 1991 and did not reflect the likely impact of AIDS. This explains the difference in life expectancy for 2001 in Tables 8.2 and 8.3. The figure in Table 8.3 reflects the AIDS crisis.

capital. These activities have included building new roads and the expansion of existing ones, provision of water and electricity, provision of education and health facilities.

Access to education, health and clean water has improved rapidly over the years, as seen in adult literacy, infant mortality rate and life expectancy rates. There has also been considerable infrastructure development, as evidenced by increases in kilometres of tarred roads, number of registered vehicles, the amount of electricity generated and the number of connected telephone subscribers. Table 8.2 shows progress in selected social indicators over the years.

Table 8.3 shows that significant progress has been recorded in the social development sector over the years. Botswana's relatively good performance in the social sector can be further appreciated if the country's performance is compared with others. This could be done by using the United Nations Development Programme's Human Development Index (HDI). According to the HDI, and using 1993 figures, Botswana ranked 71 out of 178 countries in the world. In Africa, Botswana was only surpassed by Mauritius, Seychelles, Libya and Algeria (Hope 1996). While the position of some poor people may have improved both directly and indirectly, the high growth in Botswana has not ameliorated socioeconomic inequalities long existing in the country. The Gini index of inequality barely changed between 1985 and 2001, and remained in excess of 0.5 (CSO 2001). Besides, Botswana's HDI rank deteriorated sharply in subsequent years. It was ranked 126th out of 173 countries on the UNDP Human Development Index in 2002, with Swaziland, Equatorial Guinea, and Gabon all doing better. The very high incidence of HIV/AIDS partially explained these differences, but policies that specifically favoured the rich did so too (Good 2003: 23).

Provision of social services

In the pre-colonial and colonial period, response to need was situated within the traditional tribal framework, with the extended family playing a major

Table 8.3 Key socioeconomic indicators

Indicator	*Value*	*Year*	*Source*
Population size (million)	1.7	2001	Population Census
Annual population growth rate (%)	2.3	2001	Population Census
Total life expectancy at birth (years)	56	2001	Population Census
Male life expectancy at birth (years)	53	2001	Population Census
Female life expectancy at birth (years)	59	2001	Population Census
Real GDP per capita (US$)	7,820	2001	UNDP HDR 2003
Real GDP per capita (pula)	9,788	2002	CSO-National Accounts
Human Development Index (rank)	125	2003	UNDP HDR 2003
% of population below national poverty datum line	37.4	2001	Poverty Reduction Strategy
Prevalence of HIV/AIDS (15–19) years	35.4	2002	Sentinel Survey 2003
% of underweight children (under 5 years)	6	2003	Ministry of Health
Infant mortality [per 1,000]	56	2001	Population Census
Under-5 mortality [per 1,000]	74	2001	Population Census
Maternal mortality [per 100,000]	326	1991	Estimated from Census
Total adult literacy (%)	68.9	1994	Literacy Survey
Male adult literacy (%)	66.9	1994	Literacy Survey
Female adult literacy	70.3	1994	Literacy Survey
Net enrolment in primary education 7–13 years (%)	95.3	2001	CSO-Education Statistics
Population without access to safe drinking water (%)	12.1	2001	Population Census

Source: UNDP 2004.

role. The family, neighbours, community members and the chief played a pivotal role in this regard. Children, the poor, the aged and the disabled were cared for by various members of the family in a fixed order of responsibility. Provision of such essential services as housing was the responsibility of household heads, assisted by relatives, neighbours and other members of the community. Due to urbanization, migration and other social change factors, these forms of social security have been weakened or disappeared. Modern governments are now faced with challenges to provide more formalized services.

The performance of the economy has enabled government to increase resources for its development budget. For example, during 1999/2000, the total development budget was P3.450 billion, the bulk for social services, which included education, health, food, housing and social welfare programmes. The second largest share went to economic services such as agriculture, roads, electricity and water supply. This is aimed at achieving access to social and economic services to improve the quality of life in line with the

Table 8.4 Social expenditure as a per cent of public sector expenditure (million pula)

Year	*Social sector expenditure*	*Public sector expenditure*	*Social sector expenditure (%)*
1981/82	107.6	321.2	33.5
1982/3	129.8	386.7	33.6
1983/84	142.8	411.1	33.9
1984/85	172.3	551.9	31.2
1985/86	201.8	673.9	29.9
1986/87	311.4	977.5	31.8
1987/88	407.7	1,243.9	32.9
1988/89	513.2	1,693.6	30.3
1989/90	645.8	1,969.4	32.9
1990/91	828.0	2,506.3	33.0
1991/92	1,150.4	3,092.3	37.2

Source: Molutsi 1994.

aspirations of Botswana's long-term Vision 2016. Table 8.4 shows the trend in social spending for the period 1981/2–1991/2. Government has consistently spent over 30 per cent of its total expenditure on the social services.

Table 8.5 provides current figures on social expenditure. It shows the functional breakdown of total recurrent and development expenditure for 1997/98 and 2002/03 along with the respective shares and percentage growth over the period of National Development Plan 8 (1997–2003). This high allocation to the social sector has brought positive results and these are briefly discussed below.

Education

Education is the single largest expenditure item in the fiscal budget, averaging more than a fifth of the total. In 2003, it accounted for 24 per cent of the total fiscal spending up from 22 per cent in 1981, and 29 per cent of the recurrent expenditure. At present, Botswana has achieved universal access to primary education. From 1995 to 2000, the estimated net enrolment rate (NER) for children aged 7–13 was consistently above 95 per cent, peaking at 100 per cent in 1999 and 2000. Over the same period, the gross enrolment rate (GER) was at 11 per cent higher than the NER, in part because some children start school late but also because some dropouts return to school (UNDP 2004: 29). In the process, Botswana has generated sufficient institutional capacity to guarantee every child of schoolgoing age ten years of basic education. Measures that have been adopted to improve access include among others: (i) the abolition of school fees from primary to tertiary institutions, including the university; (ii) buying school uniform and other items for destitute persons and San/Basarwa or remote area dwellers; and (iii) providing school feeding programmes. Based on these trends, Botswana will make significant gains in literacy by 2016 (CSO 2001).

Table 8.5 Functional classification of government development and recurrent expenditures in 1997/98 and 2002/03 (million pula – current prices)

Functional category	*1997/1998*		*2002/2003*		*Growth in total expenditure (%)*
	Total expenditure	*Percentage share*	*Total expenditure*	*Percentage share*	
Education	1,787,80	24.14	3,820,80	21.95	133.6
Health	411.2	5.55	1,130.80	6.50	175.0
Food and social welfare programmes	160.3	2.16	168.3	0.97	5.0
Housing, urban & regional development	430.2	5.81	1,269.90	7.30	195.2
Other community and social services	131.4	1.77	580.5	3.33	341.8
Economic services	1,701.80	22.98	3,133.50	18.00	84.1
Local authorities	887.2	11.98	2,341.68	17.85	163.9
Financial Assistance Policy (FAP) grants	102	1.38	154	0.88	51.0

Source: Ministry of Finance and Development Planning 2002; 1997.

Health

The health status of the nation also recorded positive trends in almost all the indices used to measure progress in this area. For example, it is estimated that 88 per cent of Batswana are within 15 km of a health facility and 81 per cent within a 10 km radius. As a result, health care indicators show that infant and child mortality has declined considerably (BFHS Report, 1996; 1988). However, since the advent of HIV/AIDS, both the infant and under-five mortality rates have been rising. From the mid-1990s, the child mortality rates increased to levels experienced in the 1960s and 1970s. However, with the introduction of anti-retroviral therapy and country-wide implementation of the Prevention-of-Mother-to-Child Transmission (PMTCT) programme, the situation is coming under control and may help reverse the trend in both infant and child mortality (CSO 1999).

It is important to note that health services in Botswana are offered free of charge to all citizens and a patient is only required to pay a small fee of P2.00

(an equivalent of 40 US cents). However, no one is denied health services because of inability to pay the P2.00. Government and parastatal sector employees have an option to join a contributory medical aid scheme, in which the employer contributes 50 per cent and the employee 50 per cent. Private sector employees also have access to such schemes with varying employer contributions. Most government and private sector employees prefer to participate in contributory medical aid schemes because they are prestigious. They operate like a health insurance scheme and through them one is able to access the best private medical doctors and services at a private clinic or hospital within and outside the country, while government hospitals are overcrowded and regarded as providing poor quality medical services.

Housing

The post-independence period also witnessed the rapid development of the housing sector but, in contrast to education and health, this sector did not provide universal coverage as it was mainly concentrated in the urban areas to cater for the large numbers of people who migrated from rural areas to seek employment. Entities such as the Botswana Housing Corporation (BHC) and the Self-Help Housing Agency (SHHA) were established to respond to housing problems. Because the BHC could not cater for the low-income households living in urban centres, SHHA is the main instrument through which they can gain access to affordable housing. However, the rural areas only saw the introduction of SHHA in the late 1990s. Because of rural–urban migration, housing is becoming a serious problem, resulting in the mushrooming of slum areas, with implications for social protection and provision of social services. It is also important to note that persons registered under the Revised Destitute Policy (Ministry of Local Government 2002) are entitled to basic shelter on assessment. The District/Town and City are required to construct municipal shelters to accommodate destitute persons and their dependents.

Water and sanitation

Available data reveal that nearly all Batswana, regardless of economic status, have access to safe and clean water. The 1991 census revealed that 89 per cent of the population had such access and in 2001 96 per cent. In the rural areas, 77 per cent of the population had access to standpipes or boreholes whereas this figure was 100 per cent in the urban areas. Water supply is being made available to the rural people in their homes at a minimal cost of only P439 per connection. Large-scale developments to improve the supply of water have been completed in major villages (MFDP 2001). With respect to sanitation, this has been made available in the urban centres. In rural areas, sanitation facilities are being improved through the National Rural Sanitation Programme under the Ministry of Local Government. According to the 1991 census, only about 40 per cent of the rural households had access to safe sanitation, with less than 30 per cent in the more remote areas and small settlements (CSO 2001).

Poverty and HIV/AIDS

According to UNDP-Human Development Report (2005) Botswana's rapid economic and human development has not been perfect and the country still faces a number of problems and challenges such as poverty, inequality, unemployment, excessive dependence on the state, a slow pace of citizen economic empowerment, and HIV/AIDS. These problems threaten to reverse the economic and social gains made in recent years and also have implications for democratization processes and the development of an effective social policy. According to BIDPA (1997) about 47 per cent of Batswana, an equivalent of 38 per cent of households, were living in poverty in 1993/94. In absolute numbers, approximately 623,100 people (representing 109,503 households) were very poor. The same study revealed that poverty was most acute in the rural and remote areas. An estimated 384,344 persons in rural areas were poor or very poor, compared to 149,734 in urban villages and 89,021 in urban areas. This meant that 62 per cent of poor or very poor Batswana were living in rural areas, 24 per cent in urban villages and 14 per cent in urban areas. Poverty was found to be most severe in rural/remote southwestern Botswana, in Gantsi, Kgalagadi and Southern Districts. Poverty was made worse by the HIV/AIDS rate, which is considered one of the highest in Southern Africa affecting approximately 37 per cent of the population.

Since 1992, Botswana has been monitoring the HIV/AIDS epidemic through annual sentinel surveillance of pregnant women attending antenatal clinics. The most current sentinel survey was conducted in 2003 in all 22 districts and a total of 7,251 pregnant women participated in the survey. Overall, countrywide, a prevalence rate of 37.4 per cent was recorded. Unlike the previous studies, the latest survey Botswana AIDS Impact Survey (CSO 2004) found that the overall HIV prevalence in the general population aged 18 months and older was estimated at 17.3 per cent. The most affected age groups range from 25–44 with a prevalence rate of 30.5 to 40.7 per cent respectively. This shows that HIV prevalence is very high at the prime of childbearing ages. In terms of the impact of the epidemic, the latest figures reveal that about 18 per cent of all deaths were attributed to HIV/AIDS and these are concentrated in the prime ages (NACA 2003). HIV/AIDS dramatically affects labour, setting back economic activity and social progress. There are a number of different prevention programmes. These include public education and awareness, condom distribution, PMTCT and Voluntary Counseling and Testing (VCT).

Development of welfare policy in Botswana

Botswana does not have a statutory national welfare policy. Instead, the country has a variety of policies and specific welfare programmes that provide social protection for different population groups. For example, there are policies and programmes that target citizens in formal sector employment and those that focus on the non-formal sector. There is also universal provision of social services, such as health and education, as well as those that target specific ethnic groups such as the San/Basarwa in the form of the Remote Area Development Programme (RADP). The Department of Social Services in the Ministry of Local Government develops, coordinates, monitors and evaluates the implementation of social programmes. Through the above activities, a caring and supportive environment has been created by empowering and rehabilitating individuals, groups and communities.

Social protection measures in the formal sector

Social protection is crucial for the improvement of living conditions of people. In the formal sector, this includes pensions and gratuities, medical aid, and maternity and sick leave. These provide varying levels of support to workers in the formal public and private sectors. In the long term, such services, if adequate, can provide social insurance and reduce the dependency of employees on the state. Some social protection benefits in the formal sector are briefly discussed below.

1. *Pensions and gratuity*

The Pensions Act (GoB 1988) provides for the payment of pensions and gratuities to public officers in prescribed circumstances such as early retirement at age 45 or compulsory retirement at age 60. On retirement or resignation, public officers employed on permanent and pensionable terms are entitled to a pension, which was fully financed by the government until 2002. However, after 2001 government introduced an optional contributory pension scheme in which government contributes 15 per cent and an employee 5 per cent of the gross salary of an employee. There is, however, no similar arrangement for non-formal sector employees. Most employers in the formal sector provide pensions to their employees under different discretionary pension schemes. Most of the schemes are compulsory, contributory and provided under an insurance scheme. Usually the employer and employee both contribute 50 per cent. On the death of an employee, benefits are paid directly to the beneficiaries as indicated by the deceased.

2. *Medical aid, and sickness, maternity and disability benefits*

The Botswana government operates a medical aid scheme in which all public officers are entitled to participate and become members. Botswana's Public Officers Medical Aid Scheme (BOPMAS) commenced operation in the early 1980s and covers the officer, spouse and all the dependent children under the age of 21. The government contributes 50 per cent and the employee 50 per cent. For every visit to the medical practitioner, the officer pays only 10 per cent of the medical bill and the balance is paid for by the medical aid scheme. This arrangement has enabled public officers and their dependants to acquire the best medical services in the country. It is important to note that coverage is extended to medical facilities in neighbouring countries, in particular South Africa.

The Employment Act (GoB 1982) provides for sick leave and remuneration during ill health. An employee is entitled, after completing a year at work, to sick leave on full pay. Those working in government and statutory corporations and large private sector organizations have better terms. For example, the public service regulations and some major parastatal organizations provide for sick leave of six months on full salary. Most private organizations offer health insurance under the Botswana Medical Aid Scheme (BOMAID), in which the employer contributes 50 per cent and the employee 50 per cent. Other employers in private and parastatal organizations provide reimbursement for medical expenses in varying percentages. The Employment Act (1982) also provides for a minimum period of maternity leave. Women are entitled to 42 days leave on full pay. They are also protected from dismissal on the grounds of pregnancy and they have a right to return to work. Women are also given some time off during working hours for childcare as part of their family responsibilities. However, there is no provision for paternity leave. And the Workmen's Compensation Act (GoB, 1998) provides for compensation for all injuries suffered or diseases contracted by workers in the course of their employment or for death resulting from such injuries or diseases.

3. Welfare protection in the non-formal sector

Welfare protection in the non-formal sector tends to be universal in nature. Under such arrangements, the state undertakes responsibility to provide social protection and social assistance for all its citizens. Examples of such assistance programmes are summarized in Table 8.6.

4. Programmes for destitute persons

This is a social safety net programme operated by the state. The National Policy on Destitute Persons was first introduced in 1980. The purpose of this policy was to ensure that government provides minimum assistance to the needy to improve their health and welfare. In March 2002, the existing policy was amended to take into consideration the changing economic challenges faced by the poor and needy. The policy defines a destitute as an individual who, due to disabilities, old age or a chronic health condition, is unable to engage in sustainable economic activities and has insufficient assets and sources of income such as land, cash and livestock, is earning or receiving income of less than P120 per month and is without any other means of support.

Eligibility for destitute benefits is clearly defined, targeted and conditional. The scheme does not discriminate on the basis of age, gender or ethnicity and destitute persons are classified into permanent and temporary categories – the former being those whose socioeconomic conditions render them completely dependent. They are eligible for benefits for life, with no conditions apart from an annual assessment by social workers. Temporary destitute persons, on the other hand, are those who are temporarily incapacitated by ill health or natural disasters (Ministry of Local Government

Table 8.6 Selected public policies and welfare programmes

Policy/programme	*Year*	*Main objective*	*Estimated current cost (pula million)*
Bechunaland Soldiers Benefit Fund	1946	– assist ex-servicemen to re-establish themselves into the economy	Financed by colonial administration. Not available
Creation of Bechunaland welfare department	1959–1962	– provide welfare to the needy	– welfare fund established. Not available
Labour-based drought relief programme	1960, 1970s to date	– provision of temporary supplement to rural incomes through wage employment for those most affected by drought.	Not available
Remote Area Development Programme	1974–to date	– achieve sustainable social and economic development for residents of remote areas (San/Basarwa)	P61.100.000 during NDP 9 2003/04 – 2008/09. Source: BIDPA 2003
Destitute	1980 revised 2002	– provide assistance to people categorized as genuinely destitute	Cumulative Exp. Up to April 2005 for both district/town & city councils (35,800 destitutes) P89.879.705.48
		– ensure destitute persons health and welfare	Source: Dept. of Social Services, 2005.
Universal old age pension	1996	– provide financial security to the elderly citizens	2004/2005 Expenditure as at Dec. 2004 P131.132.961.40 Source: Social Benefits Division Annual Report 2004.
Second World War Veterans	1998	– provide financial security to world war veterans, surviving spouse or children under 21 years	2004/2005 Expenditure P11. 022. 598.31 Source: Social Benefits Division Annual Report 2004.
HIV/AIDS Programmes: Community Home-based Care (1995); PMTCT (1999); Isoniazid Preventive Therapy (IPT) (1999); Voluntary counseling and testing (2002); Routine HIV testing (2004)	1999	– ensure quality care for patients in the home – provide food baskets – provide opportunities for HIV testing in the whole country – raise the uptake of HIV testing – prevent TB among HIV infected persons – reduce the impact of AIDS through treatment – provide opportunities for HIV testing in the whole country – to raise the uptake of HIV testing	2004/2005 Expenditure: Total government spending on HIV/AIDS as at March 2005: P517.883.767.32 (This includes spending on all the goal areas of Prevention, Treatment, Impact Mitigation and Psycho-social Support). Source: NACA, 2005.

Source: BIDPA 2003; Department of Social Services 2005 & 2004; NACA 2005.

2002). Deserving individuals are provided with cash entitlements; access to social services, including rehabilitation; provision of funeral expenses; and shelter. Temporary destitute persons residing in rural areas are entitled to P181.90 (US$33.68) worth of food per month, whereas those in urban areas receive P181.60 (US$33.62). Included in this amount is P61.00 cash for personal items. Permanent destitute persons are entitled to P210.90 (US$39.05) per month in rural areas and P211.40 (US$39.15) worth of food items in the urban centres. Children under the age of 18 benefit from food rations. They also receive assistance in the form of school uniforms, toiletries, transport, protective clothing, boarding, tuition in private and vocational schools, payment of additional fees required by the school such as touring fees, sports fees, and development fees. The number of needy students registered throughout the country is 15,612 (Ministry of Local Government 2002).

All categories of destitute persons are exempt from payment of publicly provided services such as medical fees, school fees, water charges, service levy and electricity. Furthermore, when a destitute person dies, the burial expenses are fully covered by local authorities. Social workers also provide rehabilitation and psycho-social support to enhance the quality of life of destitute persons. The destitute programme is fully funded by the government. The number of registered destitute persons is currently estimated at 35,800, which cost the government P2,183,800 per month in cash for personal items alone (i.e. 35,800 × P61.00) (US$436,760). The new programme costs well over P90 million per annum. The figures change all the time as the number of destitutes increases.

5. *The Orphan Care programme*

The Ministry of Local Government (1999) defines an orphan as 'a child below 18 years who has lost one (single parent) or two (married couples) biological or adoptive parents. The definition also incorporates children who are abandoned by parents who can no longer be traced. In 2003–2004 there were approximately 42,511 orphans registered with the Department of Social and Community Development (Department of Social Services 2005). Following a Rapid Assessment on the Situation of Orphans in Botswana (1998), a decentralized, multi-sectoral Short Term Plan of Action (STPA) (Ministry of Local Government 1999) was commissioned to mitigate the impact of orphanhood. The STPA, among other things, recommended the strengthening and delivery of social welfare services to orphans. Recently, the second Botswana AIDS Impact Survey (BAIS II) (CSO 2004) has indicated that 34.3 per cent of households contain orphans in need of care and support. Unlike the destitute programme, the orphan care programme is not means tested. Eligibility is open to all Batswana children under the age of 18 who do not have parents and therefore may lack access to basic human needs such as food, clothing and shelter. Currently, 92 per cent of the registered orphans are receiving assistance and only 8 per cent are supported by relatives.

Orphans receive a food basket of P216.00 per month irrespective of their geographic location. Orphans also receive additional support, ranging from clothing and educational assistance to counseling and protection from abuse. They also receive transport allowance, free medical support, water and electricity. Ways are being explored to provide quality and specialized care for orphans who are disabled and mentally handicapped. Since the inception of the Orphan Care programme, there has been a steady increase in the number of beneficiaries and a proportionate increase in the budget allocation. When the Orphan Care programme was introduced in 1999/2000 there were only 28,000 registered orphans and the budget expenditure was P28 million. The 2003/2004 budget expenditure stands at P162 million, approximately 478.5 per cent increase since the inception of the programme.

6. Universal old-age pension

The old age pension scheme was introduced in 1996. The major objective of the scheme was to provide financial security to elderly citizens without means of support due to the disintegration of the extended family support system. The Ministry of Local Government currently administers the scheme. By October 2000, the number of beneficiaries stood at approximately 80,000, 58 per cent of whom were female and 42 per cent male. The huge majority of pensioners (95 per cent) are concentrated in the rural areas. Eligibility for the scheme is currently defined by age 65 and above and only Batswana citizens qualify. Special efforts are made to ensure that the elderly poor who reside in isolated remote areas are covered. The allowance is universal, not means tested and non-contributory. Mentally ill patients, whether hospitalized or taken care of by their family, are also entitled to receive the old-age pension. Beneficiaries of the scheme currently receive P166.00 (US$33.2) per month. The Old Age Pension Scheme costs government approximately P15 million (US$3 million) per month. Concerns have been raised regarding sustainability of the programme, given its non-contributory nature. However, the Revised Policy on Rural Development (2002) reiterates government's commitment to offer this package as it is until it becomes fiscally unsustainable.

7. Second World War veterans allowance

The Second World War veterans allowance was established in 1998. The allowance is tailored to meet the needs of Second World War veterans, their surviving spouse/s and children below 21 years. As at December, 2004 there were 4,510 registered beneficiaries receiving P272.00 (US$ 54.4) per month in recognition of the services rendered during the Second World War. The allowance is also by extension payable to First World War veterans or their surviving spouses. Those who have emigrated or have repatriated do not qualify for this allowance. Where the veteran had more than one spouse or more than one child, the allowance is divided equally among the recipients.

8. *Supplementary feeding for vulnerable groups*

This is a social programme aimed at providing protection to vulnerable groups, namely pregnant and lactating mothers, nutritionally at risk under-fives and primary schoolchildren. The programme is funded by the Botswana Government and managed by the Ministry of Local Government. Health care workers implement the programmes. Children who are under-weight are given preference. It is noteworthy that child malnutrition in recent years has been exacerbated by HIV/AIDS and that breast feeding, the long recommended source of nutrition and protection from disease for infants, is no longer a viable option for HIV positive mothers because of the risk of transmission of infection from mother to child. The public health system provides infant formula for 12 months as a substitute for breastfeeding to mothers who enrol in the PMTCT programme.

The school feeding programme is another welfare protection strategy that is implemented in all public schools. It has a universal coverage. The objective of the programme is to provide at least two meals a day to all primary and secondary school children regardless of their socioeconomic status. The school feeding programme also serves as an incentive for disadvantaged children to be enrolled and retained in schools.

9. *Labour-based drought relief programmes*

During drought years, the president normally declares that drought relief programmes be implemented by the Ministry of Local Government through District Councils. During drought interventions in the late 1960s and 1970s, payment for participation in drought programmes was in the form of 'food for work'. The objective of these programmes has now shifted to provision of temporary supplements to rural incomes through wage employment for the most affected areas. The Labour Based Drought Relief project benefits all able-bodied persons in the rural areas who have lost their livelihood due to drought. No means testing is used in selection of participants. Available data show that in the 1980s, 296,000 job opportunities were created under this programme, employing 20 per cent of the rural working population, 80 per cent being women. During the 1992/93 drought year, 400,000 people received food aid and about 100,000 people were employed in the drought relief projects (MFDP, 2001). The 1995/96 drought on the other hand, created a total of 38,558 jobs involving 61,693 workers (BIDPA 1997). A daily allowance of P6.00 is given to participants. The amount is adjustable given the cost of living index in a given period. During the fiscal year 1995/96, government spent P300 million on drought relief projects implemented throughout the country.

10. *Coverage for people living with HIV/AIDS*

An estimated 300,000 people in Botswana are infected with the HIV virus and the impact of HIV/AIDS on overall economic development cannot be underestimated. Botswana has mobilized the political will to fight the epidemic and has invested substantial resources in the campaign to address related issues. In response, specific social programmes have been developed, such as provision of ARVs, home-based care, ITP, and routine HIV testing. ARV is now universally available/accessible. Apart from treatment of opportunistic infections and psycho-social support, AIDS patients are also given a monthly food basket to the value of P216.00 (US$43.2). An estimated number of 3,494 patients are currently being assisted with food out of a total of 5,471 patients. The criterion for qualification is that one should be HIV positive with CD4 count of less than 200 (NACA, 2004). In 2004, a policy was adopted on routine HIV/AIDS testing in health facilities to increase the uptake of HIV/AIDS testing, care and support services with a view to promoting positive behavioral change. This is a courageous step on a sensitive issue.

11. Social rights

Social rights have been defined as rights to adequate income, housing, education and health care, and have constitutional and statutory frameworks for their protection. At present, most of the social security programmes do not have a legal basis i.e. they cannot be claimed as rights. The constitution of Botswana contains a bill of rights, with political and civil rights known as first generation rights. However, it does not contain socioeconomic rights, also known as second generation rights, as in countries such as South Africa, whose new constitution provides for access to social security and social assistance. The Botswana constitution is silent in this respect. To this end, most social programmes do not originate from a legal source, except for a few such as the Worksmen's Compensation Act (1998). The absence of legislation to enforce social rights means that most social security programmes are offered as a matter of social policy only, and not as a right to social security and social assistance. Botswana has not ratified any international convention on social security, nor are there at present plans to do so. Neither the International Labor Organization Convention 102 (1952) nor the International Covenant on Social and Cultural Rights (UN 2001) have been ratified.

This section has shown that the Botswana government has been successful in basic service provision in that it has significantly expanded services in education, health, housing and water. The government has also provided social welfare and protection for some vulnerable population groups. However, these achievements, good as they may be, tend to obscure the realities of the excluded majority of the poor Batswana who have fallen through the cracks of the limited social safety net. The poor here refers to the youth, the unemployed and the disabled who have no basic income support. For example, the data show that education, health and housing account for about 36 per cent of development and recurrent expenditure and social welfare programmes a paltry 0.97 per cent. This means that Botswana's social policy is biased towards provision of basic social services at the expense of redistributive social welfare policies. It is reasonable to conclude that over 50 per cent of the population remains unprotected against basic social security risks. These and other factors force large numbers of Batswana to rely on informal social security mechanisms such as the extended family and kinship-based informal social security. However, these informal structures have begun to show signs of weakness, could no longer shoulder the burden of welfare and have generally disintegrated, especially in towns and cities.

Secondly, social welfare protection schemes tend to focus largely on the formal public, parastatal and private sector at the expense of the majority of the people in the informal sector. Given Botswana's high unemployment level and dependence of the majority of people on the informal sector for a livelihood, the neglect of the informal sector leaves a large number of people without adequate social protection. This is the case, despite the numerous programmes outlined above that tend to have universal coverage.

Thirdly, it is important to note that although Botswana has done very well in both the economic and social sectors, it has been unable to effectively translate its high per capita income, currently estimated at P22,013 (US$4,403) (2003/4) into commensurate improvements in livelihood for the majority of its citizens (CSO 2004). To compound these problems, it is important to note that in the last two decades, HIV/AIDS has emerged as one of the major development challenges. HIV/AIDS poses a great threat to continued economic growth, mostly because of its impact on the labour force, savings and investment. Thus, impressive gains in the economic and social spheres are being reversed by the ravaging effects of HIV/AIDS. For example, the increase in the mortality rates have impacted negatively on life expectancy at birth, which has fallen dramatically over the years from 65.3 years in 1991 to an average of 56 years in 2001, a loss of approximately 10 years (CSO 2001). This has far-reaching implications for social policy and democracy. More funds are being diverted into HIV/AIDS at the expense of other social sectors, leaving many discontented people. Discontent breeds anger and frustration and may be a threat to democracy.

Botswana's democracy: a historical overview

Many Botswana believe that the pre-colonial *Tswana* political tradition, particularly the *Kgotla*[1], was democratic and thus provided a historical basis for the liberal democracy that subsequently emerged. According to Ngcongco (1989), the democratic heritage of traditional government centres on the *Kgotla* and its role in policy making. A striking aspect of contemporary government in Botswana has been its ability to communicate local development issues with the people through the *Kgotla* and *dikgosi* (chiefs). The old Tswana proverb *mafoko a Kgotla a mantle otlhe; mmualebe o a bo a bua la gagwe* (to err is human) forms the bedrock of Botswana's liberal democracy. The conferment of full participation on the individual both guarantees the integrity of the person and is a recognition that the individual is mature and responsible enough to take decisions that affect his livelihood.

However, Molutsi (1998) argues that the traditional decision-making forum, the *Kgotla,* did not represent any genuine democratic tradition. The *Kgotla* was a vehicle to mobilize public support for decisions already made by the ruling elite. Women, young males and minority groups were excluded from the *Kgotla* discussions, and if there was any opposition it was bound to be cautious and could not be done openly. This should not, however, be misunderstood to mean that the traditional Tswana political system was not democratic. However, the liberal democratic system (which is 40 years old) is being built on, and continues to find its support and continuity in the foundations of the traditional political system.

In terms of the development of modern democratic institutions, Molutsi (1994) identified three historical features of Botswana's past in relation to the development of the modern society. First, Botswana has a long history of paternalism. For example, over a period of 80 years, Botswana was ruled indirectly by Britain. Within this system, traditional rulers held authority in their respective ethnopolities as dictated by their traditional constitutions, which were based primarily on male primogeniture. Second, the people of Botswana have, for decades, lived in poverty with no modern education facilities, no health services and very poor infrastructure. The coming of independence, with its unprecedented economic fortunes, invoked 'messianic' feelings especially among the adult population. Third, an important feature of Botswana's past was a clear absence of a radical elite similar to those found in countries such as Zambia, Kenya and Ghana. In these countries, the enclave colonial economy created a small radical elite, which became the main opposition to colonial rule and ultimately the bearers of nationalist struggle. On the contrary, Botswana at independence was characterized by a poverty-stricken, politically conservative society and an embryonic conservative elite, which was happy to peacefully acquire leadership of the post-colonial state.

Botswana's democracy was imposed by the British Protectorate Administration collaborating with a small elitist class during colonial rule when the country was known as the Bechunaland protectorate. Botswana never resisted British colonialism and was willing to accept any form of ideology from the colonial master, including democracy. While this argument may be valid, there are several fundamental factors that enabled Botswana to achieve and sustain its present democracy. First, Botswana enjoys a high degree of cultural homogeneity. About 75 per cent of the people belong to the ethnic Tswana-speaking groups and non-Tswana groups are very small in numbers. Tswana culture is characterized by openness, participation in decision making, stability and accountability. Second, there are only two official languages – Tswana and English – which are spoken widely throughout the country. This, in various ways, minimized potential ethnic rivalries. Third, Sir Seretse Khama, the founding father of the nation-state, was tolerant, open and accountable, an exemplary and consummate builder of national unity. Fourth, opposition parties and civil society organizations in Botswana tend to be weak – or even non-existent. In general, Batswana are skeptical of opposition parties since they appear to be more radical and subscribe to the communist and socialist ethos, and, more importantly, they have never been tried and tested. This has given strength to the ruling party, which now believes it is the only party that can offer Batswana democracy. Given that Batswana value democracy and will settle for nothing less, they continue to support the Botswana Democratic Party in large numbers.

The quality of Botswana's democracy: implications for social policy and welfare

Botswana has never had a war, and is peaceful, politically stable, and economically successful. These characteristics, ideally, should create a conducive environment for more inclusive policies that promote social development. It has been able to satisfy what has been referred to as the 'threshold' of liberal democracy, but the critical issue is what this democracy has achieved for Batswana. The greatest challenge is whether or not the people of Botswana who have lived in a democracy for the past four decades are qualitatively different; whether they are better placed to influence policies and programmes of their government, and to register and actually vote in large numbers. In assessing quality, it is important to examine the extent to which the development of social policy and democracy have been mutually reinforcing. To do so effectively, we should go beyond structures, institutions and economic growth measures, important as these are, and address the qualitative issues in people's social lives (Molomo 2000).

Botswana is a functional democracy. Institutions such as parliament, local councils and district and village committees are well established. In addition, the media, trade unions, women's groups, faith-based organizations, and other civic bodies are allowed freedom of association and protected by the constitution. However, opposition political parties, parliament and civil society are weak. The opposition parties are ineffectual, poorly organized and without well-written manifestoes. As such, they are unable to engage in serious policy debates on matters such as poverty, unemployment and inequality. For example, in the nine elections held since 1965, the combined opposition parties have failed to win even one-third of the seats in parliament. This has effectively made Botswana a de facto one-party state. As a consequence, the opposition's contribution to social policy debate is limited. The ruling party believes it does not need to consult opposition parties on matters of policy because of the perception that such parties have been rejected continuously by the electorate.

The National Assembly is also generally weak relative to the executive. The role of parliament appears to be that of endorsing or rubber-stamping policies already decided by the executive. This means that most of the discussions in parliament, including those relating to development plans and social policies, are a mere formality. Given the weak opposition and apparent lack of effective linkages between them and other organized interest groups such as trade unions, the ruling BDP has over the years imposed its will or policies in parliament, even though most of the policies, such as the Remote Area Development Programme (RADP), have failed to improve the quality of life of intended beneficiaries.

Civil society is also weak in Botswana and its organs, such as the media, trade unions, church organizations, environmental groups, women's organizations and many others are fragmented and unable to collectively influence the social policy agenda. Given the apparent inactivity and non-participation of civic organizations in the policy-setting agenda processes, the government has tended to ignore them in the policy-making process and has not taken their contributions seriously. Civil society faces numerous problems, usually perpetrated by the state. For example, in the case of trade unions, government has, through legislation, restricted their participation on labour issues: For example, trade union committee members are not allowed by law to be full-time officers of the union and all labour unrest in Botswana has been declared illegal. The legislation is generally hostile to the development of a strong trade union movement in Botswana. In addition, government has not ratified some of the most important International Labour Organization (ILO) instruments. Other organizations such as the media and women's groups and teachers' unions have been the subject of constant criticism and threats by government ministers. For instance, women's organizations have been chastised as misguided groups of foreign-inspired individuals and teachers' unions and church groups have also been accused of being politically inspired by the opposition when they raise grievances on matters that affect them. The attitude of the state has adverse implications for the rights of workers to form and belong to trade unions freely and this conduct is unjustifiable and at variance with the values of a democratic society.

The question to be asked is: if the Botswana government has been and continues to be hostile to opposition parties and civic organization, why does it remain popular, democratic and politically stable? The answer to this question is that the Botswana state has been, until now, fairly successful economically. Molutsi (1994) argues that not only has the economy been doing well for the larger part of the post-independence period, but the state, during this time, emerged as the wealthiest institution in society enabling it to consistently deliver on its promises. The rallying slogan since the 1960s has been 'mining for development'. The emphasis is on ensuring that the majority of Batswana benefit from the fruits of development in line with the government's 'trickle down' policy.

The politics of social provision in Botswana

Botswana's monumental economic growth has been accompanied by one-party predominance. The Botswana Democratic Party (BDP) has won all the elections since independence and has performed consistently better in the rural areas. There is ample evidence to suggest that most social policies and programmes were introduced at the time of elections and were particularly targeted at the rural poor. For example, most agricultural policies, such as the Arable Land Development Programme (ALDP), preceded election years. Picard (1987) postulates that the ALDP was introduced in 1974 by the BDP so that it could perpetuate its political hegemony in the rural areas. It is also argued that such programmes as the Old Age Pension (1996), Vision 2016, Youth Policy (1996) and programmes for women and disabled persons were all introduced ahead of the 1999 general elections to woo the voters to the side of the BDP. Matsheka and Botlhomilwe (2000) also observed that social and economic factors played an important part in explaining Batswana's voting behaviour. They found an emergence of an issue-based electorate in Botswana that is now voting with economic considerations in mind. The BDP government has made itself visible to the majority of rural voters throughout the country. Physical projects in education, health, agriculture and social welfare are on the ground and the base for a 'caring' state has been established. In this way, the government has been able to build what most commentators on the Botswana economy refer to as 'paternalistic democracy' (Holm 1988). This has obviously paid dividends to the BDP since it has consistently won all the elections (see Table 8.7).

Table 8.7 shows that since 1965 the BDP has won every election with an overwhelming majority, except in the 1994 and 2004 elections. Government social spending has remained consistently over 30 per cent in the last 30 years. Historically, the ministries of Education, Local Government and Health always got the largest share of both the recurrent and development expenditure. The trend is still evident, as reflected in the last budget allocation in February 2005, in which the Ministries of Education, Local Government and State President accounted for 59 per cent of the total ministerial recurrent budgets, with HIV/AIDS programmes claiming the largest share of the development budget (Gaolathe 2005). Clearly, the BDP has used paternalistic social provisioning to entrench itself in power.

However, it would appear that government has used its wealth to appease the voters with the introduction of social policies and implementation of social programmes a few years before or after the elections. Although the BDP's share of the total vote has declined over the years, they have managed to secure a two-thirds majority in parliament since independence because of the first-past-the-post electoral rules that govern elections. The BDP remains the favourite party for the majority of Batswana mainly because of its paternalistic welfare policies. In particular, the BDP has been able to attract more rural elderly voters, mainly through their 'carrot'-like policies in agriculture, such as ALDEP and more recently the Old Age Pension. As a result, the BDP support increased in the rural areas supporting the notion that the BDP government is caring and compassionate as stated in Vision 2016. Although some commentators have argued that issue politics

Table 8.7 Social policies/programmes, social expenditure and electoral performance

policy/programmes	*Year introduced*	*Election year votes*	*BDP share of seats in parliament (%)*	*Social expenditure*	*BDP % share of votes*	*Opposition% share of vote*	*BNF % Opposition vote*
Drought relief	1965	1965	90	Food for work	80.4	19.6	0
Accelerated rural development Programme, ALDEP	1974–79	1974	84.4	over 30 per cent total GDP	76.6	23.4	49
F.A.P	1982	1984	85	over 30 per cent total GDP	68	32	63.75
No significant policy passed	Decline in economic growth	1994	67.5	Less government spending	54.7	45.3	81.6
Old-age pension (1996), Public sector salary increase (1998); SMME	1996	1999	82.5	over 30 per cent total GDP	57	43	60.5
Destitute policy	2002 (revised)	2004	77	over 50 per cent	52	48	Not available
HIV/AIDS policy	2002 (under review)				total GDP		

Source: Independent Electoral Commission (2004).

are absent in Botswana, for the conservative older rural voter, it is clear that welfare policies have had a bearing on and influenced their voting behaviour. Older people register and do vote in large numbers while youth participation in electoral politics has been very low, much to the disappointment of opposition parties, which believed they have massive support among the youth.

The distribution of votes among political parties (Table 8.7) reveals a progressive decline of voter support for the BDP and a steady rise of the opposition share of the vote, especially the main opposition, the Botswana National Front. The BDP's share of the vote was as high as 80.4 per cent in 1965, and declined to 52 per cent in 2004. Several reasons can be advanced for the poor performance of the BDP in the urban centres and a rise in the opposition. The 1990s marked the end of the economic boom. It is believed that the BDP has become very stubborn and insensitive to the needs and aspirations of the urban voter. The long history of 'ill fare' and exploitation of the poor in the urban areas and huge inequalities between urban elites and urban poor have resulted in an urban backlash. Poverty, unemployment, crime and shortage of accomodation is very high in urban centres due to increased rural–urban migration, but welfare provisions and social transfers to address these problems are very low and government does not treat social policy as a social right. This has resulted in the emergence of a political agenda that reflects the needs and socioeconomic problems of the urban areas in the 1990s. Major urban areas started to experience increasing political participation of a protest form. In the 1994 general elections, the opposition BNF won all the traditional BDP parliamentary seats in urban areas. The urban political agenda, premised on provision of basic needs, including jobs, is different from the traditional rural preoccupation with subsistence and may be responsible for the demise of the BDP in the urban centres. The alarming reduction in the margin of victory, and the corresponding gains by the opposition in the 2004 general elections, is a wake-up call to the BDP. It has brought up the once-unthinkable reality that the party, which at one point looked at itself as invincible, can easily be defeated by the opposition.

Some contradictions in democracy, development policy and social welfare

It is clear that Botswana's development policy is full of contradictions. Botswana has frequently been referred to as 'a model of success in Africa' in terms of its unparalleled economic growth, social spending and liberal democracy. The much-talked-about success promoted the mining industry, which has a limited potential to ameliorate poverty through employment creation. This is so because the mining industry is both capital and skill-intensive. There is no doubt that Botswana has amassed a lot of wealth through the sale of diamonds. However, the bulk of this wealth has not 'trickled down' to any significant extent but is concentrated in the hands of the state. Put differently, the Botswana state is rich, as reflected in billions of

Pula in foreign reserves, but the majority of Batswana are wallowing in poverty and without sufficient social protection. The Botswana state has not been able to effectively translate its wealth into commensurate levels of human development. Abject poverty coexists with ostentatious wealth concentrated in the hands of the state and a minority of business persons in the commercial, manufacturing and construction sectors (Tsie 1998).

Although Botswana is an upper-middle-income country, one of the only six in sub-Saharan Africa,[2] it is not known for generous welfare programmes towards the poor and vulnerable. Again, its pension scheme for the elderly is lower than in Namibia and South Africa. Good (2003: 24) argues that the country's Poverty Datum Line was purposely set much higher than commonly used measures of poverty elsewhere, such as the international standard of a dollar a day. A dollar a day would represent good money for the poor in Botswana. Serious inequalities and injustices exist in Botswana today. And when existing socioeconomic and political institutions are closely examined, the much acclaimed vibrant liberal democracy does not measure up to international standards on human rights.

Within Botswana's vibrant liberal democracy, with its open multi-party system and regular, free and relatively fair elections, many limitations exist. For example, public sector employees are prohibited from speaking to the press or forming unions. There exists no freedom of information legislation and no whistle blower laws are in place. The *Kgotla*, the traditional community political forum, is not helpful either. It is dominated by the chief (who is also a civil servant) and other bureaucratic elites and therefore offers no possibilities for an organized opposition that can put pressure on the government to implement its decisions for policy reform. Instead, in the *Kgotla,* most people tend to stress Botswana's achievements regarding democracy and stability and avoid critical socioeconomic and political issues relating to redistributive justice. Compounding the above problems are fragmented and weak opposition political parties, which have never come closer to winning elections over the last forty years since the first elections in 1965. Although the BDP's share of votes continues to decline, the party continues to enjoy a comfortable majority in parliament and as such does not see the opposition forming an alternative government in the foreseeable future. Without a credible opposition, the watchdog role of parliament has been eroded, leading to a paternalistic democracy.

Conclusion

This chapter has shown that economic policies are critical in determining the social and democratic status of the country. In Botswana, the 'mining for development' approach has played a major part in determining the extent to which the people of Botswana have had access to basic social services. Botswana has a strong economic base and a stable political system. These have proved to be necessary, if not sufficient, preconditions that must be satisfied if the objectives of effective social policies are to be achieved. Economic development and democratization appear to be mutually reinforcing and provide the basis for more inclusive redistributive welfare policies. These two must be strengthened because economic performance is expected to raise standards of living and lead to higher levels of democratization. However, experience in Botswana shows that, despite the phenomenal growth rates, levels of unemployment, poverty and inequality remain high. The wealth of the country has not sufficiently trickled down to benefit the poor. Instead, an enclave economy has been created. The rich are becoming richer and the poor poorer. Given the above, the challenge for Botswana is to:

- Develop a comprehensive social protection system that promotes integration and inclusiveness, and provides security from social and economic shocks.
- Provide a legal base for social security programmes.
- Strengthen and promote informal social security programmes, such as *metshelo* (helping hand).
- Introduce reforms in the existing social security system by extending protection to the majority of citizens, particularly those living in the remote areas.
- Revitalize the economy and create more jobs.

Notes

1. The Kgotla is a place, a meeting, a court of justice and the sole legitimate forum for community decision-making. Once a decision was made at a Kgotla, it was binding on the whole community.
2. The other Middle Income Countries were: South Africa, Mauritius, Gabon, Seychelles and Mayote.

References

Bank of Botswana. 2001. *Annual Report 2000*. Gaborone.

Birdsall, N., D. Ross, and R. Sabot. 1995. 'Inequality and Growth Discovered: Lessons from East Asia.' *The World Bank Economic Review*, 9(3), 477–508.

Botswana Institute of Development Policy Analysis (BIDPA). 1997. *A Study of Poverty and Poverty Alleviation in Botswana*. Gaborone: Botswana Institute of Development Policy Analysis.

Botswana Institute of Development Policy Analysis. (BIDPA) 2003. *A Review of the Remote Area Development Programme*. Gaborone: BIDPA.

Central Statistics Office (CSO). 1988. *Botswana Family Health Survey Report II*. (BFHS II). Gaborone: Government Printer.

Central Statistics Office (CSO). 1995. *Household Expenditure Survey 1993/94*. Gaborone: Government Printer.

Central Statistics Office (CSO). 1996. *Botswana Family Health Survey Report III*. Gaborone: Government Printer.

Central Statistics Office (CSO). 1999. *Health Statistics Report*. Gaborone: Government Printer.

Central Statistics Office (CSO). 2001. *National Population and Housing Census*. Gaborone: Government Printer.

Central Statistics Office (CSO). 2003. *Informal Sector Survey Report*. Gaborone: Government Printer.

Central Statistics Office (CSO). 2004. *Botswana AIDS Impact Survey II*. (BAIS II). Gaborone: Government Printer.

Centre for Economic Policy Research (CEPR). 2002. *An African Success Story: Botswana*. Gaborone: CEPR.

Department of Social Services (DSS). 2005. *Orphan Care Programme – Annual Report*. Gaborone: Government Printer.

Department of Social Services (DSS). 2005. *Cumulative Expenditure for Destitutute Report, April 2004 to April 2005*. Gaborone: Government Printer.

Department of Social Services (DSS). 2004. *Social Benefits Division Annual Report, 2004*. Gaborone: Government Printer.

Friedrich Ebert Stiftung. 2003. *Trade Unions in Botswana: Country Report*. Gaborone: Friedrich Ebert Stiftung.

Gaolathe Baledzi. 2005. 'Budget Speech.' Speech given at the 9th session of Parliament. Botswana Parliament – Gaborone, 7th Feb, 2005.

Good, K. 2003. *Bushmen and Diamonds (Un) Civil Society in Botswana*. Uppsala: Nordiska Afrikainstitutet.

Government of Botswana (GoB). *Trade Dispute Act 2004*. Gaborone: Government Printer.

Government of Botswana (GoB). 1998. *Workmen's Compensation Act*. Gaborone: Government Printer.

Government of Botswana (GoB). 1988. *Pensions Act*. Gaborone: Government Printer.

Government of Botswana (GoB). *Employer Organization Act*. Gaborone: Government Printer.

Government of Botswana (GoB). 1982. *Employment Act*. Gaborone: Government printer.

Government of Botswana (GoB). 1966. *Constitution of Botswana*. Gaborone: Government Printer.

Government of Botswana and United Nations Development Program. 2002. *A Review of Anti-Poverty Initiatives in Botswana: Lessons for a National Poverty Reduction Strategy*. Gaborone: UNDP.

Harvey, C. 1992. 'Botswana: Is the Miracle Over?' *Journal of African Economies* 1, No. 3 (November), 335–68.

Hedenquist J.-A. 1992. *Introduction to Social Work and Community Development in Botswana*. Gaborone: Government Printer.

Holm, J. D. 1988. 'Botswana: A Paternalistic Democracy', in L. Diamond, J. Linz and S. M. Lipset (eds), *Democracy in Developing Countries*. London: Lynne Rienner Publishers.

Hope, K. R. 1996. 'Growth, Unemployment, and Poverty in Botswana.' *Journal of Contemporary African Studies*, 14(1), 53–67.

Independent Electoral Commission (IEC). 2004. *An Analysis of Botswana's Election Results 1965–2004*. Gaborone: IEC.

Matsheka, T. and Z. Botlhomilwe. 2000. 'Economic Conditions and Election Outcomes in Botswana: Is the Relationship Spurious?' *Pula: Botswana Journal of African Studies*, 14(1), 3–22.

Ministry of Finance and Development Planning (MFDP), 1991. *National Development Plan 7, 1991/1996*. Gaborone: Government Printer.

Ministry of Finance and Development Planning (MFDP). 1997. *National Development Plan 8, 1997/2003*. Gaborone: Government Printer.

Ministry of Finance and Development Planning (MFDP). 2001. *Annual Economic Report*. Gaborone: Government Printer.
Ministry of Finance and Development Planning (MFDP). 2002. *National Development Plan 9*, 2003/04–2008/09. Gaborone: Government Printer.
Ministry of Local Government. 1999. *Short-Term Plan of Action on Care of Orphans in Botswana*. Gaborone: Government Printer.
Ministry of Local Government. 2002. *Revised National Policy on Destitute Persons*. Gaborone: Government Printer.
Mogalakwe, M. 1995. 'State–Labour Relations in an Emergent Capitalist 'Democracy': The Case of Botswana', *LABOUR, Capital and Society*, 28(2), 146–74.
Molomo, M. (ed.) 2000. 'Elections and Democracy in Botswana', *Pula: Botswana Journal of African Studies*, 14(1), 1–2.
Molutsi, Patrick. P. John, Holm, D. (eds). 1989. *Democracy in Botswana*. Gaborone: Macmillan. – now Palgrave Macmillan.
Molutsi, P. P. 1994. 'Botswana Democratic Institutions: Their Strengths and Prospects', in Botswana Society, *Botswana in the 21st Century*. Proceedings of a Symposium organised by the Botswana Society, October18–21, 1993. Gaborone: Botswana Society.
Molutsi, P. P. 1998. 'Elections and Electoral Experience in Botswana', in W. A. Edge and M. H. Lekorwe (eds), *Botswana Politics and Society*. Pretoria: Van Schaik.
National AIDS Coordinating Agency (NACA). 2003. *Botswana Second Generation HIV/AIDS Surveillance: A Technical Report*. Gaborone: NACA.
National AIDS Coordinating Agency (NACA). 2004. *Botswana Second Generation HIV/AIDS Surveillance: A Technical Report*. Gaborone: NACA.
National AIDS Coordinating Agency (NACA). 2005. Report on total expenditure by Botswana Government on HIV/AIDS as at March, 2005. Gaborone: NACA.
Ngcongco, L. 1989. 'Tswana Political Tradition: How Democratic?', in J. D. Holm and P. Molutsi (eds), *Democracy in Botswana*. Gaborone: Macmillan.
Picard, L. 1987. (ed.). *Politics and Rural Development in Southern Africa: The Evolution of Modern Botswana Politics*. London: Rex Collins.
Siddiqi, M. 1999. 'Botswana: The African Success Story', *Africa Economic Digest*, 20(10).
Tsie, B. 1998. 'The State and Development Policy in Botswana', in K. R. Hope and G. Somolekae (eds), *Public Administration and Public Policy in Botswana*. Capetown: Juta, pp. 1–20.
United Nations. 2001. *International Covenant on Economic, Social and Cultural Rights*. New York: UN Publications.
United Nations Development Programme (UNDP). 2005. *United Nations Development Report – Botswana Country Report 2005*. Gaborone: UNDP.
United Nations Development Programme (UNDP). 2005. *Human Development Report 2005. International Cooperation at a crossroads: Aid, Trade and Security in an Unequal World*. New York: UNDP.
United Nations Development Programme (UNDP). 2004. *Botswana Millennium Development Goals Status Report 2004*. Gaborone: UNDP.

9
The Ballot Box and Social Policy in Mauritius

Sheila Bunwaree

Introduction

Mauritius's record of economic achievements in the 1980s and 1990s, as well as its social cohesion, led to it being given the label of the 'Little Tiger' of the Indian Ocean. In less than 20 years, resource-poor, isolated and vulnerable Mauritius has become a middle-income country with a GNP per head of approximately US$5,000. Mauritius also experiences regular, free and fair elections. The peaceful alternation of parties, coupled with a very efficient electoral supervisory commission that sees to the good conduct of elections with all norms and procedures being respected, testify to a strong ballot culture in the country. Mauritius does not have an army, it has a police force and its expenditure on defence remains relatively small. Democracy is firmly rooted in the country even if some democratic deficits still persist. Whilst the democratic deficits do not threaten the welfare state in any particular way, addressing them, particularly the marked underrepresentation of women in parliament, could help to make the Mauritian state even more inclusive. What may pose a threat to the welfare state is the current decline of the economy. Despite the growing budget deficits and the slowing down of the growth rate, the Mauritian state continues to pump resources into the welfare state. Is this fiscal irresponsibility – or is it the normal behaviour of political parties that have a socialist inclination? Or is it rather the quest for power and the need to ensure that they obtain the necessary votes to gain or retain office? This chapter argues that the right to social welfare is embedded in the average Mauritian psyche, including that of the politicians, and that no government or political party contesting elections will dare come up with a programme that suggests any major form of welfare downsizing. Lingayah (1997) argues that social welfare is politically rooted and that the consequence of this is that expectations of social services are constantly raised. Such expectations therefore make it very difficult for governments to make policy decisions regarding cuts in social expenditure.

Elections have been contested eight times since independence – in 1976, 1982, 1983, 1987, 1991, 1995, 2000 and 2005 – but social policies and the welfare tendencies of the major political parties have never been a subject of contention. Political parties are very conscious that the population regards their social rights as 'acquired rights' and that it would not be in the politicians' best interests to attempt to tamper with these rights. Trade unions have played a very strong role in defending these rights and fighting for the development and maintenance of different forms of welfare. Whilst it is true that the current rate of unionization is only around 20 per cent and that the power of trade unions has eroded, trade unions had an important influence on the two most important political parties – the Mauritius Labour Party (MLP) and the Mouvement Militant Mauricien (MMM) – especially from the 1930s to the late 1970s. Mauritius has a history of sustaining its welfare system despite very harsh economic conditions, such as in the 1980s when it had to embark on structural adjustment programmes and again now when the economy is facing the vagaries of globalization and losing almost all its preferential arrangements in the international market. Some economic analysts suggest that the country needs a growth rate of between 7 per cent and 9 per cent to meet the costs of the welfare state, but the country is currently experiencing only 3–4 per cent growth. Soaring unemployment exacerbates poverty in the country. The riots of 1999 are a manifestation of the growing alienation and frustration of certain segments of the society.[1]

The chapter is divided into three parts. The first part provides a brief history of the country and the development of the welfare regime. It shows how the development of the welfare state is tied to the efforts of the labour movement of the colonial period. It discusses the various factors that have shaped the welfare regime and the history of the Labour Party, which governed the country during the first 13 years of independence. The next section explores the relationship between politics and economics. It highlights the factors that usually push the electorate to sanction one government or the other. This discussion is interspersed with the political history of the MMM. It is noted that the brief period of authoritarianism and repressive measures displayed by the ruling party towards the rising MMM opposition did not affect social services and welfare development. Then we examine the Mauritian economy and the challenges it confronts. The contraction of the sugar economy and the export processing zone (EPZ) are highlighted as well as the growing feminization of poverty. It argues that despite demands for the streamlining of welfare, successive governments have remained committed to maintaining the welfare state. The chapter concludes that it is important for the state to protect the most vulnerable and deprived in these globalizing times, otherwise Mauritius' democracy will lose its significance and the Mauritian volcano may erupt again.

Development and consolidation of the welfare state

Brief history of the country

Mauritius is an island state located in the Indian Ocean about 800 kilometres east of Madagascar. It has a population of almost 1.2 million people, all of whom constitute a 'deterritorialization' of people from across the globe. There is no indigenous population. The island was first settled by the Dutch, followed by the French, after which it became a British possession. The Dutch did not stay long. According to Toussaint (1977), the Dutch's failure to stay could be attributed not only to a shortage of food on the island but also to their deficiencies as settlers and administrators. The island was deserted by the Dutch in 1710 and the French took control in 1715.

Sugar cane was introduced by the Dutch, but the French are the ones who expanded the sugar industry. Slaves were brought in from Pondicherry and Chandernagore in India but much bigger contingents of slaves came from Africa (Baker 1972). Madagascar and Mozambique were the two great sources of slaves for Mauritius. French colonial rule came to an end in 1810. The British ruled the island from 1810 to 1968, the year in which the country gained its independence. The abolition of slavery in February 1835 and the end of the apprenticeship system soon after, caused the settlers to tap new sources of labour. Indentured labourers were brought from India. Mintz (1985: 71), a leading scholar of the sugar colonies, notes: 'The link between sweated tropical colonial labour and non-White labour was preserved, largely undisturbed by the end of slavery.'

India provided a good resource to meet the insatiable demands of the plantocracy for cheap labour. According to many critics, including Best (1965), Beckford (1972) and Tinker (1974), the indentured labourers represented another form of slavery. The peopling of Mauritius explains the heterogeneity of the island in terms of ethnic groups based on language and religious differences. The major ethnic communities are Hindus, Muslims, Creoles, Franco-Mauritians (Whites) and Chinese. Creoles and Franco Mauritians are lumped together in a category known as 'Population Générale'. The category 'Population Générale' consists of a small group of White Franco-Mauritians (about 2 per cent of the current population, following a large wave of emigration after independence), and a much larger category of Creoles (usually defined as Catholics of African or mixed African–European, African–Indian and/or African–Chinese descent). Unlike other groups, this group cannot be said to constitute a sociocultural entity (Eriksen, 1998). The only common element within this group is their Christian religion.

Although in many countries, independence was fuelled by nationalist sentiments, Mauritius experienced a different situation. Anti-colonial feelings were expressed by the Hindu majority, but the other ethno-religious groups preferred to maintain ties with the mother country. Mauritius was divided as it negotiated its way towards independence. 44 per cent of the population voted against independence. The inter-ethnic tensions and the economic morass prevailing during that period could have led to a social explosion. But the country's development was steered in such a manner that the 'disaster' alluded to by Kearney (1990) was averted.

The beginning of political agitation: trade unions and the labour party

Although the British took over in 1810, politics on the island was dominated by the Franco-Mauritians and a small group of wealthy, conservative Creole allies. This conservative coalition was known as the 'Oligarchs'. British presence on the island remained minimal. The governor, the colonial secretary, some heads of departments, and some Supreme Court judges were British. The magistrates and senior police officials were Franco-Mauritians, whilst officials in the lower echelons were the Creole middle class. Some Indians were gradually given jobs in the lower echelons of the colonial bureaucracy.

Political agitation started to gain significance in the 1930s and 1940s. The main political issue was the deep economic crisis and hardships faced by the working class. Riots and strikes became a common feature in the late 1930s and early 1940s. During this period, several organizations, such as the Mauritius Labour Party, the Engineering and Technical Workers' Union, the Mauritius Agricultural Labourers' Association and the Indian Cultural association emerged. These organizations brought Creoles and Indians together to press for their rights. Amongst the most important of these was the Mauritius Labour Party, which was founded in 1936 by Dr Maurice Curé, a well-known Creole politician. Unlike other Creole efforts, the Labour Party had Indians in prominent positions. The party brought together the urban (Creole) workers and rural Indian labourers. Two key figures – Emmanuel Anquetil and Guy Rozemont – played a very important role in the development of the party. Anquetil also set up a new left-wing newspaper *Le Peuple Mauricien*. Rozemont was one of the editors and a strong advocate of trade union organization and labour law reform. The Labour Party's main objectives were to give the labouring class the same rights, privileges and working conditions enjoyed by workers in other countries. Curé, Rozemont and Anquetil were the initiators of the trade union movement on the island.

The trade union movement played a very important role in postwar labour relations. Members of the Labour Party criticized the various forms of oppression and injustices that the population was going through. They campaigned intensively for the introduction of social legislation and changes in the franchise to include workers' representation in the colonial executive council. The refusal of the white sugar plantocracy to entertain these demands led to a labour strike in August 1937 in the districts of Flacq and Grand Port, when five workers were shot dead (Mannick 1979). The government was then compelled to revise labour conditions and to set up a commission of enquiry. The commission condemned the abuses of the sugar planters and supported the setting up of a Labour department as well as legislation on trade unions. In short, the Labour Party sought political reforms, broader representation in the Council of Government and better laws.

Seewoosagur Ramgoolam, who was to become the prime minister in 1968, played a vital role in the upliftment of the human condition well before he actually took the reins of power. Ramgoolam returned to Mauritius in 1934 after spending many years in London training to be a doctor. Together with a few other prominent leaders within the Indian community, he set up a newspaper called *Advance*. In 1940, Ramgoolam was nominated to the Council of government and he rarely missed any opportunity to draw the attention of the authorities to the inhuman condition in which vast segments of the population were living. Riots and strikes in different parts of the island became common and some positive changes started to occur in the late 1940s.

In 1950, Ramgoolam and his associates joined the Labour Party, which was still led by Rozemont; this marked a momentary alliance between the Hindu elite and the Creole and Hindu workers. The minority groups, such as the Franco-Mauritians, conservative Creoles and Muslims, came together to form the Ralliement Mauricien in 1952. This group opposed the Labour Party and its goals of universal suffrage as well as the progressive shift of power from the colonial to the local government (Bowman 1991).

Introduction of some welfare schemes during the colonial period

The Beveridge Report of 1942 on social reform, published in England, had an impact on Mauritius. Simmons (1982) argues that a newly empowered British Labour government passed the Colonial Development and Welfare Act of 1946, allocating a budget for social programmes in the colonies. Sir Mackenzie Kennedy, who was governor from 1942 to 1948, introduced pensions for employees, particularly on the sugar estates and cooperative societies in which small planters could help each other, and a few public libraries. In 1947, a new constitution brought about changes that had been schemed, planned and hoped for in the past 40 years (Mannick 1979). Gayan (1990), citing Veerasamy Ringadoo on Ramgoolam's contribution as a nominated legislator, notes that Ramgoolam pleaded for the workers and the downtrodden and gave a clear indication of the policies he would like the government to take in education, health and welfare generally. He was already indicating his concept of a welfare state, which was to become a reality as a result of his patience, steadiness and sense of social justice.

The social security system was born in 1950. Non-contributory pensions were established for Mauritians over 60 years. In an initial phase, the government increased spending on public health, including a malaria eradication campaign that halved the infant mortality rate (from 155 per 1,000 to 67 per 1,000) in a little over a decade. Mauritius did not have a free national health service, but prices for medical services were kept low through some form of price controls and some groups received free health care, including labourers working for the government, police and prison officers (Titmuss and Abel Smith 1968).

The welfare state in post-independence Mauritius

Six major factors influenced the evolution and consolidation of the welfare state in the post-independence period. These were: (1) the country's rapid economic development and full employment for most of the 1980s till the mid-1990s; (2) the leaders of the immediate post-independence period who were inspired by Fabianism; (3) the development and strengthening of the developmental state; (4) the sugar boom between 1971–75 and the sugar export tax; (5) a human-faced structural adjustment programme in the late 1970s and early 1980s; and (6) welfare-related expenditures during electoral cycles.

Table 9.1 below shows the evolution of social expenditures between 1970 and 2004 and Table 9.2 shows more specifically the percentage of government expenditure that the different sectors represent from the late 1990s onwards. The abolition of subsidies on rice and food in the early 1980s led to some criticisms by the opposition but did not become a big issue for the population, perhaps because conditions of living had improved for almost everyone. Spending on defence represents a very small percentage of government expenditure, highlighting the fact that resources are allocated in more welfare-oriented programmes rather than on the military, as is often the case in some other developing countries. Social security and welfare constitutes the bulk of government expenditure. Apart from the universal non-contributory old age pension, the government has also established a National Pension scheme. A National Pensions Act was passed in 1976 but its coverage does not extend to workers in the informal sector. A Social Aid Act was passed in 1983, but this had a gender bias (Bunwaree 2004). The Competitiveness Foresight report (2004: 15) notes that 'the rising public debt and recurrent deficit put at risk the maintenance of the welfare state. Social expenditure has risen from 10.7 per cent to 15.1 per cent of GDP between 1985 and 2001.'

Rapid economic development, full employment and unemployment

The Mauritian economy managed to lift itself out of stagnation in the post-independence period. Between the 1970s and late 1990s, it has steadily maintained an average real GDP growth rate of about 5 per cent per annum. The successful and rapid diversification of the economy from a monocrop sugar economy into three other engines of growth, such as the textile and garment sector, the tourism industry, and the offshore and financial sector account largely for the high growth rates and full employment between the mid-1980s and the 1990s. More recently, attempts are being made to develop the Information Communication Technology (ICT) sector as well and make the Mauritian economy become a knowledge hub. Various factors, such as the

Table 9.1 Social Expenses – Budget 1967 – 2004

Budget/Year	*1967/68–1970/71 average*	*1975/76*	*1980/81*	*1985/86*	*1990/91*	*1991/92*	*1992/93*	*1993/94*	*1994–95*	*1995–96*	*1996–97*	*1997–98*	*1998–99*	*1999–00*	*2000–01*	*2001–02*	*2002–03*	*2003–04 estimation*
per cent Education	**38.4**	**29.34**	**39.42**	**35.8**	**34.9**	**32**	**29.3**	**32**	**34.4**	**32.6**	**32.9**	**31.6**	**29.6**	**29.6**	**28.1**	**26.3**	**31.4**	**29.7**
per cent Health	**25.12**	**20.62**	**18.54**	**20.5**	**20.7**	**18.3**	**20**	**18.4**	**17.2**	**17.1**	**15.2**	**15.9**	**16.3**	**16.2**	**16.4**	**15.9**	**15.3**	**17.2**
per cent Social Security	**32.72**	**16.32**	**17.34**	**36.9**	**33.5**	**34.4**	**34.1**	**32.5**	**33.8**	**37.7**	**36.9**	**38.2**	**39.3**	**39.9**	**39.7**	**37**	**35**	**34.8**
per cent Subsidy on Rice and Flour	—	**28.22**	**20.16**	—	—	—	—	—	—	—	—	—	—	—	—	—	—	—

Sources: Compiled by Author from Central Statistical Offices' Digests of Public Finance (from 1967 to 2004) and Mauritius Economic Reviews, Port Louis, Mauritius. Ministry of Economic Planning and Development. 1981–83, 1975–77, 1972–74, 1970–72.

Table 9.2 Functional classification of government expenditure, 1997/98–2000/01

	1997/98 (%)	*1998/99 (%)*	*1999/00 (%)*	*2000/01 (%)*	*2001/02 (%)*	*2002/03 (%)*	*2003/04 (%)*
Education	16.0	15.0	14.7	13.8	14.4	14.5	15.3
Health	8.1	8.3	8.3	8.1	8.8	8.2	8.9
Social security and welfare	19.4	19.9	20.5	19.5	20.3	18.2	17.9
Housing and community amenities	5.7	5.0	6.3	6.4	9.9	8.6	8.0
Defence	0.9	0.8	0.9	0.8	0.8	0.8	0.8
Public order and safety	7.6	7.8	7.4	6.9	7.6	7.5	8.0
Public debt interest	(16.0)	(14.8)	(14.5)	16.4	13.8	16.6	16.2

Source: Central Statistical Office. 2004.

presence of a national bourgeoisie and a substantial amount of local sugar capital in the different sectors, the successful fertility and population control, a literate and adaptable workforce, important flows of direct investment, protected markets and guaranteed prices, account for the Mauritian success story.

The full employment of the 1980s and 1990s is now giving way to a rapidly growing unemployment problem. Two sectors that are most hit are the agricultural and the garment/textile sector. The unemployment rate in the country has increased from 8.8 per cent in 2000 to 10.2 per cent in 2003.

Fabianism and welfare in Mauritius

The history of concern for social welfare is heavily dominated by Fabianism. The first prime minister of the island, Sir Seewoosagur Ramgoolam, and a number of other leaders had studied at the London School of Economics where they were influenced by the model of gradual socialism advocated by Fabianism. Mulloo (2000), citing Ramgoolam himself, notes: 'Fabian socialism suited my temperament and I have been a Fabian all my life... I have tried to cultivate the indefatigable patience of the Fabian philosophy and the Fabian belief in moderation and conviction in parliamentary reform and the concept of welfare state wherein the state is viewed as the representative and trustee, guardian and protector of the people'. The 'social conscience' of the nation was developed from very early on. Carroll and Carroll (1999) comment that Mauritius escaped the worst excesses of leadership found in newly independent states as the commitment to Fabian socialism of the country's first prime minister and his allies meant that they did attempt to improve conditions for ordinary workers: 'They were neither gangster politicians using the state to enrich themselves, nor factional leaders committed only to the welfare of their own members.'

The developmental state

In his paper entitled the 'Mauritian developmental state', Meisenhelder (1997) shows the extent to which Mauritius's bureaucracy and political elite are autonomous of the economic elite. Political power was transferred successfully to the large Hindu majority group whilst economic power remained in the hands of the whites. The bureaucracy, which was also filled by people of Indian origin, and the political elite worked together towards the implementation of policies that were in the interests of large sections of the society. Expenditure on health, education and social security is central to the social policies that the state and Mauritian bureaucracy formulated and implemented (Dommen and Dommen 1999).

The Mauritian developmental state has also been committed to a whole range of other non-contributory social benefits, such as Social Aid, Food Aid and Unemployment Hardship Relief. The state has also played a very important role on the economic front. The state provides a host of incentives to the private sector and has developed a strong private–public partnership. It has also used tools of 'economic diplomacy' to obtain various preferential arrangements on the international market, thus facilitating trade and improving the balance of payments in the 1980s and 1990s.

The sugar export tax

A couple of years after independence, from 1971 to 1975, the price of sugar on the international market was very high, leading to a sugar boom, which encouraged and facilitated the introduction of a sugar export tax. This tax provided a large amount of the revenues needed to consolidate the welfare state. The idea of a sugar tax was not new; the Mauritius Labour Party of 1949 had already mentioned it (Seegobin and Collen 1977). Its advocates were convinced that the sugar marketing arrangements negotiated by the state guaranteed planters a healthy and substantial profit, which justified the tax. The relatively autonomous nature of the state bureaucracy explains the effective implementation of the sugar levy.

Table 9.3 shows how the percentage of sugar tax over total tax revenue has evolved, but it has not been possible to obtain data regarding the amount of sugar tax revenue that has actually been pumped into the welfare sector. Interviews carried out with some politicians and policy makers/technicians within relevant ministries confirm that the revenues obtained from the sugar export tax helped enormously towards the consolidation of welfare. Writing about the sugar export tax in *Week-end*, a weekly newspaper, Dommen (1996, March 10) argued: 'The tax allowed government to fund its social programme, health, education and food subsidies, and... rural electrification... The expenditure was a way of meeting important consumption needs so that social peace could be maintained while wages were low'. Contrary to the advice offered by Meade (a British academic who was invited by the colonial government in 1961 to report on the economic and social

Table 9.3 Sugar tax and percentage of total tax revenue, 1962–1994 (Rs Millions and %)

Budget Year	*1962/ 63–66/ 67 Ave*	*1967/ 68–70/ 71 Ave*	*1971/72*	*R. E 1971/73*	*1973/74*	*1974/75*	*1975/76*
Amount export taxes	15.6	16.7	19.6	29	48.1	129.8	126.1
Tax revenue budgetary accounts	141.7	158.7	199.7	264.3	386.9	653.4	937.6
% sugar tax11 over total Tax Revenue	10.5	9.81	10.97	12.43	19.86	13.44	11.81
Budget Year	*1985/86*	*1986/87*	*1987/88*	*1988/89*	*1989/90*	*1990/91*	*1991/92*
Amount export taxes	459.3	549.8	606.6	606.3	370.3	427.6	416.3
Tax revenue budgetary accounts	3482.3	4546.6	5728.1	6809.8	7804.6	9025 7	9552.1
% sugar tax over total Tax Revenue	13.18	12.09	10.58	8.9	4.74	4.73	4.35

Sources: Compiled by author from National Accounts and Bi-Annual Digests of Public Finance (for various years),

conditions of the island), the enacted sugar tax applied most harshly to the large estates, while small cane growers were assisted and subsidized by the state. This reversal of the agricultural priorities of the colonial state was in part due to the new Mauritian government's need to be responsive to its own constituencies and electoral supporters.

The issue of the sugar export levy was so controversial that the Parti Mauricien Social Democrate (PMSD) led by Gaetan Duval, which represented the oligarchy, left the coalition government led by the Mauritius Labour Party (MLP) when the tax was decided. The tax remained contentious and was redebated every time the levy was raised. The large planters consistently opposed the sugar tax and any increase in its terms. But the state showed its autonomy by implementing it, increasing it and maintaining it for a good number of years. The sugar export tax was abolished in 1984. The argument that was put forward for its abolition was the depressing sugar price on the international market and the need to modernize and make the sugar sector more efficient. Fiscal Policy was readjusted. A sales tax was introduced for the first time. This, coupled with other forms of direct and indirect taxes, loans that the government struck and the various forms of aid and grants that it obtained from its two former colonial powers – England and France – as well as other countries, such as India and China, helped to sustain the welfare state.

1976/77	*1977/78*	*1978/79*	*1979/80*	*1980/81*	*1981/82*	*1982/83*	*1983/84*	*1984/85*
124.9	145.2	287.3	268.2	377.8	416.4	416.4	442	369.9
1057	1227.4	1540.8	1761.2	1927.4	2397.7	2430.5	2791.7	2977
11.82	18.64	15.22	19.6	17.36	17.13	15.83	12.42	

1992/93	*1993/94*	*1994/95*	*1995/96*	*1996/97*
433.8	400.3	—	—	—
10360.2	11611.6	11242.5	11662.5	14000.9
4.18		—	—	—

Ministry of Finance, Port Louis, Mauritius.

Human-faced structural adjustment

As the 1970s drew to an end, sugar prices fell, cyclones hit the country and the soaring price of oil had a negative impact on the economy. Meanwhile, the funding of the state's social welfare programmes led to larger debts and public deficits. By the end of the decade, the state was experiencing recession and rising unemployment. The state had no option but to adopt structural adjustment policies. The MMM's landslide victory in 1982 ushered in a new era in the elaboration and implementation of the adjustment policies. The 1982 budget speech highlighted the philosophy of dialogue adopted by the new government. According to Bheenick (1991), the government was committed to reform but maintained an 'intensive policy dialogue' with the World Bank, which meant that the structural adjustment loan was Bank-supported rather than Bank-dictated.

Contrary to many other developing countries, Mauritius did not succumb to the IMF/World Bank conditionalities of reducing government expenditure. It did not abolish free education and free health. The state did not roll back, but instead persevered in the delivery of these social services. This does not mean that the adjustment policy was painless. Very little research has been done on the social impact of SAPs in Mauritius. Gulhati and Nallari (1990) are among the very few who have drawn attention to the plight of the underprivileged in the context of SAPs in Mauritius: 'The government persevered with reforms even though it meant a considerable loss in momentum of economic growth and a perceptible setback in the welfare of low income groups. Very little was done to 'sweeten the pill' for the underprivileged social groups'. The devaluations that accompanied the structural adjustment programmes led to an erosion of the purchasing power of all Mauritians but the impact was most significant amongst the poorest stratum of Mauritian society. Moreover, the unemployed had no income at all since there was no dole system in place.

Welfare expenditures and electoral cycles

Secondary free education was introduced in 1976 by the Labour Party of the time and it is generally argued that it was largely a political bait or an electoral bribe. It was the last card that the increasingly unpopular Labour government could play. In fact, the Labour Party came back to power in the general elections of 1976 but with only a very thin majority. It quickly went into a post-election coalition with the Parti Mauricien Social Democrate and led the government until 1982 when the MMM won a landslide victory of 60–0. The opposition did not win any seat.

When the MMM came to power in 1982, they could not touch free education since many MMM members themselves promoted and demanded free education in the mid-1970s. Moreover, abolishing free education would have caused the newly elected government to lose its popularity very quickly. Politics in Mauritius is marked by a number of alliances and coaltions and this is what Bowman (1991) describes as 'political stability à la mauricienne'.

Table 9.4 captures the different political alliances and coalitions and how politics and economics are closely connected. As most parties embrace social democratic policies, there are no major differences on programmes and manifestos (Sithanen 2003). The continuous state expenditure on welfare-related items from one year to the other is testimony to the government's unflinching support to expand the welfare state. It is true that welfare expenditure on certain social items continue to increase, but the budgets preceding each general election indicate even greater generosity by the government and are often regarded as electoral bribes. In each electoral year, we find the government of the day providing important benefits to the population. During the electoral campaign, political parties often promise important welfare measures, such as the recent promise by the Social Alliance led by the Labour Party to provide free transport to all students as well as re-establishing universal old age pensions for all. The MMM/MSM government, which was in power from 2000 to 2005, had in 2004 decided to bring in some minimal element of targeting by eliminating from the old age pension all those earning more than Rs 20,000 per month. The Social Alliance quickly reacted to this and as soon as they came to power in July 2005 reinstated the universal old age pension and implemented their promise of providing free transport to all students.

Table 9.4 State expenditure on various welfare items in a political perspective

Month and year of budget presentations	*Month and year of elections*	*Parties in power at the time of budget presentations*	*State expenditure on various items of welfare*
May 1976	**December 1976**	**MLP/CAM/PMSD**	Total expenditure on social services rose from Rs90 million in 1967–1968 to Rs368 million in 1974–1975. Social transfers of various kinds – old-age pensions, family allowances, outdoor relief, most of all in terms of expenditure, food subsidies. Expenditure on social assistance more than doubled between 1967–68 and 1975–76 from Rs30 million to Rs64 million, but expenditure on food subsidies at Rs142 million was 24 times as great in 1975–76 as in 1967–68, when they totaled Rs5.8 million. Welfare benefits, such as Family Allowance, Old Age Pension and Outdoor Relief, be Rs68 million as compared to Rs62 million
May 1981	**June 1982**	**MMM**	The subsidy on rice and flour increased from Rs203 million to Rs230 million Expenditure on education went up from Rs407 million to Rs426 million, on health increased from Rs208 million to Rs216 million and on social security benefits increased from Rs198 million to Rs205 million. The balance of about Rs 650 million expended on a wide variety of essential services, including subsidy to local authorities.
July 1982	**August 1983**	**MMM/PSM**	Rs403 million for pensions and social security benefits, Rs200 million for food subsidy
June 1986	**September 1987**	**MSM/MLP**	Provision for social security increased from Rs367 million to Rs427 million to reflect government's commitment to give maximum protection to the less fortunate of the society, health raised from Rs306 million to Rs334 million, education increased from Rs540 million to Rs570 million to meet the full cost of maintaining free education and provision of Rs75 million made for subsidy on rice and flour.
June 1991	**September 1991**	**MSM/MLP/PMSD**	Budget of the Ministry of Social Security increased from Rs828 million to Rs1,076 million – that is, an increase of Rs248 million. Budget for education increased from Rs477 million in 1981/82 to Rs1,190 million in 1990/91. Budget

(Continued)

Table 9.4 (Continued)

Month and year of budget presentations	*Month and year of elections*	*Parties in power at the time of budget presentations*	*State expenditure on various items of welfare*
			expenditure increased to Rs284 million. In the area of training, increasing its provision from Rs130 million to Rs165 million, that is by 27 per cent
June 1995	**December 1995**	**MSM/MMM/MTD**	Budget of the Ministry of Social Security rises to Rs2 billion. Increased the budgetary allocation for assistance and training of disabled persons to Rs7 million, that is by 17 per cent. Increased the budgetary support to NGOs. Old-age pensioners, widows, orphans, invalids and other needy categories have seen their social benefits increased by 31 per cent. Total budgetary allocation for the Ministry of Health being raised by 12 per cent to nearly Rs1.42 billion.
June 2000	**September 2000**	**MLP**	*Education*: Total budget allocation to education is Rs4.2 billion. *Social Welfare*: The total budgetary provision for the National Pension fund – Rs3.5 billion. Increasing the grant to the NGO's Trust Fund to Rs22.5 million. The charitable organizations raised to Rs28.5 million and that for social aid to Rs150 million. *Health*: Increasing the provision for the health sector to Rs2.2 billion.
April 2005	**July 2005**	**MSM/MMM**	Increasing provisions for assistance and training of disabled person Rs12 million. Allocating of Rs40 million to complete construction of a Disability Centre at Pointe aux Sables. Provision for Social aid increased from Rs225 million to Rs261 million and increasing grants to Charitable institutions from Rs40 million to Rs42.5 million. Budgetary provisions for the Ministry of Social Security, National Solidarity and Senior citizens welfare increased from Rs6 billion to Rs6.8 billion-an increase of 13 per cent. Budgetary provision training staff increased by 140 per cent to Rs12 million Allocating Rs470 million for medicines and medical disposables. Increasing the provision to NATReSA by 35 per cent to Rs29 million. Overall budgetary provision for the Ministry of health and Quality of life increased by nearly Rs4 billion – an increase of 9 per cent.

Sources: Bérenger, 1982; Bunwaree, 2000–2001. Jugnauth, 2005–06; Jugnauth 1991–1992. Lutchmeenaraidoo, 1986–1987; Ringadoo 1981; Ringadoo 1976; Sithanen 1995–96.

Commenting on the pre-electoral budget of 2005–2006, a Mauritian weekly newspaper – the *Mauritius Times* of 11th April 2005 – states:

> The other disquieting aspect of the exercise concerns the deliberate attempt to buy last minute voter sympathy after four long years of pronounced difficulties. In addition to its various largesse, the minister of Finance has announced his intention of making Mauritius a duty free island and he has removed duties and taxes on some 1,800 articles.

The nexus between politics and economics

There is a strong nexus between politics and economics in Mauritius. Economic conditions play a major role during each election and have been determining factors for change, except perhaps in 1995 when, although the economic conditions were relatively good, Jugnauth was ousted from power. The factors that have often contributed to the downfall of governments in Mauritius are very much the same. Apart from the state of the economy, other elements such as corruption scandals, arrogance, waste of resources (often reflected in the Auditor's report), disconnection with the reality, the perception of some ethnic groups of marginalization, and politics of incumbency/abuse of state power are often the trigger to sanction the government.

In 1982, after being in power for more than 13 consecutive years, Sir Seewoosagur Ramgoolam lost the elections. There are many reasons for his downfall: the disastrous state of the economy with heavy debts and balance of payments deficits, corruption scandals, intergenerational conflicts within the party, and, more importantly, the MMM's campaign that was based on a sense of Mauritianism and class ideology. The worn-out Labour Party of the time was seen as bourgeois-oriented and exploitative, protecting the interests of a Hindu-dominated political elite. The population latched on to the MMM for change. Slogans such as 'Unity in diversity' and 'One People, One Nation' contributed to the success of the MMM.

Mauritius alternates parties in a peaceful manner and has consolidated its democracy in various ways, but the change in government by the ballot box has become so embedded to the system that Mauritians do not pay much heed to policies. Carroll and Carroll (1999) argue that 'Mauritians are limited in their capacity to determine policy outcomes through their votes, since the composition of the government is likely to change between elections and the various parties have only the loosest commitments to particular policy positions.' The question that should be asked instead is whether they can adopt particular policy positions and whether the latter are so markedly different to tilt the electorate in one direction or the other.

Change in social policies or programmes has hardly ever been the cause of a sanction by the electorate as no party has dared to challenge the fundamentals of the welfare state. The only time that the government actually tried to restructure and revisit the welfare state was when the Movement Socialiste Mauricien (MSM), led by Aneerood Jugnauth, abolished subsidies on rice and flour in the 1980s and more recently when old-age pensions were abolished for those earning more than Rs 20,000 by the same political party, but this time led by Jugnauth junior.

The MSM, in alliance with the MMM, lost the elections in 2005. This loss cannot be attributed to the targeting introduced on the old-age pensions. Other reasons, such as the ones mentioned above, are responsible for the defeat of the MMM/MSM. The budget deficit has increased, inflation is on the rise, the balance of payments deficit has worsened and unemployment has reached double-digit figures of more than 10 per cent. The continued depreciation of the Mauritian rupee poses various challenges since Mauritius does not possess any natural resources and is highly dependent on imports.

The MSM is perhaps the most 'neoliberal' of the parties and in fact party members describe themselves as 'pragmatic'. As opposed to the MSM, the MMM started off with a strong left ideology and has had an indelible impact on the country. The section below describes the political history of the MMM and how the response of the ruling government to the rise of the MMM was, in some ways, a threat to democracy.

A brief threat to Mauritian democracy

The MMM was created in 1969 by a group of radical left-wing intellectuals largely inspired by the student movement of 1968 in France. The MMM gathered increasing support in the early 1970s and even won a by-election for a vacated seat in Ramgoolam's home constituency of Triolet. The MMM candidate obtained 70 per cent of the votes. Very quickly, the leader of the MMM changed its discourse from a revolutionary one to one guided by moderation. He acknowledged that a revolution was not possible and that it was necessary to reach out to the country's progressive and democratic elements.

In the 1970s, the Labour Party started experiencing a sense of discomfort with the rising popularity of the MMM and reacted immediately to the victory of the MMM in the by-election. The government amended the constitution to push the next general elections from 1972 to 1976 and to abolish by-elections. At the end of 1971, the government also declared a state of emergency, arresting many union and MMM leaders without charges, closing down *Le Militant*, the MMM's newspaper, and banning most union and political activity. Ramgoolam described the emergency powers as 'armouries of a democratic government, and they must be there to be resorted to swiftly and without delay when required. They are not intended against the people, but against those who are out to uproot our liberal institutions, for which all Mauritians have struggled over the years.'

Ramgoolam used the argument that the MMM was a bunch of communists using subversive action to bring dictatorship and chaos to the country. And meanwhile, the MMM had realized that Mauritians were not generally inclined towards revolution and that the route to power lay in electoral politics. The MMM came to power in 1982. But the MMM soon split and a breakaway faction, called the Mauritian Socialist Movement (MSM) and led by Sir Aneerood Jugnauth, ruled from 1983 to 1995, the year in which Ramgoolam's son led the Labour Party/MMM alliance to another landslide victory. This alliance did not last long; it broke up in June 1997. All but one of the ministers left the government. The cabinet was constituted by the MLP alone from June 1997 to September 2000. In its issue of March 1998, Mauritius News of London commented: 'All the way since 1968, it has been a combination of alliances, endless quarrels and endless reconciliations, friends today, foes tomorrow, this goes on and on in Mauritian politics.'

From the very start, the MMM attempted to modify political thinking from a communal one to a class one and therefore focused its energies on building and developing a power base with the trade unions. Dockers and sugar and transport workers rallied in great numbers around the radicalism of the left-leaning MMM party. From September to December 1971, Mauritius was hit by MMM-supported strikes in several major economic sectors: transport, sugar, docks, public service and electricity. The strikes were very disruptive and led to various kinds of economic and social problems, including mounting violence in the country. The MMM went into an alliance with Boodhoo's PSM in order to ensure the support of the rural Hindus as well. During the campaigning period, the Labour Party was taken to task for high levels of corruption, nepotism, and the mismanagement of public funds. In large rallies throughout the country, the MMM/PSM alliance accused the Labour Party of having favoured and supported the white sugar plantocracy. Promises were made to redesign the tax system, and to re-examine wealth distribution and make it more equitable.

Trade unions in contemporary Mauritius

The history of both the MMM and the Labour Party has been largely infused by trade union activities, but unions' links with political parties have been greatly reduced. Their power is largely eroded and the domain that they mostly engage in is centralized wage bargaining. Mauritius is often cited as a country where tripartite negotiations work rather well. Negotiations take place between government, trade unions and the business sector and, for many years now, the main area of these negotiations is the indexation of salaries/wages to the cost of living and compensation for workers. On most occasions, some kind of consensus is reached. There is, however, an increasing level of debate about the need to index salary increases to productivity, but this has not yet been implemented.

Table 9.4 shows the unionization rate between 1981 and 1996. The relatively low rate of unionization during the 1980s and 1990s can perhaps be explained by the fact that work conditions had substantially improved by the 1980s and the diversification of the economy had made it possible for people to enter emerging work sectors, some of which did not encourage union membership. Trade unions in modern Mauritius do not have the right to strike. They have been claiming for a revision of the Industrial Relations Act of 1975. The latter was passed as a response to the wildcat strikes that paralysed the economy in the late 1960s and early 1970s. When political parties are in opposition, they often argue that they will review and revise the legislation but once in power, they conveniently forget it. For Cuttaree, the chairman of the select committee that was instituted in 1982 to revisit the industrial relations act, this act is 'based on fundamentally anti-democratic options' and was a 'piece of repressive legislation' (cited in Dukhira 2002: 180).

Although trade unions no longer have the same links with political parties as in earlier periods, they still play a relatively important role in trying to contain the vulnerabilities that some workers experience. The biggest employer in Mauritius is the civil service, currently employing some 10 per cent of the labour force and each time that there has been some attempt to make the civil service leaner by retrenching workers, the unions have acted vociferously and prevented this from happening. Unions have also prevented the privatization of certain sectors and the loss of jobs that this may entail, but they do not have much influence on macro economic policy making and on the resulting labour dynamics. What is more worrying is that there are no trade unions defending the rights of workers in the informal sector and yet the latter is becoming a major absorber of labour.

The Mauritian economy and the challenges it confronts

As Mauritius steps further into the twenty-first century, its economy faces some important challenges. The NPCC Report 'Competitiveness Foresight: What Orientations for Mauritius?' (2004: 6) notes: 'Mauritius is now in a situation

Table 9.5 Trade union density rate and industrial stoppages, 1981–1996

Year	*Union membership*	*Unionization rate*	*Year*	*Total man-days Lost in 1000s*
1981	70,478	20.9	1987–1988	16.5
1983	83,202	23.0	1988–1989	22.2
1986	102,317	24.0	1989–1990	5.4
1989	113,160	28.9	1990–1991	0.3
1992	104,311	32.2	1991–1992	1.8
1994	107,659	22.5	1992–1993	4.1
1996	108,106	21.8	1993–1994	1.4
			1994–1995	2.7

Note: Values for 1981–86 and 1989–96 are from different sources and may therefore not be completely consistent with each other.

Sources: Ministry of Labour and Industrial Relations 1988. Mauritius Employers Federation 1997. Ministry of Labour and Industrial Relations 1998.

where the economy is emitting several signs of approaching distress.' The slowing down of the country's growth rate, the increase in the level of unemployment, the rise in public debt, and a social budget that keeps increasing are cited as elements of distress. However, despite the growing budget deficits, the state is not really inclined to cut down on social expenditure. The major challenge of Mauritius is to expand growth and create employment, but this seems very difficult for an economy where size, location and limited workforce are inherent handicaps with which it needs to live. To make matters worse, the traditional pillars have been seriously shaken and foreign direct investment has declined substantially during the last years.

Tables 9.6 and 9.7 show the relatively poor performance of some key macroeconomic indicators.

Table 9.6 Macroeconomic indicators for Mauritius, 2000–2003

Macroeconomic indicators for Mauritius	*2000*	*2001*	*2002*	*2003*
Population (000)	1,186.9	1,199.9	1,210.2	1222.8
GDP at market prices (Rs M)	119494	132092	141903	156906
Per capita GDP (Rs)	100,677	110,086	117,256	128,317
Growth rate of per capita GDP (%)		9	7	9
Real GDP growth rate (%)	9.3	5.8	2.5	4.4
Inflation rate (%)	4.2	5.4	6.4	3.9
Budget deficit (% GDP)	3.8	6.7	6.0	6.0
Internal debt (% GDP)	39	40	47	55
Total public debt (% GDP)	65.8	64.4	70.5	80.5
Debt services (% exports)	7.9	9.8	8.4	8.2
Gross domestic fixed capital formation (% GDP)	26.9	25.4	25.9	26.2
Foreign direct investment inflows	276.8	11.5	27.6	5.1
Unemployment rate (%)	8.8	9.1	9.8	10.2
Trade				
Total exports (Rs M)	40,882	43,628	43,022	54,164
as % GDP	39	37	34	40
Total imports (Rs M)	54,928	57,940	64,608	66,384
as % GDP	53	49	52	48
Sugar exports (Rs M)	5,544	8,557	8,529	8,430
as % GDP	5	7	7	6
EPZ exports (Rs M)	30,961	33,695	33,502	32,052
as % GDP	30	29	27	23
Tourist earnings (Rs M)	14,234	18,166	18,328	19,397
as % GDP	14	15	15	14
Ratio of imports to exports	1.34	1.33	1.50	1.23

Source: National Productivity and Competitiveness Council 2004.

Table 9.7 Performance indicators, 1996–2004/5

Performance indicators	*1996–2000*	*2001–05*	*2004/5*
GDP growth (average for period) (%)	6.0	4.0	3.8
GD investment (as % of GDP)	25.3	22.1	21.7
Of which: Private Investment Public	17.0	14.8	14.5
Investment	8.3	7.3	7.2
GD Savings (%)	26.0	24.6	19.5
Savings–Investment Resource Gap:	+0.7	+2.5	−2.2
Unemployment (%)	5	6	11
Core Inflation	4–5	3–4	5–6

Source: Bank of Mauritius 2005.

Confronting various challenges

One of the most important challenges confronting the Mauritian economy is the loss of guaranteed prices and protected markets for its sugar in the context of the European Union sugar regime. The marketing arrangements that had been in place since 1951 – the Commonwealth Sugar Agreement (CSA) – provided a guaranteed price and market to the sugar-producing countries of the Commonwealth. The CSA came to an end in 1974, and since then Mauritian sugar has been marketed under the sugar protocol attached to the Lomé Convention. The marketing arrangements are perhaps the *sine qua non* of the sugar industry, but contemporary Mauritius is struggling to retain its protected markets for sugar. According to a study carried out by the Overseas Development Institute in Great Britain, with the advent of the dismantling of the sugar protocol, Mauritius is one of the 'great losers' amongst the ACP countries (*Le Mauricien*, 2 March 2005). The threat to the Mauritian sugar industry became a nightmare when the EU resolved that it will cut the price of sugar it imports from the ACP countries by a staggering 39 per cent by 2009. Though the sugar industry in Mauritius has entered a process of reform through a policy of centralization and a voluntary retirement scheme, the future of the industry remains very bleak. More importantly, the unemployment problem that the Voluntary Retirement Scheme (VRS) is provoking may have important social implications.

The other main engine of growth – the textile and garment sector within the export processing zone – is also facing serious difficulties. The dismantling of the Multi-Fibre Agreement (MFA) and the lifting of quotas in 2005 is a heavy blow on the Mauritian textile and apparel sector. The invasion of the world market by Chinese textiles has become a real danger and Mauritius has not been spared. The other associated challenge with the Mauritian EPZ is that Mauritius has failed to diversify its products. Overdependence on one or two products and the country's inability so far to develop linkages with the rest of the economy therefore make it more fragile and vulnerable. Wong, the director of the Mauritius Export Processing Zone Association (2005), argues that unless Mauritius is innovative enough and diversifies its products quickly, it will not be able to take full advantage of the African Growth and Opportunity Act and obtain a reasonable share of the American market.

Although the tourism industry is still doing well, it is not without threats. The tourism industry continued to grow in 2003 with tourist arrivals increasing from 681,648 in 2002 to 702,018 in 2003. In addition to tourism taking its toll on the environment, the tourism industry suffered a setback after the Tsunami. Natural disasters coupled with the fear of terrorist attacks can have a damaging effect on the industry.

The inadequately trained human capital also poses a challenge. Almost 40 per cent of the student population failed the last year of primary school, representing an important wastage of the country's human capital (Bunwaree 1997; Lall and Wignaraja 1998). Now that education has been made compulsory up to the age of 16, a large number of the children failing the academic stream are pushed into vocational and technical education but with a gender bias against girls.

The rapidly ageing population and accompanying deterioration in the worker–pensioner ratio also presents a problem (Government of Mauritius 1998). Social security expenditure is growing very fast as a result of the greying population and productivity is not growing as rapidly.

The steep contraction of the EPZ and the sugar sector is leading to important job losses. Unemployment rates amongst females is rising fast and is accompanied by a feminization of poverty. But the paradox of the Mauritian labour market is that whilst it sheds off labour from the EPZ, there are increasing numbers of foreign workers, especially young women from China, coming to work in the EPZ. The loss of jobs resulting from the changes in the international regulation of trade and markets, has affected workers' entitlements on pensions, redundancy payments and social assistance. The new labour market scenario, including the rapidly growing informal sector, poses important challenges to industrial relations and democracy.

Like most other developing countries, the Mauritian informal sector is very heterogeneous and increasing numbers of women are being absorbed in the sector. The findings of a recent study undertaken by Bunwaree and Juwaheer (2005) for the Mauritius Research Council highlight the rapid expansion of the sector, although it was not possible to measure its extent and magnitude. Some people argue that the sector helps to control theft and criminality and that it is where people are at risk and exposed to various health and environmental hazards. There is an absence of social protection for the workers. Doing informal sector work is a survival strategy and large segments of the poorest stratum of Mauritian society seek their livelihoods within this sector.

Painful economic decline: need for targeting and restructuring?

The challenges discussed above have led some commentators to advocate targeting and restructuring of the welfare state. Sarris (1998) and Mistry

(2005) have evoked the urgency of streamlining the welfare state. Sarris (1998) argues that

> Public resources should target only the genuinely needy. The welfare state needs streamlining not only to reduce fiscal imbalances, but also to ensure that public resources are not wasted and that incentive frameworks are not distorted.

However, most governments have resisted pressures to downsize the welfare state. Political parties are fully aware of the extent to which government social expenditure legitimizes the state. The popularity of the party in power depends heavily on the continued financing of the welfare state. In addition to consolidating their own vote banks, the state is also conscious of the important role of a strong welfare state in supporting the economic growth of the country. This is fully captured in the government's Vision 2020 report (1996: 5) which states:

> Some people marvel that we have achieved so much economic success despite the burden of our welfare state. It can well be argued that in reality it was the other way round. We achieved economic success because of the strength of our welfare system. For it is free education, social security and health and welfare services which have given the high education levels, high health standards and above all the exceptional social cohesion which have underpinned our past economic development.

Conclusion

Whether it is a strong welfare state that has contributed to the economic development of the country or vice versa, the reality now is that the contemporary economic conditions will make it very difficult to maintain such a welfarist orientation. In an interview accorded to the *Mauritius Times* of 22 September 2005, Percy Mistry, Chairman of the Oxford International group notes that a growth rate of 7–8 per cent is necessary for Mauritius to be able to afford its welfare state. He also notes that Mauritius has

> probably overdone the dimensions of its welfare state before Mauritius can really afford it. It has built up expectations of guaranteed entitlements of social provision and protection, as well as of eternally free public services, that are way above what a society at Mauritius's level of development can deliver. The social overhead cost definitely gets in the way of its competitiveness... Mauritians seem to put populist-pandering politics above good economics. As a result they get both bad politics and bad economics...

It is not quite clear what is meant by bad politics in this context, but if politics is truly about transforming people's lives and improving the standard of living of the average citizen, about ensuring a good dose of social citizenship, then it is clear that Mauritius has fared quite well so far. Almost all political parties in Mauritius have a strong socialist inclination and none of them would dare challenge the embeddedness of the Mauritian welfare state. The country is currently going through very uncertain times and sustaining the welfare state would no doubt pose a challenge to the state. Only the future would tell us how the Mauritian state would cope with this challenge and how it would juggle around with various policies so as to redefine good economics and good politics the Mauritian way.

Note

1. The riots of February 1999 are largely attributed to the malaise Creole. The latter refers to the deplorable conditions in which large sections of the Mauritians of African descent, usually called the Creoles, live in. Tensions flared during a public meeting organized by the Mouvement republicain, a small political party which was asking for the depenalisation of *gandia*. Police had subsequently arrested some participants for smoking banned substances. Amongst those detained was Kaya, one of the country's leading 'seggae' singers. His arrest and death in police custody triggered a series of protest marches in major forms, amid allegations that he had been beaten to death by police officers.

   The demonstrations of February 1999 paralysed the country for almost a week. Various symbols of capitalism and wealth were targeted. Although the unrest of February 1999 degenerated into some form of communal attacks between the Creole community on the one side and the Muslims and Hindus on the other, some people's readings and interpretations of the riots are that they are much more an indication of the frustration of the working class and that Kaya's death was simply a detonator.

References

Bank of Mauritius. 2005. *Annual Report*. Port Louis, Mauritius.

Baker, P. 1972. *Kreol: A Study of Mauritian Kreol*. London: Hurst and Hurst.

Beckford, E. L. 1972. *Persistent Poverty: Underdevelopment in Plantation Economies of the Third World*. Cambridge, Ma: Oxford University Press.

Bérenger P. 1982–1983. 'The Budget Speech'. Speech given at National Assembly Mauritius, July 1982.

Best, L. 1965. 'A biography of Labour'. Caribbean Economy Monograph, Jamaica Institute of Social and Economic Research.

Bheenick, R. 1991. 'Beyond Structural Adjustment'. Paper presented to seminar on 'Deficit Financing and Economic Management', University of Mauritius.

Bowman, L. W. 1991. *Mauritius: Democracy and Development in the Indian Ocean*. Boulder, CO: westview Press.

Bunwaree, S. 2004. 'Export Oriented Employment and Social Policy – The Case of Mauritius', in S. Razavi, R. Pearson and C. Danloy (eds), *Globalization, Export-Oriented Employment and Social Policy: Gendered Connections*. Basingstoke: Palgrave – now Palgrave Macmillan.

Bunwaree, S. 2001. 'The Marginal in the Miracle: Human Capital in Mauritus.' *International Journal of Educational Development*, 21(3).

Bunwaree, S. 1997. 'Education and the Marginalisation of Girls in the Post-GATT Era', *COMPARE*, 27, 297–317.

Bunwaree, S. and Juwaheer 2005. 'A Study of the Informal Sector'. Draft Mimeo, Mauritius Research Council, Rose-Hill, Mauritius.

Bunwaree, V. 2000–2001. 'The Budget Speech'. Speech given at National Assembly Mauritius, June 2000.

Carroll, T. and B. Carroll 1999. 'The Consolidation of Democracy in Mauritius', *Democratization*, 6(1), 179–97.

Central Statistical Office. 2004. *Digest of Public Finance 2003 Vol. 15*, Ministry of Finance, Port Louis, Mauritius.

Central Statistical Office. Digests of Public Finance (from 1967 to 2004). Port Louis, Mauritius: CSO.

Dommen E. and Dommen B. 1999. *Mauritius: An Island of Success*. Wellington: Pacific Press.

Dukhira, C. 2002. *History of Mauritius: Experiments in Democracy*. New Delhi: Brijbasi Art Press Ltd.

Economist. 1998. 28 February.

Eriksen, T. 1998. *Common Denominators: Ethnicity, Nation Building and Compromise in Mauritius*. Oxford: Berg.

Gayan, S. N. 1990. *An Act to Serve: Sir V. Ringadoo (Debates and Speeches)*. Moka, Mauritius: Mahatma Gandhi Institute.

Government of Mauritius. 1998. *Battersby Report: Actuarial Review as at 30 June 1995*. Mauritius National Pensions Fund.

Gulhati, R. and Nallari, R. 1990. *Successful Stabilisation and Recovery in Mauritius*, EDI, Policy Cast Series. Washington DC: World Bank.

International Herald Tribune. 1999. 17 June.

International Herald Tribune. 1993. 20 September.

Jugnauth Sir A. 1991–1992. 'The Budget Speech'. Speech given at National Assembly, Mauritius, June 1991.

Jugnauth P. 2005–2006. 'The Budget Speech'. Speech given at National Assembly, Mauritius, April 2005.

Kearney, R. C. 1990. 'Mauritius and the NIC Model Redux: Or How Many Cases Make a Model?', *Journal of Developing Area*, 24 (2), 195–216.

Lall, S. and G. Wignaraja. 1998. *Mauritius: Dynamising Export Competitiveness*. London: Commonwealth Secretariat.

Le Défi-Plus, 4-10 August 2001, Mauritius, pp. 22.

Le Mauricien, 2 March 2005, Mauritius.

Le Mauricien, 25 November 2000, Mauritius.

Le Mauricien, 17 June 2000, Mauritius.

Lingayah, S. 1997. *Social Welfare in Mauritius: A Critical Analysis of Social Service Provisions*. Kent, UK: Sankris Publishing, Ltd.

Lutchmeenaraidoo, S. 1986–1987. 'The Budget Speech'. Speech given at 'National Assembly, June 1986.

Mannick, A. R. 1979. *Mauritius: The Development of a Plural Society*. Nottingham: Spokesman.

Mauritius Employers Federation. 1997. *Annual Report*. Port Louis, Mauritius.

Mauritius Times, 16 September 2005, Mauritius.

Meisenhelder, T. 1997. 'The Developmental State in Mauritius.' *Journal of Modern African Studies*, 35(2), 279–97.

Ministry of Economic Planning and Development. 1970–72. *Mauritius Economic Review*. Port Louis: Mauritius.

Ministry of Economic Planning and Development. 1972–74. *Mauritius Economic Review*. Port Louis: Mauritius.

Ministry of Economic Planning and Development. 1975–77. *Mauritius Economic Review.* Port Louis: Mauritius.

Ministry of Economic Planning and Development. 1981–83, *Mauritius Economic Review.* Port Louis: Mauritius.

Ministry of Economic Planning and Development. 1996. 'Economic Indicators.' No. 245. Port Louis: Mauritius.

Ministry of Economic Planning and Development. 2002. 'Economic and Social Indicators.' No. 397. Port Louis: Mauritius.

Ministry of Finance, *Bi Annual Digests of Public Finance* (1962–1997), Port Louis, Mauritius.

Ministry of Finance, *National Accounts* (1962–1997). Port Louis, Mauritius.

Ministry of Labour and Industrial Relations. 1988. *Annual Report.* Port Louis, Mauritius.

Ministry of Labour and Industrial Relations. 1998. *Annual Report.* Port Louis, Mauritius.

Mintz S. W. 1985. *Sweetness and Power: The Place of Sugar in Modern History*. New York: Elisabeth Sifton/Viking.

Mulloo, A. 2000. *Father of the Nation – The Story of Mauritius 1900–2000*. New Delhi: Vision Books.

National Productivity and Competitiveness Council. 2004. 'Competitiveness Foresight: What Orientations for Mauritius?' Discussion Paper, Port Louis, Mauritius.

Ringadoo Sir V. 1976–1977. 'The Budget Speech'. Speech given at 'National Assembly Mauritius', May 1976.

Ringadoo Sir V. 1981–1982. 'The Budget Speech'. Speech given at 'National Assembly Mauritius', May 1981.

Sarris, M. 1998. 'Presentation Round table with the Government of Mauritius.' Maritim Hotel, Balaclava, Terre Rouge, March 25–27, Mauritius.

Seegobin, R. and Collen, L. 1977. 'Mauritius: Class Forces and Political Power.' *Review of African Political Economy*, 4 (8), 109–118.

Simmons, A. S. 1982. *Modern Mauritius: The Politics of Decolonization*. Bloomington: Indiana University Press.

Sithanen, R. 2003. 'Coalition Politics Under the Tropics: Office Seekers, Power Makers, Nation Building – A Case Study of Mauritius'. Paper presented at the Electoral Institute of South Africa (EISA) Round Table, Cape Town, Draft mimeo.

Sithanen R. 1995–1996. 'The Budget Speech'. Speech given at 'National Assembly Mauritius', June 1995.

Tinker, H. 1974. *A New System of Slavery: The Export of Indian Labour Overseas, 1830–1920*. London: Oxford University Press.

Titmuss, R. M. and B. Abel Smith, assisted by T. Lynes. 1968. *Social Policies and Population Growth in Mauritius*. London: Frank Cass & Co. Ltd.

Toussaint, A. 1977. *History of Mauritius*. London: Macmillan.

Vision 2020. 1996. *The National Long Term Perspective Study.* Mauritius Government: Printing Press.

Week-End, 10 March 1996, Port Louis, Mauritius.

Wong, D. 2005. 'AGOA and its Future in Mauritius.' In *Mauritius Chamber of Commerce and Industry (MCCI)*, Chamber News, 29 July.

10

Democracy and Social Policy in Jamaica

Jennifer Jones

Introduction

This chapter looks at the social policy and democracy of Jamaica in the context of its economic and political evolution. Although Jamaica achieved its independence in 1962, it had put into use most of the institutions of democracy, including universal suffrage, parliament and a multi-party system, since 1944. It had lacked only sovereignty over external affairs and, in the early years, full ministerial control.

An island in the Caribbean, its indigenous Amerindian population was wiped out during the Spanish occupation from 1493, followed by the British in 1655. Under Spanish and British rule over two million West Africans were transported across the Atlantic to work as slaves on sugar plantations. Today Jamaica has a population of 2.6 million, 90 per cent of African descent in all shades of black to light brown, with the remainder of European, Indian, Chinese and Middle Eastern origin. Its per capita income of US$4,104 (2003) puts it in the lower-middle-income category. Experiencing negative or low growth from the mid-1970s to the present, with only a brief positive spike in the late 1980s, Jamaica has been a leading developing country example of failed structural adjustment policies.

Jamaica's geopolitical position has played a critical role in its history. Its proximity to both the USA and Cuba (144 kilometres away) has had a profound impact on political and economic events – intensely during the Cold War years – on migration, and on social psychology. It is estimated that a number equal to its island population live in the Diaspora, clustered especially in the USA, Canada and the UK.

Social complexity is another important factor in Jamaica's profile. Jamaica existed for centuries under a racist value system which attempted to justify the enslavement of the majority of inhabitants by a small white minority. Acculturation resulted in the internalization of this racist ideology and elements have remained to this day. Jamaica's history produced 'Two Jamaicas'[1] divided by contiguous race, class and cultural lines. Jamaican anthropologist

Barry Chevannes notes that the majority of Jamaicans still live under a dual system: legal land titling alongside family-shared land not legally recognised, legal marriage only after years of common-law union with children, and religious practice that includes membership simultaneously in the socially respectable European established Sunday churches and the Afro-Christian churches of lower class communities (Chevannes 2006).

Jamaica was among the 22.5 per cent whose democratic path was incorrectly predicted by Przeworski *et al.*'s (2000) empirical study of 141 countries between 1950 and 1990. It was predicted (by 0.58) to have been a dictatorship from 1962 to 1983, as was India (more strongly by 0.83) during a specific period. A major finding of this study is that high per capita income has a strong positive impact on the survival of democracy. It can be argued that formal democracy is deeply entrenched in the Jamaican cultural psyche because democratic politics has been long perceived as linked to civil and social rights, and liberation from colonialism. In the century following Emancipation there was a continuous struggle, led by outstanding black leaders, for voting rights, the right to be elected to the Legislature, the formation of political parties, freedom from colonial rule and independence – all linked to issues of equity and social equality.

Today the question for the majority of Jamaicans is whether 45 years of formal democracy as an independent nation has produced equitable development. Social policy and programmes are important indicators of equity. What has been the quality of these in a country that had the highest murder rate in the world in 2005?[2] Where at the beginning of secondary school only half the students are at the required level in English and Maths, and at the end only a quarter can matriculate in English and less than a fifth in Maths? Where more than one in two inner-city residents are unemployed in a rapidly urbanizing society? What do these facts mean for a sustainable democracy?

A weakened democratic state does not necessarily lead to coups or one-man dictatorships in a country with a non-military tradition like Jamaica, whose small army is highly respected for its non-partisan history. It can lead to alternative systems, existing side by side with the formal system and over which the state has weak authority. In Jamaica these include the alternative informal economy, now estimated to account for over 40 per cent of GDP (Grade/IDB 2002); alternative systems of welfare in certain inner-city communities (known as political 'garrisons') usually run by leaders with 'unconventional' income sources (once from politics, now from drugs or extortion); and alternative violent systems of justice in those same communities where these 'dons' are also 'enforcers' through their access to illegal arms. In the twenty-first century this is further complicated by Jamaica's position as a trans-shipment point for the Columbian–US drug trade.

Is democracy in Jamaica consolidating or disintegrating? Can it answer the urgent social needs? Are we in a transition period of both opportunity and risk, when it is too soon to foresee the outcome? To answer these questions this chapter will focus in succession on Jamaica's political economy, evolving democracy, and social policy and expenditures.

Political economy

Jamaica developed as an agricultural economy producing sugar and bananas for export. After Emancipation in 1838 poor working conditions and appallingly low wages were the experience of the majority. A hundred years later, Jamaica's greatest labour revolt took place, bringing profound changes in the political and social landscape that led inexorably to self-government in 1944, followed by independence in 1962. Jamaica's persistent challenge since has been to link sustainable economic growth with social development for the majority of its people.

In the early period the new government adopted the 'industrialization by invitation' and 'import substitution' models, focusing heavily on economic growth, and initially appearing to have great success. Between 1950 and 1960 GDP moved from £70 million to £230 million, a rate of growth exceeded only by Puerto Rico and Japan. The international climate was favourable for foreign direct investment, mainly for extractive industries, and during the 1960s bauxite mining replaced agriculture as chief foreign exchange earner. However, the economy was basically fragile: the external accounts showed persistent current account deficits, offset only by the heavy direct investments. Nobel prize winner and Caribbean economist W. Arthur Lewis, who promoted these economic models, commented on the intractability of Jamaica's economic problems – how could a country from 1950 to 1960 double its output, lose 11 per cent of its labour force by migration, and still have 12 per cent unemployment? His answer: foreign investment was 'producing more goods without employing more people' (Gray 1991: 241).

There were also other factors involved. 'Predominantly agricultural production continued to be organized on a plantation-capitalist basis despite over half a century's recommendations that the development of peasant farming on a large scale was both socially desirable and economically productive…' (Munroe 1972: 98) Against these recommendations strongly put forward by Royal Commissions (1885, 1897, 1928 and 1938) stood the tenacity of the plantation aristocracy, the weakness of the small farmer organizing capacity, and the non-transformational orientation of the early national governments. Rural poverty led to increasing migration to the capital city of Kingston where the masses lived in squalid informal settlements of shacks and 'lean-to's'. Land reform remains an urgent requirement for greater equity.

The new bauxite and tourist industries could not absorb the surplus and mainly unskilled labour. The tourist industry failed to create backward linkages with the economy, increasing the country's food import bill. Much of this was explained by the extent of foreign ownership, which included the largest sugar estates, the bauxite industry, most hotels, all banks and insurance companies, and basic utilities such as telephone and electricity. Jamaican economist Owen Jefferson has described the period as '"a form of perverse growth".... (and)... calculated that between 1959 and 1969 the funds flowing out of the Jamaican economy actually exceeded all the incoming investments attracted by official incentive policies.' (Payne and Sutton 2001: 65–6). By 1972 (an election year) unemployment had reached 23 per cent and inequality had increased – the share of the poorest 40 per cent declining from 7.2 per cent in 1958 to 5.4 per cent in 1968 (Table 10.1). Sometimes characterized as a period of 'growth without development', it culminated in the irony of the first independence decade (1962–72) becoming a decade of *social* frustration.

A change of government in 1972 brought a fresh approach. Critical of the extent of foreign control, the new leadership under Michael Manley felt that the policies of the 1950s and 1960s had emphasized economic growth to the neglect of social welfare. The government began a policy of distributive justice to decrease social inequalities, passing key laws to protect labour, women and children, and attempting to restructure the economy through nationalization (with compensation) and redistribution of idle land to small farmers and sugar worker cooperatives.

However, as it began on this new path the Manley government encountered major external economic pressures: major oil shocks in 1973 and 1978 and recession in the world economy just as initial bauxite investment dried up with the capital investment cycle completed. There was sharp GDP (gross and per capita) contraction. Social spending opened up large fiscal deficits (25 per cent of GDP in 1976), which were financed by printing money. Through heavy borrowing of petro-dollars 'to sustain the level of imports deemed necessary for the economy... the external debt... from 1975 to 1980... increased by over 100 per cent to US$1.9 billion' (Davies and Witter 1989: 86). Stephens and Stephens, while acknowledging 'the crying needs of the underprivileged', felt the government's policy 'was too distributionist, much like that of the new socialist governments of Chile in 1970 and France in 1936...' (1986: 340). Meanwhile Jamaica's policy of self-reliance, with exchange, trade and price controls, its 1974 declaration of democratic socialism, its state directed development and pro non-aligned movement stance with close ties with Cuba, attracted US hostility.

The economy came to the verge of collapse.[3] Production was down, private foreign investment and government private borrowing had literally dried up, hospitals were dangerously short of drugs, and food shortages were serious. With acute balance of payments problems, and despite its previous scathing criticisms of the Bretton Woods institutions, the government felt it had little option in 1977 but to turn for assistance to the IMF and its Special Drawing Rights programme. Following a minor failure on the first Test, the second brought new and much harsher terms including an immediate 25 per cent devaluation followed by a 15 per cent 'creeping devaluation' over 12 months, wage controls of 15 per cent beside a projected 40 per cent inflation rate,

Table 10.1 Selected social and economic indicators, 1957–2004

	1957	*1962*	*1968*	*1972*	*1976*	*1980*	*1984*	*1988*	*1992*	*1996*	*2000*	*2004*
Real GDP Growth (%)	11.3	2.1	4.8	7.5	−6.1	−5.4	−0.88	2.9	1.5	−1.3	0.8	1.2
% contribution of services to GDP	51	53	52	51	57	68	64	57	56	57	67	67
% levels of employment in service industries				47	46	48	49	49	56	58	62	64
Unemployment Rate (%)		12	19.7	23.2	22.4	27.3	25.5	18.9	15.7	16	15.5	11.7
Exchange Rate (J$:US$1)			0.83[1]	0.77	0.91	1.78[2]	3.55	6.17	23.01	37.02	43.32	61.39
Inflation (consumer prices)	3		6	8	8	29	31	8	40	16	6	14
% Consumption of poorest 40% of households	7.2		5.4						17.3	18.3	17.3	16.6[3]
Incidence of poverty (%)									33.9	26.1	18.7	19.7[3]

Notes:
1. 1969. 2. 1979. 3. 2002.
Sources: Central Planning Unit 1958; Dept. of Statistics 1959; National Planning Agency (formerly CPU) 1975: 1978/79/81; Planning Institute of Jamaica (formerly NPA) 1983: 1985: 1987: 1990: 1993: 1996: 1999: 2003: 2004.

expenditure cuts and new taxes. Even the private sector complained about the harsh terms and the unions uniformly condemned them.[4] The IMF prescriptions failed to stimulate growth. GDP declined, inflation was 49 per cent in the first year, average weekly incomes declined by 30–35 per cent, and unemployment had increased to 28 per cent by the end of the period.

After another failure, with even more stringent conditions proposed, the government broke with the IMF and held early elections based on a non-IMF path. They suffered a huge defeat. '[T]he tragedy of all this is that the IMF recipe could not work for a structurally dependent economy like Jamaica's, so lacking in productive capacity. It is now a commonplace of political economy analysis to say this, in good part as a result of Jamaica's experience' (Payne and Sutton 2001: 81).

In 1980, the new prime minister, Edward Seaga, was rewarded for his anti-Cuba[5], pro-capitalist and pro-US stance by softer IMF conditionalities and generous US government loans[6]. Foreign direct investment was encouraged, investor confidence was restored, the macro-economy stabilized and there was growth in GDP. Export processing zones were established and some trade restrictions relaxed. However, in this new import deregulation environment, the use of loan funds was not sufficiently focused on the rehabilitation of traditional industries and on stimulating new export-oriented ones. A consumer boom in imported goods, including cheap food imports, put many small farmers out of business; it worsened the balance of payments and deepened the associated debt problem. Following this boom, tight fiscal and monetary policy under IMF directed parameters led to severe public sector retrenchment. Even Seaga broke with the IMF in 1986 with the help of the windfall from the decrease in international oil prices. However, balance of payments problems led to another agreement signed in 1987. By the end of the period there were fiscal surpluses and inflation was down.

The labour market saw significant changes. Agriculture's share of jobs declined, both for wage workers and for self-employed, from 39 per cent in 1980 to 28 per cent in 1989 and there was an absolute decline in the numbers employed (Anderson and Witter 1994: 29–30). After 1983 unemployment steadily declined throughout the period and into the 1990s. However, most of the new jobs, located in the informal sector or in the less-skilled secondary sector of the labour market, 'were characterized by low wages, low skills, job instability and the virtual absence of worker protection… [T]he trade-off from structural adjustment was that where employment increased, job adequacy in terms of earnings decreased' (Anderson and Witter 1994: 23)

Returned to power in 1989, Michael Manley this time adopted a market-oriented economic approach. Liberalization of exchange controls and imports and elimination of trade barriers were rushed in under private sector and external pressure. Inflation rose dramatically, peaking around 80 per cent for two (2) years (1991–2) (Fig 10.2), as the Jamaican dollar plunged in the absence of the requisite regulatory mechanisms. The rapid influx of cheap imports caused the further collapse of some manufacturing and farming businesses. The new and growing local financial sector exploited the situation, indulging in a credit boom. The bubble burst in 1995 and there was a financial 'shake-out'. Several local banks and insurance companies folded. Fearing an Argentinian-style middle-class revolt, the government chose to bail out all depositors, small, medium and large. This was a difficult judgement call, but it was not a choice for social equity. It left the country with a massively increased internal debt with severe repercussions for social programmes, a scenario which has not changed.

Hyperinflation was brought down and foreign reserves built up, releasing Jamaica from the grip of the IMF Special Drawing Rights programme in the mid-1990s, and improving Jamaica's credit rating, enabling successful floating of government bonds on international markets, massively improving access to foreign exchange. The fiscal deficit is now financed by debt instead of printing money.

However, the economy has been stagnant for the entire period. There has been considerable informalization of the market with self-employed workers, contractors and generally lower level workers in demand (Alleyne 2001: 98), as the structure of the economy changes from production of goods to production of services (Table 10.1). Productivity has not risen significantly, however, while employment has expanded at the lower and upper ends of the market, suggesting that 'the phenomenon of "deskilling" and "upskilling"...is simultaneously taking place' (Alleyne 2001: 98) in an economy in transition. Lacking has been any serious focus by the government on small and micro-business, key to wealth creation and employment. The continuous use of 'government paper' to control inflation has caused a significant transfer of wealth from the poor to the rich in a context of high interest rates with no incentive for capital to risk new business investment. The incidence of poverty, by a consumption-based measure, fell from 33.9 per cent in 1992 to 18.7 per cent in 2000 but is now rising again, as is inflation. Tourism has taken over from bauxite as the major foreign exchange earner, equalled however by remittances in 2004. A positive of this period is the growing strength of a number of globally competitive Jamaican businesses, especially in the tourism and food processing sectors.

Evolving democracy

The 1938 labour revolt and the formation of political parties

The 'democratizing moment'[7] for Jamaica came in 1938 through a great labour revolt, preceded by nearly two decades of worsening economic and social conditions at the time of the Great Depression. It opened the path to self-government and independence with the support of critical middle-class leaders. This first phase ended with universal suffrage and internal self-government in 1944 – Jamaica led the colonial world in this achievement.

The rebellion was started spontaneously by grossly underpaid sugar workers in western Jamaica. There was a cascade of work stoppages and marches all over the island, on a scale that was unprecedented. In a revolutionary alliance, the historical mistrust of the brown middle class by the black lower class was overcome. The Kingston marches were led by Alexander Bustamante, an unorthodox charitable moneylender and an outstanding orator, also called upon by militant dockworkers to represent them, and eventually imprisoned during one of the marches. As the protest intensified, Norman Manley, an eminent and brilliant criminal lawyer and a leading figure in the island, offered legal assistance to any group of workers with grievances. With Bustamante in prison he negotiated on behalf of the dockworkers and assisted in Bustamante's release.

The uprising was the cause and catalyst of many developments. After 100 years, sugar workers' wages increased – by approximately 25 per cent for labourers and 75 per cent for skilled workers. Before the end of 1938, the national movement, which had been in formation since the end of the previous century, had coalesced into a political party, the Peoples National Party (PNP), led by Norman Manley; and five small unions had merged to form the Bustamante Industrial Trade Union (BITU), led by its namesake.

Political unionism and middle-class leadership

From the beginning, Jamaica's major unions were linked umbilically to the political parties. This has had both negative and positive consequences for the development of democracy and social policy. In 1939 the Trades Union Congress (TUC) was formed, led by radical Marxist PNP members. A year later the PNP, strongly influenced by the British Fabian Socialist movement, took the decision to adopt a socialist ideology. Bustamante, a masterful tactician, seized on the political opportunity afforded him by this move. He equated socialism with communism, communism with tyranny, slavery and godlessness, and the PNP's adoption of socialism with the tyranny of the brown middle class, proceeding to form Jamaica's second political party, the Jamaica Labour Party (JLP). The success of his tactic is demonstrated in the JLP's victories in the first two elections from 1944, despite Manley's acknowledged leadership in negotiating the Constitution. The PNP did not win its first election until 1955 after a "purge" of four radical Marxist leaders from the party.

It was critical to both parties to win the allegiance of the workers. After 1944 there was a period of violent rivalry between the TUC and BITU. This led to the banning of public meetings by the governor in 1946, 1947, 1949, and 1951. Jamaican political scientist Trevor Munroe notes that these powers were invoked not to protect the colonial regime but to keep Jamaicans from attacking each other. This, he suggests, provides an important insight into the emerging style of mass politics: '[T]he short-run need to get votes took primacy. This meant effectively the suppression of the long term aim of transforming the social order... Both parties became firmly fixed as vote-catching mechanisms'

(Munroe 1972: 114) This structural alliance between unions and rival political parties split the working class movement and weakened the unions' ability to independently represent labour and the lower class interests. It partly explains why democratic politics in Jamaica has not brought greater development for the majority. Union leaders frequently moved on to become political leaders, including Norman Manley's son, Michael, and Bustamante's protégé, Hugh Shearer, weakening the union leadership base, the underlying message being that the unions were a stepping stone to the more important political arena.

A positive outcome of this link, it can be argued, has been the influence of the unions on the 'labour consciousness' of Jamaica's political leaders. Trade union density in Jamaica is one of the highest in the Caribbean, peaking at 43 per cent at the end of the 1970s and around 25 per cent today, and many major historic laws protecting workers' rights were passed in the 1970s. These laws include the Labour Relations and Industrial Disputes Act (LRIDA), the Employment Termination Redundancy Payment Act and the Equal Pay for Men and Women Act. The first guarantees the right of workers to be represented by a trade union and lays out the procedures to ensure that there can be no avoidance due to unclarity; the second protects workers' rights by making arbitrary and unfair dismissal illegal and also provides for redundancy payments, particularly important in the 1970s when fly-by-night foreign investors were common.

Trade unions remain a strong force, critical for the social contracts that have been attempted, recently successfully, for a joint approach to social crises. Jamaica and the English-speaking Caribbean in general have a history of a comparatively strong defence of workers' rights putting them, in some respects, at a disadvantage in international trade. Jamaican workers' wages have never reached the lowest wage levels of workers in Mexico, Central America and in Caribbean islands such as the Dominican Republic.

Another critical influence in the development of Jamaican democracy was the middle-class nature of its early political leadership. The PNP was led by the middle class who advocated for self-government that was 'democratic and *fundamentally British*' (Leader Article, *Public Opinion*, Sept 2, 1939, the paper of the national movement, *their emphasis*, Munroe 1972: 22). Decolonization came through a constitutional struggle led by professionals, not a struggle involving people and their organizations.[8] The perspective was elitist.

The Jamaica Labour Party (JLP) governed in the first decade following the 1944 constitution. Bustamante's biographer, George Eaton, has analysed in Bustamante's own philosophy and approach, part of the reason for the non-transformatory character of this period:

> Alexander Bustamante had brought the working class into the mainstream of Jamaican political life. As a leader, effectively of a worker's party, he was given a unique opportunity, had he been so inclined, to pursue a 'political economy' which might have made it possible, through either

> restructuring of the economy or refashioning of the instruments of economic control, for the working class to have been brought into the mainstream of economic activity. But he was inhibited by his own conservative... philosophy (as well as that of the working class) from using political power as the primary instrument for achieving social and economic justice.[9] Instead, he continued to rely on collective bargaining as the primary institutional means for achieving distributive justice and used the political agency to redress specific inadequacies of collective bargaining. (Eaton 1995: 155)

Independence constitution: powerful prime minister, two parties entrenched

The authors of the 1962 Jamaican Constitution chose to continue the autocratic tradition of the plantation. If faced with a motion of no confidence the prime minister is authorized to dissolve Parliament and call new elections rather than resign.[10] The Constitution provides for a Leader of Opposition whose position is entrenched – an indication of genuine commitment by the two major parties to a power-sharing system. However, it has also been self-serving, leading to a virtual political cartel as third parties cannot be represented in the upper house, whose members are appointed by the prime minister and by the leader of the opposition. The rapid decline in support for third parties can be seen in Table 10.2. In the 1990s a new party, the National Democratic Movement (NDM), raised hopes when its leader, Bruce Golding, brought a new dynamic to the Jamaican political culture by admitting to, and renouncing, his former involvement as a member of the JLP in political violence. Although it has virtually collapsed since he returned to the JLP, succeeding Edward Seaga in 2004 as Opposition Leader, for a few years it opened a new space – offering a critique of the Constitution and strengthening the shift against the *tribalist* and violent two-party politics of the traditional parties.

The context for this constitutional dictatorship is a Parliament of 60 members, in which cabinet ministers make up 40–50 per cent of the government MPs. This has resulted historically in a weak backbench. Such a dynamic does not exist in the home of the Westminster model where among hundreds of government MPs ministerial chances are nearer to 1 in 20 than 1 in 2.

The local government system of parish councils has not yet fulfilled its potential as a vehicle for decentralization and deepened democracy, bringing governance closer to the people. A 1963 report commented that 'local government has been left out of the mainstream of national development.' (Jones and Mills 1989: 124). Some steps have been taken over the last decade but they have been slow and halting.

Clientelist democracy and 'garrison constituencies'

Starting with the trade union rivalry from 1944 which split the working class, the development of partisan 'political tribalism' from the mid 1940s increasingly interfered with and eventually poisoned national development.

Table 10.2 Political systems and elections in Jamaica, 1944–2002

Election Year	*No. of electors*	*Per cent voting*	*No. of seats*	*Won by*	*Comment*
1944 Universal Suffrage, Limited self-government	633,069	55.2	32	JLP	Universal suffrage for all aged 21 & over. JLP win 22 seats (41.4 per cent of votes), PNP 5, Independents 5, Jamaica Democratic Party representing the white elite, 0 (latter 2 get 35.1 per cent of votes).
1949	732,217	63.8	32	JLP	JLP win 17 seats (42.7 per cent of votes), PNP 13 (get most votes – 43.5 per cent), Independents 2.
1955	761,238	63.9	32	PNP	PNP win 18 seats (50.5 per cent of votes), JLP 14. No Independent gets seats (10.5 per cent of votes).
1959	853,539	65.4	45	PNP	PNP win 29 seats (54.8 per cent of votes), JLP 16.
1962 Independence	796,540	72.3	45	JLP	JLP win 26 seats (50 per cent of votes), PNP 19.
1967	543,307 see 'Comment'	81.5	45	JLP	JLP win 33 seats (50.7 per cent of votes), PNP 20. Voter registration reduced by changes in registration system.
1972	605,662	78.2	53	PNP	PNP win 37 seats (56.4 per cent of votes), JLP 16.
1976	870,972	84.5	60	PNP	PNP win 47 seats (56.8 per cent), JLP 13. Changes in registration system reversed. Voting age lowered to 18.
1980	990,417	86.1	60	JLP	JLP win 51 seats (58.9 per cent of votes), PNP 9.
1983	90,019 see under "Comment"	28.9	60	JLP	PNP boycotts the elections.
1989	1,078,760	77.6	60	PNP	PNP win 45 seats (56.6 per cent of votes), JLP 15.
1993	1,002,600	66.7	60	PNP	PNP win 52 seats (61.3 per cent of votes), JLP 8.
1997	1,182,294	65.2	60	PNP	PNP win 50 seats (55.7 per cent of votes), JLP 10. NDM get 4.8 per cent of votes but no seats.
2002	1,301,638	57.3	60	PNP	PNP win 34 seats, JLP 26.

Source: Electoral Office of Jamaica (2005).

Jamaican political scientist Carl Stone suggested that Jamaican politics is based on a structure of patron-clientelism which makes it a distinct system, not simply a sub-type of the class-based politics of liberal democracy in advanced capitalist countries.[11]

This power structure characteristically emerges in Third World countries when imperialist interests hand over the machinery of government to the politically dominant petty bourgeois party leaders. The underdevelopment of local capitalism due to the hegemony of foreign capital has facilitated state power in competing with, and eventually subordinating, the power base of capital and property ownership. Domestic capitalist interests court party leaders on terms controlled by the latter, thus becoming their clients, since they lack the independent control of material forces characteristic of corporate capitalist interests in the metropolitan centres of world capitalism (Stone 1980).

For the ordinary citizen housing became a key benefit under party patronage, manipulated from the 1940s by successive governments, leading to the phenomenon known as 'garrison constituencies'. 'In the typical case, JLP and PNP governments pack the housing schemes they construct with persons who are party supporters. The result is the creation of... politically partisan communities that reflect one-party tendencies' (Stone 1989b: 26). In garrison constituencies the election of the representative of the party that built the housing scheme is secure. Party activists have ensured voter intimidation and fraudulent voting practices with vote counts of over 100 per cent. Intense tribalist loyalty in these communities accompanied by murderous violence have been the tragic consequences of this garrison culture, referred to as 'tribalist politics'.

Political patronage also extended to jobs, an increasingly scarce benefit in the post-independence period. From 1968 to 1973 employment in the public sector almost doubled, from 57,000 to 107,000, in part the result of 'considerable "welfare" and "political" recruitment to lower level Civil Service jobs as well as within the parastatal sector' (Jones and Mills 1989: 111). Elections became bitterly and violently contested events, critical for the survival of sections of the poorer classes, since they meant gain or loss of jobs, housing and other 'scarce benefits'. The political cycle in the 1970s and 1980s was accompanied not just by material bribes but also by the lethal political practice of distributing guns as the ultimate means of intimidation in garrison constituencies. Notable in their open rejection of such political handouts were the Rastafarians for whom all such manipulation was another demonstration of the evil 'Babylon system'.

Democratic socialism 1972–80: precursors and impact

The first decade after Independence was a time of intense social and political ferment. Left-wing political groups such as the Young Socialist League of young PNP members aiming to politicize youths and reform the party, and the Workers' Liberation League (WLL), forerunner to the Marxist Leninist

Workers Party of Jamaica (WPJ), were formed. Demands from Rastafarians and others for recognition of the black heritage of Jamaica's people reached a crescendo. Young Guyanese History lecturer at Jamaica's UWI campus, Walter Rodney, took his teaching on Africa from packed campus classes into Rastafarian camps and the poorest districts in West Kingston. Another group critical of government policy in the 1960s and involved in actions around employment on inner city sites, was the Unemployed Workers Council (UWC), an early advocate of worker self-management and independence from political unionism. The intelligentsia were represented by the university-based New World Movement who provided a radical critique of the economic and social policies of the Independence governments across the Caribbean.

Faced with a ferment of critical, revolutionary, anti-establishment ideas, the JLP government responded with repressive anti-civil liberty measures. It banned literature deemed 'communist' or associated with black power ideas, seized passports, approved the re-introduction of 'cat-ó-nine-tails' and the tamarind switch in the prisons, and handed out long prison terms for the possession and use of marijuana. In 1968, while Rodney was off the island attending a conference, it refused him re-entry and tear-gassed the ensuing peaceful university protest march, provoking a serious riot downtown.[12]

Coming against this background, 'Michael Manley carefully constructed a broad alliance of the nationalist and progressive elements... The PNP victory of 1972... was a coming together of three important currents: the radicalism of the youth and particularly the progressive intelligentsia, the cultural mass movement emanating out of the Rastafari, and the reorganization of the PNP as a mass political party:' (Beckford and Witter 1980: 78–9) The outcome was a raft of outstanding social legislation but also, later, intense political and class polarization: between socialist and capitalist, PNP and JLP, 'sufferer' and 'big man', downtown and uptown, pro-Cuba/Third world[13] and pro-America. The entire society was involved in this ideological confrontation and there were high voter turnouts in elections: 78.2 per cent in 1972, 84.5 per cent in 1976 and 86.1 per cent in 1980.

The PNP's explanation of democratic socialism adopted in 1974 was published in a newspaper supplement. It included the following:

- '[G]ives practical expression to the Christian ideal of the equality of God's children'
- 'Socialism recognizes that democracy is fundamental to the *creation of a society in which each individual* has equal opportunities in... the process by which decisions on matters of public interest are made and implemented.' (*their emphasis*)
- 'Private business... can exist either in a capitalist or in a socialist society...Under Socialism private business is required to work within the bounds of the national interest and people's rights and welfare.' (Stephens and Stephens 1986: 107)

Listed as examples of 'nations with democratic socialist governments' were Australia, Britain, Sweden, Israel, Malta, New Zealand, Singapore, Tanzania, Guyana, Germany, Holland, India, Denmark and Sri Lanka. There is no indication from Manley's words or deeds that there was ever any intention to work outside the structure of parliamentary democracy. He spoke of a 'third path' between the capitalist and the socialist models of the Cold War.

Under democratic socialism, democracy for many in the population became more meaningful because it touched them directly: the new government opened critical legislative, economic and social 'space', heretofore closed, for low-status sugar and domestic workers, so-called 'illegitimate' children, workers and women in general, and youth, the latter enabled to vote at the age of 18 years. Social policies included the Status of Children Act, which removed the stigma of bastardy applicable to the majority of children and gave equal rights to all children, Maternity Leave (including for domestic workers who were specially provided for under National Insurance), historic laws protecting workers' rights, Special Employment Programmes developed to provide immediate unemployment relief, and the National Housing Trust (NHT), a compulsory national savings scheme based on 3 per cent payroll tax and 2 per cent of employees' gross earnings. Housing distribution is by lottery not patronage – the NHT is an extremely successful institution still in operation. A communist third party, championing the cause of the workers, was allowed freedom to operate as a legitimate political entity.

In the government's thrust towards a more egalitarian society there were also intangible social gains, hard to measure but no less real, that irreversibly raised the status and self-esteem of the black majority whose ancestors had been slaves. Symbolic messages were conveyed in many ways, including dress codes. Some ministers adopted the beards and tams associated with Rastafarians; Manley himself wore a kareba, a tie-less one-layer suit with short or long-sleeves. Added as official formal wear for Parliament, it was a cooler Third World alternative to the western suit, until then de rigueur. The wardrobe and look of the Prime Minister's third wife, Beverley Manley, a black woman, had a huge impact – she wore her hair in the natural Afro style, beloved of the Black Power movement, and sometimes wore a 'tie-head' – a scarf tied in a certain style associated with market women; she might turn up to welcome a visiting head of state in a traditional African gown. The culture of the African majority received validation from the top, and the self-esteem of the lower class was thereby strengthened. All this had a revolutionary effect on the way the society thought and behaved. 'I think our biggest success was the extent to which... we were able to raise the level of consciousness of the people. People were saying for the first time 'is black man time now'. *For example, domestic servants, for the first time, felt entitled to walk through the front door*' (PNP leader quoted in Stephens and Stephens 1986: 293, my emphasis).

This decade turned on its head the colonial Eurocentric 'white bias' which had persisted into independence. An overarching and lasting achievement was the active promotion of a sociocultural model based on the premise that all Jamaicans were of equal worth and value, and the opening up of opportunities to facilitate the material expression of this. The strength of leadership required to undertake this, working as it was against deeply vested interests and colonial cultural overhangs, should not be underestimated. At the same time it was often the organized sociopolitical groups that pushed the government into taking the action to match its words: the socialist-oriented originally Catholic NGO, Social Action Centre, mobilized the sugar workers to insist on the cooperatives and backed them against the sabotage from many estate managers; it took a two-year campaign to ensure the government passed the Maternity Leave Law, despite opposition from the business class and the single very influential daily newspaper, *The Daily Gleaner.* Initiated by the National Union of Democratic Teachers (NUDT), it was then carried by the PNP's own Women's Movement headed by Manley's wife, strongly supported by the WPJ-allied Committee of Women for Progress (CWP). Women's organizations insisted on the government paying attention to critical issues that affected families and children, such as the availability of food. They agitated for Voluntary Price Inspectors (VPIs) and were able to prove, through the inspection of storerooms, that supermarkets were indeed hoarding basic items absent from the shelves, as part of private sector action to provoke a government fall. The communist WPJ was a key force behind many of these thrusts through its members in the leadership of the NUDT, CWP, Press Association of Jamaica (PAJ) and some government media houses.

Unions became increasingly militant, the incidence of strikes doubling during this period, as much a reflection of labour's confidence in its ability to pressure employers as of economic discontent. The University and Allied Workers Union (UAWU), linked to the Marxist-Leninist WPJ, became a significant force and is now one of the three major general unions, with the BITU and National Workers Union (NWU – formed by the PNP to take over from the TUC after the 1955 'purge' of the Left), although the WPJ became defunct at the end of the 1980s. Fatally weakened by their non-ideological tradition, the unions' contribution to social transformation in the 1970s, however, was slight. The UAWU excepted, they were unenthusiastic, for example, about the sugar worker cooperatives and worker participation schemes.

In 1972 Manley had turned the PNP into a party that both accommodated a left wing and *initially* managed to coalesce a multi-class coalition around him. He attracted not only ministers of a left-wing persuasion but also brought with him liberals in the capitalist class who shared strong feelings of nationalism. It was the skills of leading businessmen combined with the daring of Manley's tactics that negotiated a revolutionary 'bauxite levy' with the bauxite companies to assist Jamaica to cope with the phenomenal changes in oil prices after the OPEC increases.

In his second term, however, as fears of a communist-style takeover arose, unnecessarily as an objective analysis would suggest but fostered by Manley's rhetoric in 'the charismatic moment' and his friendship with Castro, the business class would turn solidly against him – the support of the capitalist and high-income professionals going from 60 per cent in the 1972 elections to 20 per cent in 1976, dropping even further in 1980 (Kaufmann 1985: 192, based on polls by Carl Stone).

The social gains of this period – the cultural gains were less affected – were undermined by clientelist politics and by the internal and external economic challenges discussed earlier. Even as egalitarian gains were deepening democracy at one level, ironically the formal democratic system came under threat. In 1976 alleged evidence of a military coup linked to organized violence in inner-city communities led to a State of Emergency being declared. Bitter political tribalism resulted in violence which reached its culmination in near civil war in the election year of 1980, when 889 were killed (a 253 per cent increase in murders in one year) and elections saw stuffing and stealing of ballot boxes, all fuelled by a clientelist patronage system. Jamaica was one of the arenas in which the Cold War was played out.[14] Its population became bitterly divided as events led one half of the country to fear CIA involvement in Jamaica's political process, with a US government allied to large businesses prepared to sabotage the Manley government and its gains for the lower class; while the other half heard, in Manley's rhetoric, foreign policy and the imprisoning of some Opposition members under the State of Emergency, along with the existence of a small but activist Marxist Leninist third party, clear evidence that Jamaica was about to become a Cuban-style Russian-linked communist state, which would suppress private capital and civil liberties.

Structural adjustment, 1980–89

Radical economic and social changes were rejected under the political ideology of the new JLP government. They favoured an incrementalist approach to policy changes and defended capitalist free enterprise. Their chief contributions to social policy in this period were in providing an important focus on skills training for employment through the creation of the Human Employment and Resource Training (HEART) agency, and in social protection through a targeted programme of food stamps to compensate for removal of food subsidies – beneficiaries of non-contributory schemes jumped from 63,000 in 1978 to almost 500,000, a fifth of the population, in 1986. HEART is funded through a levy on all medium to large employers unless they choose to apprentice a HEART graduate for one year after training. Initially open only to high school students, it has since expanded to take in lower-level applicants and is now attached to a national certification body. Like the NHT this is an indigenous institution that has been creatively and viably funded from within the internal economy. The same approach is now being applied to the new National Health Fund (NHF), which provides selected medications at drastically reduced prices subsidized by a 'sin tax' on alcohol and cigarettes.

The government closed down the new economic structures focused on equity – like the sugar worker cooperatives, the Land Lease programme leasing idle government and private land at nominal rates to over 40,000 small farmers, and the community economic organizations. Their policy thrust was to focus on the economic – an election mandate, since this was where the PNP had failed – but using an economistic neoliberal market-led approach in which social policy was a separate issue. Government was to be run as a business because, in the words of the JLP leader, 'It takes cash to care'. Under structural adjustment social policy was on the back burner, severely constrained under the terms and conditions of IMF and World Bank agreements. Areas such as health and primary/secondary education suffered major damage.

Strengthened though they were under the PNP in the 1970s, the unions proved unable to withstand the onslaught of structural adjustment combined with the tough and determined leadership of Edward Seaga. Their weakness became clear when they attempted Jamaica's first (and only) General Strike in mid-1985, the year of the most severe IMF conditionalities, only to have it collapse because of BITU vacillation (an instance of partisan loyalties) and the non-participation of the civil service union, as well as organizational weaknesses.

Following the failed General Strike the Seaga government undertook severely repressive measures against labour. Invoking the Essential Services clause of the 1975 Labour Relations and Industrial Disputes Act (LRIDA), it fired 200 militant electricity workers who had shut down the island's power system. Later settled in a redundancy action, this provoked bitter anti-government sentiments. The government implemented layoffs in the areas of local government allegedly most militant in the strike, suspending 1,200 firefighters. This was followed by the introduction of the Fire Brigade Act depriving these workers of the right to join a trade union. The Act was only withdrawn after the case was taken to the ILO.

While the unions were weakened, the NGO movement strengthened in this period as some left forces went into development agencies as social workers and development professionals. The traditional umbrella Council of Voluntary Social Services (CVSS) was joined by newer, more developmentally oriented umbrella NGOs – the Association of Development Agencies (ADA), environmental and women's umbrella groups. They received financial support from international British, European and Canadian NGOs in particular. The result was significant capacity building at the grassroots among community-based organizations. For many it was their first experience, since Jamaica Welfare, of tangible assistance that did not come politically attached. Jamaica Welfare was an NGO established in 1937. It pioneered a method of community development in rural communities that provided a model emulated not only in the Caribbean, but also in parts of Latin America and Africa. It later became a state agency under another name, becoming increasingly centralized and dropping many of its original participatory methods.

As in the previous decade, the formal democratic system came under threat. The experience of structural adjustment in the 1980s was devastating and two years after their election, by October 1982, despite some improvements in the standard of living, the JLP had already lost majority support according to Carl Stone's unerringly accurate polls (Stone 1989a: 27). However, Edward Seaga cleverly built on the Jamaican revulsion at Maurice Bishop's murder in Grenada[15] to call a successful snap election in 1983, boycotted by Manley because agreed electoral reform had not been implemented. For almost six years Jamaica was ruled under a one-party Parliament while the PNP opposed through public meetings. Public opinion would not have countenanced any abuse of their position by the JLP nor is their any evidence that they intended to do so, and when they called elections by the constitutionally due date in 1989 they were voted out.[16]

The recent period 1989–2004

The PNP returned on a different platform – they were still seen as the party that 'puts people first' (their 1989 election slogan), but now Manley had made firm alliances with the private sector and took a market-oriented approach to the economy.[17] He stepped down due to ill health during his first term and was succeeded by Percival James Patterson, a non-charismatic, non-confrontational but astute politician, respected abroad for his diplomatic skills.

The mood of the country was also changing. There was increasing dialogue between groups that would not have sat across a table from one another in the 1970s. The media has played a major role in facilitating this change. There are now three television stations, 12 locally based cable stations, and 20 radio stations, all privately owned except one cable and one radio station, up from one and two respectively in the 1970s (when two out of three were publicly owned). They include a university station, a religious station, and a local NGO-run station for inner-city Kingston residents, all playing a critical role in giving voice to multiple interests. A talk show hosted by two former political opponents, Manley's former wife and a former JLP cabinet minister, led the way, breaking new ground in getting ministers and opposition spokesmen to talk on the programme and to respond to criticisms and controversy, and taking the programme into warring inner city areas. The democratic tradition of free speech in Jamaica is such that in the popular radio call-in programmes the most frank and open criticisms against all and sundry are made by both callers and hosts. With competition and the final breaking of the print media monopoly of one daily newspaper, investigative journalism has improved. Media exposure has become an important modality for communicating the concerns of civil society. It was the media's support for the voice of one individual, later assisted by a human rights NGO, that pressured the government into investigating a scandal surrounding children's homes. A commission provided further damning evidence and there is now a Child Care and Protection Act with teeth, a new Child Development

Agency and a Children's Advocate. The media is providing a key mechanism for political accountability.

Although the garrison communities still exist, there has been a strong trend towards detribalizing the political culture. On the partisan front on both sides, responding to the national mood, there has been some 'ideological demobilization of supporters' (Gray 1991: 1). The 1993 election was widely criticized for corruption, although the overall outcome was accepted. The electoral system has since been largely cleaned up, thanks to Citizens' Action for Free and Fair Elections (CAFFE), established in 1994, and to legislation giving power to an independent Electoral Advisory Committee (EAC) to declare an election void if certain abuses are verified. Used in one constituency in the 1997 Election, it reversed the result in favour of the Opposition. The EAC's secretariat, the Electoral Office of Jamaica, has weeded political activists from among electoral officials, successfully got volunteers to train and act as Election Officials, and set up a fingerprint voter identification system as the country moves towards electronic voting. The 2002 General Election was considered to have been conducted at a high standard of fairness.

Island-wide roadblocks and riots over gas price increases in 1999 leading to nine deaths and millions of dollars of damage were a catalytic event for civil society and government action. The crisis was resolved nine days later after the Prime Minister invited a committee of the business sector and civil society/NGO representatives to make recommendations. The tax was reduced by 45 per cent and the balance recouped from the wealthier classes by a tax on interest earned from commercial paper. These protests were the trigger for the formation of Jamaicans for Justice (JFJ), a human rights group led by middle- and upper-class persons. Derided not only for its class origins but also falsely for connection to the political Opposition, then for supporting criminals against the police, the JFJ has gained respect from all levels of the society for exposing police brutality and for insisting on accountability from the government. It has taken action through a variety of methods including demonstrations but also via legal action. Through its efforts the families of victims of police killings now have the right to be represented at autopsies, and government has passed legislation to end the 'packing' of juries in Coroner's courts. JFJ has taken the Government to the Organization of American States (OAS) over an alleged police brutality case and, in alliance with the Jamaica Bar Association and the Independent Jamaica Council for Human Rights, won a case in the British Privy Council forcing government to withdraw accession to the new Caribbean Court of Appeal without full consultation with the Jamaican public.

The government has adopted a more rights-based and participatory policy approach. One of the highpoints of this approach is the Access to Information Act, passed in 2004, now being actively used by the media and citizens to probe expenditures, parliamentary attendance, etc. The government has also opened up to the public the proceedings of critical Parliamentary Committees, such as the Public Accounts Committee (PAC) to review government expenditures, which it has put under Opposition chairmanship. It has set up the offices of Contractor-General, Public Defender, and Political Ombudsman. It has formally adopted a participatory social policy framework and action plan, the Jamaica 2015/Jamaica Social Policy Evaluation (JASPEV), with technical and funding assistance from the UK government. Under this project innovative governance mechanisms are being tested including people-centred policy-making in 46 communities island-wide with Opposition involvement; a progress report using social, environmental and economic indicators to measure progress towards long-term social goals, written by a 'joined-up' group of voluntary public sector and civil society experts; a planning and budgeting network within government for a more coherent and participatory government budget process.

Government and unions for the first time in Jamaica's history succeeded in signing in 2003 a three-year social contract, with the support of the Opposition, to halt public sector layoffs and to keep inflation down for three years in exchange for a wage freeze, in order to enable Jamaica to achieve critical fiscal targets. It is unlikely to be renewed, however, in the face of government's failure in its inflation targets and the refusal of the Police Federation to sign the agreement leading to protests and a wage increase in late 2005.

Other successes from a more partnership mode have included the 2002 National Committee on Crime and Violence, with leading politicians from both sides, along with private sector and church representatives, which issued a well-received report; a 2003 bipartisan parliamentary agreement on Education; a Peace Management Initiative (PMI) with a team from government and opposition, the police and civil society (chaired by an evangelist bishop), which intervenes in communities with gang conflicts, originally along political borderlines, employing social workers and facilitating developmental interventions.

Regulatory mechanisms, such as the Contractor-General's and the Auditor-General's reports to Parliament, are frequently very critical of specific public sector bodies and procedures. However, there have been several scandals and the general view is that corruption has increased under the present PNP regime and that, despite the mechanisms, accountability is lacking *because there are no penalties and no enforcement*. In addition, many of these agencies are understaffed – the Corruption Commission, for example, has a staff of only ten. The government has been singularly unsuccessful in developing an independent police investigative mechanism trusted by citizens. The rate of police killings is still among the highest in the world. Indeed many credit the PNP's historic and unprecedented four terms in office (a record 18 years) as much to the former Opposition Leader Edward Seaga's general unpopularity and autocratic leadership of the JLP, resulting in frequent internal wrangling, as to ongoing public satisfaction with the PNP. Voter turnout has consistently declined in the last three elections (Table 10.2).

Social policy and patterns of expenditures[18]

From the colonial pattern of low social sector expenditures and high national security expenditures, after self-government (1944) Jamaica began to move in the opposite direction, increasing its social expenditures and lowering its security budget. Debt began to threaten the budget following the oil shocks of the early 1970s and impacted particularly on social expenditures. Figure 10.1 shows the inverse correlation between social expenditures and debt payments as a percentage of the government's budget. The period under Democratic Socialism (1972–80) was significant for the attempt to address social justice through an emphasis on social policy and on mechanisms to address economic inequity. However economic growth eluded the government under the influence of a multiplicity of factors and social expenditures began to fall below 28 per cent of the budget after 1975, deepening this fall under the IMF agreements from 1977. While during the 1980s structural adjustment heavily reduced the public sector, frequently in an arbitrary manner, and social expenditure only reached the level of the early 1970s in 1986 under the windfall from lowered oil prices, it remained above 20 per cent because of the generous aid received by the JLP under Seaga. It is since

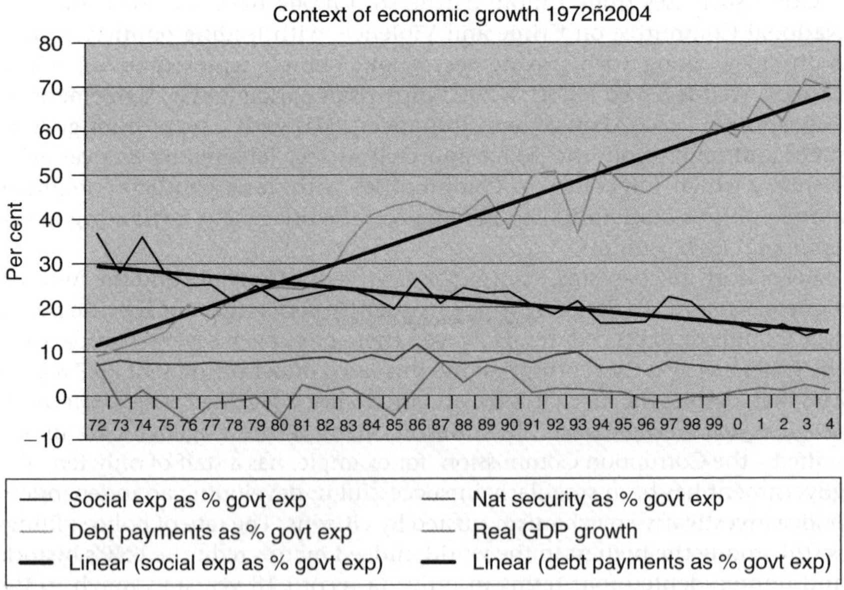

Figure 10.1 Social expenditures compared to other government expenditures in the context of economic growth, 1972–2004

Source: National Planning Agency (NPA) 1975: 1978: 1979: 1981; Planning Institute of Jamaica (formerly NPA) 1983: 1985: 1987: 1990: 1993: 1996: 1999: 2003: 2004.

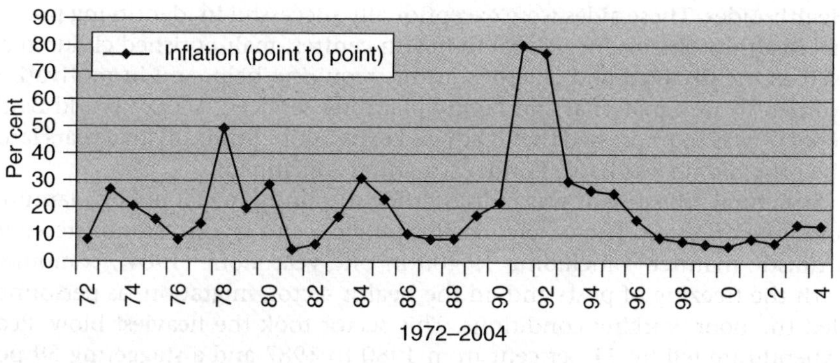

Figure 10.2 Inflation, 1972–2004
Source: National Planning Agency (NPA) 1975: 1978: 1979: 1981; Planning Institute of Jamaica (formerly NPA) 1983: 1985: 1987: 1990: 1993: 1996: 1999: 2003: 2004.

the 1990s that it has fallen below 20 per cent of the government budget (except in 1997–8) and in 2004 was only 14 per cent (Figure 10.1). The general decrease in social expenditures in the 1990s is directly related to the debt burden, which saw a phenomenal increase after the 1991 financial crisis, which also precipitated hyperinflation (Figure 10.2).

The area of most progress in social policy has been health and many of Jamaica's vital statistics put it on par with upper-income countries (for example, life expectancy is 73.3 yrs). However the high debt servicing allocation in the budget (69.9 per cent in 2004) continues to seriously undermine the public health system and all social policy areas. Education has been the least successful social policy area: fairly high literacy levels (79.9 per cent – higher among females, but 43 per cent functional illiteracy among males) mask deep educational weaknesses. Public housing has been considerable, but the social benefits have been critically marred by political patronage. Finally social welfare provision has been inadequate and more recent attempts at targeting may be wide of the mark in terms of poverty reduction. The next sections will briefly explore the three areas of health, education and social welfare.

Health

After the damning report of the Moyne Commission (1938) a colonial development fund was established in 1942 and a primary health care system for all signalled a new approach focused on prevention. Its impact was seen in the reduction in preventable illnesses and increases in life expectancy from 61 years in 1950 to 67 years in 1970; and dramatic decreases in infant mortality: from 81 deaths per 1,000 live births in 1950 to 40 per 1,000 live births in 1970, and 19.2 deaths per 1,000 births in 2004. Many health units were built during the 1970s. This period also saw the delivery of public health care carried out free of cost. Hospitals were managed by regional boards that were mostly autonomous, and outreach services expanded the use of Community

Health Aides. These aides were exceptionally successful in identifying potential health problems for referral to health centres, malnourished children as well as the disabled and elderly shut-ins requiring help, and in motivating women to seek maternal and family planning services. A 1979 World Bank report[19] was so impressed that it advised expansion. Ironically five years later the programme was halved under structural adjustment.

Structural adjustment was a disaster for sustaining social policy planning and programming. There were massive public sector layoffs, administered in a drastic manner,[20] including 19,400 in one year alone (1984), combined with the freezing of posts and, in the health sector, migration, as personnel fled the poor working conditions. This sector took the heaviest blow. Real expenditure fell by 24 per cent from 1980 to 1987 and a staggering 59 per cent reduction was seen in key health personnel including nurses, medical technologists, pharmacists and public health inspectors (Jones 1995: 133). This had serious practical consequences. The October 1989 newsletter of the Medical Association of Jamaica reported that:

> in Spanish Town Hospital... nursery wards were often staffed by just one registered nurse; sometimes there was no nurse at all in pediatrics...; in the University Hospital of the West Indies, 3 out of 21 wards closed due to nursing shortage, only 3 out of 8 intensive care unit beds could be used, and operating theatre time was down by 50 per cent; and in the Kingston Public Hospital, 4 out of 16 wards were closed... some surgeons [were] only able to operate every other week.

Now a middle-income country, Jamaica's epidemiological profile is changing, with chronic non-communicable lifestyle diseases accounting for half of total annual deaths. HIV/AIDS is the second highest cause of death for men and women aged 30–34 years and for children aged 1–4 years. It is estimated to have caused productivity losses of 4 per cent of GDP. Government has a well-planned internationally funded HIV/AIDS programme.

The progress in overall statistics is, however, masking the present impact of expenditure cuts on day-to-day health care. This public letter from a medical intern refers to his/her experience in Jamaica's largest public hospital:

> On entering the wards, the congestion and overcrowding were the first things apparent. Second was the stress and anxiety on the faces of doctors and nurses. The shortage of basic equipment was alarming... From syringes, to branulas, to antibiotics and pain medication, KPH runs short on a chronic basis... Hospital diagnostic units are overwhelmed by sheer volume and backlog. It takes two months if not more to get an ultrasound as an outpatient at KPH... Overwhelmed technicians have to play 'trouble-shoot that machine' each night to get ageing machines to work magic... (*Sunday Gleaner*, 18 September 2005)

Targets in child nutrition, reduction of anaemia in pregnancy, and drug supplies to clinics and hospitals were not reached in 2004 due to resource constraints in materials and staff linked to the declining budget.

One programme successfully reaching a vulnerable group has been the Drugs for the Elderly Programme, now absorbed by the NHF, which has extended the programme to all ages. It has reduced the cost of drugs for the most common chronic diseases by 88–96 per cent.[21]

The cost-sharing approach was introduced in 1991 and user fees have increased from 1 per cent of the budget in 1991 to 14 per cent in 2004. Officially no one is turned away from a public health facility on the basis of inability to pay but anecdotal evidence suggests otherwise.

Education

The system that emerged after emancipation maintained the racial/social cleavages of slavery, confining education for the African majority to the elementary (primary) school while the light-skinned minorities received upgraded high school education, and white expatriate children went to boarding school in England.

Following independence, the government introduced a 'New Deal in Education', building many more secondary schools and introducing the Eleven Plus Examination (later called Common Entrance) to provide opportunities for scholarships to fee-paying high schools. These prepared students for academic subjects and allowed for social mobility. It further introduced a regulation that reserved 70 per cent of high school places for examination entrants from government primary schools, the remaining 30 per cent going to entrants from fee-paying private preparatory schools.[22] During the 1970s all secondary and tertiary education became free and there was a vibrant literacy programme with thousands of volunteers, on a scale never since repeated.

Nonetheless, the elitist two-tier system persists. A 1983 UNESCO report described the situation:

> The variety of types of secondary schools appears confusing but, actually, boils down to two: the high schools and the others. The differences can be seen in admission criteria, type of curriculum, enrolment patterns, future promise, social currency and unit expenditure... The High Schools hold the promise of post-secondary studies, have a much higher social currency, spend more money per student, experience a continually higher demand for admission and have an academically oriented programme. By contrast the New Secondary Schools enjoy noticeably lower esteem on the part of pupils/parents, which is reflected in a declining tendency of enrolments and transition rates. The curriculum is heavily biased towards pre-vocational, non-academic subjects. (Task Force on Educational Reform 2004: 18)

Under structural adjustment graduate teachers, who had alternative career options, moved out of the educational system. In 1976, 64 per cent of teachers in traditional high schools had degrees. This percentage had dropped to 28 per cent by 1989. During this period per capita expenditure on primary education, already far behind Caribbean sister islands such as Barbados and Trinidad and Tobago, fell even further. Whereas Jamaica had spent the equivalent of US$119 per primary school child in 1976, increasing to US$141 in 1981, by 1990 this had dropped to US$90, while in that year Barbados spent US$600 per child. The comparative figures for 2001 were US$323 per Jamaican primary school child and US$1,871 per Bajan child.

The impact can be seen in the rate of functional illiteracy among primary school leavers. This had been halved between 1971 and 1983 – from 54 per cent to 26 per cent. By 1989 functional illiteracy had started to rise again to 33 per cent among the same group (Errol Miller and Manley Thompson in Jones 1995: 142). Over the following 14 years there has barely been any improvement – functional illiteracy among the same group was 30 per cent in 2003 (Task Force on Educational Reform 2004).

In the 1980s cost sharing was introduced for tertiary-level education although it is still heavily subsidized (80 per cent) and in the 1990s cost sharing was brought back for secondary-level schools.

In 2000 the Common Entrance Exam was replaced by the Grade Six Achievement Test (GSAT), as part of a National Assessment Programme. Former new secondary schools have been 'upgraded' to high schools and follow a curriculum leading to matriculation exams for tertiary-level education. However, these newly upgraded schools remain under-resourced. Meanwhile an elite selection system remains, operated by the Ministry of Education, whereby the highest GSAT achievers go to traditional high schools, the highest scorers among them going to the best resourced. Parents and teachers focus as frenetically as ever on GSAT 'passes', i.e. those mark levels in the examination that will enable their children, under this selection system, to enter the traditional high schools. The residual problem lies in the fact that there are far too few well-endowed and well-resourced high schools to serve the growing population, reflecting the continuation of insufficient policy commitment to equitable educational opportunities.

Education has been the social policy area of greatest public focus and controversy in recent years[23] because of poor student performance at the end of the secondary school system. Only 17 per cent of the eligible cohort passed the matriculation exam in Mathematics in 2003 and only 25 per cent passed in English Language.[24] In the same year only one in 10 students of the eligible cohort matriculated, i.e. passed 4 subjects including Maths and English Language (JASPEV 2004). This pattern has been repeated for years. Debt payments are consuming higher and higher portions of the budget and the percentage allocation to the Ministry of Education, although it receives the highest portion of the budget after debt payments, has steadily dropped in recent years – from 14.9 per cent in 1997 to 9.2 per cent in 2004. Expenditure on education is now the subject of a bipartisan agreement signed between the government and opposition in 2003 incorporating a five-year plan to carry expenditure on education to 15 per cent of the budget, shift more resources to early childhood and primary levels, and focus on improvement in teacher quality.

In 2004 the government commissioned a Task Force on Educational Reform and its frank report, combined with the political will, led to the establishment of a Transformation Team with a mandate to work to transform the education system over the next five years. Massive funding assistance is being sought. Despite Opposition fears that a dangerous precedent is being set, the government has drawn on NHT funds[25] at an equivalent of over US$73 million to support the first five years of the new transformation plan.

Social welfare and development

The new independence government introduced social reform legislation, the most important of which was the National Insurance Act in 1965, providing very minimal old-age pensions (now about US$63 per month), invalidity benefits and disablement benefits. Many formal sector jobs carry their own pension schemes, but with the decline in this sector and the growth of the informal sector, estimated to employ 53 per cent of labour (GRADE/IDB 2002), there has been a decline in pension coverage. There are no unemployment benefits.

A National Minimum Wage, although very small (presently about US$39 per week), was established under Democratic Socialism to give protection to vulnerable groups including domestic workers in a country where 45 per cent of households are female-headed. The primary school feeding programme, also introduced in the 1970s, tried to compensate for the severe educational disadvantage faced by poor children who were undernourished. The programme has since been supplemented by government-subsidized lunch programmes at the secondary level. During the 1970s price controls were introduced on those basic goods used most by the poor but were removed under structural adjustment. Under the present regime some are zero-rated under the 16.5 per cent General Consumption Tax (GCT).

Under structural adjustment in the 1980s, food stamps were introduced as a social safety net for the vulnerable. In 2000 PATH (Programme for Advancement Through Health and Education) replaced a number of welfare programmes, including food stamps, in an approach that is intended to be more developmental. Continued receipt of benefits is tied to compliance criteria: minimum school attendance of 85 per cent among 6–17 year olds and prescribed clinic attendance for children up to six years and for the elderly. Benefits are very minimal (about US$6.5 per beneficiary per month) and are funded by an international development partner, leading to questions about sustainability.

In a sharp and rigorously argued critique of the present approach to poverty reduction through social targeting, Patricia Anderson suggests that youth 'are more marginalized and excluded than any other generation' (Anderson 2001) and points out that in 1998 unemployed youth of 14–24 years represented 52 per cent of all unemployed workers and that 7 out of every 10 unemployed workers in Jamaica were below the age of 30. Given the logic of social targeting, however, 'there is a refusal to consider that the risk of poverty may be spread throughout entire strata of the population, who are distinguished by their current or former relationship to the labour market' (Anderson 2001: 2). Instead the benefits are provided to their children and grandmothers, who they could be supporting if employed. Analysis by age of the rising incidence of murder and shootings provides worrying support for Anderson's concerns. In 2004, 50 per cent of total admissions to adult correctional centres were of persons of 17–30 years of age. Moreover, this age group provided 62 per cent of admissions for murder, 71 per cent of admissions for shooting with intent, and 77 per cent of admissions for possession of illegal firearms (Planning Institute of Jamaica 2004).

Conclusion

The issue for democracy in Jamaica is not whether the country has democratic institutions and values – its history proves that these are well established – but the substance and quality of this democracy. If democracy is to be sustained it has to go beyond its minimalist definition to ensure equitable development. This issue confronts southern societies more urgently than northern societies because of the significant numbers of their citizens who are deprived of basic social rights, such as sanitation, adequate food, ready access to quality health and educational services, and whose civil and social rights are often slighted on the basis of their class, usually combined with race/ethnicity. The conclusion of this chapter is that democracy in Jamaica has not brought sufficiently equitable development – that holistic nexus where economic and social policy must cohere – and it has not yet brought social cohesion.

The risk Jamaican democracy runs is the risk of a level of redundancy – of being relevant to only part of the society, while the other part works outside a system which has failed to help them to escape from poverty and to achieve personal progress. The analysis of a number of commentators in Jamaica is that the rising crimes of aggression are rooted in social exclusion. The majority of these crimes are committed by youth 30 years and under against, in a bitter irony, their own age group, who provide the majority of victims. Many inner-city communities in Kingston are currently traumatized by an implosion of violence, unprecedented in its magnitude and in its merciless killing of women and children.

The policy approach has not consistently prioritized equity. This is elucidated for the 1950s and 1960s by Phillip Sherlock and Hazel Bennett who, comparing the Jamaican and Puerto Rican approaches in that period, point out that

> whereas Jamaica concentrated on economic growth through incentive legislation, Puerto Rico made this part of a *larger programme for social change*.....[E]very effort was made to increase social mobility through quality of educational opportunity. *The result was that social cohesion was strengthened and a sense of unity enforced by the impressive economic growth.* (Sherlock and Bennett 1998: 386–7, my emphases)

In the same period the 1960 University of the West Indies (UWI) report on the Rastafarian community, which highlighted the social cleavages in Jamaican society, identified the colonial system of education as their underpin.

A review of social expenditures (Figure 10.1 and Table 10.3) shows that over the past 23 years there has been a steady overall decline of 15 per cent in their relative percentage of government expenditures and a whopping overall increase of 57 per cent in the relative percentage of government expenditure on debt payments. The critical context for understanding the exponential impact of this is the stagnant one per cent real growth over the same period. In the context of a 41 per cent population increase[26] this suggests serious negative social consequences are virtually inevitable.

All governments from 1972 to 2004 have placed great importance on social programming, all have given comparable, although declining budgetary weight to the social sectors, and all have been seriously constrained at various times by economic crisis, structural adjustment and other external forces, such as oil prices and natural disasters. However, there is a significant difference between what was achieved by social policy under the Michael Manley government of 1972–80 and all other subsequent governments. The raft of social and economic legislation and programmes of that government, specifically aimed at increasing equity and inclusion, have not been repeated since. The difference inheres in political approach and will – Manley's government prioritized social justice and equity while all succeeding governments have prioritized economic growth, albeit with little success over 25 years. It must be acknowledged that no government since 1980 has experienced the level of negative growth that developed under Manley in the late 1970s, although there were probably powerful external factors of a political as well as economic nature contributing to, but not alone responsible for, this. There was indeed a spike in economic growth under Seaga from 1987 to 1990. However, this was accompanied by the repression of trade unions and workers' rights and Seaga was rejected in the 1989 elections. When social policy is not built around a social equity paradigm that combines the social and the economic, the efficacy and impact of social expenditures on social progress is reduced. Furthermore, the social equity paradigm is likely to inhere in the same paradigm that produces the thrust to deepen democracy beyond its minimalist definition.

Table 10.3 Expenditures (recurrent plus capital) on education, health and social security as a percentage of total government expenditures, 1943–2004

	1943	*1954*	*1962*	*1968*	*1973*	*1976*	*1979*	*1982*	*1985*	*1988*	*1991*	*1994*	*1997*	*2000*	*2004*
Education	9.6	15.1	15.3	14.7	18.3	16.0	15.0	14.9	12.6	12.7	12.4	9.2	14.9	11.0[1]	9.2[1]
Health	10.1	20.2[2]	17.3[2]	8.9	8.3	6.7	7.8	7.7	6.9	6.1	6.4	6.1	6.2	4.3	4.7
Social Security	7.7	7.4	10.0	5.7	1.5	2.3	2.1	1.0	1.7	5.5	1.6	3.3	4.1	0.7	0.8

Sources: Colony of Jamaica 1943; Dept. of Statistics, 1959: 1968; Central Planning Unit (CPU), 1958: 1969; National Planning Agency (NPA, formerly CPU), 1975: 1978: 1979: 1981; Planning Institute of Jamaica (PIOJ formerly the NPA) 1983: 1985: 1987: 1990: 1993: 1996. 1999: 2003: 2004.

Notes:

1 Includes youth.

2 Health allocation included water and sanitation.

From this review of democracy and social policy in Jamaica we can identify what conditions drove a focus on social policies and programmes, and especially those that simultaneously promoted equity, and what conditions weakened or de-emphasized a focus on the social:

1. In Jamaica the main driver of improved social policies has been social movements, from the rebellions of the nineteenth century, through the organizing of Marcus Garvey and others leading to the 1938 labour uprising, followed by the Rastafarian movement culminating in the critical ferment of the 1960s, the activist social groups of the 1970s and, in recent years, human rights movements, supported by a more probing media.
2. A democratic quality or tradition in Jamaica that respects the right of the people to voice their concerns, and to take action to promote them, has assisted these social movements in obtaining a political response. Even repressive regimes in Jamaica's democratic history, like the JLP government in the latter part of the 1960s, operated within certain limits (Gray 1991).
3. Enlightened political leadership has also been a key driver for improved social policies, especially Michael Manley and his political colleagues under democratic socialism, but also Edward Seaga with his creation of HEART in the 1980s, and the present PNP leadership through its legislation of rights-based mechanisms.

The factors weakening a focus on social policy have been:

1. The economistic approach to public policy in the last two and a half decades directly associated with neoliberalism. This dismisses the socio-economic policy nexus of a holistic approach. Instead it is a matter of sequence – a country must develop economically first, and then it will have the funds for social development. As Sherlock and Bennett (1998) suggest, in the past an economistic focus did not lead to social cohesion but to social turmoil.
2. External forces have been able to exert a powerful influence on Jamaica's policy direction. The US government's role in its opposition to democratic socialism and the multilateral financial institutions promoting structural adjustment from 1977 to the mid-1990s weakened social policy.[27]
3. A local political elite prepared to subordinate everything to partisan power and only shifting when pushed by strong social movements, usually from the lower classes, or by international pressure. This elite has thrived on the contradictions of Third World weakness not only by its division of working people along party lines but also by its unabashed use of patronage and violence, one moment encouraging thuggery by its supporters, the next moment suppressing it. Clientelist politics have ensured that this elite is well represented in top positions in the public sector where it has influenced policy formulation.

Democracy in Jamaica is linked in its history with the liberation of the poor majority, their economic and social progress, and their social movements. These movements in the last two centuries have come in approximately 35-year cycles.[28] Another cycle of social movements in response to increasing social pressure is now in progress. Jamaica is presently suffering from the highest murder rate in the world.[29] The inflation rate, which since 1997 has been kept to single-digit figures, is rising again – 14 per cent in 2003 and 2004 – and heading for several points higher in 2005. In a context of rising oil prices and increasingly intense hurricanes[30] this inflationary situation is not likely to change in the immediate future. Unless there is an increase in general productivity and in micro and small business start-ups the man and woman in the street are unlikely to prosper, despite the tourism and bauxite investments taking place. There is increased social and political activism with the rise in civil society movements and the change of leadership underway in both parties for the next elections, constitutionally due by 2007.[31]

What could be said to be new about this period is the lack of unity around a national goal or vision, which guided previous turning points in Jamaican history. Jamaica is in transition: whether to a new vision and a more united country or to anarchy and a weakened state is still to be resolved.

Notes

1. The title of a book by Phillip Curtin, published in 1955 by Greenwood Press.
2. Passing South Africa and Columbia (of those countries which fully record their murder rates).
3. This period, in contrast to the previous, is sometimes described as 'development without growth'.
4. '[O]ne of the most savage packages ever imposed on any client government by the IMF' was Manley's verdict in his 1982 book *Jamaica: Struggle in the Periphery*.
5. Immediately after the Election the Cuban Ambassador was declared 'persona non grata' and diplomatic relations with Cuba severed.
6. Seaga was the first Head of State to be hosted by newly elected Ronald Reagan at the White House.
7. Fatton 2002: 1.
8. Trevor Munroe entitled his book on the period 'Constitutional Decolonisation'.
9. In contrast to the earlier political leaders referred to in the Introduction.
10. Norman Manley saw it as power to 'bully' cabinet and the rest of the party, eventually accepting 'continuous dictatorship' for 5 years in the interest of stable government. Edward Seaga, who later became JLP leader, had no such concerns: 'Quite right and if any Minister can't get along, the Minister must resign as only one Minister must rule' (Verbatim Record 1961–2: 320–3 in Munroe 1972: 169–70).
11. Trinidad & Tobago, Grenada, Barbados, Costa Rica, India, Malaysia and Singapore were other democracies Stone included (*Democracy and Clientelism in Jamaica*).
12. Two rioters were shot dead, 90 buildings and 100 buses were damaged (30 were write-offs).

13. Fidel Castro, Samora Machel and Julius Nyerere all made state visits during this period.
14. A comment recently made by Beverley Anderson-Manley, Manley's former wife, on her radio talk-show.
15. Jamaica participated in the invasion of Grenada, which was condemned by the UN (and by the PNP).
16. For this reason Jamaica is counted by Przeworski *et al.*'s study as remaining a democracy in this period.
17. However, the PNP continued to pursue a more third world-oriented foreign policy – a key indicator of this being the renewal of ties with Cuba, which have remained ever since.
18. The author wishes to acknowledge the assistance of Brigette McDonald-Levy in preparing this section and of Dr Michael Witter in interpreting the economic data. All errors are her own.
19. World Bank. *Project Performance Audit Report, 1st Population Project.* April 1979 (Jones 1995: 132).
20. Often apparently without any strategy or aforethought, e.g. the Water Commission soon after found itself without the personnel who knew the lock-off points in the Kingston Metropolitan system.
21. This is presently the only component of the National Health Fund.
22. Up to today, all those who can afford it send their children aged 6–11 years to private prep schools as their average performance in Grade 4 and 6 tests far exceeds primary school students (JASPEV 2003).
23. Now being surpassed by Human Security as Jamaica's murder rate climbs to the highest in the world.
24. In the best traditional high schools these percentages jump to 70–98 per cent (JASPEV Annual Progress Report, vol 2, pp. 50–65, found on www.jaspev.org).
25. Acknowledged by all including the Opposition to have the necessary safe 'depth'.
26. 1970–2001 intercensal period (Statistical Institute of Jamaica).
27. However, in the more recent period, international aid agencies have been pushing for a more social policy orientation in a pro-poor human rights context, the gaps in the neoliberal economistic approach now recognized.
28. 1832 (Sam Sharpe), 1865 (Morant Bay Rebellion), Bedward in the early twentieth century, 1938, 1960s.
29. Among those countries which fully record their murder rates (e.g. this is not true of some in Central America).
30. Jamaica has suffered 3 in the last two years.
31. On 31 March 2006 Jamaica's first female Prime Minister, Portia Simpson-Miller, who boasts of her grassroots and inner city origins, replaced P.J. Patterson, who had indicated he would step down before the 2006 Budget. A huge wave of popularity has surrounded her ascension to office, which followed the longest and most contentious intra-party campaigning ever seen. Her rallying cry has been national unity.

References

Alleyne, D. 2001. 'The Dynamics of Growth, Employment and Economic Reforms in Jamaica', *Social and Economic Studies*, 50(1), 55–126.

Anderson, P. 2001. 'Poverty in Jamaica: Social Target or Social Crisis?' *SOULS: A Critical Journal of Black Politics, Culture, and Society*, 3(3), 39–55.

Anderson, P. and M. Witter. 1994. 'Crisis, Adjustment and Social Change: A Case Study of Jamaica', in E. LeFranc (ed.), *Consequences of Structural Adjustment: A Review of the Jamaican Experience*. Kingston: Canoe Press, University of the West Indies, pp. 1–55.

Beckford, G. and M. Witter. 1980. *Small Garden… Bitter Weed: Struggle and Change in Jamaica*. London: Zed Books Ltd.

Chevannes, B. 2006. *Betwixt and Between: Explorations in an African-Caribbean Mindscape*. Kingston and Miami: Ian Randle Publishers.

Central Planning Unit. 1958. *Economic Survey of Jamaica 1957*. Kingston: Government of Jamaica.

Central Planning Unit. 1967. *Economic Survey of Jamaica 1968*. Kingston: Government of Jamaica.

Colony of Jamaica. 1944. *Finance and Appropriations for the Year Ending 31st March, 1943*. Kingston.

Davies, O. and M. Witter. 1989. 'The Development of the Jamaican Economy since Independence', in R. Nettleford (ed.), *Jamaica in Independence: Essays on the Early Years*. Kingston: Heinemann Caribbean, pp. 75–104.

Department of Statistics. 1968. *The National Income and Product of Jamaica 1966*. Kingston: Government of Jamaica.

Department of Statistics. 1959. *National Accounts Income and Expenditure 1950–57*. Kingston: Government of Jamaica.

Eaton, G. E. 1995. *Alexander Bustamante and Modern Jamaica*. Kingston: LMH Publishing.

Electoral Office of Jamaica, Kingston. Response to request for information in August 2005.

Fatton, R. 2002. *Haiti's Predatory State: The Unending Transition to Democracy*. Boulder, CO: Lynne Rienner Publishers.

GRADE/IDB. 2002. *Informal Sector Study for Jamaica. Final Report*. Washington and Jamaica: GRADE/IDB.

Gray, O. 1991. *Radicalism and Social Change in Jamaica, 1960–1972*. Knoxville: University of Tennessee Press.

JASPEV, Cabinet Office. 2004. *Annual Progress Report on National Social Policy Goals 2003*. Jamaica.

Jones, E. and G. E. Mills. 1989. 'The Institutional Framework of Government', in Rex Nettleford (ed.), *Jamaica in Independence: Essays on the Early Years*. Kingston: Heinemann Publishers (Caribbean) Ltd., pp. 105–30.

Jones, J. 1995. 'The Impact of Structural Adjustment Programmes on the Public Sector in Jamaica', in Trevor Evans (ed.), *Structural Adjustment and the Public Sector in Central America and the Caribbean*. Managua: CRIES, 100–65.

Kaufmann, M. 1985. *Jamaica under Manley: Dilemmas of Socialism and Democracy*. London: Zed Books.

Moyne Commission 1938. *Report (with appendices) of the Commission to enquire into the Disturbances which occurred in Jamaica between the 23rd May and the 8th June 1938*. Kingston.

Munroe, T. 1972. *The Politics of Constitutional Decolonization: Jamaica, 1944–62*. Jamaica: Institute of Social and Economic Research, University of the West Indies.

National Planning Agency. *Economic and Social Survey of Jamaica 1975*. Kingston: Government of Jamaica.

National Planning Agency. *Economic and Social Survey of Jamaica 1978*. Kingston: Government of Jamaica.

National Planning Agency. *Economic and Social Survey of Jamaica 1979*. Kingston: Government of Jamaica.

National Planning Agency. *Economic and Social Survey of Jamaica 1981*. Kingston: Government of Jamaica.

Payne, A. and P. Sutton. 2001. *Charting Caribbean Development.* London and Oxford: MacMillan Education Ltd.

Planning Institute of Jamaica. 1984. *Economic and Social Survey of Jamaica 1983.* Kingston.

Planning Institute of Jamaica. 1986. *Economic and Social Survey of Jamaica 1985.* Kingston.

Planning Institute of Jamaica. 1988. *Economic and Social Survey of Jamaica 1987.* Kingston.

Planning Institute of Jamaica. 1991. *Economic and Social Survey of Jamaica 1990.* Kingston.

Planning Institute of Jamaica. 1994. *Economic and Social Survey of Jamaica 1993.* Kingston.

Planning Institute of Jamaica. 1997. *Economic and Social Survey of Jamaica 1996.* Kingston.

Planning Institute of Jamaica. 2000. *Economic and Social Survey of Jamaica 1999.* Kingston.

Planning Institute of Jamaica. 2004. *Economic and Social Survey of Jamaica 2003.* Kingston.

Planning Institute of Jamaica. 2005. *Economic and Social Survey of Jamaica 2004.* Kingston.

Planning Institute of Jamaica and the Statistical Institute of Jamaica. 2003. *Jamaica Survey of Living Conditions 2002.*

Przeworski, A., M. E. Alvarez, J. A. Cheibub and F. Limongi. 2000. *Democracy and Development: Political Institutions and Wellbeing in the World, 1950–1990.* Cambridge: Cambridge University Press.

Sherlock, P. and H. Bennett. 1998. *The Story of the Jamaican People.* Kingston: Ian Randle Publishers; Princeton: Markus Weiner Publishers.

Stephens, E. H. and J. Stephens. 1986. *Democratic Socialism in Jamaica: The Political Movement and Social Transformation in Jamaica.* New Jersey: Princeton University Press.

Stone, C. 1980. *Democracy and Clientelism in Jamaica.* New Brunswick and London: Transaction Books.

Stone, C. 1989a. *Politics versus Economics: The 1989 Elections in Jamaica.* Kingston: Heinemann Publishers (Caribbean) Ltd.

Stone, C. 1989b. 'Power, Policy and Politics', in Rex Nettleford (ed.), *Jamaica in Independence: Essays on the Early Years.* Kingston: Heinemann Publishers (Caribbean) Ltd, pp. 19–54.

Task Force on Educational Reform. 2004 (Revised Edition). *A Transformed Educational System 2004: Final Report.* Jamaica.

Index